A
Civil War
Treasury

A Civil War Treasury

Being a Miscellany of Arms and Artillery,
Facts and Figures, Legends and Lore,
Muses and Minstrels, Personalities and People

Albert A. Nofi

CASTLE BOOKS

This edition published in 2003 by
CASTLE BOOKS ®
A division of Book Sales, Inc.
114 Northfield Avenue
Edison, New Jersey 08837

This edition published by arrangement with and permission of
Da Capo Press, a subsidiary of Perseus Books L.L.C.
387 Park Avenue South
New York, New York 10016-8810

First Da Capo Press edition 1995. The Da Capo paperback edition of *A Civil War Treasury* is an unabridged republication of the edition published in Conshohocken, Pennsylvania in 1992. It is reprinted by arrangement with Combined Books.

Library of Congress Cataloging in Publication Data

Nofi, Albert A.
  A Civil War Treasury: being a miscellany of arms and artillery, facts and figures, legends and lore, muses and minstrels, personalities and people / Albert A. Nofi.
    p. cm.
  Previously published: Conshohocken, PA: Combined Books, c 1992.
  Includes bibliographical references and index.
  1. United States—History—Civil War, 1861-1865—Miscellanea. I. Title.
E468.N75 1995   94-31227
973.7—dc20   CIP

ISBN: 0-7858-1686-0

Printed in the United States of America

To M.S.N.
For putting up with it all.

Contents

Acknowledgments

A great many people were of considerable assistance in the preparation of this volume, and, though I selfishly reserve for myself credit for any errors, I would like very much to thank them.

Dr. David G. Martin, of Longstreet House, was an invaluable source of advice, ideas and information, which he culled from his extensive collection. Helena Rubenstein, Daniel Scott Palter, Jeff Briggs and the other fine folks at West End Games were generous in providing access to their fine company library. Prof. John Boardman, of Brooklyn College, was very helpful in certain matters linguistic, mathematic and heraldic and also for Renfrew. Kelly Richter made several useful contributions and is, moreover, a devoted student of the war, dioramist and friend of the Harbor Defense Museum at Fort Hamilton, New York. I owe Anthony Staunton, from "Down Under," thanks and a cold one for use of his Medal of Honor materials. Richard L. DiNardo, Dennis Casey, Jay Stone, James Dingeman and several other stalwarts of the New York Military Affairs Symposium provided a number of interesting items. The people at the Hunter College Library, CUNY Graduate Library and the Brooklyn College Library were of great help, while those at The New York Public Library were enormously cooperative, and particular thanks must go to the folks in the Rare Book Collection, the Newspaper Division, and to Margaret Moore, for her ever-cheerful welcome. Matilda Virgilio Clark graciously provided access to certain family records. Among other people whom I would like to thank are Eric Smith, James R. Furqueron, Dave Wesley, Robert Capriotti and Daniel David of Sky Books International; Linda Grant DePauw, Editor of *Minerva*, a unique journal dedicated to the study of women and the military; Mike and Danny Kilbert of the New York Complete Strategist; Thomas Brooks, John Southard, and William Koop, the editor of *The Volunteer*, and Valerie Eads, former editor of *Fighting Woman News*, for advice and assistance. Nor should I neglect to mention James F. Dunnigan, who, while editor of *Strategy & Tactics*, helped shape my approach to military history; nor Daniel and Diana Alejandro, who want to write books someday.

I owe a particular debt of gratitude to the officers and men of the recreated *15th New York Engineers, Co. A, 124th New York Volunteers, Clark's Battery (B, 1st New Jersey Artillery)* and the *1st New Jersey Cavalry,* who greatly assisted in the preparation of this volume by means of their demonstrations of Civil War kit, equipment and tactics, their cheerful responses to questions and their interest in and devotion to the study of the Civil War.

Bob Pigeon, John Cannan, David Martin and Kne Gallagher of Combined Books, deserve special mention for coming up with the idea for this volume.

Finally and particularly I would like to thank my wife and daughter, Mary S. Nofi and Marilyn J. Spencer, for their support, cooperation and understanding.

—A.A.N.

Preface

This volume, entitled *A Civil War Treasury*, does not pretend to be a sweeping historical account of the greatest crisis in the life of the Republic. Rather, it looks at that monumental struggle in terms of bits and pieces of reality. Herein are anecdotes of encampments and battles, of soldiers and citizens. There are extracts from memoirs and letters, profiles of people and regiments and ships, songs and poems, newspaper clippings and notices and not a few serious treatments of particular aspects of the war, such as musketry and artillery. No attempt has been made to attain completeness or balance, for much must be left out so that much may be included. The object is to give the reader a deeper understanding of the human side of the struggle and a look at something of its more technical aspects as well, both topics alike frequently neglected in more traditional treatments. Thus, there is no continuous narrative nor is there much logical continuity. The materials are, however, arranged in a roughly chronological fashion and there is a brief introduction to each chapter which outlines the principal political and military developments of the year in question. In addition, several major themes link the longer pieces together, so that, for example, a camp recipe appears under "Army Life," while the adventures of a lady spy fall under "Incidents of War," and a discussion of railroads under "The Ways of War." In the interests of economy, references have been kept to a minimum, although they have been maintained in the original.

Some of the items in *A Civil War Treasury* have been taken exactly as found in letters, newspapers and early books on the war. A few will be familiar, others obscure. Many are well documented, others but poorly so. At times a tale likely to be apocryphal has been included if it seems to show the spirit of the times, or just because it's too good to omit, though care has been taken to note the dubious provenance of such items. It should be remembered that many Civil War stories are genuine folk tales and exist in several versions, often involving different people at different times and in different places. As the Civil War was an era of particularly formal and florid speech, a number of original items have been rewritten to make them both shorter and more readily understandable to our simpler tastes, when the flavor will not suffer from the operation. At times language which would today be considered offensive has been permitted to stand; in such cases the reader is reminded that the age was one of particularly open bigotry, directed in various degrees against blacks and other non-whites, as well as most immigrants and non-Protestants.

Unless materials are being quoted directly, a number of a historical conventions have been adopted in accord with modern practice. Spelling conforms with current usage, so that, for example, "reconnaissance" and "center" have been used rather than the more authentic "reconoissance" and "centre." Similarly, military terminology has usually been modernized so that, for example, army corps have been given roman numerals, which was not the case during the Civil War. To facilitate distinguishing Union formations from Confederate ones, the designations of the former have been given in *italics*.

I

The Eve of War

The American Union: it must and shall be preserved.
—Andrew Jackson

How can the Union be preserved?
—John C. Calhoun

The irrepressible conflict.
—William H. Seward

Government cannot endure permanently half slave, half free.
—Abraham Lincoln

The crimes of this guilty land will be judged away but with blood.
—John Brown

*T*he American Civil War was long in coming. The question at issue was a simple one, secession, the separation of a state from the Union of States, a subject on which the Constitution was silent.

Secession became a divisive issue in American society because there developed significant social, cultural and economic differences between the Southern states and the rest of the nation. The South, rural, agricultural and aristocratic, saw its interests threatened as the rest of the nation became increasingly urban, industrial and democratic. This divergence of interests between the South and the rest of the country existed even before the Revolution, and the differences increased into the early nineteenth century. There were disputes over tariffs, over government sponsored internal improvements and over the distribution of public land, all of which the Northerners and Westerners favored, and the Southerners opposed, since they were of little benefit to its primarily agricultural economy. Complicating the issue was the fact that the population of the North and the West grew at a rate faster than did that of the South, a development itself largely a result of the divergent character of the regions. This trend led to a decline in Southern influence in the Congress, as the House of Representatives took on an increasingly Northern character. Then Southern influence in the Senate began to be threatened as new states tended towards a Northern or Western socio-economic pattern. Even without further complicating factors, the differences between the sections would have been sufficient to raise tensions, though it is hardly likely that these tensions would have led to an open break. Throughout history the "right of rebellion" has been morally justifiable and, given the differences between North and South, an argument could be made in favor of secession on this basis. But exercise of the "right of rebellion" is contingent upon several important moral questions: ultimately it boils down to a question of whether or not the majority of the people involved are suffering some form of oppression which cannot be resolved by any other fashion than a resort to arms. In the case of the

Civil War there was no such justification. Indeed, there was more justification for rebellion against the South. For there was one complicating factor which simultaneously was at the root of and more important than all the other issues taken together. It was a factor of overwhelming importance: slavery.

Slavery was the cause of the differences between the South and the rest of the Union. Slavery had created the planter aristocracy of the South. Slavery, which had made the South the preeminent agricultural region of the world, had hampered its industrialization. Slavery retarded the growth of the Southern population by discouraging the immigration which swelled the ranks of Northerners and Westerners.

Moved by practical and moral considerations, many perceptive Southerners had raised objections to slavery in the period after the Revolution, not least among them Thomas Jefferson and George Washington. And, indeed, the institution seemed to decline in the early years of the nineteenth century, but began to revive with the introduction of the cotton gin. In addition, the character of the society created by slaveholding, the enormous profits, the gentility, the elegance, blinded most, both North and South, to the pernicious effects of the institution on the nation.

By the middle of the nineteenth century—when the rest of the Western world had abandoned the institution—most of the white people of the South, relatively few of whom actually owned slaves, had come to view slavery as vital to the survival of Southern society. There had developed in the South an almost spiritual belief in the righteousness of slavery. The slaveholders represented wealth and status, something to which the non-slaveholders could aspire. The fact that slavery had a racial dimension enhanced the status of the impoverished white: whatever else he was, he was "free, white and twenty-one," a matter which was of considerably greater importance to the average Southerner than states' rights. This development was in direct contrast to the growing belief in Western civilization that slavery was inherently wrong. By 1840 the United States was the only major Western country in which slavery was still legal. Nor was there an absence of opposition to slavery.

Active resistance to slavery was remarkably widespread, among both blacks and whites. The Underground Railroad operated everywhere, involving people from every level of society, in both the North and South. Though initially resisted even in the North, the Abolitionist movement grew steadily. Slavery came under fire in books and plays and songs, in sermons and editorials and lectures. Southerners continuously tried to defend the institution, but slavery was indefensible, regardless of the arguments advanced. In the end, the advocates of slavery converted only themselves, while its opponents gradually converted most Northerners and not a few Southerners. The impact of the debate over slavery was tremendous, totally distorting legitimate concerns over states' rights, concerns which even Northern states possessed, but concerns which would never have become so inflammatory save for slavery.

Slavery was the overriding issue of the age. Families were broken up, friendships dissolved. Every major Protestant sect in the nation split in two, one branch opposing slavery and one favoring it. While Northerners snapped up 300,000 copies of Harriet Beecher Stowe's *Uncle Tom's Cabin* within a year of its publication in 1851, Southerners avidly read detailed rebuttals by pro-slavery authors. While former slaves—such as Frederick Douglas, Sojourner Truth and Harriet Tubman—and Abolitionists —such as William Lloyd Garrison and Charles Sumner—stumped the North pointing out the evils of slavery, pro-slavery advocates toured the South, lecturing on its importance to "civilized living." Some extremists even advocated reopening the trans-Atlantic slave trade.

Violence grew commonplace. It became impossible to publicly express anti-slavery views in the South and an incipient Southern Abolitionist movement was destroyed in a series of lynchings and riots. Though a few Southerners, such as Robert E. Lee, were committed to the notion that slavery was a moral outrage, they largely kept their opinions to themselves thereafter. The situation of pro-slavery advocates in the North was little better, and there were sometimes riots when slaveholders attempted to reclaim their "property" under the Fugitive Slave Act. Compromise was several times attempted, but each time came to naught. The fundamental issue was individual freedom, and despite constitutional sanction, slavery was inherently incompatible with the promise of America.

Despite the acrimony, the generation before the Civil War was one of expansion, as the increasingly divided United States grew and prospered on an unprecedented scale, finding time to expand into the sparsely inhabited West and to wage a successful war on Mexico which added greatly to the national territory. But even these achievements were tainted with the quarrel over slavery. The question of permitting slavery in newly acquired territories became a burning issue. Fanatical slavocrats sought national expansion specifically for the purpose of securing new slave states, and American filibusters were active in Mexico, Nicaragua and Cuba. By the mid-1850s the issue had become one without reasonable solution or compromise. The lines were drawn, the tinder was ready. And the tinder began to take fire.

In 1854 Congress passed the Kansas-Nebraska Act, in effect, a final effort at compromise. The idea seemed reasonable: let the citizens of each territory decide whether they wished to become a free state or a slave state through election. But a number of factors were at play. Both territories were relatively unsuited to slaveholding on a significant scale. In addition, with Northerners far more numerous than Southerners, it was not difficult to predict the probable outcome of any exercise in "popular sovereignty." So war came to Kansas, as pro-slavery thugs invaded the state to keep free soilers out, while anti-slavery fanatics retaliated in kind. The disorders continued into 1859, with the anti-slavery faction gradually gaining the upper hand. By then, the Supreme Court had dealt the final blow to any possibility of compromise. In 1857 the Dred Scott decision was handed down, which effectively ruled that no state could bar slavery from within its borders and went on to declare that even free blacks could not be citizens, both provisions alike being viewed as gross violations of states' rights and civil liberties throughout the North and West. Tensions rose still higher. In late 1859 John Brown, a veteran of "Bleeding Kansas," attempted to spark a slave insurrection, sending thrills of horror throughout the South. And in 1860, the Democratic Party fell to pieces, so that Abraham Lincoln, a mildly successful Republican lawyer from Illinois, was elected president by 39.9 percent of the voters.

Lincoln's views on slavery could hardly be called radical. Nevertheless, he was a opponent of the institution, believing it morally wrong, though he was not inclined to abolition. But he was opposed to the further extension of slavery. And that alone was too radical a position for the slaveholding fanatics. On 20 December 1861, as the results of the election became clear, South Carolina, in which slaves actually outnumbered freemen, passed an "Ordinance of Secession." With that, civil war was a virtual certainty.

Incidents of War

The Orphan Commission

As the coming of war causes armies to expand, it is not unusual for the number of high ranking officers to expand as well. Nor is it unusual for fierce competition to develop as to who should get to fill the newly created slots. And so it was in the Mexican War. Up to a point. On 3 March 1847 Congress authorized an increase in the number of generals in the army to serve for the duration of the war. President James K. Polk found little difficulty in filling most of the slots available, as there was considerable competition to secure the coveted promotions. But one major generalcy seems to have been cursed.

The president first offered the commission to Sam Houston of Texas, a wise choice given the man's military and political reputation. But Houston had just been elected senator from Texas and declined. So the president turned to Texas' other senator, Thomas J. Rusk, a man of considerable military experience—he had been surgeon general of the Army of the Republic of Texas and a regimental commander at San Jacinto—who, however, also preferred to remain in the Senate. And so, the president tried again, offering the commission to Senator Thomas Hart Benton of Missouri. Benton was politically a wise choice. A moderate on slavery, he had opposed the annexation of Texas, but had become a strong supporter of the war. And Benton was willing to accept the job. But he attached a condition, supreme command. This the president wisely rejected, considering that Winfield Scott was the obvious man for that task. That made three times that the commission had been spurned.

At this point Polk decided to offer the post to a man whom he had already appointed a brigadier general of volunteers, Gideon J. Pillow. Pillow gladly accepted. Totally without military experience, Pillow was otherwise well qualified for the job: he was a power in the Democratic Party, had been the principal architect of Polk's nomination for the presidency, and was Polk's law partner.

Pillow commanded a division during Winfield Scott's Mexican Campaign with little skill, though some courage, acquiring two wounds. He engaged in continuous quarrels with his superior, and was constantly in communication with the president. Polk, claiming that Pillow was being persecuted, sustained him in his quarrels with Scott, a Whig and potential presidential candidate. As a result, Pillow continued to be a thorn in the latter's side throughout the war.

With the coming of peace, Pillow returned to politics in Tennessee, failing in two bids to become vice-president. In 1860, Pillow became a Douglas Democrat. On the secession of Tennessee his political clout and alleged military reputation secured for him command of the state's troops. He shortly afterwards transferred to Confederate service as a brigadier general, expressing considerable annoyance that he was not appointed to a higher post, such as supreme commander. Pillow's career in the Civil War was even less distinguished than it had been in the Mexican War; his principal feat of arms being at Ft. Donelson, where he accepted command from the fainthearted John B. Floyd, only to pass it on to the honorable Simon Bolivar Buckner, so that the latter could surrender the place while Pillow and Floyd escaped. So perhaps Houston and Rusk and Benton were prescient in turning down the commission which Pillow so eagerly accepted.

In the Matter of Bragg vs. Bragg

Braxton Bragg, who would eventually rise to the highest levels of the Confederate Army, was not an easy man to get along with. Indeed, he seems to have quarreled with everyone in the service from the time he graduated from West Point. U.S. Grant once recounted a tale which, whether true or not, gives some notion of Bragg's temperament.

It seems that Braxton Bragg was once the quartermaster on a small frontier post. As the second ranking officer, he naturally assumed command when the senior officer had to absent himself for a time. Bragg performed his duties as acting post commander with great diligence, and, of course, had to tend to the quartermaster's duties as well. It chanced that, in the course of his duties as post commander, Bragg made a request of the post quartermaster. Due to some technicality, the post quartermaster found it necessary to reject the request.

The rejection caused an inquiry from the acting post commander, to which the post quartermaster replied. Several such communications passed back and forth, and the matter remained unresolved. Finally the real post commander returned. Reviewing the actions which the acting post commander had taken in his absence, the post commander came upon the correspondence between the latter and the quartermaster, that is, between Mr. Bragg and Mr. Bragg, with the result that he cried out, "My God, Mr. Bragg, you have quarreled with every officer in the army, and now you are quarreling with yourself!"

The Men

Winfield Scott

The most distinguished American soldier between Washington and the Civil War, Winfield Scott (1786-1866), was born near Petersburg, Virginia. As a young man he briefly attended William and Mary College, but left in 1805 because he disapproved of the irreligious sentiments of most of his fellow students. Scott read law and was admitted to the Virginia bar in 1806. In 1807, caught up in the war fever sparked by the *Chesapeake-Leopard* affair, Scott enlisted as a private in a local militia cavalry troop. Finding the military persuasion to his liking, he secured a commission in the Regular Army in May of 1808, being posted to New Orleans.

Scott's early career was marred by a court martial for having called his commanding officer, Brig. Gen. James Wilkinson—who never won a battle nor lost a court martial—as big a traitor as Aaron Burr, with the result that he was suspended from active duty for a year, 1809-1810. Returning to service, Scott was made a lieutenant colonel upon the expansion of the army at the outbreak of the War of 1812.

Scott had a notable career in the second war with Britain. By the end of 1813 he had served with distinction at Queenston, Ft. George and in the abortive Montreal Campaign; this last under the command of his nemesis Wilkinson. In March of 1814 Scott was promoted brigadier general and given a brigade under Maj. Gen. Jacob Brown, one of the nation's finest—and least remembered—field commanders. Scott's brigade fought well at Chippewa (5 July) and with particular distinction at Lundy's Lane, (25 July), during which Scott was severely wounded. For his performance at Lundy's Lane Scott became a national hero and was breveted a major general. With the coming of peace, Scott proved to be as able an administrative soldier as he was a combat soldier.

In the immediate aftermath of the war, Scott was placed in charge of the selection board which oversaw the reduction of the Regular Army, revised the standard drill manual and had the pleasure of heading the board of inquiry investigating James Wilkinson's disgraceful performance during the late war; true to his reputation, and through no fault of Scott's, Wilkinson got off on a technicality. Over the following decade Scott made two trips to Europe to keep abreast of military developments, headed various boards and commissions and prepared or revised a number of manuals. Passed over when Jacob Brown retired as general-in-chief in 1828, Scott attempted to resign, but was refused. The next few years were busy ones for the energetic Scott. He was peripherally involved in the Black Hawk War, negotiated treaties with several Indian nations and, in late 1832, was sent by President Andrew Jackson to deal with the Nullification Crisis.

Nullification, a theory advanced by John C. Calhoun, held that the laws of the United States did not necessarily apply to the individual states; a state could, if it desired, enact legislation to "nullify" a particular law with regard to itself. In the early 1830s this notion became popular in South Carolina, highly resentful of protective tariffs, which it perceived as harmful to its agricultural trade with Europe. As a result, in 1832 South Carolina, confident in the support of the other Southern states, nullified the tariffs of 1828 and 1832. Jackson, although himself a Southerner and slaveholder, was determined to assert the primacy of the Federal government. Securing from Congress the "Force Bill," which authorized the use of the army if necessary to suppress defiance of Federal law, Jackson sent Scott to Charleston to secure compliance with the tariff. Scott performed his task perfectly. A judicious show of force and considerable tact, plus a broad lack of support from the other Southern states and some modification of the tariff, caused South Carolina to back down, though still asserting the verity of nullification; indeed, the state legislature nullified the Force Bill! The Nullification Crisis further enhanced Scott's already high prestige.

Scott's career over the next decade reads like a catalog of American military activities. He commanded in the early part of the Second Seminole War (1835-1837), in which War Department mismanagement, disloyal subordinates and Seminole tenacity combined to cause his only failure. He helped resolve the "Aroostook War"—a potentially dangerous border dispute which had already involved the militias of Maine and New Brunswick—with Canada (1837-1842) and he directed the removal of over 16,000 Indians from the Southeast to the Indian Territory (1838). Finally, in 1841 he was promoted major general and named general-in-chief.

Scott's principal activity as general-in-chief was the conduct of the War with Mexico (1846-1848). Initially a supporter of Zachary Taylor's invasion of Northern Mexico, Scott became convinced that the only way to "conquer a peace" was to seize Mexico City, and he bent all his efforts towards that objective. The invasion of Mexico was effected with tremendous daring—the Duke of Wellington said, "Scott is lost"—and extraordinary success, at remarkably little cost, despite a number of disloyal subordinates and a hostile president. The Mexican War confirmed Scott's reputation as a talented soldier and brought him considerable fame abroad. But while Zachary Taylor's bloody though indecisive victories secured for him the White House, Scott's political ambitions were frustrated when he was decisively defeated by Franklin Pierce in 1852, though by way of consolation he was made a lieutenant general by brevet in 1855, the only man in American history to hold that rank. In the years between the Mexican War and the Civil War, Scott continued to command the army, most often from New York City, about as far from the War Department bureaucracy as he could conveniently get. During this period he continued to write, helped settle the Northwest Boundary dispute with Britain and supervised the resolution of the "Mormon War" and the Kansas-Nebraska troubles. A stickler for military propriety—which earned him the nickname "Old Fuss and Feathers"—and increasingly infirm, Scott nevertheless continued to be an able administrator with an alert mind.

Although Scott, himself a Southerner, disapproved of secession, he did not believe that the Federal government had the constitutional authority to use force to prevent it. Nevertheless, when called upon, he was ready to serve. Despite his age and extreme infirmity, Scott probably had the clearest understanding of what was coming. However, when he asserted that the war would be long, he was regarded by most people—though apparently not by Lincoln—as a senile old fool. Even before the fighting began, Scott outlined what his enemies contemptuously called the "Anaconda Plan." This called for the imposition of a naval blockade on the South, the concentration of enormous armies in Virginia and the Mississippi Valley and a long war. Scott also realized that there was no one who had experience commanding such enormous forces—his own largest command in Mexico had been fewer than 20,000 men—but believed that Robert E. Lee might have the makings of a good general. When Lee turned him down, he selected Irvin McDowell, who was replaced after Bull Run by George B. McClellan.

Scott and McClellan ought to have made a good team. But the latter's flaws of character—and lack of intestinal fortitude—created tensions between the two. As a result, Scott retired from the army on 1 November 1861, concluding a military career of over 53 years. Even after he was gone, Lincoln would say of him "I cannot but think we are still his debtors."

Scott died at West Point a little more than a year after the war had ended, largely on the basis of his "Anaconda Plan."

Although always counted among the nation's greatest soldiers, Winfield Scott's reputation is overshadowed by the overwhelming drama of the Civil War. As a result, Civil War commanders of far less skill are much better known. Nevertheless, his Mexican Campaign was among the most remarkable in history, with little, if anything in the Civil War surpassing it for daring, economy and decisiveness. It is difficult to escape the conclusion that, few, if any, American commanders since Washington were Scott's equal.

Josiah Henson

Josiah Henson (1789-1881) was born a slave in Maryland. After passing through a series of owners, he ended up on a plantation near Rockville. As a boy Henson developed a desire to learn to read. By selling apples he raised the eleven cents necessary to buy a copy of Webster's speller and proceeded to teach himself. The first words he wrote, tracing them in charcoal, were "Isaac Riley," his master's name. The latter, however, took a dim view of slaves reading and administered a savage beating, with the result that Henson gave up the attempt. As he grew older, "Sie" Henson became a trusted retainer of the Riley family and was often taken on business trips by his master. On one such trip to Kentucky, Henson became a Methodist preacher. On his return to Rockville, Henson continued his duties, while tending to the spiritual needs of the Riley slaves and was once credited with calming a potentially disastrous outbreak by some 400 slaves. Meanwhile, Henson worked towards his freedom and in 1828 bought himself and his family out of servitude, removing to Kentucky.

After a short time in Kentucky, Henson's former master began to dun him for additional money. Henson began to suspect that his former master was about to double-cross him, claiming that he was not in fact free, and sell him "down the river" to New Orleans, a not uncommon swindle. His suspicions being confirmed—any white person could lay claim to any free black with relative impunity under the "Fugitive Slave Law"—, Henson took his family off to Canada in 1830, to the great disappointment of his former master, who put a price on his head. In Canada, Henson found the freedom which he desired, prospered and finally learned to read. Becoming involved in the problems of fugitive slaves, some hundreds of whom trickled into Canada each year, he joined with several other successful former slaves to found the British-American Institute, a school for the "coloured inhabitants of Canada." Between times he became involved in the Underground Railroad and over the years is credited with helping 118 slaves escape bondage, often undertaking risky journeys into the South in the course of his work. Meanwhile he found time to write, and in 1849 published *The Life of Josiah Henson, formerly a Slave, Now an Inhabitant of Canada.*

Henson's memoirs came to the attention of a Brooklyn woman, who was of a literary inclination. Combining this with her anti-slavery activities, the woman, Harriet Beecher Stowe, sister of the prominent Abolitionist the Rev. Henry Ward Beecher, used Henson's memoirs to provide the background for a 40-part serial which she wrote for *The National Era*, an anti-slavery newspaper. So popular was this venture that Stowe turned the serial into a novel, calling it *Uncle Tom's Cabin, or Life Among the Lowly*, one of the greatest "best sellers" in history, a work which sparked much controversy in its day and ever since as well. Stowe, when challenged as to the veracity of anything in her book, would ever afterwards refer to Henson's memoirs.

Henson himself grew quite wealthy, richer, he observed, than his former master. After the Civil War he toured England, lecturing and meeting the greats of the land, including Queen Victoria and the Archbishop of Canterbury, to whom when asked where he had been educated, he replied "I graduated, Your Grace, from the University of Adversity."

In 1877 Henson toured the United States, visiting President Rutherford B. Hayes at the White House and paying a call at the old Riley Plantation. When his former master's invalid widow, upon recognizing him, said "Why, Sie, you are a gentleman," he replied, "I always was, madam."

Henson was proud to have been the model for Uncle Tom in Harriet Beecher Stowe's novel, commenting, "If my humble words have in any way inspired that gifted lady to write such a plaintive story that the whole community has been touched with pity for the sufferings of the poor slave, then I have not lived in vain."

Sylvanus Thayer

A native of Massachusetts, Sylvanus Thayer (1785-1872) graduated from Dartmouth in 1807, and then entered West Point, graduating in 1808 and being commissioned in the Engineers. Save for a brief tour as an instructor at the academy, he spent the next four years working on coast defenses in New York and New England. On the outbreak of the War of 1812 he served as engineer on the staffs of Henry Dearborn and Wade Hampton on the

Canadian border. Although he saw no action in the war, he emerged as a captain and brevet major. He spent 1815-1817 touring European military academies and in July of 1817 was appointed superintendent of West Point, which was then virtually a dying institution.

Thayer spent 16 years at West Point and is the founder of the academy as a genuine institution of higher learning and military art. Effecting a thorough reform of the academy, he instituted a formal, four-year academic curriculum, created the post of Commandant of Cadets, prescribed regular military exercises, established stringent entrance and academic requirements and recruited capable instructors such as Dennis Hart Mahan. Not all of Thayer's reforms were welcome, and there were student riots in 1818 and 1826, which he put down firmly. In 1833 Thayer clashed with President Andrew Jackson when the latter reinstated some cadets who had been expelled. As a result, Thayer requested that he be relieved.

Thayer spent the next 25 years engaged in harbor improvements and coast defense work in New England, while serving on various army boards. In 1858 ill health forced him to go on leave of absence. He was promoted colonel of engineers and brevet brigadier general upon his retirement in 1863. After the war he endowed a school of engineering at Dartmouth and lived quietly in his native Massachusetts. One of the most important soldiers in American history, Thayer had an enormous influence on the development of engineering, education and technology in the United States, and was the true founder of West Point.

John C. Fremont

On the eve of the Civil War no American soldier was better known than John C. Fremont (1813-1890). A native of Georgia, Fremont had a varied and adventurous life. Expelled from Charleston College at 18, the influence of South Carolina's Joel R. Poinsett secured for him an appointment as teacher of mathematics aboard the sloop-of-war *Natchez*—midshipmen in those days learned their trade at sea. In 1838, Poinsett—after whom the plant is named—managed to get Fremont made a second lieutenant in the prestigious Corps of Topographical Engineers. Over the next seven years Fremont was engaged in surveying and exploring the West. In 1841 he wed Jessie Benton over the objections of her father, the powerful Senator Thomas Hart Benton of Missouri, who later did well by his son-in-law, promoting various expeditions which the latter led.

Fremont's trips into the Rockies had already made him something of a national hero when, acting on secret orders, he led a column into California on the eve of the Mexican War, sparking the so-called "Bear Flag Rebellion" and being instrumental in securing the territory for the United States. Fremont was shortly appointed governor by Commodore Robert F. Stockton, but soon ran into difficulties with Brig. Gen. Stephen W. Kearny, who had arrived with orders to set up a civil government. Placed under arrest, Fremont was subject to a court martial. Though cleared of mutiny charges, he was found guilty of disobedience and conduct prejudicial to military order. Although President James K. Polk intervened to suspend sentence, Fremont resigned in early 1848.

Settling in California, Fremont soon acquired vast lands, grew rich from the gold rush, and was elected to the Senate. Meanwhile, various railroad interests employed him to explore possible routes over the Rockies. An early supporter of the infant Republican Party, Fremont was its first candidate for president, going down to defeat in 1856 at the hands of James Buchanan; had he won he would have been the youngest man ever elected.

The outbreak of the Civil War found him in California. In a move designed to cement various elements to the Republican Party—the Blair family, the Abolitionists and the German-Americans, among all of whom Fremont was immensely popular—Lincoln made Fremont a major general of volunteers on 14 May 1861 and sent him to command in Missouri.

Fremont's war service was acrimonious, but important to the Union cause, despite the fact that he was uniformly unsuccessful in the field and occasionally embarrassing to the president. He helped in holding Missouri for the Union, but issued a premature order freeing the slaves which Lincoln was forced to retract. Combined with a lack of success in the field, this prompted Lincoln to remove him in November of 1861, despite the hysterical pleadings of Jessie Fremont and an absolutely dishonest and dishonorable attempt by Fremont to avoid receipt of the appropriate orders. As a political sop, Fremont was placed in command of West Virginia in March of 1862, and he promptly involved his forces in a series of reverses at the hands of Thomas "Stonewall" Jackson, culminating in his defeat at Cross Keys on 8 June. When his command became the *I Corps* of John Pope's *Army of Virginia* shortly thereafter, Fremont asked to be relieved rather than serve under an officer who was his junior in rank. He did not return to active duty.

In 1864 Fremont was briefly involved in an attempt by some Radical Republicans to prevent the renomination of Lincoln. For the balance of his life he devoted himself to his business affairs, suffering a series of devastating failures, including an *in absentia* conviction for fraud by a French court, and was only kept solvent by the literary efforts of his wife. From 1878 to 1887 he was governor of the Arizona Territory and at his death was receiving a pension as a major general on the retired list. As with most "political" generals, whether North or South, there were sound reasons for Fremont's appointment. Unlike most, his prewar achievements to some extent justified the confidence initially placed in him. His failure as a commander was due to his ambition, his indecisiveness and his penchant for the dramatic.

Samuel P. Houston

One of the giants of American history, Sam Houston (1793-1863) was a native of Virginia. After his father died when he was 14, Houston's mother took her nine children to Tennessee. Houston, who was largely self-edu-cated—he nevertheless managed to secure a solid knowledge of classical literature—ran off to join the Indians about 1808, living with the Chero-kee for three years, among whom he acquired the name "The Raven." In 1812 he ran a school for a time, but the following year volunteered for the war with Britain. Houston's war service was entirely in the then southwest, against the Creek Indians. During his five years of military service he was severely wounded, became a close friend of Andrew Jackson and rose to first lieutenant.

In 1818 Houston resigned his commission rather than take part in Indian removal. He became an Indian agent among the Cherokee, while he read law. Admitted to the bar in Tennessee, Houston acquired a consider-able reputation, became a major general of militia and was elected to Congress in 1823 and again in 1825. In 1827 Houston was elected gover-nor of Tennessee. By the age of 34 Houston's career had been remarkable, and great things might well have been expected of him. But in January of 1829 he made a disastrous marriage which lasted less than three months and about which he never afterwards spoke. He resigned his governorship and headed west for Arkansas, where the Cherokee had been "removed."

Houston lived among the Cherokee for three years. Despondent, he took to drink for a time, earning the name "Big Drunk," but then married Tiana Rogers, a Cherokee woman—a collateral ancestor of Will Rogers—who helped reform him. Meanwhile, the pressures for Indian "removal" were again at work and in 1832 Houston went to Washington to see what his old friend Andrew Jackson, now president, could do to protect the Cherokee. In Washington he got nowhere, for Jackson was a strong backer of Indian removal. Worse, he had a violent encounter with an anti-Indian member of the House and was sentenced to a public condemnation for contempt of Congress. However, since the speaker was a Jackson man, Houston's formal condemnation sounded more like a commendation. While Jackson could not—or would not—do anything for the Cherokee, he suggested that Houston go to Texas—at that time a part of Mexico which had been heavily settled by Americans—to negotiate with various Indians who were raiding into the United States. Houston took up the assignment and headed west. For the rest of his life he was closely identified with Texas.

Troubles between the Texans, both American and Mexican, and the Mexican government of Antonio Lopez de Santa Anna had been brewing for a long time, and reached a boiling point in late 1835. The Texans resorted to arms and Houston was named a major general and commander of the revolutionary army. Shortly after Texas declared its independence from Mexico—on 2 March 1836, his birthday—Houston led the revolutionary army to victory at San Jacinto (21 April 1836). Three months later he was elected president of the Republic of Texas. Houston served two terms as president of Texas (1836-1838 and 1842-1844). When Texas was admitted to the Union—a matter which was long delayed because of its slaveholding status—Houston was elected to the United States Senate, serving until 1859, when he was elected governor of Texas, becoming the only man in American history to have been the governor of two states. But Texas had changed, and Houston had not. Over the years the original small population had been swamped by outsiders, mostly from the South. The political status of the Mexican-Texans had deteriorated tremendously, while the old Americo-Texans had lost power to the newcomers. A strong Union man, Houston found that Texas was heavily secessionist.

Houston's years in office were difficult ones. He openly opposed secession, believing it would be a disaster for the South, and remained staunchly Unionist to the end. When, in March of 1861, he refused to endorse the Ordinance of Secession and would not take the oath of allegiance to the Confederacy, he was removed from office in an illegal proceeding. Houston died a broken man in 1863, with "Texas" on his lips, one of the forgotten heroes of the Civil War.

Dennis Hart Mahan

Although raised in Virginia, Dennis Hart Mahan (1802-1871) was born in New York. He entered West Point in 1820 and was intimately connected with it for the rest of his life. Mahan's intellectual brilliance soon attracted the attention of the superintendent, Sylvanus Thayer, who appointed him an acting instructor in mathematics while still a cadet. Graduating first in the class of 1824, Mahan was commissioned in the Engineers and assigned at Thayer's request as a faculty member at West Point. He spent 1826-1830 in France, studying the military educational system there and completing the prescribed course at the School of Application of Engineering and Artillery at Metz. Upon his return to West Point he began a notable academic career, holding several professorships and becoming dean of the faculty in 1838. Mahan's work affected virtually every aspect of the academy's curriculum. He wrote at least six textbooks which remained standard for many decades, introduced the study of the Napoleonic Wars as interpreted by Baron Henri Jomini, and furthered the work, begun by Thayer, of turning the academy into one of the foremost military and engineering institutions in the world, while educating virtually all of the men who would rise to the highest levels of military leadership during the Civil War. Mahan's most important work, *Elementary Treatise of Advance-Guard, Out-Post, and Detachment Service of Troops* (1847), popularly known as *Out-Post*, became the standard handbook of military training for the regular army and militia.

In 1871 Mahan stepped off the side of a river steamer in the Hudson, apparently a suicide, as he was despondent over a recommendation that he retire. His son, Alfred Thayer Mahan, had a distinguished naval career and was the author of the popular *The Influence of Sea Power Upon History*.

The Women

Harriet Tubman

Nicknamed "Moses," Harriet Tubman (c. 1821-1913), who became the most famous "conductor" on the Underground Railroad, was named Araminta when born as a slave on a plantation in Dorchester County, on Maryland's Eastern Shore. At the age of 22 the young field hand was forced to marry John Tubman, a fellow slave. In 1849 she left him, and slavery forever, fleeing northwards and adopting the name Harriet.

Tubman, a small, uneducated woman who never lost her slave accent, became involved with various Quaker anti-slavery groups and was soon active in the Underground Railroad. Over the next decade she conducted 20 hazardous missions into the South, bringing more than 300 people to freedom. A hard, tough, fearless and at times ruthless woman, she was almost caught several times, but always managed to elude her pursuers. In a remarkable coup, she brought both her parents out of bondage in 1857 and settled them at a house which she had acquired in Auburn, New York. Ms. Tubman, who was a legend among the slaves and well known in the Abolitionist community—John Brown counted her among his friends—, never held a formal position with any organization, supporting herself by working as a cook, lecturer and contributor to various Abolitionist journals, dictating what she wished to say, since she never learned to write.

On the outbreak of the Civil War, Ms. Tubman went to the Carolina Sea Islands, where her fame had not reached, to serve the black community there, helping to finance a school and working as a nurse. She became involved in a number of military operations, as spy, scout and, in one instance, leader of a raiding party. After the war she continued to work for the rights of black Americans and founded a home for indigent freemen.

Lincoln

Young Abe at War

In 1830 Congress passed the Indian Removal Act, which called for the relocation of all Eastern Indians to lands west of the Mississippi, for which the munificent sum of $500,000 was appropriated to pay "compensation." Removal brought great suffering upon tens of thousands of Indians. There was also a great deal of bloodshed in Illinois and Wisconsin.

Dissatisfied with the lands allocated to them by the Federal government, lands which they had to dispute with their blood enemies, the Sioux, Omaha and Menominee, and longing for their ancestral Illinois—guarantied to them in perpetuity by a treaty dating from 1804—500 Sauk and Fox warriors crossed the Mississippi into Northern Illinois in April of 1832. Under the leadership of Black Hawk (c. 1767-1838), a Sauk, and accompanied by some 1,500 women and children, the movement was more of a migration than a raid. Nevertheless, panic spread rapidly among the white settlers. As nearly 5,500 militiamen and volunteers turned out, the Federal government began moving over 1,300 regular troops from Jefferson Barracks in Missouri and various coast defense posts in the East.

The Indians won a skirmish with the militia at Stillman's Run, but, concluding that the odds against them were too great, decided to retire into Wisconsin. A few days later the militia caught them as they were attempting to cross a river. Although the Indians came off with the worst of it in the ensuing Battle of Wisconsin Heights, they did succeed in escaping. By this time some 400 regulars had turned up. Not being a stupid man, Black Hawk endeavored to surrender, only to have his offer rejected twice. Aided by about 900 militia, the Regulars, under Brig. Gen. Henry Atkinson, began driving the Indians westward. On 2 August Col. Zachary Taylor—who later went on to greater things—led a column of troops through swampland to corner Black Hawk's band against the Bad Axe River, just south of La Crosse, Wisconsin. The next day there occurred the so-called Battle of the Bad Axe, a massacre which left only 150 survivors. American casualties in the war were 26 killed and 38 wounded. Many of the Indians

33

were driven into the river at bayonet point and shot down in the water or drowned. Thus was Illinois made safe for civilization. Black Hawk himself was soon captured and imprisoned for about a year in Fortress Monroe. Upon his release, he settled in Iowa, where he helped drive out the Sioux, Omaha and Menominee to establish a Sauk reservation. However, his influence over his people soon passed to the younger Keokuk, who became a great favorite with the Americans.

Among the many men who served in the militia during the Black Hawk War was Abraham Lincoln, then aged 23. Lincoln volunteered on 21 April and was immediately elected captain of his company—his first success at the polls. He appears to have been popular with the men, not the least for his willingness to help with the chores. On one occasion, Lincoln wrestled another captain to see whose company would get a more desirable camp-site; he lost, but history has failed to note the name of the man who beat him. Although the story is probably as old as close-order drill, Lincoln is alleged to have been the green officer who forgot the proper sequence of commands which would get the troops through a defile and so ordered them to "break ranks and reform immediately on the other side of that gate." Lincoln's company was mustered out on 27 May. Military life appears to have agreed with young Abe sufficiently to prompt him to reenlist on 29 May. This time, however, he served as a private, being mustered out on 16 June. Lincoln saw no action during his 53 days of military service. Much of his time was spent slogging through swamps in search of Black Hawk and his men. He did, however, endure some physical hardship and helped to bury five men who had been killed and scalped by the Indians. During his brief military career Lincoln was twice under arrest for minor infractions of military law.

In later life, Lincoln rarely referred to his military service, and then only with some self-denigrating bit of humor. Nevertheless, he seems to have been mildly proud of having served. How well his brief brush with the military life served him when he was commander in chief of the greatest armies and navies the Republic had ever put in the field cannot be determined. But Lincoln's military experience—or lack of it—seems to have stood him in better stead than Jefferson Davis'.

The "Railsplitter's" Maiden Speech

Lincoln first stood for public office in 1834, running for the Illinois legislature as a Whig. He had a number of strikes against him. He was young, awkward and unknown. Moreover, the flowery "speechifying" of his opponents and their supporters and of his supporters as well, had gone on for some time, with much tooting of personal horns and praises about individual virtues, so that they had "rolled the sun nearly down." In short, the crowd was getting bored. And then it was Lincoln's turn.

> Gentlemen, fellow-citizens: I presume you all know who I am. I am humble Abraham Lincoln. I have been solicited by many friends to become a candidate for the legislature. My politics are short and sweet, like an old woman's dance. I am in favor of a National Bank. I am in favor of the internal improvement system and a high protective tariff. These are my sentiments and political principles. If elected, I shall be thankful; if not, it will be all the same.

Though no masterpiece of rhetoric, Lincoln's little speech must have done the trick. He won the election, served several terms in the legislature and later went on to the House of Representatives, where his opposition to the War with Mexico later cost him his seat.

The Units

The Old Army

The United States Army on the eve of the Civil War was remarkably small given the population, wealth, and extent of the nation. Yet it was sufficient unto the need. Under no immediate threat from any power, the United States required an army primarily for police duties on the frontier and as a national cadre which would provide the leavening to turn the militia into a combat-ready force in the event of mobilization. This system had worked rather poorly during the War of 1812 (1812-1814), due largely to sectional disunity, political ineptitude and poor leadership. But the Mexican War (1846-1848) had turned out quite well, due to a considerable measure of national unity, reasonably sound political direction and excellent leadership, not the least because of the presence of a goodly number of West Point graduates in both the Regular and Volunteer establishments.

At the end of 1860 the Regular Army had an authorized strength of 16,367 officers and men, of whom 14,663 were actually present with the colors. The combat strength of the army comprised ten regiments of infantry, four of artillery and five of mounted troops. These totaled 198 companies, of which 183 were normally stationed west of the Mississippi. Although every four years several thousand men were brought to Washington for presidential inaugurations, it was unusual for so many troops to be in one place at the same time. As a result, when it became necessary to concentrate a considerable force, as during the Mexican War or the Utah Expedition, a great administrative muddle often ensued.

The ten infantry regiments each comprised twelve companies in three battalions on paper, but in practice had only ten companies active. Although the oldest regiment dated back to 1784, their enumeration had suffered considerably from a series of consolidations at the end of the War of 1812, when, among other peculiarities, the senior regiment acquired the designation *3rd Infantry*, which it still bears. The *1st Infantry* was formed in 1791, the *2nd* and *5th* date to 1808, the *4th*, *6th* and *7th* to 1812, the *8th* to 1838 and the *9th* and *10th* to the expansion of the Regular Army in

1855. Although on occasion all ten companies of a regiment might serve together, this was a rare occurrence in peace time, when many army posts had but one or two companies. The principal peace-time role of the infantry was to assist the mounted troops in policing the frontier.

Prior to 1821 the artillery had constituted a corps on the model of the Royal Artillery. In that year the existing autonomous batteries—several of which dated back into the eighteenth century and one to 1776—were grouped into four regiments. This was a purely administrative measure, however, designed to provide jobs for colonels of artillery, and the batteries continued to be deployed individually until the twentieth century. Each artillery regiment comprised ten foot companies and two light companies. A number of the foot companies were assigned to coast defense duties; the garrison of the Charleston harbor forts in December of 1860 comprised two companies totaling 65 officers and men, plus eight bandsmen. The balance of the artillery was scattered in the West, where most served as infantry, since artillery was of little use against Indians.

There were three types of horse soldiers in the army: dragoons, mounted rifles and cavalry. Despite the different designations, all three types had the same organization: initially ten companies divided into five squadrons, an additional squadron was added shortly before the Civil War, permitting the formation of three battalions at need. The *1st Dragoons*—which served as cavalry, not dragoons, a form of mounted infantry—had been organized in 1833, as the frontier began to move onto the prairies, and the *2nd Dragoons* was added in 1836. The *Regiment of Mounted Rifles* was raised in 1846 for service in the Mexican War, and rendered excellent service, being dubbed "Brave Rifles" by Winfield Scott. In 1855 two cavalry regiments were added, the *1st* and *2nd*, to provide additional mounted troops to help police the vast territories recently annexed from Mexico.

In addition to the combat arms, the Regular Army included the Corps of Engineers and the Corps of Topographical Engineers. The Engineers performed numerous civil and military services, designing coast defenses, supervising harbor development, clearing obstacles to navigation on the Western rivers, and the like. The "Topos" were generally considered the intellectual elite of the army, and were responsible for surveying the Western territories, no minor task. Although the Corps of Engineers included a small contingent of enlisted personnel, the Topos were composed entirely of officers.

The administrative needs of the Regular Army were tended to by a number of staff departments which were often mired in bureaucratic detail. These included the Adjutant General's Department, the Inspector

General's Department, the Judge Advocate General's Department, the Quartermaster General's Department, the Subsistence Department, the Medical Department, the Pay Department, and the Ordnance Department. There was, in addition, a Chief Signal Officer, but he had neither staff nor department.

If the Old Army was small, it was well officered. Very few of the officers lacked serious military training or experience. Of the 1,080 officers on active duty at the end of 1860, some 821 (76 percent) were graduates of West Point. A number of the others had graduated from one of the dozen or so private or state military high schools and academies which existed at the time. In addition, a small percentage had risen from the ranks. All of the senior officers were combat veterans, some, like general-in-chief Winfield Scott, having distinguished themselves in several wars. Nor were the men they led unworthy of them. Although the troops were by no means the best representatives of American manhood, being prone to desertion, brawling and drunkenness and frequently not American at all but Irish or German immigrants, they were good material. Well trained, they proved intensely loyal, only 26 deserting to join the Confederacy.

On 3 May 1861, shortly after the Civil War broke out, the Regular Army was expanded. Nine new infantry regiments were authorized, numbered *11th* through *19th*, each to comprise three battalions of eight companies. In addition the *3rd Cavalry* was raised and the *5th Artillery*, comprised of a dozen light batteries. But this may well have been an error. Had Regular Army personnel been dispersed among the Volunteers, the latter would have been brought up to a relatively high degree of military skill rather rapidly. Certainly those Volunteer Army regiments and brigades which had former Regulars officers and enlisted men in their ranks became militarily proficient far sooner than those which lacked such experienced personnel. Although some individuals recommended such a course, the political and military leadership of the nation decided against it. So the Regular Army, which enrolled about 75,000 men during the war, but peaked at about 50,000, served in separate regiments and brigades and divisions, discharging its duty with great courage and skill wherever it served, and providing a mark against which the officers and men of the Volunteer Army could measure themselves. It was not, perhaps, the best way for the Old Army to have served, but it served honorably and well.

War and Society

The Militia in Pre-War America

It has been customary to deride the military policy of the United States in the period before the Civil War. Indeed, it occasionally has been said that the United States had no military policy in that period. Citing the experience of the Civil War, some authors have suggested that the nation was woefully unprepared for war. This is unreasonable. In fact, quite the reverse was true, for the nation had a realistic and intelligent military policy, given the war which was expected, as demonstrated by the experience of 1812-1814, 1846-1848, 1898, 1917-1918 and even 1941-1945.

The expected war was a conflict with an overseas power, and most specifically with Britain, which was, after all, the only country in the world having the wherewithal to seriously threaten the United States. The principal underpinning of American military policy for most of the nation's history was the triad of the navy, the coast defense system and the militia. A British invasion of the United States would require a prodigious effort, one which would take months or even years to mount. During this grace period the navy would harass British merchant shipping while the militia would have time to turn out and, leavened by the Regular Army, be brought to a reasonable degree of efficiency. By the time the British were in a position to assault American shores or drive southwards from Canada, considerable forces would be available for service either in the field or behind the most elaborate coastal fortifications in history.

Given the war which was expected, this was a reasonable strategy. But the war which was expected was not that which occurred. Nor was there very much which could have been done to prepare for the war which happened. As a result, the nation was indeed unprepared, unprepared for an internal conflict. So the militia had to go to war with little or no serious preparation.

The history of the militia in the United States has been long and varied, and its popularity and effectiveness have risen and fallen over the years. In the period immediately after the War with Mexico the militia of most states was relatively good. In 1852, for example, New York State had over 45,000 active militiamen in eight divisions, plus a regiment each of riflemen and cavalry and a small corps of artillery, all relatively well-armed and well-drilled. But through the 1850s the popularity, and, more importantly, the effectiveness of the militia declined. The institution virtually ceased to exist in several states; Jacob D. Cox, a lawyer who became one of the best amateur soldiers of the war, did not even own a uniform in 1861 despite being a brigadier general in the Ohio militia. In many states the militia became little more than an excuse for the local menfolk to get together occasionally and have a few. Although by and large the militia in the Southern states seems to have been marginally better than that in the North, if only because of the potential danger of slave insurrections—a danger more apparent than real since the last serious outbreaks occurred in the 1830s—, no state was really prepared for war in 1860, not even for a limited war. New York, noted for maintaining an effective militia—Canada was right next door, and it was also useful in suppressing urban riots—had less than 20,000 active militiamen on the eve of the Civil War.

The militia began to become popular again late in the 1850s, as much for its social, political and entertainment value as for its military. Famed drill masters, such as the young Ephraim Elmer Ellsworth of the *Chicago Zouaves*, toured the country with their regiments, holding drill competitions and exhibitions in many cities, providing a showy, romantic notion of the military life which would eventually be shattered on the battlefield; Ellsworth himself was among the first to fall, shot by James T. Jackson on 24 May 1861, as he pulled down the Confederate flag which had flown over Jackson's hotel in Alexandria, Virginia.

In 1860 there were about 4,200,000 men liable for service under the terms of the Militia Act of 1792. On paper several states had substantial contingents. Maine, for example, had 60,000 men enrolled in the state militia, while Tennessee had over 150,000. But the important figure was that of active militia, men who were organized, uniformed, equipped and drilled in some fashion, and on that score Maine had only 1,200 militia and Tennessee about twice as many. Nevertheless, despite its very uneven military quality, it was the militia which provided the backbone of both armies in the early months of the war, many militia outfits enlisting together for war service. The accompanying table gives an approximate estimate of the strength and effectiveness of the militia of several states in 1860.

State or Territory	Men (1,000s)	Quality
Alabama	2.5	Fair
Arkansas	1.5	Poor
California	1.0	Fair
Colorado Territory	0.0	
Connecticut	1.0	Fair
Dakota Territory	0.0	
Delaware	0.2	Poor
District of Columbia	0.5	Poor
Florida	0.5	Poor
Georgia	2.0	Fair
Illinois	1.0	Poor
Indiana	0.5	Poor
Indian Territory	0.0	
Iowa	1.5	Poor
Kansas Territory	1.0	Fair
Kentucky	4.0	Fair
Louisiana	3.0	Good
Maine	1.2	Poor
Maryland	1.0	Poor
Massachusetts	5.6	Good
Michigan	1.2	Fair
Minnesota	1.5	Fair
Mississippi	2.5	Fair
Missouri	1.5	Fair
Nebraska Territory	0.5	Fair
New Hampshire	1.0	Poor
New Jersey	1.0	Satisfactory
New Mexico Territory	0.5	Fair
New York	19.0	Good
North Carolina	1.5	Satisfactory
Oregon	0.5	Poor
Ohio	5.5	Poor
Pennsylvania	19.0	Fair
Rhode Island	2.0	Fair
South Carolina	7.0	Good
Tennessee	2.5	Fair
Texas	1.5	Fair
Utah Territory	2.0	Fair
Vermont	0.9	Fair
Virginia	13.7	Good
Washington Territory	0.0	
Wisconsin	2.0	Fair

As can be seen, there were perhaps 115,000 active militiamen in the United States on the eve of the Civil War, mostly of indifferent quality. By no stretch of the imagination was any state actually ready for war in 1860, at least not that which came in the following year. Although South Carolina, where secession had become something of a secular religion, had made some efforts to build a state arsenal and accumulate arms, its preparations were trivial compared with the demands of even a small war.

The secessionist states—Virginia, the Carolinas, Georgia, Florida, Alabama, Mississippi, Louisiana, Texas, Arkansas and Tennessee—had about 38,000 active militiamen in 1860, while the three Border States—Maryland, Kentucky and Missouri—had some 6,500 more, most of whom would "go South" in the secession crisis. Deducting those portions of the Virginia and Maryland militia which adhered to the Union, the Confederacy started off with over 40,000 relatively trained and equipped men, while perhaps 75,000 militia remained in the loyal areas, along with about 16,000 men of the Regular Army. Of course, the Confederacy began mobilizing before the Union. By 1 April 1861 the seceded states—South Carolina, Georgia, Florida, Alabama, Mississippi, Louisiana and Texas—had at least 45,000 men under arms in Confederate service, of whom about 5,000 were at Charleston and some 2,000 at Pensacola, when the Union had yet to call a single man. The secession of the "Upper Tier" slave states and disloyalty in the Border States over the next few weeks would immediately add over 25,000 more. Of course, by then Northern manpower began to muster.

The Mormon War

The Mormons had a long and difficult struggle to establish a niche in American society. Founded by Joseph Smith in Fayette, New York, in 1830, the "Church of Jesus Christ of Latter Day Saints" was dogged by religious intolerance from the start. As a result, its adherents were driven several times to relocate, often under severe pressure and even armed force; the Missouri militia destroyed a Mormon settlement in 1838, as did the Illinois militia in the mid-1840s. Finally, after the murder of Smith at Navuoo, Illinois, in 1846, Mormon leadership decided to seek safety in an unsettled region in the west. Since the United States was then at war with Mexico, President Polk, who, like most Americans lacked sympathy for the Mormons, decided it would be in the national interest to be nice to them, lest "they turn up in California at some delicate moment in the progress of the conquest." As a result, the government granted the Mormons permission to settle in Utah. To further secure the adherence of the Mormons to the national cause, Polk authorized the recruitment of a Mormon battalion for war service.

The Mormons responded well to the appeal for troops, almost 550 men were mustered into service at Ft. Leavenworth in June of 1846, representing about a fifth of military-aged Mormons. The Mormon battalion served for a year. Initially under the command of Lt. Andrew Jackson Smith of the *2nd Dragoons*, a "gentile" who would later become a Union major general, the battalion was shortly taken over by Capt. Philip St. George Cooke of the *1st Dragoons*, later a Union brigadier, who commanded as acting lieutenant colonel; among Cooke's officers was George Stoneman, who later commanded the cavalry of the *Army of the Potomac* for a time. Cooke whipped the battalion into shape, discharged unfit personnel and took off for California, blazing a new trail from Santa Fe, New Mexico, along the Gila River and thence westwards to San Diego, along a route which was later followed by many of the "'49-ers" and eventually by the Southern Pacific Railroad. The Mormon battalion, which saw no combat but lost about 30 percent of its strength to disease, mustered out in California in June of 1847. About 50 of the men reenlisted, and a few settled in California, but most went to Utah, where in the interim Brigham Young had settled the first Mormon families.

In 1848, of course, Utah officially became part of the United States, along with most of the rest of the Southwest. The rapidly growing Mormon community in Utah petitioned for statehood in 1849. This was rejected, and Utah was established as a territory, though as a concession to the Mormons, Brigham Young was made governor. Over the next few years relations between the Mormons and the United States deteriorated steadily. Things came to a head in the mid-1850s. California-bound wagon trains passing through Utah began to be harassed by Mormon extremists. A number of clashes occurred, and several massacres took place. Meanwhile, the impression grew that the Mormons were contemplating separating themselves from the United States. This impression was fueled partially by the Mormon extremists' arrogant attitude towards non-Mormons, partially by Mormon practices such as polygamy, which were in violation of American law, and partially by Young's dictatorial style of leadership. Further "proof" of disloyalty was to be found in the "Danites," a 2,000-strong militia which the Mormons had organized for self-defense against Indians and other marauders. Convinced that treason was afoot, President James Buchanan removed Brigham Young from office and appointed Alfred Cumming of Georgia. Young refused to step down, whereupon a military expedition was authorized to "quell the rebellion."

Early in the summer of 1857 some 2,500 troops were despatched from Ft. Leavenworth to reestablish Federal authority in Utah. The expedition, commanded by Col. William A. Harney, comprised the *5th* and *10th Infantry Regiments*, two batteries of light artillery and Col. Albert Sidney Johnston's *2nd Cavalry*, which included Robert E. Lee, George H. Thomas and William Hardee among its field officers. Harney, a fair cavalryman, was nevertheless a poor administrator and the expedition got off to a bad start. The Danites proved able irregulars, and harassed the advancing column in a variety of ways, attacking supply trains, stampeding horses and cattle, and setting grass fires. Poorly led and ill-supplied, the troops proved unable to effect an advance on Salt Lake City, falling back on Ft. Bridger. That November Johnston was breveted a brigadier general and assigned to command, by which time the campaigning season had passed. The expedition wintered at Ft. Bridger amid considerable privation, until Johnston was able to sort out the administrative mess. Meanwhile, among the Mormons, the extremists appeared to have gained the upper hand. Additional attacks on wagon trains occurred, efforts were made to stir up the Indians, and preparations were taken in hand for the defense of Salt Lake City. A major clash appeared inevitable.

In the spring Johnston was ready to advance, reinforced with both regulars and volunteers to about 5,500 men. With the renewal of the advance, however, came efforts at mediation. As a result, Brigham Young decided to rein in his more extreme followers, disowned any suggestion of disloyalty and agreed to step down in favor of the new governor. In June of 1858 the Utah expedition entered Salt Lake City. Direct occupation of the Mormon capital was brief, however, for the troops were shortly relocated to Ft. Floyd, a newly constructed post about 60 miles to the southwest. This effectively ended the "rebellion," though Federal troops remained in the territory for several years.

A great many of the officers who would later distinguish themselves in the Civil War took part in the Utah expedition. In addition to Johnston, Lee, Hardee and Thomas, Barnard E. Bee—who fell at Bull Run after bestowing upon Thomas J. Jackson the nickname "Stonewall"—commanded a battalion of volunteers, and Winfield Scott Hancock, later a Union major general and hero of the Battle of Gettysburg, also took part. Altogether it appears that at least 50 future Union generals and 30 future Confederate generals served on the expedition to suppress the alleged Mormon attempt to secede from the Union.

The Seminole Wars

The Indian Wars are an inherent part of the folklore and history of the United States. Yet the most difficult of these, the three Seminole Wars, are among the least well known, perhaps because, in the end, it was the Indians who won.

The Seminoles are by origin natives of Georgia, a branch of the Creek nation who migrated into Florida in the mid-eighteenth century, primarily to get away from Britain's American colonists. As a result of the American Revolution, Florida passed to Spain. The Seminoles were not inclined to cross the border into the United States looking for trouble. Indeed, the trouble went in the other direction. Knowing that the racially tolerant Seminoles would give them refuge, blacks fleeing bondage would often head south. This presented a problem for slaveholders in Georgia, concerned about the security of their "property." As a result, slave catchers would sometimes cross into Florida, where they would often be given a warm welcome by the Seminoles. In complete violation of international law, some of these slave catching expeditions were accompanied by American troops, who received much the same treatment at the hands of the Seminoles. Things came to a head in 1817.

On the assumption that the Seminoles were being subsidized by a foreign power, about a thousand regulars and nearly 7,000 militiamen and volunteers under Maj. Gen. Andrew Jackson deliberately invaded Florida and seized several Spanish posts. A number of Seminole chiefs and two British merchants were executed out of hand, a matter which caused a furor in Congress and in Parliament, though Jackson weathered the storm. Thus ended the so-called "First Seminole War." As Spain was incapable of defending its interests in Florida, it sold the place for $5,000,000 and the United States took possession in 1821, with Jackson as governor. Seeing the way the wind was blowing, the Seminoles retreated into the swamps and jungles. An uneasy peace prevailed for a decade. Then, in 1830, with Andrew Jackson in the White House, the Indian Removal Act was passed, a massive swindle designed to grab the remaining Indian holdings east of the Mississippi through so-called "compensated" relocation to the Indian Territory, in what is now Oklahoma. By 1835 it was the turn of the Seminoles.

The Seminoles were not interested in relocating, having grown attached to the local swamps. A bloody war ensued. Led by several able war chiefs, including Osceola (c. 1800-1839), some 3,000 to 5,000 poorly equipped Seminole warriors led over 11,000 regulars—virtually the entire Regular

Army and the Marine Corps—and 30,000 militiamen and volunteers on a merry chase through the bogs and marshes and jungles for seven years. The struggle degenerated into the most brutal guerrilla warfare. Osceola himself was captured in 1838 through the treacherous violation of a safe conduct; imprisoned in Charleston, he died there the following year. But there were other chiefs to take his place, notably Alligator, Jumper and Micanopy and they carried on the struggle. By 1842 perhaps $40,000,000 had been spent. The death toll was enormous, at least 2,000 whites and an unknown number of Seminoles and blacks had died. Some Seminoles, perhaps 3,500, had been relocated, but the outcome seemed hardly worth the effort. As a result, Congress decided to drop the matter. Thus ended the Second Seminole War.

Three years later Florida entered the Union as a slave state. Things remained calm for another decade. Then, with increasing settlement, concern arose anew about the remaining Seminoles. A new effort was mounted to convince the Seminoles to go west. They refused. And so there was a Third Seminole War.

The new war was a desultory affair, involving less than 3,000 troops, all militiamen save for some regular officers and staffs. The Seminoles stayed in their swamps and the army pretty much stayed out of them. There was little fighting. In 1858 a negotiated settlement was reached in which most of the Seminoles agreed to move to Oklahoma for a substantially better financial deal than any other Indians had ever received. Nevertheless, not all the Seminoles left Florida. Some retired deep into the Everglades. Not until 1934 was a treaty of peace concluded with the descendants of these holdouts.

The Seminole Wars brought no honor to the nation and little luster to American arms. But they did provide a remarkable number of Old Army officers with a lot of hard experience. Among the veterans of the Seminole Wars who would rise to prominence in the Civil War were Robert Anderson, George H. Thomas, Nathaniel Lyon and John Gibbon, as well as Braxton Bragg. Although exact figures are difficult to determine, at least 100 future Union and Confederate generals fought in the Seminole Wars.

Army Life

Water and Molasses

When, from time to time higher powers decreed that the troops deserved a party, careful preparations were made to ensure that a good time would be had by all without discipline suffering in the bargain.

Typically on such occasions a whole beef was provided for each company, to be split and roasted over open fires. Regimental bands supplied the music and the troops themselves would often sing or dance for the entertainment of their comrades, while the officers might kick in for an extra special treat, such as something sweet. The most delicate aspect of such regimental parties was the matter of drink.

Feelings about drink ran deep in mid-nineteenth century America. It was a hard drinking time, though the temperance movement was strong. To provide alcoholic refreshments to the troops might engender serious political problems for an ambitious officer. Moreover, the real stuff loosened the bonds of discipline. Yet how could one have a party without a little taste of something interesting? As a result, an Old Army expedient was often resorted to, "water and molasses."

Water and molasses was easy to make. For each company one mixed together:

1 barrel water
3 gallons molasses
1 quart undiluted vinegar
0.5 pounds ginger

The resulting concoction was actually quite good as a substitute for the harder stuff. The ginger provided flavor and the vinegar a certain bite, while the molasses gave color and enough sugar to hike up one's metabolism a mite. Given the circumstances, water and molasses was just the thing to provide a little extra to ensure a convivial atmosphere at a regimental blow-out. As one observer noted, it would "cheer but not inebriate."

War and the Muses

Dixie

Perhaps the most popular of Civil War songs, and certainly the most enduring, the sprightly "Dixie" was written in April of 1859 by a Northerner, Daniel D. Emmett of Ohio. A well-known tunesmith of the era, Emmett—composer of the popular "Old Dan Tucker" and "The Blue-Tail Fly" (better known as "Jimmy Crack Corn")—wrote it to fill a hole in a so-called "Negro minstrel show" in New York. In 1861 Herman Arnold, a German who had immigrated in 1852, added a few notes and rescored it somewhat, apparently in the belief that he was adapting an old folk song. On 18 February 1861 Arnold's band played his version for the first time, during the parade marking the inauguration of Jefferson Davis as provisional president of the Confederacy; the escorting 1st Alabama had the distinction of being the first regiment to march to the tune. The new version proved immensely popular and soon became the unofficial anthem of the South, a status which it enjoys to this day, despite the fact that Emmett is said to have written an anti-Southern version, which included lines like ". . . the land of treason." Impressively, the tune was only a little less popular among Northerners, and on 8 April 1865 Lincoln requested an army band play it for a visiting foreign dignitary, "It has always been a favorite of mine, and since we've captured it we have a perfect right to enjoy it."

> ### *Dixie*
> I wish I was in de land ob cotton,
> Old times dar am not forgotten,
>   Look away, look away, look away, Dixie Land!
> In Dixie Land whar I was born in,
> Early on one frosty mornin',
> Look away, look away, look away, Dixie Land!
>   Den I wish I was in Dixie
>   Hooray, hooray!
>   In Dixie land I'll take my stan'!

To lib an' die in Dixie
Away, away,
Away down south in Dixie
Away, away,
Away down south in Dixie
Ole Missus marry "Will-de-Weaber,"
William was a gay deceber
    Look away, look away, look away, Dixie Land!
But when he put his arm around 'er
He smiled as fierce as a fourty-pounder
Look away, look away, look away, Dixie Land!
His face was sharp as a butcher's cleaber,
But dat did not seem to grieb 'er,
    Look away, look away, look away, Dixie Land!
Ole Missus acted de foolish part,
An' died for a man that broke her heart,
    Look away, look away, look away, Dixie Land!
Now, here's a health to de next ole Missus,
An' all de gals dat want to kiss us,
Look away, look away, look away, Dixie Land!
But if you want to drive 'way sorrow,
Come 'an hear dis song to-morrow,
    Look away, look away, look away, Dixie Land!
Dar's buckwheat cakes an' Injun batter,
Makes you fat, or a little fatter,
    Look away, look away, look away, Dixie Land!
Den hoe it down and scratch your grabble,
To Dixie's Land I'm bound to trabble,
    Look away, look away, look away, Dixie Land!

The Portent

Though noted principally as the author of *Moby Dick*, *Typee* and other great novels of men and the sea, Herman Melville was also a poet of considerable ability. His *Battle-Pieces* and *Aspects of the War* (1866) includes a number of important works, among them this short poem.

The Portent

Hanging from the beam
   Slowly swaying (such the law),
Gaunt the shadow on your green,
   Shenandoah!
The cut is on the crown
   (Lo, John Brown),
And the stabs shall heal no more.
Hidden in the cap,
   Is the anguish none can drown;
So your future veils its face,
   Shenandoah!
But the streaming beard is shown,
   (Weird John Brown),
The meteor of the war.

II

1861

She has left us in passion and pride.
—Oliver Wendell Holmes, Sr.

Justifiable cause.
—Jefferson Davis

Combinations too powerful to be suppressed by the ordinary course of judicial proceedings.
—Abraham Lincoln

This strange sad war.
—Walt Whitman

A nine inch shot is a terribly effective argument.
—David Dixon Porter

A band of brothers fighting.
—John Gibbon

What gives the wheat fields blades of steel?
—John Greenleaf Whittier

Through the winter of 1860-1861 secession fever swept the lower tier of Southern states. By early February, Mississippi, Florida, Alabama, Georgia, Louisiana and Texas had joined South Carolina, forming The Confederate States of America. President James Buchanan, well-meaning but untalented, proved incapable of acting with decision, seeking, on the one hand, to preserve the prerogatives of the Federal government, while not precipitating an open break with the secessionists in the hope that a peaceful solution might be found. Many others, both North and South, shared this hope. But it was futile. Though several last-ditch compromises were proposed, none had much chance of success.

Meanwhile, the seceded states occupied—had to occupy to assert their sovereignty—Federal installations on their territories, so that by the time Lincoln was inaugurated, in early March, the "Stars and Stripes" could be found flying over but three places in the entire South, all isolated posts, Fort Pickens off Pensacola Harbor, Fort Taylor in the Florida Keys and Ft. Sumter in Charleston Harbor. And it was at Sumter that the issue boiled over into war. On 12 April 1861, after over four months of blockade and negotiation and hopes and prayers, Confederate artillery under Brig. Gen. Pierre G.T. Beauregard opened fire on the small Federal force holding the incomplete fort. Within 48 hours the garrison surrendered with the honors of war.

Fort Sumter proved the tocsin call. The tiny Regular Army, little more than 16,000 strong and losing officers daily as they resigned to "go South," could scarcely muster 4,000 men in one place at a time when the Confederacy had already some 45,000 men under arms, with nearly 60,000 more authorized. So on 15 April Lincoln issued a call for 75,000 volunteers to put down "combinations too powerful to be suppressed by the ordinary course of judicial proceedings."

Shocked at the threatened use of force against the secessionists, the remaining slaveholding states, hitherto tentatively loyal to the Union, wavered. Most soon threw their lot in with the Confederacy: Virginia on 17 April, followed within weeks by Arkansas, North Carolina and Tennessee, while Maryland, Kentucky and Missouri were held to their loyalty only by extreme measures. North and South, men sprang to arms in the hundreds and thousands, all alike desirous of taking part in the glorious adventure which all save a handful believed would be short. In vain did a few suggest that the war would be long and hard, among them old brevet Lt. Gen. Winfield Scott, hero of the Mexican War and general-in-chief of the United States Army.

Over the next few weeks, as men poured into recruiting stations both North and South, fighting began to spread all across the land. It began in small ways. There were relatively bloody riots at Baltimore and St. Louis, and there were virtually bloodless skirmishes at Harper's Ferry, Fairfax Courthouse and Philippi in Virginia. By then the dead from a handful of riots and skirmishes already numbered in the dozens. Meanwhile large forces began to concentrate, notably at Washington and in northern Virginia and in Missouri.

Fighting became more common and more intense. On 10 June the first real battle of the war occurred at Big Bethel in Virginia, a mere skirmish by later standards, but at the time viewed as a great victory for the Confederacy and a disastrous defeat for the Union. It was not until 21 July that the war began in earnest, when, in a confusing, ill-managed, but hard-fought encounter along the Bull Run, a small creek in northern Virginia, a Confederate army under Gen. Joseph E. Johnston and Brig. Gen. Pierre G.T. Beauregard defeated a Union one under Brig. Gen. Irvin McDowell, with nearly 3,000 Union killed, wounded or captured as against less than 2,000 Confederate casualties, appalling losses for the times.

Though Bull Run elated the South and depressed the North, it was but the beginning. In the East both sides pulled back, the Confederates almost as disorganized in victory as the Federals in defeat, each side seeking to strengthen itself for a future effort. Though numerous skirmishes would take place, little of importance would happen in the field through the end of the year, but much in camp and cabinet. A new man came to the helm of the Union forces, Maj. Gen. George B. McClellan, and he began to create a real army out of the inchoate mass of volunteers about Washington, even as, a scant 50 miles away in Virginia, his Confederate counterpart, Gen. Joseph E. Johnston, undertook the same task, the end result being the creation of two armies whose fate and honor would be eternally linked, the *Army of the Potomac* and the Army of Northern Virginia.

In the West it was different. There, the war grew bitter, with major clashes at Wilson's Creek and Lexington in Missouri and scores of little fights in which, by and large, the Union slowly gained the upper hand and secured control of most of the state, while Kentucky, vainly trying to maintain its "neutrality," found itself being drawn into the struggle.

At sea the United States Navy began, somewhat feebly, to impose a blockade on the South, and even, in August, in cooperation with the army, to essay a successful amphibious operation against Hatteras Inlet, while sustaining the isolated garrison at Ft. Pickens in Pensacola Harbor.

It was a decisive year, 1861, though not perhaps in terms which most could understand. It was not the issue which was decided, but rather the shape of the war. Though many did not yet see it, the war would be long and hard and bloody.

Incidents of War

Mrs. Anderson Reinforces Ft. Sumter

The position of Major [Robert] Anderson and his little band [in Fort Sumter], composed of ten officers, fifteen musicians and fifty-five artillerists—eighty in all—was an extremely perilous one. His friends were uneasy; his wife, a daughter of a gallant soldier, General Clinch of Georgia, was in New York City. She knew her husband was exposed to ferocious foes without and possible traitors within the fort.

In the emergency she remembered a faithful sergeant who had been with her husband in Mexico, but she had not seen him in seven years. His name was Peter Hart. She knew him to be a tried and trusty friend, on whom she could rely in any emergency and she resolved to find him and place him by the side of her husband within the walls of Fort Sumter.

For a day and a half she sought a clew by visiting the residences of the various Harts named in the City Directory. She was an invalid. Her physician protested against her project, as he believed its execution would imperil her life. She would listen to no protests, but found Hart and the two started the next day for Charleston. They traveled without intermission and reached Charleston at the end of forty-eight hours.

The cars were crowded with recruits hastening to join in the attack on Fort Sumter. She neither ate, drank, nor slept and heard her husband threatened with instant death should he fall into their hands. Their language was very violent especially respecting the destruction of the old flag-staff at [Fort] Moultrie, which was considered such an insult to the South Carolinians as might not be forgiven. At the Mills House, Mrs. Anderson met her brother. She found no difficulty in procuring a permit from Governor [Francis] Pickens, who was her father's old friend, to go to Fort Sumter.

The Governor refused one for Hart, saying he could not allow a man to be added to the Sumter garrison. She scornfully asked if South Carolina, claiming to be a sovereign power among the nations of the earth, would be endangered by the addition of one man to a garrison of seventy or eighty, while thousands of armed hands were ready and willing to strike them.

The Governor, seeing the absurdity of his refusal, gave a pass for Hart, requiring from Major Anderson a pledge that he should not be enrolled as a soldier. A small boat carried them to Sumter. On every hand she saw strange banners and warlike preparations. Nearing Sumter, she turned and saw the national ensign floating over the fort, the only one in the whole bay. "The dear old flag!" she exclaimed, and burst into tears.

Reaching the fort, her husband caught her in his arms, whispering, "My glorious wife!"

"I have brought you Peter Hart," she said. "The children are well. I return to-night."

In two hours, Mrs. Anderson was placed in the boat by her husband, and rowed back to the city. The same evening she started for the national capital. Her mission ended, she was utterly prostrate. A bed was placed in the car for her comfort. She was insensible when she arrived in Willard's Hotel, Washington, and after forty-eight hours of suffering from exhaustion, she proceeded to New York and rejoined her children.

This brave woman had done what the government failed to do—she had not sent, but had taken, reinforcement to Fort Sumter.

—The Soldier in Our Civil War (1884)

"How I Joined the Army"

John N. Opie, son of a prosperous Virginia farmer, was 17 when the war began. His wartime experiences were many and varied. He served under Thomas "Stonewall" Jackson and later J.E.B. Stuart before being captured in late 1864, an experience from which he barely emerged alive. After the war he practiced law and served in the Virginia State Senate. His memoirs, *A Rebel Cavalryman with Lee, Stuart, and Jackson* (Chicago, 1899), are lively and amusing, as can be seen from the following excerpts which cover the period from his enlistment through his initiation into military life in the early months of 1861.

My Father, Col. Hierome L. Opie, who was a well-to-do farmer, resided in the beautiful and fruitful County of Jefferson, now West Virginia, until 1856, when, anticipating the impending struggle between the States, he moved up the Valley of Virginia and purchased a farm one mile from the city of Stauton, where we were living at the outbreak of the war. On the 16th day of April, 1861, I, a boy seventeen years of age, was seated in a school room vainly wrestling with a proposition in analytical geometry. Not being able to master my mathematical problem, I was revolving in my mind how I should cut the Gordian knot, when I was informed that my father wished to see me.

I went to the door, and, to my great surprise, he informed me that the volunteer companies were ordered into service, and that, in fulfillment of a promise made a year previous, I could go with them; but it was his wish that I would not go, on account of my youth. I desired very much to please my noble father; but two mighty influences actuated me: one my unsolved mathematical problem; the other, the effect of having just read [the novel] *Charles O'Malley, the Irish Dragoon*, the reading of which induced me to believe that war was a glorious thing; and so I went, with many other thoughtless men and youths, and plunged heedlessly into a long and deadly war, without, at the time, being able to give a reasonable why or wherefore.

If there was any mischief or fun or devilment abroad, I was always implicated. I was a very polite boy, and I believe that, if on my way to Hades, I would bow politely to and exchange greetings with the Devil; but, if his Satanic Majesty desired or sought other than friendly relations, he would surely have been gratified, such was my accommodating nature and disposition.

In war, I ran when it was necessary, fought when there was a fighting chance, burned fence rails when cold, stole when hungry, and was oftentimes insubordinate.

* * *

It was [at Harper's Ferry] that the first Virginia army, which was composed of volunteer militia, assembled.

When we reached the place, where a Government armory and arsenal were located, we found that the small Union force had fled, first setting fire to public buildings. We succeeded, however, in saving most of the machinery and some hundred stand of muskets. Our stay here was spent organizing and drilling. I was detailed to assist Maj. John A. Harmon, afterwards Jackson's quartermaster, my duty being to quarter the troops as they arrived. The Major at first gave me the countersign every evening, until, he remarked to me, "Your father has asked me not to give you the countersign." I replied that, being an enlisted man, I was no longer under his authority. I had, that evening, an engagement, and must have the countersign, so I got my musket; and buckled on my belt, determined not to be circumvented. I took the post at the mouth of an alley, and marched up and down as a sentinel, until, finally, hearing someone advance I brought up my gun to a charge and gave the usual command, "Halt! Who comes there?" "Friend with the countersign." "Advance, friend, and give the countersign." The officer advanced and gave me the countersign, when, returning to the office and divesting myself of gun and accoutrements, I pursued the even tenor of my way. This I continued to do, for several nights, until, at last, one night I heard some one approach, and, upon going through the usual ceremony, I found that I had halted the major himself, who, recognizing me, exclaimed, "You d— little rascal!" After this he always gave me the countersign. This mode of procuring the countersign I used during the whole war, together with the following plan: When there was a cordon of sentinels around the camp, and there was no possibility of making a new post, I wedged in between two sentinels and walked the beat until I met one, when, having forgotten the countersign, I would ask him for it. He, supposing I was a sentinel, invariably gave it to me.

General Cheatham's Escape from the Yankees

On the morning of 7 November 1861, Union Brig. Gen. U.S. Grant began advancing a mixed force of over 3,000 men against Belmont, a small Missouri town on the Mississippi. In an effort to see what Grant was up to, Confederate Brig. Gen. Benjamin Franklin Cheatham went out a little in advance of the Confederate lines. As the area was rather wooded, he tarried a little too long beyond Confederate lines. Quite suddenly a small contingent of Union cavalry came upon him as he stood on a country lane. As the Union troopers spotted him almost as soon as he saw them, escape was impossible. Thinking quickly, Cheatham—who, in common with several other Civil War commanders, including Grant, was not what one would term a natty dresser—rode *towards* the column, and the Yankee cavalrymen halted. At a distance of a few yards, Cheatham reined in, asking, "What cavalry is this?"

The officer in command replied promptly, "*15th Illinois Cavalry*, sir."

"Oh, Illinois cavalry. All right, just stand where you are."

With an exchange of salutes, Cheatham and his orderly rode on, passing the halted troopers, passing an infantry regiment which halted behind them, and then doubling back through the woods and on to the safety of their own lines.

The First to Answer the Call

John T. Hunter of Philadelphia is generally considered the first man to volunteer for the Union. Almost as soon as Gov. Andrew Gregg Curtin of Pennsylvania issued the call for volunteers in response to Lincoln's appeal of 15 April 1861, Hunter telegraphed his willingness to serve. Hunter enrolled in the *Logan Guards*, a militia company from Mifflin, Schuylkill and Berks counties, under Capt. John B. Selheimer, which was the first company of volunteers to reach Washington, on 18 April, and the first to be accepted for service by the Adjutant General of the United States Army.

However, Hunter's claim, and that of the *Logan Guards*, is disputed by one Josias R. King and the *1st Minnesota*. It seems that on 14 April, the very day on which Sumter fell, while Lincoln was still composing his appeal, Gov. Alexander Ramsey of Minnesota, who chanced to be in Washington, walked into Secretary of War William Cameron's office and offered 1,000 men for service, which was immediately accepted. Ramsey at once wired St. Paul, where King signed up that very evening, though the regiment was not completed and mustered into Federal service until 29 April.

While the rival claims of Hunter and King cannot be resolved, those of the *Logan Guards* and *1st Minnesota* can. The *1st Minnesota* was accepted for Federal service before the *Logan Guards*, but the latter was mustered into service before the former, so, in a sense, both were the first, depending on how one counts these things. One thing is certain, however, the *27th Pennsylvania*, in which the Logan Guards formed Company A, was the first volunteer unit to suffer a casualty.

The Logan Guards together with four other companies from Pennsylvania, totaling about 460 men, plus one Regular Army company from Minnesota, reached Baltimore at 2:00 p.m. on 18 April. Because there were no through rail connections, the troops—who were not armed—had to march across town to "take the cars" for Washington. As they did, they came under some abuse from secessionist hooligans. Some debris was thrown and Nicholas Biddle, a black freeman serving as an officer's orderly, was struck and injured by a brick-bat, thus becoming the first man injured by hostile action. The troops managed to get through the mob without further injury and reached Washington several hours later, arriving at 7:00 p.m. This took place one day before the more famous attack upon the *6th Massachusetts*, to which the regiment replied with lethal effect, which incident caused the first "combat" deaths in the war, Pvts. Sumner Needham, Luther C. Ladd, Addison O. Whitney and Charles A. Taylor, plus a dozen civilians.

A Postal Affair

For some months after the formation of the Confederacy the United States Post Office Department continued to deliver the mails throughout the

South. Not until 1 June 1861, six weeks after the firing on Fort Sumter, did the Confederate Postal Department take over, in a remarkably smooth operation by which the postal workers carefully completed all the paper-work demanded by the Post Office Department of the U.S.A on the 30th of May and then, the next morning, went to work at precisely the same jobs, with precisely the same ranks and salaries, for the Post Office Department of the C.S.A. It was a transfer which undoubtedly warmed the hearts of many a bureaucrat.

In any event, the U.S. Post Office promptly discontinued deliveries to the South, and the South immediately reciprocated. As a result, postal communication between the two parts of the country was almost completely severed, which, of course, created enormous problems. However, it was possible to pass mail through Kentucky, which was attempting to maintain a precarious neutrality in the first months of the war. And one Northern man wishing to communicate some good news to his Southern kin took advantage of this, solving his problem in an elegant fashion.

One day a letter turned up at the post office in Louisville, Kentucky, having been routed there from somewhere north of the Ohio. On it, in addition to the stamp and address, was a bit of verse.

> Feds and Confeds, let this go free
> Down to Nashville, Tennessee;
> This three-cent stamp will pay the cost
> Until you find Sophia Yost.
> Postmasters North, or even South,
> May open it and find the truth;
> I merely say my wife's got well,
> and has a baby, cross as . . . ,
> you know!

A Problem in the Ranks

In the spring of 1861 newly minted Brig. Gen. William T. Sherman commanded a brigade in the army which concentrated at Washington. After Bull Run (21 July 1861), at which the brigade was heavily engaged, his troops held part of the defenses of the city as the army was reorganized. There were a lot of problems, for the troops were all ill-trained militiamen. A major difficulty developed over the terms under which the men enlisted, 90-days. The principal issue lay in the definition of when the period in question began. A number of men claimed that their 90-days began when they enlisted in their regiments, usually in their home towns, while the

War Department contended that it began only when the regiment was accepted for service. But let Sherman tell the story, in a slightly edited version of his own words, from *Memoirs of General William T. Sherman* (New York, 1875).

By the 25th [of July] I had collected all the materials, made my report, and had my brigade about as well governed as any in the army; although most of the ninety-day men, especially the Sixty-ninth [New York Militia], had become extremely tired of the war, and wanted to go home. Some of them were so mutinous, at one time, that I had the battery to unlimber, threatening, if they dared to leave camp without orders, I would open fire on them. Drills and daily exercises were resumed, and I ordered that at the three principal roll-calls the men should form ranks with belts and muskets, and that they should keep their ranks until I in person had received the reports and had dismissed them. The Sixty-ninth still occupied Fort Corcoran, and one morning, after reveille, when I had just received the report, had dismissed the regiment, and was leaving, I found myself in a crowd of men crossing the drawbridge on their way to a barn close by, where they had their sinks; among them was an officer, who said: "Colonel, I am going to New York today. What can I do for you?" I answered: "How can you go to New York? I do not remember to have signed a leave for you." He said, "No; he did not want a leave. He had engaged to serve three months, and had already served more than that time. If the Government did not intend to pay him, he could afford to lose the money; that he was a lawyer, and had neglected his business long enough, and was then going home." I noticed that a good many of the soldiers had paused about us to listen, and knew that, if this officer could defy me, they also would. So I turned on him sharp, and said: "Captain, this question of your term of service has been submitted to the rightful authority, and the decision has been published in orders. You are a soldier, and must submit to orders till you are properly discharged. If you attempt to leave without orders, it will be mutiny, and I will shoot you like a dog! Go back into the fort *now*, instantly, and don't dare leave without my consent." I had on an overcoat, and may have had my hand about the breast, for he looked at me hard, paused a moment, and then turned back into the fort. The men scattered, and I returned to the house where I was quartered, close by.

That same day, which must have been about July 26th, I was near the river-bank, looking at a block-house which had been built for the defense of the aqueduct, when I saw a carriage coming by the road that crossed the Potomac River at Georgetown by a ferry. I thought I recognized in the carriage the person of President Lincoln. I hurried across a bend, so as to stand by the road-side as the carriage passed. I was in uniform with a sword on, and was recognized by Mr. Lincoln and Mr. Seward, who rode side by side in an open hack. I inquired if they were going to my camps, and Mr. Lincoln said, "Yes; we heard that you had got over the big scare, and we thought we would come over and see the 'boys.'" The roads had been much changed and were rough. I asked if I might give directions to his coachman, he promptly invited me to jump in and to tell the coachman which way to drive. Intending to begin on the right and follow around to the left, I turned the driver into a side-road which led up a very steep hill, and, seeing a soldier, called to him and sent him up hurriedly to announce to the colonel (Bennet, I think) that the president was coming. As we slowly ascended the hill, I discovered that Mr. Lincoln was full of feeling, and wanted to encourage our men. I asked if he intended to speak with them, and he said he would like to. I asked him then to please discourage all cheering, noise, or any sort of confusion; that we had had enough of it before Bull Run to ruin any sort of men, and that what we needed were cool, thoughtful, hard-fighting soldiers— no more hurrahing, no more humbug. He took my remarks in the most perfect good-nature. Before we had reached the first camp, I heard the drum beating the "assembly," saw the men running from their tents, and in a few minutes the regiment was in line, arms presented, and then brought to an order and "parade rest."

Mr. Lincoln stood up in the carriage, and made one of the neatest, best, and most feeling addresses I ever listened to, referring to our late disaster at Bull Run, the high duties that still devolved on us, and the brighter days to come. At one or two points the soldiers began to cheer, but he promptly checked them, saying: "Don't cheer, boys. I confess I rather like it myself, but Colonel Sherman here says it is not military; and I guess we better defer to his opinion." In winding up, he explained that, as president, he was commander-in-chief; that he was resolved that the soldiers should have everything that the law allowed; and he called on one and all to appeal to him personally in case they were wronged. The effect of this speech was excellent.

We passed along in the same manner to all the camps of my brigade; and Mr. Lincoln complimented me highly for the order, cleanliness, and discipline, that he observed. Indeed, he and Mr. Seward both assured me that it was the first bright moment they had experienced since the battle.

At last we reached Fort Corcoran. The carriage could not enter, so I ordered the regiment, without arms, to come outside, and gather about Mr. Lincoln who would speak to them. He made to them the same feeling address, with more personal allusions, because of their special gallantry in the battle under Corcoran, who was still a prisoner in the hands of the enemy; and he concluded with the same general offer of redress in case of grievance. In the crowd I saw the officer with whom I had had the passage at reveille that morning. His face was pale, and his lips compressed.

I foresaw a scene, but sat on the front seat of the carriage as quiet as a lamb. This officer forced his way through the crowd to the carriage, and said: "Mr. president, I have cause for grievance. This morning I went to speak to Colonel Sherman, and he threatened to shoot me." Mr. Lincoln who was still standing, said, "Threatened to shoot you?" Yes, sir, he threatened to shoot me." Mr. Lincoln looked at him, then at me, and stooping his tall, spare form toward the officer, said to him in a loud stage-whisper, easily heard for some yards around: "Well, if I were you, and he threatened to shoot, I would not trust him, for I believe he would do it." The officer turned about and disappeared, and the men laughed at him. Soon the carriage drove on, and, as we descended the hill I explained the facts to the president, who answered, "Of course I didn't know any thing about it, but I thought you knew your own business best." I thanked him for his confidence, and assured him that what he had done would go far to enable me to maintain good discipline, and it did.

Mrs. Hancock's Dinner Party

On 15 June 1861 Captain and Mrs. Winfield Scott Hancock gave a farewell dinner party at Los Angeles for several officers who had recently resigned their commissions in order to join the Confederacy. The guest of honor was Col. Albert Sidney Johnston, but lately Acting Commander of the Department of the Pacific, who would later die leading a Confederate army at Shiloh in early 1862. Despite the somewhat awkward circumstances, the evening passed in good spirits and everyone parted on friendly terms. It had been an unusual dinner in many ways, and the aftermath was to be even more so. Years later Mrs. Hancock observed that three of the officers present died at Gettysburg during Pickett's Charge against her husband's position along Cemetery Ridge on 3 July 1863. Two of these were the then Capt. Richard B. Garnett and the then Maj. Lewis A. Armistead, who had given Mrs. Hancock a prayer book on that last happy occasion, both of whom led brigades against Hancock's *II Corps*, with the death of the latter marking the instant of the "High Tide" of the Confederacy. Mrs. Hancock could not recall the name of the third, nor has his identity been established with any degree of satisfaction.

Stonewall Jackson's Railroad Movement

Thomas J. Jackson's campaign in the Shenandoah Valley in the spring of 1861 is widely recognized as a stellar example of the military art, as he successfully out-marched and out-fought less ably led but greatly superior

Union forces, a campaign which has provided inspiration to succeeding generations of soldiers. However, Jackson's earlier tenure in the Valley in mid 1861, is often overlooked, which is unfortunate, for during that period occurred one of the most innovative and clever maneuvers of his career, his rail movements in May and July. It must, of course, be understood that it was not Jackson who was moving by railroad, but rather Jackson who was moving the railroad, or, rather, some valuable pieces of it.

Harper's Ferry, the principal town at the lower end of the Shenandoah Valley, was an important junction in the Baltimore & Ohio Railroad, the most southerly and most direct connection between Washington and Ohio, a link of inestimable value to the Union, if only because it was the principal carrier of coal to Washington and Baltimore. While the iron logic of war dictated that this line be cut, important political considerations dictated otherwise. The B&O was a Maryland railroad and ran mostly through that border state. Despite swift action by the Lincoln Administration to keep Maryland to her loyalties, it was widely believed in the South that Maryland might yet throw her lot in with the Confederacy, and thus it was necessary to avoid antagonizing the people of the state. As a result, B&O freight trains were permitted to pass through Harper's Ferry despite the fact that the place was in Confederate hands.

As time went on, it became increasingly clear that Maryland was not going to secede and Jackson began to contemplate action against the railroad. He began in a small way. In mid-May the president of the B&O, John W. Garrett, received an unusual message from Jackson. "The noise of your trains," he wrote, "is intolerable. My men find their repose disturbed by them each night. You will have to work out some other method of operating them." Since Garrett was quite aware that the continued operation of the line depended on Jackson's good will he acted with commendable speed. Schedules were shortly revised so that trains passed through Harper's Ferry only during daylight hours. But Jackson complained again, for the increased traffic interfered with the daily routine of the troops, who were drilled in the mornings and inspected in the afternoons. Could Garrett make some additional modifications to the schedule? Once again Garrett complied, arranging for all traffic to occur from 11:00 a.m. to 1:00 p.m. Soon the double traced line was "the liveliest railroad in America" for two hours each day as heavily ladened trains carried coal eastbound and empty ones rumbled westwards.

This new arrangement suited Jackson very well. On 23 May he made his move. At 11:00 a.m. Capt. John D. Imboden of the Staunton Artillery blocked the eastbound track at Point of Rocks, in Maryland, about 20 miles east of Harper's Ferry, though permitting traffic to continue westwards from that point. Then, at 1:00 p.m. Col. Kenton Harper of the 5th Virginia cut the westbound track at Martinsburg, about 18 miles west of Harper's Ferry. Altogether 42 locomotives and 386 cars were taken, a valuable prize indeed for the rolling stock-starved Confederacy. Jackson immediately began to send cars south, along the rickety tracks of the Winchester & Potomac. Unfortunately, only four small locomotives could make the run. And since the Winchester & Potomac was a deadend line, the additional rolling stock was of limited use. Limited, that is, until the ingenious Jackson—he would not become "Stonewall" for some weeks yet—got to thinking. At Winchester the locomotives were stripped and taken off the rails. Teams of horses were attached to them and they were hauled over the hard, dry Valley Pike for 20 miles, to Strasburg, on the Manassas Gap Railroad, which connected with the rest of the Southern railroad system. There they were rerailed, refitted and pressed into service. Jackson's clever trap and resourceful movement of the captured locomotives was very valuable to the Confederacy. And within weeks he did it again.

In mid-June, Union forces in southern Pennsylvania began to show signs of moving south, as did those concentrating about Washington. On 14 June Maj. Gen. Joseph E. Johnston, Jackson's newly appointed superior, ordered him to evacuate Harper's Ferry. Over the next few days Jackson demolished everything of value within miles of Harper's Ferry, including the rail and road bridges, the rail yards, all remaining rolling stock and the former United States arsenal. Jackson's long arm reached even to Martinsburg, where, in addition to important machine shops, there was considerable rolling stock, including fourteen big locomotives. Whatever couldn't be evacuated had to be destroyed, but Jackson hesitated over the engines. And decided that what could be done once, could be done twice, and bigger and better at that. He ordered them prepared to be towed overland to Strasburg, 38 miles on the Valley Pike.

It required over 200 men—six machinists, ten teamsters, scores of laborers—with 40 horses to haul one 50-ton locomotive. The work was hard. After a preliminary stripping of all removable parts, each locomotive was jacked up so that the front wheels and all drive rods could be removed. The front end was then lowered onto a heavy wooden truck provided with wide, thick wooden wheels and secured in place, so that the engine now rested on the wooden truck and its rear wheels. The horses were then hitched in place at the end of a 100 foot chain. When all was in readiness, the horses were whipped up and slowly the behemoth began to move.

The movement required four days. The first stage, from Martinsburg to Winchester, was fairly easy, 18 miles of relatively flat going. But the 20 from Winchester to Strasburg was more difficult, as it covered hilly country. It required as many as 200 men heaving on ropes to help the horses haul a locomotive up some of the grades, and as many more to help them down again. But the work was done, despite the enormous obstacles and some harassment from Union snipers. At Strasburg the engines were re-railed, reassembled and dispatched to Richmond for overhauls. In all, Jackson had added 18 locomotives to the slender rolling stock resources of the South. And then, a couple of days later he turned up at Bull Run.

"Self Defense, Sir"

There is a tale which is told of both armies, at various times, in numerous different regiments, but apparently having its origins in the very first months of the war. There are several versions of the story, but all retain the same essential elements, specifically an officer, a private and a pig.

One day a private walked nonchalantly into camp with a rather large, bulky object concealed under his coat. An officer espied the fellow and challenged him.

"What's that you've got there under your coat, soldier?"

"Why, sir, it's a pig," replied the young man.

"Don't you know it's against regulations to take livestock from the local people?"

"Yes, sir, I known that, but I killed the pig in self defense."

"How was that?"

"Well, I was coming down the road just outside of camp when I heard a loud noise. Looking about, I spied this pig charging down on me. Having no choice, I raised my musket and fired, killing him dead."

"Oh, I understand," said the officer, "and, of course, I will have to examine the evidence." Thereupon the private was permitted to go on his way, though with his burden somewhat lightened by that portion of the "evidence" which the officer required.

The Eleven Hour Day

During the Confederate siege of Lexington, Missouri, (12-20 September 1861) there was an elderly Texan who served as a free-lance infantryman for the cause. The old gent would arrive at the siege lines each day at 7:00 a.m., dressed in buckskin, toting an old flintlock with a generous supply of ammunition and carrying a full dinner pail. Selecting a good position in the works, he soon settled himself in and then proceeded to bang away at the Yankees. Promptly at noon the gentleman would cease firing for an hour, during which he had his lunch and took a little rest. Then, at 1:00 p.m. he would resume his "work," banging away until six in the evening, when he would knock off for the day, carrying his musket and dinner pail back home, where supper and a good night's rest would ready him for the next day's business.

The Men

Jefferson F. Davis

One of the most influential men in the country long before the Civil War, Jefferson Finis Davis (1808-1889) was born in Christian County, Kentucky, into a family in comfortable circumstances. Though a Baptist, he received his early education at a Catholic school, and then attended both Jefferson College, near Natchez, Tennessee, and Transylvania College, at Lexington, Kentucky, before enrolling in West Point in 1824. Davis' career at the academy was unspectacular, and when he graduated in 1828 he was 23rd in a class of 32. He served as a junior officer of dragoons until 1835, when he resigned to become a planter in Mississippi. That same year he married the daughter of Col. Zachary Taylor, one of the most distinguished officers in the army, but she died of malaria just three months later. Over the next decade Davis built a considerable fortune as a planter, introducing innovative agricultural and management methods: his slaves were governed by an elective body of their own choosing. In 1845 Davis married again, to the considerably younger Varina Howell (1826-1905) of Natchez, who proved an important influence in his life. That same year he entered politics, successfully running for the House of Representatives and immediately establishing a reputation as a champion of "Southern rights." An enthusiastic expansionist, on the outbreak of the Mexican War in 1846 he resigned his seat in the House to serve as colonel of the *1st Mississippi Mounted Rifles*.

In Mexico, Davis served with distinction under his former father-in-law, Zachary Taylor, until severely wounded at Buena Vista. Mexico made him the most popular citizen in Mississippi, and upon his discharge he was elected to the United States Senate. Davis resigned his seat in the Senate in 1851 to make a bid for the governorship of Mississippi. Although he lost, in 1853 Franklin Pierce, who had succeeded to the presidency upon the death of Zachary Taylor, asked him to serve as secretary of war. Davis proved an excellent secretary, and under his aegis the organization, administration and equipment of the army underwent extensive examination.

Several new regiments were added, officers—including Capt. George B. McClellan—were dispatched to observe the British and French military in action during the Crimean War, a new musket was adopted and an experimental camel corps was organized, while military engineers undertook surveys to determine the optimal route for a transcontinental railroad. Meanwhile Davis managed to acquire considerable political influence, and helped secure passage of the Kansas-Nebraska Act, which seriously worsened sectional tensions over slavery. When Pierce left office in 1857, Davis was returned to the Senate by the Mississippi legislature.

Over the next four years Davis became an increasingly strident spokesman for states' rights and slavery, even advocating the reopening of the African slave trade. Despite this, he was viewed by some as a compromise Democratic candidate for president in 1860. But the party split into three parts and Republican Abraham Lincoln was elected. Lincoln's election sparked the "Secession Winter," which seemed to forebode the imminent dissolution of the Union. Mississippi passed an "Ordinance of Secession" on 9 January 1861, the second state to do so. Davis lingered in Washington for a bit, apparently in hopes that a pro-southern "compromise" could be worked out, and then, on 21 January made an eloquent farewell address to the Senate and resigned his seat.

Returning to Mississippi, Davis served briefly as commanding general of the state's military forces before he was elected president of the Confederacy. He served in that post for a little more than four years, guiding the fortunes of the South through one of the most arduous and devastating wars in the history of any English-speaking country.

When chosen president, Davis expressed surprise and regrets at his election. This seems to have been a bit of false modesty. He could not have been so naive as to realize that given his political stature there was no other choice: no Southerner was more popular and none had a greater political reputation, nor did any have superior administrative qualifications. But Davis was, in fact, ill-suited to the task at hand. A stubborn, narrow-minded man, he was usually inflexible, touchy in matters of pride, and excessively loyal to his friends and inveterately hostile to his foes, regardless of circumstances. Moreover, he believed himself to be something of a military genius, a matter which greatly hampered the conduct of the war, and he quarreled with virtually every one of his military commanders. That the Confederacy endured for four years is far more a tribute to the dedication and sacrifice of its people, than to the will, intellect, vision and determination of its president.

When the Army of Northern Virginia was compelled to evacuate Richmond, Davis fled southwards, hoping to join Confederate forces still resisting in the West. On the evening of 10 May he was captured near Irwinville, Georgia, by a Union cavalry patrol. Davis spent two years imprisoned in Fortress Monroe, as various factions in the Federal government tried to figure out what to do with him. In the end, nothing was done. In 1867 Davis was released on bail pending a trial on charges of treason. The charges were eventually allowed to lapse and Davis spent the rest of his life unmolested.

Davis passed his last days quietly. He traveled abroad for a time, and then in 1877 settled at Beauvoir, his plantation near Biloxi, Mississippi. There he wrote his *The Rise and Fall of the Confederate Government* (New York, 1881), a tendentious, self-exculpatory work of little historical value. Never a beloved man, in his last years he attained some measure of respect and veneration as a symbol of the "Lost Cause," never requesting amnesty nor taking the oath of allegiance to the United States. So in the end, Davis attained a measure of the nobility which eluded him when he needed it most.

Pierre Gustav Toutant Beauregard

Scion of an old and distinguished Louisiana creole family, Pierre Gustav Toutant Beauregard (1818-1893) was the Confederacy's first war hero. Beauregard, second man in the West Point class of 1838, was commissioned in the Corps of Engineers, and sent to help build coast defenses and clear hazards to navigation. During the Mexican War he served with distinction as an engineer on Lt. Gen. Winfield Scott's staff, being twice wounded and earning two brevets. With the coming of peace he returned to more mundane matters. In 1858 he was made chief engineer in charge of the drainage of New Orleans, but devoted most of his time to improving navigation on the Lower Mississippi and supervising the construction of the New Orleans customs house, a white elephant project which had been dragging on for several decades and continued for several more. In January of 1861 he was briefly Superintendent of West Point, but was relieved for what Southern sympathizers term "suspicion of disloyalty," which was nevertheless a legitimate charge given that he had informed a Louisiana cadet that he would go with his state should it secede. Louisiana seceded soon afterwards and he tendered his resignation as captain and brevet major.

Within a few days he was appointed a brigadier general in the Confederate Army and sent to Charleston to supervise the investment of Fort

Sumter. Sumter made Beauregard's reputation. When he went to Virginia to assume a command under Gen. Joseph E. Johnston, he was given a hero's welcome along the entire route.

Beauregard was in direct command of the Confederate forces during the First Battle of Bull Run (21 July 1861), handing his West Point classmate Irvin McDowell a sound thrashing. As a reward, Beauregard was promoted full general in the Confederate Regular Army. He was not, however, given a command commensurate with his new rank, and ran afoul of Jefferson Davis when he brought up the subject. Davis sent him west to serve under Gen. Albert Sidney Johnston. Beauregard helped plan the Shiloh Campaign, and, when Johnston was killed on 6 April 1862, assumed command. The results of the first day's battle being so favorable, he wired Richmond word of a tremendous victory. The Union riposte on the following day convinced Davis—who bore grudges—that Beauregard was a poor commander. When, several weeks later, Beauregard abandoned Corinth, Mississippi, in the face of superior Union forces (110,000 to 66,000), Davis decided that Beauregard had to go. Rather than act aboveboard, he waited for an opportune moment. A few weeks later Beauregard fell ill and went on sick leave, temporarily turning command of the Army of Tennessee over to Braxton Bragg. Davis pounced. Claiming that Beauregard had abandoned his post without authorization, Davis relieved him of command.

For nearly two years thereafter Beauregard commanded coast defenses in Georgia and the Carolinas. While it was important work, he was probably wasted in such a limited assignment. Finally, in April of 1864 he was sent to the defenses of Petersburg. In the Drewry's Bluff Campaign (4-18 May 1864), Beauregard skillfully met, held, and beat back the initially stronger forces of Union Maj. Gen. Benjamin Butler's *Army of the James*. Several days later his command was merged into the Army of Northern Virginia and he was again unemployed. Briefly given a hollow theater command in the West, Beauregard ended the war serving with Gen. Joseph E. Johnston in the Carolinas.

After the war Beauregard became quite prosperous in railroading, did some writing and served as adjutant general of Louisiana. Although he became involved in the notorious Louisiana Lottery, he apparently never realized it was crooked: unsold tickets were included in the drawings. His military reputation remaining high, he occasionally considered seeking, and was several times offered, commissions from powers as diverse as France, Brazil, Argentina, Egypt, Romania and Spain.

Beauregard, nicknamed "The Napoleon in Gray," was short of stature, but looked every inch a soldier. He had an enormous military reputation in his lifetime—he was once mobbed by admiring New Yorkers—and much written about him since reflects this high regard. Yet there was little of substance in his career. At neither Sumter nor Bull Run did he demonstrate—nor need—any spectacular military skill. Neither his planning nor his performance at Shiloh were particularly impressive. And his opponent at Drewry's Bluff was one of the most inept in the Union Army. To be sure, his operations after Shiloh demonstrated some skill and he was a fine coast defense engineer. Moreover, he was, with Joseph Johnston, one of the few Confederate leaders to see that a concentration in the Western theater was probably the optimal Southern strategy, a view which, while militarily sound, only got him more deeply into trouble with Jefferson Davis. In the final analysis, it must be said that Beauregard's abilities were never properly tested in the field.

Nathaniel Lyon

A native of Connecticut, the short, slim, redheaded Nathaniel Lyon (1818-1861) graduated from West Point in 1841 and had a fairly typical career in the Old Army: frontier duty, service against the Seminoles, Mexico (one wound and one brevet), and a tour in "Bleeding Kansas." During the "Secession Winter" he was a captain in the *2nd Infantry*, stationed in St. Louis. Secessionists being particularly active in the state, Lyon collaborated with Frank P. Blair to organize a Unionist response. Working behind the back of Lyon's superior, the affable, but Southern-sympathizing and befuddled Brig. Gen. William A. Harney, the two organized a home guard from loyal citizens and the large German community, pinched arms from the Federal arsenal, which Lyon commanded, and in a clever coup captured the largely secessionist militia while it lay encamped just outside St. Louis. Appointed a brigadier general of state troops in mid-May, Lyon was named brigadier general of volunteers by Lincoln on the 17th. Quickly organizing an army, he led it against the superior secessionist forces of Sterling Price. Lyon conducted a series of operations which largely secured Missouri for the Union, despite his death and the defeat of his forces at Wilson's Creek on 10 August 1861. Lyon was the right man in the right place at the right time. His death in action deprived the Union of a capable soldier willing to take the initiative and not afraid to take responsibility.

Raphael Semmes

The Confederacy's first naval hero, Raphael Semmes (1809-1877) was born in Maryland. Appointed a midshipman in the navy in 1826, he did not actually serve afloat until 1832, by which time he had been admitted to the bar. His career was satisfactory, if largely uneventful save for blockade duty during the War with Mexico, out of which he got two books, one a history of Scott's campaign and the other a personal memoir. Settling in Alabama after the war, Semmes continued in the service, rising to commander in 1855. When Alabama seceded, he resigned from the service and was promptly commissioned in the same rank in the Confederate Navy.

In the tense weeks before Fort Sumter, Semmes was assigned to a procurement mission in the North, purchasing desperately needed supplies for shipment south, during which period he managed to attend Lincoln's inauguration. Briefly in charge of the Confederacy's lighthouse bureau, he was shortly assigned the task of fitting out a raiding cruiser at New Orleans. The 520 ton C.S.S. *Sumter*, was converted from merchant ship to sloop-of-war in about eight weeks, from 18 April 1861 to mid-June.

After playing cat-and-mouse with Federal blockaders for several weeks, Semmes was able to slip out of the Mississippi on 30 June and begin a rather successful career as a commerce raider. Over the next six months, *Sumter* took 18 prizes, several times eluded Union pursuers, and began the near-total disruption of American flag shipping which the war was to cause. Finally, in January of 1862, Semmes put in at Gibraltar hoping to effect some repairs to *Sumter's* increasingly failing engines. Unable to secure assistance—U.S.-British relations were just then in delicate balance—and unable to sortie because three Federal warships (one of them the U.S.S. *Kearsarge*) soon showed up on the horizon, Semmes paid off his crew, sold the ship to a British firm, and made his way overland to England.

In England, a new ship was procured for Semmes, C.S.S. *Alabama*. He took command of the vessel in the Azores in August of 1862, rapidly converted her into a commerce raider, and set out on a devastating career. In the next two years Semmes would take or destroy 69 vessels, including a Union blockader, setting a record for a raiding cruiser never since equaled. Semmes' activities led to the mass abandonment of the American flag by hundreds of merchant vessels. In June of 1864 he put in at Cherbourg, France, hoping to effect some major repairs. Finding the French government unwilling to cooperate, and with the Union sloop-of-war *Kearsarge* looming on the horizon, Semmes decided to fight it out and actually sent a formal challenge to *Kearsarge*. The two vessels dueled on 19 June, andthe sinking *Alabama* was struck after about two hours. Semmes and many of his crew were rescued by a British yacht and landed in England.

Taking a blockade runner home, Semmes was given a hero's welcome, promoted rear admiral, and assigned to command the James River flotilla, a strong squadron which helped keep the Union fleet and army away from Richmond. By this time the war was virtually over. Semmes' sole important act as commander of the flotilla was to order its destruction upon the abandonment of Richmond and Petersburg by the Army of Northern Virginia in early April of 1865. Organizing his men into a naval brigade, Semmes was made an acting brigadier general in one of Jefferson Davis' last official acts. Eluding immediate capture, Semmes and his men made their way south to join Joe Johnston's Army of Tennessee, with which they surrendered on 18 April.

Although paroled, in December of 1865 Semmes was arrested and charged with piracy, treason and a number of other crimes. After about three months, all charges were dropped. Semmes was briefly a college professor and newspaper editor before returning to Alabama to practice law and write *Memoirs of Service Afloat* and *The Cruise of the Alabama and Sumter.* His younger brother, Paul Jones Semmes (1815-1863), had a distinguished career with the Army of Northern Virginia, serving as colonel of the 2nd Georgia and later as a brigadier general until mortally wounded on the first day at Gettysburg.

Thomas J. Jackson

Among the most successful and the most daring of Civil War commanders, and certainly the most eccentric, the "Gallant Stonewall" (1824-1863) was born in poverty in what is now West Virginia. Raised by an uncle after his parents died, Jackson received a haphazard education, but nevertheless managed to secure an appointment to West Point, where his academic standing increased each year so that it was said of him "if the course had been a year longer he would have come out first." Graduating in 1846, he served in John B. Magruder's battery during the Mexican War, winning two brevets. After garrison duty in New York and Florida, Jackson resigned in 1851 to become professor of artillery and natural philosophy—physics—at the Virginia Military Institute. In 1859 he commanded a company of cadets at the hanging of John Brown.

On the outbreak of the Civil War, Jackson was promoted colonel in the militia. Soon after appointed a colonel and then a brigadier general in the Confederate Army, his first war service was as commander of the brigade which occupied Harper's Ferry. Jackson led his brigade with great distinction at Bull Run on 21 July 1861, earning for it—and himself—the cognomen "Stonewall." Promoted major general early that Autumn, Jackson was shortly sent back to the Shenandoah Valley. Although he was involved in a number of minor operations through the winter, there was nothing, not even his performance at Bull Run, to suggest that he was anything but a rather pedestrian commander. Nothing, that is, until the spring, when he undertook what would become one of the most spectacular campaigns in American history, the Valley Campaign.

Essentially a strategic diversion, Jackson's objectives in the Shenandoah Valley in the spring of 1862 were threefold: to prevent the Union from gaining control of the vital agricultural resources of the fertile Valley, to tie-down Federal forces which might otherwise be committed against Richmond and to act as a reserve for the outnumbered Army of Northern Virginia. All this Jackson achieved with remarkable skill, though himself greatly outnumbered, so that by June, he had neutralized some 50,000 Union troops while bringing nearly 20,000 men to reinforce the Army of Northern Virginia in time for the Seven Days. While his performance during the opening engagements of the Seven Days left something to be desired, Jackson steadily improved as his relationship with Gen. Robert E. Lee grew closer.

After an initially poor start at Cedar Mountain, during the opening phases of the Second Bull Run Campaign, Jackson became Lee's most effective corps commander, entrusted with the most daring missions, culminating in his spectacular envelopment of John Pope's *Army of Virginia* at Second Bull Run and timely arrival at Antietam, which probably saved the Army of Northern Virginia from destruction. Promoted lieutenant general the following October, Jackson led his II Corps at Fredericksburg and Chancellorsville, where he executed the spectacularly successful flank march which resulted in the collapse of Union Maj. Gen. Joseph Hooker's offensive. On the evening of 2 May 1863 Jackson was wounded by some of his own men as he was making a reconnaissance with his staff. Despite the amputation of his left arm, he died on 10 May.

Stonewall Jackson was a remarkable tactician, fearless of vision, bold in execution, daring in the attack and stubborn in the defense. A man of numerous idiosyncrasies—one is almost tempted to suggest that he was not quite sane—he had few, if any, equals as a soldier. A big man, about six feet tall and 175 pounds, Jackson had blue eyes and a brown beard. Extraordinarily religious, Jackson was a devout Presbyterian and did not smoke, drink, nor gamble, ate sparingly and lived simply. His death was a devastating blow to the Confederacy, Lee himself observing, "I have lost my right arm."

Irvin McDowell

Born in Ohio, Irvin McDowell (1818-1885) was educated in France before attending West Point, from which he graduated in 1838. After a short tour of duty on the frontier, he returned to the Academy as an instructor from 1841 through 1845. As an aide-de-camp to Maj. Gen. J.E. Wool in Mexico he served with some distinction, winning a brevet. After another short tour of duty on the frontier, McDowell was assigned to the office of the Adjutant General and spent many years at headquarters in Washington.

On the outbreak of the Civil War McDowell was jumped from major to brigadier general for no apparent reason other than that he was well-known to Lt. Gen. Winfield Scott and Secretary of the Treasury Salmon P. Chase. Worse yet, although he had never commanded so much as a company, McDowell was assigned to lead the army concentrating about Washington in the spring of 1861. Although his plan for what would become the Bull Run Campaign was sound, it expected too much from the green troops who would have to execute it. Only the fact that the Confederate forces opposing his advance were equally green prevented Bull Run from turning into a decisive disaster.

After Bull Run, McDowell was given a division in the newly formed *Army of the Potomac.* Early in 1862 he was made a major general and given command of *I Corps*, over the objections of the army commander, Maj. Gen. George B. McClellan. McDowell's command went through several name changes, emerging as *III Corps* of John Pope's *Army of Virginia*, which saw service in the Second Bull Run Campaign, during which McDowell clearly did not perform well. Relieved, he demanded, and received, a court of inquiry. Although the court found him not culpable of misconduct, he never afterwards commanded troops in the field. For the balance of the war McDowell served in various administrative capacities. Continuing in the service after the war, he was promoted major general in the Regular Army in 1872 and retired a decade later to become Parks Commissioner of San Francisco.

McDowell, a big, powerful looking man with a friendly manner, was a perfect example of the kind of officer who rises to high command in peace time. An excellent administrator and able planner, he was a poor commander, and very unlucky.

George B. McClellan

A native of Philadelphia, George Brinton McClellan (1826-1885) was a child prodigy, who attended the University of Pennsylvania before entering West Point at the age of fifteen. Graduating second in the class of '46, he served as an engineer in Mexico, winning two brevets. Over the next decade he had a varied career, including three years as an instructor at West Point, exploration and survey work in the West and military observer in the Crimean War. As a result of his European tour, he designed the "McClellan saddle," a comfortable and serviceable if clumsy-looking affair which remains the army's official saddle. In 1857 he resigned to become chief engineer of the Illinois Central Railroad, one Abraham Lincoln being counted among the corporation's attorneys.

At the outbreak of the Civil War, McClellan was serving as president of the Ohio and Mississippi Railroad. Commissioned a major general of Ohio troops within a fortnight of Sumter, McClellan was extremely active in preparing the state militia for war. On Winfield Scott's recommendation, Lincoln commissioned McClellan—whom he had, rather surprisingly, never met—a major general in the Regular Army on 14 May, making him the second ranking man in the army.

Given command of the upper Ohio Valley, McClellan worked energetically to hold Kentucky and western Virginia for the Union. Taking the field in the latter region, he was credited with securing what would become West Virginia for the Union as a result of the victories at Philippi (3 June 1861) and Rich Mountain (11 July). Though the actions were minor ones, the consequences were considerable and McClellan, who had not actually been present at either fight, rapidly became a major war hero, due partially to the fact that touting his success helped offset the unfortunate experience at Bull Run.

In consequence, McClellan was shortly brought to Washington and given charge of what would become the *Army of the Potomac*. Energetic as ever, he proved a capable organizer and drillmaster, turning a mass of demoralized, ill-trained volunteers into a finely-tuned fighting machine. However, soon after taking command, a certain weakness of character began to manifest itself in a variety of forms. Whatever else his talents, McClellan was also egotistical, argumentative and secretive and had a contempt for the civil authority. Disputes with General-in-Chief Scott— who had gotten him his command to begin with—led to the latter's resignation in November. Despite the fact that he had serious misgivings about McClellan, Lincoln gave him Scott's post. Although Lincoln pressed for a winter campaign, he deferred to McClellan's military opinion: not yet having learned that they were disposable, the president was at this point still in awe of generals.

McClellan devised a brilliant plan of operations for the spring of 1862, one perfectly suited to the strategic situation which confronted him through the winter: with the main Confederate force encamped at Manassas, not 40 miles from Washington, he proposed to make use of Federal sea power to interpose his army between Richmond and Confederate Gen. Joseph E. Johnston's Army of Northern Virginia. But by the time he was ready to move the situation had changed: Johnston had pulled back to a more centrally located position. Despite this reverse—a reverse which McClellan considered a victory secured by "pure military skill"—the "Little Napoleon" pressed on with his plans. The result was the Peninsular Campaign. Despite the fact that the Confederates were strategically in a much better position to respond to McClellan's movement than at the time the operation was planned, the Peninsular Campaign might well have succeeded, save for McClellan himself.

For all his brilliance and energy and popularity with the troops, McClellan proved less than spectacular on the battlefield. He was too cautious, lacked the ability to grasp the "big picture," proved unable to adequately control his subordinates and took counsel of his fears. And, although he secured several significant victories, he lacked the nerve of a Lee or the killer instincts of a Jackson, and was beaten back from literally the gates of Richmond; the campaign ended in an ignominious retreat. The *Army of the Potomac* would not again get so close to the Confederate capital for two years.

Temporarily on the shelf after the Peninsula, McClellan was recalled to command after the disasters of the Second Bull Run Campaign. Once again demonstrating his abilities, he rapidly restored the morale of the *Army of the Potomac* and at Antietam inflicted a reverse on the Army of Northern Virginia, while letting slip the opportunity to deliver a smashing defeat. McClellan had become increasingly associated with the anti-Lincoln, anti-war elements in the North and there was even some suspicion of disloyalty; certainly McClellan did nothing to discourage anti-democratic and subversive talk among his subordinates. In any case, Lincoln decided to relieve him. On 7 November 1862, McClellan was replaced by Maj. Gen. Ambrose Burnside and told to "await further orders." These never came.

McClellan became politically active, maneuvering to return to command—and indeed he was a better officer than either of his next two successors—and in 1864 he received the Democratic nomination for president. Although verbally committed to the successful prosecution of the war, he was widely regarded as a "peace at any price" candidate and went down to crushing defeat. McClellan's abilities as a soldier were distinctly mixed. A superb organizer and trainer of men, he was a brilliant commander on paper, but lacked the flexibility, imagination and will to gain smashing victories in the field.

Benjamin F. Butler

One of the most prominent and under-rated "political" generals of the war, Benjamin Franklin Butler (1818-1893) was born in New Hampshire, but spent most of his life in Massachusetts. After college he taught in Lowell until admitted to the bar in 1840. The genial, diminutive, stocky Butler rapidly built a successful criminal practice in Lowell and Boston. Entering politics as a Democrat in 1853, he served in both houses of the state legislature. In 1860 he was a delegate to the disastrous Democratic National Convention in Charleston, during which, believing that only a moderate candidate could save the Union, he supported the nomination of Jefferson Davis through 57 consecutive votes. He subsequently took part in the rump convention at Baltimore which nominated the more extreme John C. Breckinridge.

Despite this highly conservative record, Butler proved a staunch Unionist upon the fall of Fort Sumter. A brigadier general of Massachusetts militia, his first war service was early and important. Accompanying the *8th Massachusetts* en route to Washington, he arrived in Philadelphia on the afternoon of 19 April to learn that secessionists in Baltimore had attacked the *6th Massachusetts* earlier that same day. The next morning, as the *7th New York* arrived, he learned that secessionists had burned several railroad bridges, thus isolating Washington from the North. Showing great presence of mind, he took off by steamer for Annapolis, arriving on the 21st, and sent both regiments on to Washington on the 24th, thus reopening communications with the capital. Little more than three weeks later Butler occupied restless Baltimore in a swiftly executed operation on 13 May, thereby ensuring rail communications with the North. For his efforts he was named a major general of volunteers, the first such created in the war and was soon transferred to command Fortress Monroe, a Federal toehold on Virginia's Chesapeake shore.

Butler's tenure at Fortress Monroe was acrimonious. Although he was largely responsible for the Union reverse at Big Bethel (10 June 1861), he gained a considerable measure of fame when, unwilling to return fugitive slaves to their so-called masters, he declared them "contraband-of-war," thus bringing the ire of the slaveholding class down upon himself. Lincoln shortly afterwards gave him command of the expedition which seized Hatteras Inlet, an operation which was efficiently executed by the Navy on 27-29 August. Butler received a great deal of credit for the success of the expedition and was authorized to return to Massachusetts and recruit more troops for further coastal ventures. In the spring of 1862 Butler was given a command in the Gulf, with orders to occupy New Orleans.

The occupation of New Orleans was a simple affair, the city having surrendered to David Glasgow Farragut's squadron on 25 April. Butler's troops moved in on 1 May, and he rapidly established a firm grip on the strongly secessionist city. Already a target of Southern wrath, his actions brought still more opprobrium upon his name. William Mumford, a citizen who had defaced the first American flag raised over the city upon its fall, was hanged. Discovering that the Dutch consul had colluded to conceal funds earmarked for the purchase of arms in Europe, he confiscated the entire sum, about $800,000. He hit his stride when he ordered that any female resident of New Orleans who by word or deed showed disrespect to the Union uniform be "treated as a woman of the town plying her avocation," an order which was condemned in newspapers, from pulpits and in legislative houses throughout the English speaking world, and caused Jefferson Davis to order that Butler be instantly executed should he be captured. Strongly backed from Washington, Butler remained in power, raising some of the first black regiments to muster into Union service, thereby attracting still more Southern vituperation. He was called "Beast Butler" and "Spoons Butler," allegedly for stealing said items from fashionable New Orleans homes; though he did turn a dishonest nickel or two, it was through speculation in cotton, a business in which those who lampooned him took a large part, rather than from loot. Crude tales of his vices, his greed, and his stupidity were widely circulated, much to his enjoyment most of the time. Despite his reputation, Butler worked tirelessly to care for the hordes of fugitive slaves and impoverished whites who crowded the city, and was solicitous of the welfare of the seriously ill wife of Confederate Gen. Pierre G.T. Beauregard. Not until December of 1862 was Butler relieved. Held on the shelf for a time, in late 1863 he was returned to Fortress Monroe to command the *Army of the James*. Butler was given a crucial role in Grant's Overland Campaign in 1864; while Grant and the *Army of the Potomac* held Lee's attention north of Richmond, Butler was to advance up the James River, seizing Petersburg, threatening the Confederate capital from the southeast. It was an undertaking far beyond Butler's capabilities. In the brief Drewry's Bluff Campaign (4-16 May 1864), he bungled a chance to deliver a devastating blow to the Confederacy, and allowed Gen. Pierre G.T. Beauregard's outnumbered forces to bottle up his army at Bermuda Hundred.

His political influence being great, Butler was not relieved, but merely temporarily transferred to other duty. His skill as a "city tamer" being unquestioned, he was detached to New York shortly before the election of 1864 to be on hand should there be a repetition of the rioting which had prostrated the city in the summer of '63. New York remaining calm, Butler was next sent on an expedition to close the port of Wilmington, an endeavor which failed. Though the failure was not entirely Butler's fault— the Navy's David Dixon Porter must share a good deal of the blame—he was relieved at the end of 1864 and told to await orders. Those orders never came.

After the war Butler had an enormously successful career in politics. Elected to the House as a Republican in 1866, he was one of the most enthusiastic supporters of the impeachment of Andrew Johnson. Regularly reelected, he remained in the House until 1875, was reelected in 1877, and in 1879 returned as a Greenbacker. In 1883 he was elected—after trying since 1871—governor of Massachusetts, and in the following year made a bid for the presidency as a Greenback. From 1884 until his death he lived an uncharacteristically quiet life.

Butler was unquestionably an incompetent commander. But he was by no means an incapable soldier. He was a fairly good administrator and a firm military governor. In addition, he was far more willing to see value in innovative ideas than were most of the other generals in the war; an early and ardent supporter of the use of black troops, he was also an enthusiast for ballooning and the Gatling gun. Though vilified as an unsuccessful political general, his services to the nation were enormous and precisely political.

Joseph E. Johnston

A native of Virginia, Joseph Eggleston Johnston (1807-1891) graduated from West Point in 1829. He had a busy career in the Old Army, seeing service in the Black Hawk War, the Second Seminole War and on the frontier, and then spent 1837-1838 a civil engineer in Florida. Returning to the service, he compiled an impressive record in the Mexican War (five wounds and three brevets), culminating in command of the storming party at Chapultepec Castle. Thereafter he served in the Topographical Engineers, commanded the *1st* (now *4th*) *Cavalry* on the frontier and in Kansas, served as a staff officer during the Utah Expedition and on the eve of the Civil War was an acting brigadier general and Quartermaster General of the Army.

Johnston resigned on 22 April 1861 and entered the service of Virginia as a brigadier general. On 14 May he was named major general in the Confederate Regular Army and assigned to command at Harper's Ferry, where one of his subordinates was Thomas J. Jackson. Shortly appointed a full general, he was placed in command of all Confederate forces in Northern Virginia, but during the Bull Run Campaign permitted Pierre G.T. Beauregard to direct the battle. Meanwhile, Johnston commenced a lengthy bureaucratic squabble with Jefferson Davis and the War Department as to his proper status—in the Old Army he had been senior to the three generals who were now senior to him—a matter which polluted his relations with the president ever afterwards.

Johnston created the Army of Northern Virginia through the autumn and winter of 1861-1862 and led it during the opening phases of the Peninsular Campaign. Severely wounded at Seven Pines, Robert E. Lee replaced him on 1 June 1862. Johnston did not return to active duty for some time thereafter, partially because there was no suitable command for him. Finally, in November, he was placed in overall command of the Department of the West, supervising—but not really permitted to command—the operations of Braxton Bragg in Tennessee and John C. Pemberton in Mississippi. Meanwhile, his feud with Jefferson Davis resumed, since the latter flatly refused to approve Johnston's proposals for a concentration of Confederate efforts in his theater. As a result, save for Chickamauga, 1863 was essentially a series of devastating reverses for Confederate arms in the heartland: Stones River, Vicksburg, Tullahoma, Chattanooga. On 27 December 1863 Johnston was given direct command of the Army of Tennessee.

The following year, Johnston led his army with skill, courage and verve in the Atlanta Campaign, managing to slow the greatly superior Union forces of William T. Sherman to a virtual crawl by skilled maneuver, surprise attacks and well-timed retreats. As a result, between 1 May and 17 July, Sherman was able to advance little more than a mile a day, against a foe whom he outnumbered by nearly two-to-one. Such skill was not, however, appreciated in Richmond; Jefferson Davis wanted someone who could fight hammer-blow battles, and so Johnston was replaced by John B.

Hood on 17 July. Hood did fight, and Atlanta fell within six weeks, with enormous losses to the defenders.

Because of his feud with Davis, Johnston remained inactive for more than six months, until, in late February of 1865 newly appointed General-in-Chief Robert E. Lee restored him to command of the Army of Tennessee. Johnston led the remnants of this once mighty force with some skill in the hopeless Carolina Campaign. Shortly after receiving news of Appomattox, he concluded an armistice with Sherman on 18 April 1865.

After the war Johnston prospered in the insurance business, served in Congress, wrote and became excellent friends with his erstwhile foemen Sherman and Grant. A small, tough man, Johnston was an outstanding soldier, a master of the strategic defensive, whose abilities did much to sustain the Confederacy, though he was ill-rewarded for his efforts.

Sterling Price

A native of Virginia, Sterling Price (1809-1867) received a college education and later studied law before removing to Missouri at the age of 21. He had a varied career in his adopted state, farming and practicing law for some years before entering politics. He served in the state legislature and later in Congress. He resigned his seat in the House on the outbreak of the Mexican War to become colonel of the *2nd Missouri*. His war service was entirely in New Mexico, where he was military governor as a brigadier general of volunteers. After the war he returned to his adopted state and served as governor 1853-1857, a crucial period, since the Kansas-Nebraska troubles were afoot at the time. In 1860 he was named head of the state militia. Although he opposed secession, he believed the efforts of Nathaniel Lyon and Frank Blair to keep Missouri loyal were high handed and unconstitutional, and he accepted command of state troops raised to resist Union forces.

Price's command, about 5,000 men, participated in the Pyrric victory at Wilson's Creek in August of 1861. The following month he was more successful at the siege of Lexington, taking over 3,000 prisoners and much booty besides. However, he was shortly forced to retire into Arkansas in the face of a major advance by Union Brig. Gen. S.R. Curtis. Reorganizing his forces, he served under Earl Van Dorn at Pea Ridge in early 1862. As a result of this devastating blow to Confederate fortunes in the Trans-Mississippi theater, Price accepted a commission as a major general in the Confederate Army.

Ordered eastwards into Mississippi, Price commanded his reluctant

Missourians with little success in the operations around Iuka and Corinth in October of 1862. Shortly transferred back across the Mississippi, Price was again unsuccessful at Helena, Arkansas, in 1863. He performed better under Edmund Kirby Smith's overall command in 1864, but a major raid which he undertook through Missouri in September and October of that year, while beginning well, ended disastrously. At war's end Price threw his lot in with the self-proclaimed Emperor Maximilian of Mexico, but returned to Missouri in 1866. Although he attempted to rebuild his shattered fortune, Price died in relative poverty the following year. Handsome, tall, and stout, "Pap" Price was an unsuccessful commander, but was nevertheless extremely important to the Confederacy because of his immense popularity in Missouri. That alone was worth his commission.

Lincoln

No Euphemisms, Please

Early in July of 1861 President Lincoln called a special session of Congress to handle emergency matters arising out of the war. In the course of a message concerning the situation, he observed that the leaders of the South had been promoting secession for years in a variety of guises, saying, among other things, "With rebellion thus sugar-coated, they have been drugging the public mind of their section for more than thirty years, until they have brought many good men to a willingness to take up arms against the government." The speech was well received and Congress took prompt action to prosecute the war. Meanwhile, of course, the speech had to be printed in the *Congressional Record*. And it was there that it ran into some problems.

It seems that the government printer, a Mr. Defrees, found the phrase "sugar-coated" distastefully colloquial, and certainly not equal to the dignity of the *Congressional Record*. Considering the matter, Defrees decided to take it up with the president and requested a meeting.

Defrees started off indirectly, explaining to Lincoln that a message to Congress was quite a different thing than a speech before a mass meeting in Illinois, for a message to Congress would become a part of history and ought to be written accordingly.

Though a patient man, Lincoln disliked being patronized and lectured about as much as any man, and replied rather sharply, saying "What is the matter now?"

"Why," said Defrees, "you have used an undignified expression in the message," and proceeded to read aloud the offending paragraph, adding, "I would alter the structure of that, if I were you."

By now thoroughly annoyed, Lincoln said "Defrees, that word expresses precisely my idea, and I am not going to change it. The time will never come, in this country, when the people won't know exactly what 'sugar-coated' means."

The Units

The Louisiana Tigers

The "Louisiana Tigers" or "Wheat's Tigers," one of the toughest combat forces of the Civil War, was formed from the "lowest scrapings of the Mississippi and New Orleans" by Chatham R. Wheat (1826-1862). Born in Virginia of an old Maryland family, "Rob" Wheat, son of an Episcopal minister, had an extraordinary career. Graduating from the University of Nashville in 1845, he was reading law in Memphis when the Mexican War broke out. Wheat promptly volunteered and served with some distinction, emerging as a captain. Back in civilian life, he opened a law practice in New Orleans, while dabbling in politics and serving in the state legislature. Growing bored, he gave it all up to become a soldier of fortune, serving in Cuba, Mexico, Nicaragua and Italy from 1850 to 1860.

Still abroad at the outbreak of the Civil War, he hurried home to lend a hand. Upon his return to New Orleans, Wheat began to raise an infantry battalion. Meanwhile, one Alex White was raising a company from among the sweepings of the local prisons, with which he was intimately familiar. White, who had managed to convince a wealthy citizen to foot the bill to equip his company as *zouaves*, offered his company for service with Wheat's battalion. Wheat happily incorporated White's "Tiger Zouaves" into his battalion, which was mustered into Confederate service as the 1st Louisiana Special Battalion, with Wheat as its major and White numbered among the captains.

The rowdy "Louisiana Tigers" were certainly a showy outfit, with baggy blue-and-white striped trousers, red shirts, brown jackets and tasseled scarlet skullcaps, Bowie knives hanging from their belts as they trotted along in the peculiar quick-step gait popular among the French-inspired *zouave* regiments both North and South. Shortly after mustering into service the battalion went East to join the army just then concentrating in northern Virginia. When it left New Orleans, there were allegedly serving in its ranks three women, all alike uncharitably described as "women of no status," one ostensibly serving as a lieutenant and two as color bearers, carrying Louisiana's Pelican flag and the regimental banner, which ironically depicted a lamb and the slogan "As Gentle As." The battalion arrived in Virginia without the "ladies" but in time for First Bull Run.

Assigned to Col. Nathan G. Evans' provisional command, the Tigers played a crucial role early in the battle by helping to hold the left of the Confederate line as it fell back on Henry House Hill under considerable pressure from stronger Federal forces, and later joined in the counterattack which threw the Union troops back in disorder. This action gained them a reputation for considerable tenacity under fire, and unusual ferocity in the attack: they were alleged to have thrown down their muskets and charged the Yankees with their Bowie knives. Wheat himself was seriously wounded at Bull Run, a ball passing through both of his lungs. Informed that the wound was fatal, Wheat replied, "I don't feel like dying yet," and proceeded to recover nicely.

In the reorganization of the Confederate forces in Virginia following the Bull Run Campaign, the Louisiana Tigers were brigaded with four other Louisiana outfits, the 6th, 7th, 8th and 9th Louisiana Volunteer Infantry Regiments, to form the Louisiana Brigade, under Brig. Gen. Richard Taylor, one of the Confederacy's finest combat leaders. This brigade was shortly incorporated in Maj. Gen. Richard S. Ewell's division which was sent to support Stonewall Jackson's operations in the Shenandoah Valley in early 1862. The Tigers took part in Jackson's series of victories at Front Royal, Winchester, Cross Keys and especially Port Republic (20 May-9 June 1862), where they spearheaded a desperate attack against the Union left. After the briefest of rests, the Tigers were shortly transferred, along with the rest of Jackson's command, to support the Army of Northern Virginia against the *Army of the Potomac*, which was advancing up the Virginia Peninsula.

Hotly engaged at Gaines' Mill on 27 June, the Louisiana Tigers took heavy casualties, most notably Wheat himself, who was mortally wounded. With Wheat, whom they worshiped, gone, the spirit went out of the Louisiana Tigers. Worse still, without Wheat to keep them in line, the troops lost all discipline. Although the battalion served to the end of the Peninsular Campaign, it performed its duties in a perfunctory fashion, desertions soared—even a major went over the hill—and the troops proved extremely unruly. In August the 1st Louisiana Special Battalion was broken up, its men being distributed among the four regiments of the Louisiana Brigade. But if the battalion died, its spirit did not. Wheat's veterans, who together proved such poor soldiers without him, separately imparted some of their style and dash to their new comrades, no poor soldiers to begin with. And the Louisiana Brigade shortly acquired the nickname "Louisiana Tigers."

The 39th New York

Many regiments, both North and South, may have had a more distinguished battlefield record than did the *39th New York*, but certainly few were more colorful. The regiment was raised by a remarkable military adventurer, Frederick D'Utassy. Born Frederick Stasser, possibly in Vienna, D'Utassy appeared in New York during the 1850s, claiming to have been a veteran of the Hungarian Revolution of 1848-1849. For a time he made his living as a language teacher, while involving himself in various emigre circles and the city's social whirl.

In May of 1861 D'Utassy raised a regiment of European exiles with himself as colonel and two of his brothers serving as company officers. The *Garibaldi Guard* was a polyglot outfit, incorporating such diverse volunteer units as the *Italian Legion*, the *Polish Legion*, the *Netherlands Legion*, the *Hungarian Regiment* and the *German 1st Foreign Rifles*; the regiment is alleged to have included men of fifteen different nationalities. As organized, four companies, including one of Swiss volunteers, spoke German, three spoke Hungarian, one Italian and one French and one was half Spanish and half Portuguese. As a result, orders were regularly given in seven languages—English plus these six—though Spanish and Portuguese were usually omitted from recruiting posters.

The regimental uniform was loosely based on that of the famed Piedmontese *Bersaglieri*, being blue with red and gold trim, topped by a broad "Garibaldi" hat trimmed with green cock feathers, however for fatigue duties the men wore a loose red shirt with a broad belt similar to that popularized by Garibaldi and his famed "Red Shirts," and a few men wore the uniforms of their original ethnic volunteer outfits. Since it was composed of European personnel, the regiment had several *vivandieres*. As a result, the *39th New York* cut a brave figure on 4 June 1861, when it headed off to war, with the men lustily singing "Les Marseillaise" as they marched down Broadway behind an Italian flag which had flown from the battlements of Rome during Garibaldi's heroic defense of the city in 1849. It was a glorious beginning for what was perhaps the most romantic of the hundreds of regiments mustering North and South in 1861. But like most outfits which served in the war, although the *Garibaldi Guard* had a interesting record, it had but few moments of glory.

Accepted for state service on 27 May 1861, the regiment was mustered into Federal service at Washington on 6 June, to date from 28 May. At First Bull Run, the *39th New York* was part of Col. Louis Blenker's brigade in the reserve and performed well in helping to cover the retreat of the Union troops on that disastrous afternoon. In the reorganization of the Federal forces about Washington which resulted in the creation of the *Army of the Potomac*, the regiment was incorporated into by then Brig. Gen. Louis Blenker's division. Like the *39th New York*, this division was a polyglot outfit composed mostly of middle European volunteers.

In March of 1862, Blenker was ordered to take his division to the Shenandoah Valley. What resulted was one of the most mismanaged marches of the war, with the troops taking six weeks to make a movement of little more than 100 miles, amid considerable privation and contingent depredations on the part of the hungry troops. The division, and the *39th New York*, nevertheless reached the Valley in time to take part in the Union defeat at the hands of Stonewall Jackson, fighting at Cross Keys (8 June 1862).

When Blenker's division was shortly afterwards broken up, the regiment was transferred to the garrison at Harper's Ferry, where it passed the next few months. Meanwhile, the regiment began to lose some of its European character, the *bersaglieri* uniforms giving way to Uncle Sam's standard issue and the *vivandieres* gradually losing their zest for military life. D'Utassy assumed command of a brigade comprising the *111th*, *115th* and *125th New York*, green outfits all, as well as the *39th*, which passed temporarily to the command of Maj. Hugo Hildebrandt. Unfortunately the garrison commander at Harper's Ferry, Colonel Dixon Miles, proved highly inept. Neglecting the most elementary precautions, he allowed himself to be encircled and invested there by Stonewall Jackson on 12 September 1862, in the opening stages of the Antietam Campaign. Although most of his subordinates—D'Utassy among them—were inclined to attempt an escape—and one regiment did elude the trap—Miles demurred and surrendered after a brief siege. The angry D'Utassy concealed the regimental colors in his personal baggage and ordered his men to smash their weapons before surrendering. The entire brigade was almost immediately paroled, being sent to Camp Douglas, Illinois, and was shortly thereafter formally exchanged and sent to Washington, to form part of the garrison there. Although by the spring of 1863 the regiment had been but lightly engaged, in its two years of service it had lost heavily from disease and desertion.

In May of 1863 the regiment, which numbered little more than 300 men, was reorganized, forming four companies. Meanwhile D'Utassy was removed from command and eventually sent to Sing Sing Prison in New

York, having been tried and convicted of a variety of charges, most notably of having been skimming a little off the top.

In late June of 1863 the *39th New York*, now under Col. Augustus Funk, an Old Army man, was incorporated, along with its brigade mates into *II Corps* of the *Army of the Potomac*, just in time for the Gettysburg Campaign. The *39th New York* was hotly engaged for all three days of Gettysburg, its greatest moment being on the evening of 2 July, when, in a furious charge, it drove the 21st Mississippi back from a captured battery, retaking all six pieces and capturing three Rebel flags; during the three days the regiment lost 35.3 percent of the 269 men it brought into action, 95 men being killed or wounded, including six field officers. After Gettysburg the regiment was gradually brought up to strength, an additional six companies being added over the next few months. As a result, when, in May of 1864 the regiment's enlistment expired, these six companies remained with the colors, absorbing those veterans of '61 who wished to reenlist, and a seventh company was shortly added.

The *39th New York* served in *II Corps* from the Wilderness to the end of the war and was present at Appomattox. But by that time the regiment had lost its European character, the ranks being filled up with drafted men. Funk became a casualty in the Wilderness, and was temporarily replaced by Maj. Joseph Hyde, who was in turn replaced by Capt. David A. Allen, before the colonel returned to service. When mustered out in July of 1865 some 200 men were still with the colors. Of the 2,110 men who had passed through the ranks, 115 men had been killed in action, 163 had died of disease, and over 1,000 wounded, disabled by disease, or missing. Like most regiments whether Union or Confederate, the *Garibaldi Guard* rendered hard service, but garnered little fame. In the end Gettysburg was the *39th New York's* moment of glory.

The Washington Artillery

The most famous artillery outfit of the war was undoubtedly the Confederacy's Washington Artillery of Louisiana. This distinguished organization was formed at New Orleans in 1838 as the "Native American Battery" and was comprised of the finest and richest young men of the Crescent City's Creole society. When the Mexican War came, the battery reorganized as infantry and served as *Company A* of Persifor Smith's *1st Louisiana Volunteers*. Returning in glory to its native city, the company was reorganized in 1852 and renamed the "Washington Artillery."

On the outbreak of the war the battalion, probably one of the most skilled militia outfits in the country, acquired a good deal of equipment with the seizure of the Federal arsenal at Baton Rouge. Volunteering for service in the Confederate Army, the battalion mustered in on 26 May 1861. One company, the 5th, was detached from the battalion and sent to serve with the Army of Tennessee, but the other four went East together and joined the Army of Northern Virginia.

When it went to war, the Washington Artillery went in style. As was common in the early days of the war, a lot of unnecessary luxuries and personnel accompanied the battalion into the field. Its uniforms alone were estimated to have cost $20,000. The first commanding officer, Maj. James B. Walton—a wholesale grocer who helped found the outfit in 1838, went on to command the *1st Louisiana* in Mexico after Smith's promotion, and would later rise to Inspector General of Field Artillery in the Army of Northern Virginia—brought along his German-born major-domo, while the latter's wife accompanied the battalion as a *vivandiere*. M. Edouard, the chef of the famous Victor's of Carrollton, came along as well, to provide proper meals for the troops and brought along his pet fox. But if the men of the battalion liked luxury, they also knew how to fight.

The Washington Artillery compiled the most distinguished record an artillery outfit could possibly have in the war. The first four companies were engaged in every battle of the Army of Northern Virginia from First Bull Run—before there even was an Army of Northern Virginia—to Appomattox, and served with particular brilliance at Fredericksburg and at Chancellorsville. So heavily engaged was the battalion that at Gettysburg it could muster but eight guns for four batteries. The 5th Company was with the Army of Tennessee throughout the war, from Shiloh to the Carolinas. In addition, James Dearing, a West Point drop-out who joined the battalion as a lieutenant in 1861, rose to brigadier general by the war's end; one of only three Confederate gunners to become a general.

The Washington Artillery was as distinguished in camp as in the field. The battalion had one of the most famous amateur theatrical troupes in the Confederate Army. It was noted for elaborate and professional productions, to the extent that for one performance while in camp near Fredericksburg in January of 1863 a special train was run up from Richmond so that various dignitaries from the capital could attend. Robert E. Lee himself once sent formal regrets at having to miss a performance.

At the end of the war the Washington Artillery was officially disbanded. However the veterans maintained an informal association with each other until, after a year or so, they were permitted to incorporate as "The Washington Artillery Veterans Charitable and Benevolent Association," a name which belied their true purpose, to keep alive resistance to Reconstruction. With this object in mind, the veterans held secret infantry drills and acquired arms. The veterans of the Washington Artillery—and not a few new recruits—took part in a number of the demonstrations and riots which attended the overthrow of carpetbagger government in Louisiana, once even appearing in the streets with two small brass cannon! With the end of Reconstruction in 1876 the veterans association was recognized as a unit of the state militia, later becoming part of the National Guard. As such, the Washington Artillery served in Cuba and in both world wars.

War and Society

Army Officer Loyalties in 1861

The United States Army had 1,080 officers on active duty at the onset of the "Secession Winter." Over the months which followed hundreds of officers left the army. What follows is a series of tables which summarize the professional and regional origins of the officers and look at their loyalties in the crisis of 1860-1861.

It should be noted that in these tables percentage figures given in square brackets refer to the figure appearing in the left hand column. Parenthe-sized percentages on the "Total" line refer to the "Base" line entry imme-diately above, while those on subsequent lines refer to the "Total" line entry in the same column.

Origins of the Officers on Duty

	All	West Point	Civil Life
Base/Total	1080 [100.0%]	821 [76.0%]	259 [24.0%]
Of these:			
Northerners	620 (62.0%)	491 (59.8%)	129 (49.8%)
Southerners	460 (38.0%)	330 (40.2%)	130 (50.2%)

On this table, of course, the "Base" and the "Total" are the same, since it is examining the entire officer corps: including slaves, the South had about 35 percent of the population. Note that while Southerners were slightly over-represented in the officer corps, the disproportion was not great. It is, however, interesting to note that Southerners were more likely to have been commissioned from civil life than were Northerners; the ratio of officers commissioned from West Point to those appointed directly from civil life is 3.8:1 for Northerners but only 2.5:1 for Southerners.

Officers Separating from the Army

	All	West Point	Civil
Base	1080 [100.0%]	821 [76.0%]	259 [24.0%]
Total Separating	313 (29.0%)	184 (22.4%)	129 (28.6%)
Of these:			
Northerners	16 (5.1%)	16 (8.7%)	
Southerners	297 (94.9%)	168 (91.3%)	129 (100.0%)

Officers Remaining in the Army

	All	West Point	Civil
Base	1080 [100.0%]	821 [76.0%]	259 [24.0%]
Total Remaining	767 (71.0%)	637 (77.6%)	130 (50.2%)
Of these:			
Northerners	604 (78.7%)	475 (74.6%)	129 (99.2%)
Southerners	163 (21.3%)	162 (25.4%)	1 (0.8%)

Officers of Northern Origins

	All	West Point	Civil
Base	620 [100.0%]	491 [79.2%]	129 [20.8%]
Loyal	604 (97.4%)	475 (96.7%)	129 (100.0%)
Disloyal	16 (2.6%)	16 (3.3%)	

Officers of Southern Origins

	All	West Point	Civil
Base	460 [100.0%]	330 [71.7%]	130 [28.3%]
Loyal	163 (35.4%)	162 (49.1%)	1 (0.8%)
Disloyal	297 (64.6%)	168 (50.9%)	129 (99.2%)

It should be noted that although 313 officers left the army or were expelled as a result of secession, not all of them joined the Confederacy. About 1 percent of the men separated from the service retired to civilian life, being unwilling to either fight for or against the "Old Flag." The Northern men who chose to "go South" were all West Point graduates who had married Southern women. The Southern men who remained loyal were, with one exception, all West Pointers as well, though their marital status is less clear. The only officer of Southern origins commissioned from civil life who did not betray his oath to "support and defend the Constitution of the United States" was Winfield Scott, the general-in-chief and most distinguished American soldier since Washington.

The Flags of the Confederacy

The events of the "Secession Winter" saw Old Glory replaced by the state flag in South Carolina, Georgia, Florida, Alabama, Mississippi, Louisiana and Texas. With the formation of the Confederacy at Montgomery, Alabama, in February of 1861, the question of a flag for the new nation was of pressing concern.

While there was some sentiment for the so-called "Bonnie Blue Flag," with its one white star on a blue field, enthusiastic citizens from all over the South were not hesitant in submitting ideas. Most of the suggestions were essentially variants on "Old Glory," for there was much affection for the flag of Washington. Indeed, some Southern leaders, such as Jefferson Davis, believed the Confederacy should co-opt the old flag entirely, to suggest that it, rather than Yankeedom, was the true heir to the Republic. One delegate to the Provisional Congress actually submitted a bill to ensure that the new flag be "as similar as possible to the flag of the United States." These proposals, however, did not find favor among more ardent secessionists and slavocrats. Observing that the "Stars and Stripes" had inspired the flags of both Liberia and Hawaii, South Carolina's William P. Miles, chairman of the committee on heraldic devices, remarked that it would be improper to use "what had been pilfered and appropriated by a free negro community and a race of savages." Nevertheless, the influence of the old flag persisted in the design which the committee adopted on 4 March, even as Lincoln was preparing to take the oath of office in far-off Washington.

The new flag was to be a rectangle in the ratio of 1.5:1, with three stripes of red, white and red, and a blue canton on which were arranged a circle of seven white stars, one for each Confederate state at the time, the famed "Stars and Bars." A sample was hastily put together and was hoisted over the capitol at Montgomery that very afternoon by a granddaughter of John Tyler, the only ex-president living in the Confederacy. The new flag was soon seen everywhere in the South, and was often displayed by secessionists in the then still-loyal "Upper South" and border states. However, when the new flag was used in battle its similarity to the old one caused problems, particularly at a distance. At First Bull Run—by which time the "Stars and Bars" had eleven stars—Confederate troops almost fired on Brig. Gen. Jubal Early's brigade as it marched up because they could not at first discern which flag it bore. As a result, when Brig. Gen. Pierre G. T. Beauregard approached Gen. Joseph E. Johnston and suggested that the Confederacy needed a battle flag as distinct from the "Stars and Stripes" as possible, the latter expressed enthusiastic agreement. With the help of some staff officers they soon came up with a unique design.

The proposed flag was square, having a blue field charged with a red St. Andrew's cross on which were placed the stars representing the states. After some quibbles about heraldic propriety the field was changed to red and the cross to blue. The enthusiastic generals submitted their design to the Congress. Since the Congress took no action on the matter, the generals then went to the War Department. The result was that on 1 October 1861 the new design was approved for military use. Thus was born the famed Confederate battle flag.

The first Confederate battle flags were made by the vivacious and beautiful Cary girls, the sisters Hetty and Jennie of Baltimore and their cousin Constance of Alexandria, Virginia. Alas for romance, the flags were not made from their dresses nor from their undergarments; as Constance later observed, they had no "apparel in the flamboyant colors of poppy red and vivid dark blue required," and, in fact, they had trouble securing materials of the proper colors, with the result that the red silk which she obtained for her flag was of such poor quality she had to use an interlining to provide proper stiffening. On 28 November the new flags were given to the three most prominent Confederate commanders at the time, Hetty's to Joseph E. Johnston, Jennie's to Pierre G.T. Beauregard and Constance's to Earl Van Dorn; when Van Dorn was murdered in mid-1863, his flag was returned to Constance, who, along with the other girls, had by then become prominent in the social life and war work in the Confederate capital. Use of the battle flag greatly reduced confusion on the battlefield.

Meanwhile, of course, the debate over the "Stars and Bars" continued. A Richmond newspaper effectively expressed the dissatisfaction when it observed "...we took, at rough calculation, our share of the stars and our fraction of the stripes, and put them together and called them the Confederate flag." Although the Confederate Congress had more pressing business, it was constantly bombarded with suggestions for a new flag to replace the "Stars and Bars." The proposed designs were numerous and varied. Many different symbols and color combinations were proposed, including snakes, horses and the sun. One suggestion anticipated Australia a bit by incorporating the Southern Cross, which was nowhere visible in the Confederacy. And one had a white field with a black bend, which its designer—ignorant of heraldry—claimed symbolized the eternal truth of the white race dominating the black. None of these received serious consideration.

On 1 May 1863 the Congress adopted a new design, a white flag of 2:1

dimensions with the battle flag in the canton. This new flag proved even less satisfactory than the old. Unless there was a stiff breeze, the new colors could not be distinguished from a flag of truce. Moreover, it was remarkably difficult to keep clean. So the Congress went back to work. Not until 8 March 1865—when the matter was rapidly becoming academic—was a new design approved, and this merely a stop-gap expedient which added a broad red panel at the fly and returned the dimensions to 1.5:1. In any case, the white flag was the last Confederate flag to be displayed in an official capacity, being worn by the cruiser C.S.S. *Shenandoah* at the time of her surrender to British authorities in November of 1865.

The Confederacy's search for a flag is a good example of failing to see what was right under one's nose. The obvious flag for the Confederacy was the battle flag, which like Britain's Union Flag, readily could have been adapted to a wide variety of uses. But if the Confederate Congress failed to act, history and the Southern people did, and the battle flag today symbolizes the Confederacy far more effectively then the three successive national flags which were adopted. While the national colors are largely forgotten, the battle flag is widely displayed throughout the South and at Ku Klux Klan rallies as well.

What's in a Name?

Many of the actions during the Civil War are known by two or even more names. It is not uncommon for a battle to bear both a Northern and a Southern name. The practice began early in the war, on 26 June 1861, with the little action known as Patterson Creek/Kelly's Island, in Virginia, and continued right to the end, in the engagement at Amelia Springs/Jettersville, Virginia, on 5 April 1865. This multiplicity of names persists, sometimes to the confusion of even the most serious student of the struggle.

Writing after the war, former Confederate Lt. Gen. Daniel H. Hill pointed out that the "Union" name for a battle was usually that of a local terrain feature, while the "Confederate" name was frequently that of a town, "In one section the naming had been after the handiwork of God, and in the other section it has been after the handiwork of man." He advanced an elegant explanation for this: Southern soldiers, being mostly from the country, were impressed by man-made features, while their Northern counterparts, being mostly from villages, towns and cities, were more impressed by natural features.

While Hill's observation is accurate enough, his explanation is faulty; most Union troops came from very small towns or rural areas. Moreover, for a number of battles it is the Southern name which refers to a geographic feature and the Northern one which refers to a place, as in the case of Olustee/Ocean Pond. And in any case, battles are not usually named by the common soldiers. For a better explanation one must look elsewhere.

In the Middle Ages the heralds of the opposing armies would meet after a battle to decide upon an appropriate name. In modern times the two sides rarely communicate and so battles are named by generals, politicians, historians and common usage. There are sound reasons for differences in the naming of battles, not just during the Civil War, but during any war. Frequently, the name of a battle is drawn from that of the most prominent locale on the field or in the immediate vicinity behind friendly lines. It is thus perfectly possible for a different place or geographic feature to catch the fancy of one side and the other. As a result, at least 24 of the major actions of the war have two names, including some of the most famous, such as Shiloh/Pittsburg Landing and Antietam/Sharpsburg. Now this is relatively easy to understand. More difficult by far, is the fact that at least a dozen important battles have three names, at least three have four names, four have five and one glories in seven: White Oak Swamp/Frazier's [or Frayser's] Farm/Glendale/Charles City Cross Roads/Nelson's Farm/Turkey Bend/New Market Cross Roads, fought on 30 June 1862. Fortunately, time has eliminated most of these. They had their origins in the use of different names by officers making reports, by newspapermen filing dispatches and even by political leaders making public pronouncements.

The problem of names extends, of course, even to that of the struggle itself, for the name preferred in different parts of the country is still largely a matter of opinion. Although "Civil War" had some usage in the South in the early years of the conflict, no genuinely Southern name emerged until some years after Appomattox, when "The War between the States" gained favor. In the North "The War of the Rebellion" was fairly common at the time, and is, indeed, the official name by Congressional fiat, but it gradually gave way to "The Civil War." Other names for the conflict are numerous: one researcher enumerated 120 of them, and he clearly missed a few. Some of the more popular have been:

The War for Separation
The War of the Sections
The War for Constitutional Liberty
The Confederate War
Mr. Davis' War
Mr. Lincoln's War
The Southern Rebellion

The Great Rebellion
The War for Southern Rights
The War of Northern Aggression
The Reb Time
The Late Unpleasantness
The War for Abolition
The War for Southern Liberty
The Second American Revolution
The War of Yankee Arrogance
The War of Southern Arrogance
The War of the 1860s

None of these were quite satisfactory, and in common usage "The War between the States" and "The Civil War" have had no competitors for nearly a century now, despite the fact that they both refer to the same events, and that neither is particularly accurate. A civil war is, of course, a dispute over control of the state, which was not at all the issue, since—aside from some genuinely extreme fanatics—the South did not wish to take control of the United States but merely to secede from it. Similarly, "The War between the States," aside from being grammatically poor, makes equally little sense unless one subscribes to the Southern political view of the conflict. Superior names exist. "The War for Southern Independence" is certainly accurate and had some popularity in the South in the late nineteenth century, while "The War of the Slaveholders Rebellion" is also accurate and once found some favor in the North. However, neither of these are entirely satisfactory to all concerned. There is, of course, a perfectly accurate, and politically neutral name which has never found much favor, the "War of Secession."

The Ways of War

Service and Rank in the Civil War

One of the more confusing aspects of the Civil War is the matter of branches of service and rank. One can best understand this by looking at the Union forces. There were four different branches of the land forces and as a result it was possible for an officer to have several different ranks. A man might have one rank in the militia, another in the Regular Army, yet another in the volunteers, and possibly still another in the state troops.

The militia, of course, were the part-time forces which each state could muster from its own population. A rank in the militia did not necessarily have any value outside the borders of one's own state, though in emergencies the militia of one state was known to serve in another, such as when 13,000 New York militiamen went to help hold the line of the Susquehanna during the Gettysburg Campaign. At the height of the war there were some 200,000 active militiamen in the loyal states.

The Regular Army was the permanent land force maintained by the Federal government, a small band numbering little more than 16,000 at the start, and no more than about 50,000 during the war. Normally the regulars and the militia were responsible for the defense of the country. However, militia terms of service were rather short, and they served under state control. As a result, there was also the Volunteer Army.

The Volunteer Army was usually recruited by states, often drawing men from the militia, but served under Federal terms of enlistment. Some states over-filled their volunteer quotas and chose to retain the surplus troops at their own expense as permanent, standing force for territorial defense. These were the state troops, maintained by several states, the most notable of which were the famed *Pennsylvania Reserves*, thirteen regiments recruited and maintained at state expense which later passed into the Volunteer Army and proved to be among the best Union outfits; there were perhaps 50,000 troops maintained on active duty by various of the loyal states at the height of the war. Since militia and state regiments might sometimes volunteer for Federal service, some regiments had two designations, such as the *83rd New York Volunteers*, which was also the *9th New York Militia*, or the *11th Pennsylvania Reserves*, which was also the *40th Pennsylvania Volunteers*.

The situation in the Confederate Army was simpler, but only marginally so. On paper there existed a Regular Army, authorized to recruit a number of infantry and cavalry regiments, none of which were ever completed. As a result, the Volunteer Army, known as the "Provisional Army," represented virtually the whole of the national forces, supplemented by the militia and the state troops of those states which maintained such, notably Georgia. There was another way in which the Confederate differed from the Union Army. After the fighting got serious, all Confederate troops were in for the duration, a fact which many one-year volunteers resented when they found their enlistments extended in early '62. In the Union Army enlistment was in the form of a personal contract. As a result troops were enlisted for 30-days, 90-days, three months, 100-days, six months, nine months, one year, two years, or three years, a matter which greatly complicated operations; time-expired regiments sometimes marched off on the eve of battle.

In general, Civil War literature refers to regiments merely by number and state, so it is sometimes difficult to tell what type of outfit is meant, though on both sides most of the fighting was done by volunteer regiments. This plethora of branches of the service complicated the rank structure. Under prevailing terms of service, a man might be a lieutenant in his state militia, serving as a major in a volunteer regiment. Or he might be a captain in the Regular Army serving as a brigadier general of volunteers, or a Regular Army captain, a major of volunteers, and a colonel in the state troops. Only one's Regular Army rank counted towards permanent time-in-grade for purposes of post-war retention and promotion in the regulars. As if this were not confusing enough, there was also *brevet* rank.

A brevet was an honorary promotion, awarded for distinguished service. Thus, a major of volunteers might also have a brevet as a colonel of volunteers. Brevet rank conferred some prestige on an officer and did make him technically senior to another officer of equal rank under certain circumstances, such as when serving on courts martial or when in detachments composed of elements of several arms, but brought few other benefits. One could hold several brevets, for example in both the volunteers and the regulars. The Union awarded brevets with a lavish hand, including 1,700 brevet generalships, a matter which did much to discredit the practice, which gradually passed into disuse. In any case, as a result of the complicated inter-relationships of rank and service, it was at least theoretically possible for a Union officer to have eight ranks, one substantive rank and one brevet in each branch of the service—the militia, the regulars, the volunteers and the state troops—though this does not actually ever seem to have occurred.

The rank situation in the Confederacy was somewhat simpler. Save for a list of mostly senior officers, there was very little in the way of a Regular Army. An officer might be, as in Union service, a captain in the Regular Army and a colonel in the Provisional Army but the former rank was of no consequence. Moreover, the Confederacy was far more generous with rank than the Union, giving out the real thing rather than brevets to deserving officers. It was a better reward for excellent service and given the precipitous decline in the value of Confederate currency, didn't cost much.

The experience of the Civil War caused the practice of awarding brevets to be discredited. As time went on fewer and fewer were awarded, the last being during World War I, when Maj. Gen. Trasker Bliss was made a brevet general so he could hob-knob on a fairly equal footing with the marshals of the Allied Supreme War Council. But the duality of ranks between the wartime and peacetime army continued right down into World War II; at the time that Dwight D. Eisenhower was wearing four stars as commander of the largest army in the history of the Republic, his Regular Army rank was colonel.

Civil War Military Organization

Given that the military leadership on both sides was drawn largely from among West Point graduates it is not surprising that there was considerable similarity between the organization of the two armies. The basic formation was the infantry regiment. Both armies consisted largely of infantry; artillery and cavalry will therefore be treated elsewhere.

In the Old Army, regiments were on paper composed of twelve companies organized in three battalions, but in practice had only ten companies in one battalion. As it was rare for an entire regiment ever to be in one place at one time, this was not a particular problem. Militia regiments, and the quality and strength of the militia varied considerably from state to state, were usually on a ten company basis, two of which were "flank" companies, technically trained for skirmishing and other special duties. As a result, when war came, virtually all infantry regiments in both armies were composed of a headquarters and ten companies, lettered from "A" through

"K" omitting the "J", and, at least in the early period of the war, usually a regimental band as well.

Occasional regiments had a somewhat different organization, particularly at the start of the war. Thus, in April of '61 the *7th New York* had only eight companies, plus a pair of howitzers, an engineering platoon, a band and a drum corps, for a total of 991 officers and men; while the *56th New York* (the "*Tenth Legion*") had ten line companies, a sharpshooter company, two light artillery companies and two lancer companies, with only a few more hundred men; and the *2nd Massachusetts* 13 companies, with some 1,200 men. In both armies there were some separate battalions as well, usually of four companies designated "A" through "D", though in Confederate service often as many as seven companies, "A" through "G". Several new Regular Army regiments were raised early in the war which theoretically had three battalions of eight companies each, a pattern which was also used when a number of heavy artillery regiments were converted to infantry.

A Confederate regiment had a colonel, a lieutenant colonel, and a major at headquarters, plus two captains to deal with quartermaster and subsistence matters, a first lieutenant as adjutant and a second lieutenant as ensign or color bearer. In addition there was a surgeon major and an assistant surgeon, ranking as a captain. Noncommissioned staff comprised a sergeant major and three sergeants, one each to deal with quartermaster, commissary and ordnance matters. Each company had a captain, three lieutenants, five sergeants, four corporals and from 80 to 112 privates.

A Federal regiment was very similar, with a colonel, lieutenant colonel and major, plus a quartermaster captain, a lieutenant serving as adjutant and a chaplain. There was, in addition, a surgeon ranking as a major or captain and two assistant surgeons ranking as captains or lieutenants. The noncommissioned staff included a sergeant major, quartermaster sergeant, commissary sergeant, hospital steward and two musicians, plus, later in the war, the ambulance sergeant and his staff of 12, who were not normally counted on the rolls of the regiment. Each of the companies had a captain, a first and a second lieutenant, a first sergeant and four other sergeants, eight corporals, two musicians and a wagoner, plus from 64 to 80 privates and, while in camp, four washerwomen.

On paper then, a Confederate regiment ran slightly larger than a Union one, some 943 to 1173 officers and men as opposed to some 845 to 1045. But regiments were rarely full, Northern ones particularly. This was due partially to accumulated losses to disease and battle, but also to political considerations. The Confederacy generally adopted a policy of rebuilding veteran regiments by regular infusions of fresh manpower, often sending depleted outfits home to recruit back to strength. The Union generally did not do this, so that veteran outfits gradually ran down to tiny fragments of their former selves. As a result, we find, for example, that at Gettysburg, of regiments fielding ten companies, the *61st New York* entered the battle with but 104 men, though the average Union regiment ran 300, while the weakest ten-company Confederate outfit, the 15th Louisiana, had 186 men, the average strength being 340.

Above the regimental level, both armies were organized into brigades, divisions and corps, which had very small staffs. A Union brigade, for example, was supposed to have a brigadier general—though more frequently a colonel—in command, with a couple of aides-de-camp, an assistant adjutant general, a brigade surgeon, an assistant quartermaster and a brigade commissary officer, plus a couple of enlisted clerks, but often got by with less; some Confederate brigades operated with no more than two or three officers. Division staffs were not much larger, nor were corps staffs.

In the Army of Northern Virginia higher formations were invariably known by their commander's name, which leads to some confusion at times, particularly when a commanding officer was changed, since the name of his command would usually change as well. There was a tendency for Union troops to do this too, but generally Union higher formations were more often known by their official designations. However, since all divisions were numbered only within their individual corps, and brigades within their divisions, some confusion is also possible when referring to Union formations.

In general, the eastern armies were better organized at an earlier period than were those in other theaters. A look at the armies of the Gettysburg Campaign can give some notion of what was considered the norm on each side. During this campaign Confederate brigades were mostly of four or five regiments, with a few of but three and several with six, running between 800 and 2,600 officers and men. At Gettysburg five of the Confederate divisions had four brigades, two had five and one had three. In addition, each division had a battalion of four batteries of artillery attached. As a result, Confederate division strength was formidable, running between 5,500 and 7,500 men with from 15 to 19 pieces of artillery. Three divisions plus two battalions of artillery comprised an army corps, with a combat strength of around 21,000 officers and men and about 80 guns. This level of organization had been introduced into the Union armies early in 1862, with the Confederacy not following until much later that year. However, Confederate corps organization soon proved superior. By mid-1863 the Army of Northern Virginia had three such corps, plus J.E.B. Stuart's oversized cavalry division. Surprisingly, there was no army level pool of artillery, which made it difficult to shift the guns readily, nor were there any combat service troops, so that line infantry units had to serve as engineers at times, and infantry and cavalry regiments had to provide detachments for military police duties.

Most Union brigades during the Gettysburg Campaign ran four or five regiments, though several had six or more and a few had three. Brigades had anywhere from 530 to 3,000 men, due to variations in the number and strength of their regiments. Divisions had mostly two or three brigades, with one having four, which gave them a strength of from 2,400 to 5,100 combatants. Early in the war it had been the practice to add a battery of artillery and some cavalry to each division, but these had been removed long before the Gettysburg Campaign. While the loss of the cavalry contingent was not significant, the fact that the division commander had no artillery directly under his control was a serious organizational defect, one which would be remedied later in the war when a battery or two were routinely attached to many divisions. Two or three divisions plus a brigade of four or five artillery batteries comprised a corps, which averaged between 9,000 and 13,500 combatants, with from 20 to 46 pieces of artillery. Altogether, the *Army of the Potomac* had seven infantry corps and one of cavalry. There were, in addition, the *Artillery Reserve*, a brigade of engineers and a mixed brigade under the Provost Marshal General. These were a distinct asset to the *Army of the Potomac*, for there was nothing like them in the Army of Northern Virginia. The Artillery Reserve of 118 guns and over 2,500 men gave the army commander a readily deployable pool of artillery, without having to strip batteries from the individual corps. The engineer brigade had technical skills which were not available among the line troops, even when directed by trained engineer officers and the provost marshal's guard served as field police, thereby relieving individual regiments from having to provide detachments for this purpose. In addition, of course, each Federal brigade, division and corps had its ambulance corps and medical team, which facilitated treatment of the wounded. However, despite these valuable advantages, the organization of the *Army of the Potomac* was distinctly clumsy.

Operationally, on the eve of Gettysburg the *Army of the Potomac* had nine subordinates under its commander's immediate control: his seven infantry corps commanders, plus that of the *Cavalry Corps* and of the *Artillery Reserve*, who controlled nineteen infantry divisions and three cavalry divisions. In contrast, the Army of Northern Virginia commander R.E. Lee had four direct subordinates, one for each corps, plus J.E.B. Stuart for the cavalry, and only nine infantry divisions and the cavalry division, thus giving him far fewer people to supervise. So superior was the organization of the Army of Northern Virginia, that in preparation for the Campaign of 1864, Lt. Gen. Ulysses S. Grant restructured the Army of the Potomac, so that it emerged with but four corps, plus the cavalry, artillery reserve and headquarters assets, thus greatly easing the burden of command.

In general, by the middle of the war both sides had achieved a fairly satisfactory system of organization, albeit with minor problems which would be refined as time went on.

Drummer Boys

Until well into the nineteenth century armies regularly recruited young boys for service as drummers. This was not merely to provide music. As with bugles—called "trumpets"—drums formed an important part of the battlefield communications system, with various rolls signaling different commands. Recruiting boys for the work freed men for combat duty. As the boys got older they could regularly enlist in the ranks. Drummer boys were usually treated as something of a mascot by the troops, and often entrusted to the good offices of the regimental chaplain. Since they had few military duties to perform, the life of a drummer boy was not particularly onerous and appeared rather glamorous. As a result, boys of all ages tried to enlist, often running away from home. Officially there were age restrictions, but these were often ignored, and boys as young as ten were occasionally found beating the "long roll" which called the men to action.

Needless to say, drummer boys—in Confederate regiments they were sometimes black—were often in the thick of the fighting, becoming casualties on a regular basis. Many lie in unknown graves, such as the heroic boy who fell at the head of Confederate Col. James C. Tappan's 13th Arkansas in an unnamed skirmish along the Arkansas River.

A number of drummer boys greatly distinguished themselves in action, and several became rather well known. The most famous drummer boy of the Civil War was undoubtedly John Clem (1851-1937), who added "Lincoln" as a middle name in 1861. At the age of ten little Johnny ran away from home in Newark, Ohio, and tried to enlist in various regiments, until the *24th Ohio* took him on. He served at Shiloh, earning the nickname "Johnny Shiloh" for his steadiness. Later transferring to the *22nd*

Michigan, Clem drummed the long roll at Chickamauga—where he acquired the nickname "The Drummer Boy of Chickamauga"—and at Chattanooga and several other battles, occasionally finding the time to lend a hand with the fighting as well. After the war he attempted to win an appointment to West Point, but, having been otherwise occupied when most children his age were in school, he was a little weak academically. With the support of President Ulysses S. Grant, in whose army he had drummed at Shiloh, and Maj. Gen. George "The Rock of Chickamauga" Thomas, for whom he had drummed on that disastrous occasion, Clem was given a direct commission into the army as a second lieutenant in 1871, retiring 45 years later as a major general, the last Civil War veteran on active duty.

Willie Johnson, from St. Johnsbury, Vermont, was a drummer boy in *Company D* of the *3rd Vermont*. His service during the "Seven Days" retreat in the Peninsular Campaign was exemplary, and he was the only drummer in his division to come away with his instrument, by no means a trivial accomplishment. As a result, he was awarded the Medal of Honor on the recommendation of his division commander, thereby becoming the youngest recipient of the highest decoration, being then just 13 years old.

John McLaughlin, a native of Lafayette, Indiana, enlisted as a drummer in the *10th Indiana* in 1861, being then "a little over ten years of age." McLaughlin had numerous adventures. During the Henry-Donelson Campaign he put aside his drum to take up a musket and join the firing line. Subsequently transferring to a Unionist Kentucky cavalry regiment, he fought as a trooper at Perryville, where he took a wound in his leg and took part in the pursuit of Col. John Morgan, during which he received a saber cut in the same leg. His wound proving serious, he was discharged. Although he recovered only partial use of his leg, he fought the discharge, appealing to Lincoln. After a private interview with the president, McLaughlin was enlisted as a bugler in the Regular Army.

"Little Oirish" was a Kentucky lad of about eleven who enlisted in the Confederacy's famed "Orphan Brigade." At Shiloh he is credited with stemming a rout by grabbing the colors and rallying elements of the brigade which were in danger of breaking under a Federal assault.

Field Artillery

During the early nineteenth century there were significant improvements in artillery. However, as a result of the existence of the new rifled small arms, artillery service was both more difficult and more dangerous than in the past. Most artillery pieces were direct fire weapons, so the gunners had to see their targets in order to hit them. As recently as the Mexican War (1846-1848) it had been possible to site batteries within 500 yards or less of enemy formations, but this was now highly dangerous, given that rifle-armed infantry could deliver voluminous and accurate fire at such ranges, cutting down gunners and horses alike.

In an attack artillery was used to soften up the defenses, showering them with explosive shell and solid shot, inflicting casualties and destroying the cohesion of the defenders. This was most effectively done at relatively short ranges, to ensure accuracy. Unfortunately, this put the gunners within range of enemy rifle men. As a result, unless the guns could be put under cover of woods, fire had to be delivered at rather long range. At Gettysburg, for example, the Confederate batteries which fired the preparatory bombardment on 3 July were mostly sited in the woods atop Seminary Ridge, at ranges of between 1,200 yards and 2,200 yards away from the Union lines. This was one reason why the two-hour bombardment, involving perhaps 5,000 rounds, was ineffective. At such ranges, gunners were unable to observe the fall of shot and tended to overestimate the range. As a result, a substantial proportion of their fire fell behind the Union lines, rather than on them.

When it was possible to deliver a preparatory bombardment from massed batteries at closer range, as James Longstreet's batteries did during the same battle on the afternoon of 2 July against the Union *III Corps* or as Alpheus Williams' did on the morning of 3 July against the Confederate forces on Culp's Hill, the results could be effective. In these cases, of course, the guns were firing from cover, which permitted such close work.

Artillery could also be used to bring enemy artillery under fire. However, although opposing artillerymen often engaged each other in such personalized gun duels, counter-battery fire was relatively ineffective. The guns all used black powder, which generated lots of thick white smoke. As a result, after a few rounds, the guns were literally shrouded in great clouds, making it difficult to observe one's targets. Continuing to fire in such circumstances was merely a waste of ammunition. It was for this reason that most artillerymen preferred not to return fire during a preliminary bombardment; there was no point in wasting ammunition which could be put to better use in meeting an infantry attack.

As with the infantry rifle, it was in defense that artillery was particularly useful. A single well-handled battery could often hold up the advance of thousands of troops. And massed batteries could be particularly devastating, especially if the attackers had to cross wide stretches of open ground, as at Malvern Hill on 1 July 1862 or Gettysburg on 3 July 1863. An attacking formation could be brought under fire at ranges upwards of 2,000 yards, albeit with low effectiveness. As the troops drew nearer, effectiveness increased. Solid shot could bowl swathes through the attacking ranks and explosive shell could burst in the midst of the troops, both alike causing great slaughter. When the enemy was within 300 yards the gunners would switch to canister, which were giant shotgun shells capable of tearing a man to pieces. At the very last moment, the guns could be double-loaded with canister, which could be discharged right into the faces of the enemy as they reached the muzzles. Consider a charge against a battery of six 12-pounder Napoleons:

Volume of Fire Delivered Against Troops Attacking at 1,500 Yards

Attacker	Time*	Type of Projectile Fired			
		Shell	Ball	Canister	Total
Cavalry	4.9 min	42	12	12+	66+
Infantry	16.9	120	42	66+	228+

* Time required for the attackers to reach the battery at prescribed attack rates.

As can be seen, even cavalry, which charges at a much faster rate than infantry, would receive an enormous volume of fire. Given that the attackers would also be receiving increasingly accurate rifle fire as they closed with the defenses, it is not difficult to see why frontal attacks were costly.

Field Artillery of the Civil War

Type	Bore (in)	Weight (pds)	Round Proj	pds chg	Range (yds)	Notes
Howitzer						
12-Pdr U.S. 1841	4.62	788	8.9	.75	1072	A
24-Pdr U.S. 1841	5.82	1318	18.4	2.00	1322	A
Gun-Howitzer						
12-Pdr U.S. 1857	4.62	1227	12.3	2.50	1680	B
Guns						
3" U.S. Ri 1861	3.00	820	9.5	1.00	2788	C
6-Pdr U.S. 1857	3.67	884	6.1	1.25	1523	D
10-Pdr Parrott Ri 1863	3.00	890	9.5	1.00	2970	E
12-Pdr Blakely Ri BL 1859	3.10	700	12.0	1.50	1760	F
12-Pdr Whitworth Ri BL 1860	2.75	1100	12.0	1.75	8800	G
14-Pdr James Ri 1857	3.67	875	12.0	0.75	1700	H
20-Pdr Parrott Ri 1861	3.67	1750	20.0	2.00	4400	I

This table includes the specifications for the most commonly used field artillery pieces of the Civil War. Type indicates that the piece was a *Howitzer*, able to use high angle fire to drop explosive shells behind obstacles, or a *Gun*, designed for a flat trajectory, and able to fire shells or solid shot to long ranges, or a *Gun-Howitzer*, theoretically capable of being fired in either mode. The designation given a piece is the official one, with the year normally that of introduction, though sometimes that of design. *Ri* indicates a rifled piece, all others being smooth bores. *BL* indicates a breech loading-piece, all others being muzzle loaders. *Bore* is the diameter of the tube, in inches. *Weight* is the total weight, in pounds, of the piece, with carriage, but exclusive of limber, caisson, and ammunition. *Round* is the weight, again in pounds, of the *Projectile* and the propellant *Charge*; for howitzers the projectile weight is for shells, for other pieces for solid shot. Note that official pounder designations were not usually a reliable indication of actual projectile weight. *Range* is the maximum range in yards, that at which it could project rounds, though not necessarily with any accuracy; for guns the range given is for solid shot; when using explosive shell this was about 25 percent less. Effective range, that at which most of the rounds fired reached the vicinity of the target, was usually about 60 percent of maximum range. *Notes* refers to the lettered paragraphs below.

A. The standard U.S. howitzers of the pre-war period, both models, plus a lighter mountain version of the 12-pounder were widely used early in the war, but were soon phased out by both sides in the major theaters, due primarily to their short range and the difficulty of observing their fire with any accuracy. A less serious problem, that of properly setting fuzes, was shared with all artillery pieces able to fire shell. Howitzers could also fire canister. They were made of gun metal, normally called "brass," but actually a bronze of about 10 percent tin plus some other minor alloying ingredients. Cast solid, the tubes were then bored out on a lathe.

B. The famed "Napoleon," this was actually an American version of the field piece designed by Napoleon III in 1853. Though heavy and short-ranged, it was the most commonly used artillery piece of the war. A great favorite with the troops, who considered it highly reliable, the Napoleon could fire all types of ammunition, but was particularly effective firing canister in support of defending infantry. At least theoretically it could fire both as a gun and a howitzer, though rarely employed in the latter role. As with the howitzers, Napoleons were cast in gun metal, and bored out, though some Confederate versions were made of weaker cast iron, with a reinforcing jacket at the breech and were consequently much heavier.

C. Variously referred to as the "Ordnance Rifle" or "Gun," or as the "Rodman Gun" or "Rifle," or as the "Griffen Gun," this was, after the Napoleon, the most reliable piece in service and in numbers, eventually used by all Union horse artillery and many field batteries as well. The piece was so good that the 10-Pounder Parrott guns were converted to take the same ammunition. Like all rifles, however, the 3" gun was not really good at firing canister, since the latter scoured the inside of the barrel, damaging the rifling. The piece was made by welding together wrought iron strips which had been wound in a spiral around a solid core, which was then drilled out and seven rifling grooves cut into the tube.

D. The light field gun version of the Napoleon. Little used in the Eastern Theater by the middle of the war, it remained with the troops in the West rather longer.

E. Designed by Robert P. Parrott, Superintendent of the West Point Iron and Cannon Foundry, both armies made considerable use of this reliable gun, which had been designed originally with a 2.9" bore but was rebored to take the same ammunition as the 3" Ordnance Rifle in 1863. It was made of cast iron, poured solid and then bored out, and was reinforced at the breech by a wrought iron band which was shrunk on. Since Confederate attempts to duplicate the gun were not successful—the end products weighing nearly 70 percent more than the originals—the Rebels relied on captured stocks.

F. A small number of these highly unusual guns were obtained in England by the Confederacy. Although impressive enough in performance, and very suitable for horse artillery due to their lightness—indeed, Wade Hampton actually imported a battery at his own expense—they had a terrific recoil, making relaying difficult. The guns were made of cast iron poured solid and drilled out. The shells had flanges which fit the rifling grooves in the barrel.

G. Designed by Sir Joseph Whitworth, small numbers were imported by the Confederacy and a single battery by the Union. They fired a 9.6" long hexagonal shaped bolt up to five miles. However, the peculiar shape of the projectile precluded the development of an effective explosive shell, thereby restricting its use to solid shot. Although satisfactory in service, with remarkable accuracy and hitting power, the piece was a disappointment for no system existed by which the fall of shot could be observed and corrected at such ranges. The Whitworth was made out of cast steel, poured solid and drilled out in the desired diameter.

H. Invented by Charles James of Rhode Island, the James rifle proved unsatisfactory in service, due to unstable projectiles. Indeed, James himself was mortally wounded by the accidental detonation of one of his shells in 1862. Most James guns were cast in gun metal, but a few seem to have been made of high grade cast iron. Very few James rifles were actually produced, however, though numbers of existing cannon were experimentally converted to the James system and referred to as "James" guns.

I. This was a heavier version of the standard Parrott field gun, and the heaviest normally carried into the field. It was substantially similar to the 10-Pounder version.

Infantry Tactics

The infantry was the principal arm of both armies in the Civil War. The overwhelming majority of the combat casualties were suffered, and inflicted, by infantrymen. In the generation before the Civil War the old smooth bore, muzzle loading musket which had been first introduced some two centuries earlier had passed from the scene. These weapons were highly inaccurate, extremely slow firing and of very short range. As a result, battles were fought with the troops lined up shoulder-to-shoulder, firing coordinated volleys at very short ranges against enemy troops similarly arrayed, which could be devastatingly effective. This was all perfectly satisfactory for well over a century. Both organization and tactics were based on the use of these weapons.

It had long been known that the smooth bore musket was decidedly inferior to the rifle, a weapon which had shallow grooves cut into the barrel which imparted a spin to the projectile, thus helping to stabilize it in flight, thereby greatly enhancing range and accuracy. But the existing rifles were even clumsier than the smooth bore, with an even lower rate of fire, for it required very careful loading. As a result the rifle was rarely used by armies.

In 1848 a French officer, Capt. Claude Etienne Minie, invented a practical rifled musket. What Minie actually invented was a more practical bullet for the rifled musket. The so-called "minie-ball" was a cylindro-conoidal (i.e. "bullet-shaped") lead projectile with a hollow base, cast to a somewhat smaller diameter than the musket barrel. When the piece was fired the rapid generation of gas expanded the soft, hollow base of the round, forcing it to conform to the rifling grooves on the inner side of the barrel; in some early versions a small pellet of harder metal was placed at the base to help expand the round, but this was later found unnecessary. The rounds were made up into paper wrapped cartridges of about two inches in length. Loading was thus no more difficult than it was for the old smooth bore weapons, while accuracy and range were greatly enhanced. The new weapon was soon adopted by most armies, to devastating effect. One reason for the devastation was a failure of tactical doctrine.

Tactics ought to be a reflection of weaponry. By the mid-nineteenth century the optimal tactics for the smooth bore musket were well understood, having evolved over more than a century. Unfortunately, when the rifled musket was introduced its effects on tactics were not clearly understood, even when the new rifled muskets went to war. In the first wars in which rifles were widely available, the Mexican-American War of 1846-1848, the European Revolutions of 1848, the Crimean War of 1853-56 and the Italian Wars of 1859-1860, the armies continued to use their existing tactics. Casualties were often horrendous as lines of troops arrayed shoulder-to-shoulder marched up to short ranges and exchanged fire in formal Napoleonic style, or attempted heroic bayonet charges right into the face of rifle-armed foes. The lesson was plain to see, but was not noticed for a variety of reasons. The most important was probably that these wars were short, all essentially resolved in one or two major battles, often against inept opposition.

When the Civil War began both sides used the same field service regulations, William J. Hardee's *Rifle and Light Infantry Tactics*, written in 1853, which was essentially a modification of French Napoleonic practice. But the killing power of the rifle was not fully appreciated by very many military leaders, and probably by even fewer political leaders. So the troops went to war in the grand old style, made worse by the fact that everyone was very green and very brave. This led to some horrible bloodbaths; the bulk of the casualties at the First Battle of Bull Run occurred when a couple of regiments attempted to trade volleys in the old style. The problem was that the rifle had made it virtually impossible to physically assault the enemy frontally. But it took a while for this fact to sink in. As it did, tactics began to change, out of a combination of the instinct for self-preservation and an understanding of the futility of the traditional methods. Defensive tactics changed first and best.

In defense, presupposing that his flanks and rear were secure, a commander would put some of his troops out as skirmishers a couple of hundred yards before his main line. Firing from cover, their function was to entertain an advancing enemy, sniping at officers and generally attempting to disrupt the attack. As the enemy closed, the skirmishers could either filter out by the flanks, to regroup, or drift back to join the main line of resistance. Most of the troops, of course, would be on the main line. By 1863 both armies resorted to all available cover when defending, and given

time, attempted to improve their positions with rifle pits and other en-
trenchments. Firing from cover, the defenders could deliver an annoying
shower of bullets at ranges out to a thousand yards, with increasing
effectiveness as the foe came closer; since a 350-man regiment could
theoretically pour out well over 10,000 rounds in the time required for
attacking infantry to cover 1,500 yards, the defense had a distinct advantage, particularly if artillery was at hand to lend support.

Should the enemy actually reach the main defense line, hand-to-hand
combat was common, though far more frequently with clubbed rifles than
with bayonets. A wise defender usually retained a portion of his troops
behind the line as a reserve, and these could be thrown in should the enemy
begin forcing the line. In addition, if his skirmishers had regrouped to the
flanks, they could be thrown in against the attackers' flanks at the critical
moment. The Union stand on Cemetery Ridge during the Battle of Gettysburg on 3 July was a very fine example of what a properly conducted
defense was supposed to look like, once the power of the rifle was appreciated. Since the principal impact of the rifled musket was to greatly improve
the effectiveness of the defense, it made the offensive far more difficult.

No one managed to evolve proper offensive tactics during the Civil War.
Initial efforts at Napoleonic-style storming columns or linear tactics
proved disastrously expensive, but the cult of the bayonet persisted. Attacks in waves, with skirmishers to the fore were tried, to better effect, but
these were by no means widely successful. Attempts were also made to
attack with troops advancing by rushes in open order, again with mixed
results. The best way to conduct any attack was to avoid the enemy's
strength, to use maneuver and surprise to strike where he was weakest, on
an exposed flank or at a thinly held position or against a poorly deployed
formation, or one already badly battered by infantry and artillery fire. In
these circumstances, going in with the bayonet was possible, though most
of the fighting was still by fire, the principal effect of the bayonet being
psychological. It was precisely this sort of attack which Lee effected at
Chancellorsville (1-4 May 1863). However, such an attack required considerable tactical skill. Even if successful, one had to pay the price, for even
in highly adverse situations the tactical defensive was enormously strong
and anyone undertaking an offensive, even against poorly organized opposition, had to be willing to take losses. Thus, at Second Bull Run and
Chantilly (27 August-2 September 1862) the Army of Northern Virginia
lost nearly 20 percent of its strength in defeating the *Army of Virginia* and
the *Army of the Potomac*, which lost about 13 percent. This was one reason
why the Union suffered repeated defeats during the earlier period of the

war; Union forces were more often on the offensive. It also helps explain why Confederate losses were often enormous, for Rebel generals had a predilection for the tactical offensive even when on the strategic defensive. So fine a commander as Lee himself fought only one purely defensive battle, when, at Fredericksburg on 13 December 1862, he held Marye's Heights in strength and accepted the repeated frontal attacks of the *Army of the Potomac*. Both absolutely and statistically Union casualties were almost double his own, whereas when he won by a tactical offensive his casualties were almost invariably statistically greater than his opponent's.

Certainly by mid-1863 the effectiveness of entrenched infantry defending against frontal assaults had been fairly clearly established. Nevertheless, the temptation to try precisely such an assault seems to have been overwhelming. Certainly it is extremely difficult to understand such attacks as Pickett's Charge at Gettysburg on 3 July 1863, Grant's assault at Cold Harbor on 3 June 1864 and Hood's at Franklin on 30 November 1864, all against strong forces well posted and all resulting in enormous losses to no purpose. Perhaps in the end, the Napoleonic ideal was stronger than reality.

Army Life

Vivandieres

One of the more unusual phenomena of warfare in the nineteenth century was the *vivandiere*. An eighteenth century French military development, the *vivandiere* was, in effect, a paid camp follower properly enlisted on the rolls of a regiment, to serve as den mother, nurse and mascot, with eminent respectability, frequently being the wife or daughter of one of the men. Since the French were reputedly the finest soldiers in the world, the practice was widely imitated.

A number of *vivandieres* served in the early part of the Civil War, on both sides, primarily in French-style zouave regiments or in outfits with large numbers of foreigners. Like nurses, who also often served in the field, the "job description" of *vivandieres* was a non-combat one, but it at least implicitly included service under fire. These women were often up on the firing line in some of the hottest battles of the war, and a few seem to have taken at least a small part in the fighting. Three women who gained particular distinction in the role of *vivandiere* were Kady Brownell, Annie Etheridge and Bridget Divers.

Kady Brownell (1842-?), was born in Africa, the daughter of a British soldier. By most accounts an expert with pistol and saber, she enlisted at age 19 as a *vivandiere* in her husband's regiment, the *1st Rhode Island,* a 90-day outfit and carried the regimental colors at First Bull Run. When her husband reenlisted, in the *5th Rhode Island,* Kady went with him, although not carried formally on the rolls this time. She stayed with the regiment for nearly two years, often serving as color bearer under fire. On at least one occasion she saved the regiment from the fire of another Union outfit by running out into the line of fire with colors in hand. Her husband was severely wounded at New Berne on 14 March 1862. Kady spent 18 months nursing him back to health, whereupon he was discharged and they both left the service forever. Her subsequent life is obscure.

Annie Etheridge (1844-?), a some-time resident of both Wisconsin and Michigan, enlisted as a nurse-*vivandiere* in the *2nd Michigan,* later passed over to the *3rd Michigan* and in 1864 reenlisted in the *5th Michigan,* serving throughout the war. Said to have been very brave under fire, she served in most of the battles of the *Army of the Potomac,* being in the thick of things on numerous occasions, such as at Gettysburg on the second day. She was wounded only once, a graze across one hand, despite numerous bullet holes in her clothing, and at Spotsylvania was credited with rallying retreating troops in the face of the enemy. Known to the troops as "Gentle Anna" and "Michigan Annie," Phil Kearny was said to be planning to make her a sergeant-major at the time of his death, and Daniel Butterfield, his successor as division commander, awarded her a Kearny Cross. After the war she received a government job in lieu of pension.

Bridgett Divers (?-?) joined the *1st Michigan Cavalry* as a *vivandiere* when her husband enlisted in 1861 and served in numerous engagements. She subsequently worked as an agent for the Sanitary Commission. During the war she had many adventures, and was twice almost captured. On two separate occasions "Irish Biddy" was credited with rallying her regiment under fire, and was several times reported to have taken up a musket and joined the firing line. After the war she followed her soldier-husband into the Regular Army, serving as a regimental laundress for many years on the frontier.

Uniform Expenses

On the outbreak of the war both armies had elaborate uniform regulations, the Confederacy adopting virtually unchanged the prewar regulations of the United States Army. For a Union soldier a full uniform cost about $40.00, while for his counterpart in gray the price was rather higher, about $62.00, reflecting the relative shortage of manufactured goods in the Confederacy. On this basis, uniform costs for an infantry regiment were about $40,000 for the Union and about $62,000 for the Confederacy. In addition, there were equipment costs, including blankets, knapsack, haversack, canteen and the like, which added an additional $10.00 to the bluecoats' outfitting costs and, although this is less certain, perhaps $15.00 to that of his graycoated foeman, which brings regimental outfitting costs up to about $50,000 for the Union and $77,000 for the Confederacy. Then consider the price of arms. A complete stand of arms—musket, bayonet and accoutrements—seems to have run about $30.00 for the Yankee, more for the Rebel, though how much more being impossible to calculate. This brings the cost of outfitting a Union regiment of about 1,000 men up to about $80,000 without considering the cost of such necessary items as mess'pans (at $0.17 a piece), camp kettles ($0.48), axes ($0.66), spades ($0.56), picks ($0.57), bugles ($2.82), fifes ($0.45) and drums ($5.58), nor regimental colors nor supply wagons nor medical equipment, and certainly not officers kit, equipment and mounts, which they themselves had to supply. So a single regiment of infantry probably cost Uncle Sam about $100,000 in the first year or so of the war. What it cost "Uncle Jeff" is conjectural, but certainly more, even considering that the Rebels often marched off to war with a lot less than the Yankees.

Prescribed Annual Uniform Allowances,
Union and Confederate Armies, 1861

Year of Service:	1st	2nd	3rd
Hat	1		
Caps	2	1	1
Cap Cover	1	1	1
Coat	2	1	1
Trousers	3	2	2
Shirts	3	3	3
Blouse	1		
Drawers	3	2	2
Shoes, pair	2	2	2
Stockings, pair	2	2	4
Stock [tie]	1		
Great Coat	1		
Woolen Blanket	1		
Rubber Blanket	1		

In addition to these items, mounted troops—cavalrymen, artillery drivers and wagoners—were issued a stable frock each year while engineers and ordnance men received a set of fatigue overalls every other year. Theoretically each year's allotment of uniform items was divided into two batches, one for issue in the spring and one for issue in the fall.

	Initial Uniforming Costs, 1861		
	Number		Unit Cost
	Issued	Union	Confederate
Hat	1	1.98	?
Caps	2	0.63	1.00
Cap Cover	1	.25	.38
Coat	2	6.71	8.00
Trousers	3	3.03	4.00

Initial Uniforming Costs, 1861

	Number Issued	Unit Cost Union	Confederate
Shirts	3	.88	1.00
Blouse	1	2.15	?
Drawers	3	.50	1.00
Shoes, pair	2	1.94	3.00
Stockings, pair	2	.26	.50
Stock [tie]	1	.25	.25
Great Coat	1	7.20	25.00
Woolen Blanket	1	3.50	7.50
Rubber Blanket	1	1.00	?

At the beginning of the war there were many variations in the kit issued to newly mustered troops. Many militia regiments, both North and South, which were mustered into the service often had their own very elaborate uniforms and kit; the *7th New York* and the Washington Artillery come readily to mind, with their camp stools and tents and other bric-a-brac. On the other hand many newly raised regiments found themselves only partially outfitted, or outfitted in a fashion other than that prescribed in regulations, due to shortages in the availability of uniforms and equipment. It was rare, for example, for Union volunteers ever to receive a hat and blouse, which were dress uniform items. A typical example is that of the *7th Wisconsin*, outfitted at state expense, which was mustered into Federal service in August of 1861.

Initial Uniform Allotment
7th Wisconsin Infantry

	Number	Unit Cost
Cap & Cover	1	$1.00
Winter Coat & Trousers	1	9.50
Summer Coat & Trousers	1	4.63
Shirt	2	1.38
Shoes, pair	1	1.87
Stockings, pair	2	.30
Great Coat	1	7.50
Woolen Blanket	1	3.50
Rubber Blanket	1	1.00

The differences between what the state supplied and what the Federal government prescribed were eventually made good, though there was an unpleasant exchange of notes between the two jurisdictions as to who owed what to whom. Of course, the Federal supply situation grew steadily better as the war went on. Moreover, as time went on the troops found that they could manage with a lot less than the prescribed allotments of uniform and kit; the knapsack, for example, was discarded early. For Confederate troops this was making a virtue of a necessity, since their quartermaster department was never up to the task of outfitting them according to regulations anyway. They frequently made do with captured Union uniforms, eked out by civilian clothing and occasional bits and pieces of their prescribed uniforms.

War and the Muses

The Bonnie Blue Flag

In September of 1861 a New Orleans song writer, Harry McCarthy, an immigrant from Britain, wrote "The Bonnie Blue Flag" to fill a hole in a theatrical program which he was directing, with music adapted from an old Irish air by Jacob Tannenbaum, a German immigrant. The song was an instant hit, running through eleven editions during the war, and was soon popular second only to "Dixie" throughout the Confederacy. Unlike many other songs of the war, it was not popular in the North, due to its blatantly secessionist sentiments and its reference to slavery in the line "Fighting for the property we gained by honest toil." When Union forces occupied New Orleans in the spring of '62 a silly effort was made to ban it, with little success, despite a $25 fine. The song endured, though it lost some popularity when its writer abandoned the Confederacy for the North.

The Bonnie Blue Flag

We are a band of brothers, and native to the soil,
Fighting for the property we gained by honest toil;
And when our rights were threatened, the cry rose near and far:
Hurrah for the bonnie Blue Flag that bears a single star!
　　Hurrah! hurrah! for the bonnie Blue Flag
　　That bears a single star.
As long as the Union was faithful to her trust,
Like friends and like brothers, kind were we and just;
But now when Northern treachery attempts our rights to mar,
We hoist on high the bonnie Blue Flag that bears a single star.
First, gallant South Carolina nobly made the stand;
Then came Alabama, who took her by the hand;
Next, quickly Mississippi, Georgia, and Florida—
All raised the flag, the bonnie Blue Flag that bears a single star.
Ye, men of valor, gather round the banner of the right;
Texas and fair Louisiana join us in the fight.
Davis, our loved president, and Stephens, statesman are;
Now rally round the bonnie Blue Flag that bears a single star.

And here's to brave Virginia! the Old Dominion State
With the young Confederacy at length has linked her fate.
Impelled by her example, now others must prepare
To hoist on high the bonnie Blue Flag that bears a single star.
Then here's to our Confederacy; strong we are and brave,
Like patriots of old we'll fight, our heritage to save;
And rather than submit to shame, to die we would prefer;
So cheer for the bonnie Blue Flag that bears a single star.
Then cheer, boys, cheer, raise the joyous shout,
For Arkansas and North Carolina now have both gone out;
And let another rousing cheer for Tennessee be given,
The single star of the bonnie Blue Flag has grown to eleven!
    Hurrah! hurrah! for the bonnie Blue Flag
    That bears a single star.

Maryland! My Maryland!

James Ryder Randall, an expatriate Baltimorean serving as a professor at
Pydras College, in Pointe Coupee Parish, Louisiana, wrote "Maryland! My
Maryland!" soon after hearing of the bloody clash between the 6th Massachusetts and a secessionist mob in Baltimore on 19 April 1861. Shortly
after the poem was published in the *New Orleans Delta* it came to the
attention of Jennie Cary, one of the redoubtable Cary Cousins. Miss Cary
set the words to the music for "Lauriger Horatius," more familiar as the
tune of the Christmas carol "O Tannenbaum," and performed it at a
patriotic rally. The song caught on rapidly and became a favorite Southern
marching song in the early years of the war, losing little of its popularity as
the state clung to the Union. Later adopted as the Maryland state song, its
avowedly secessionist verses are a constant irritant to the state's black
population.

Maryland! My Maryland!

The despot's heel is on thy shore,
    Maryland!
His torch is at thy temple door.
    Maryland!
Avenge the patriotic gore
That flecked the streets of Baltimore,
And be the battle-queen of yore,
Maryland, my Maryland!
Hark to an exiled son's appeal,
    Maryland!
My Mother State, to thee I kneel,

Maryland!
For life and death, for woe and weal,
Thy peerless chivalry reveal,
And gird thy beauteous limbs with steel,
    Maryland, my Maryland!
Thou wilt not cower in the dust,
    Maryland!
Thy beaming sword shall never rust,
    Maryland!
Remember Carroll's sacred trust,
Remember Howard's warlike thrust,
All thy slumberers with the just,
    Maryland, my Maryland!
Come! 'tis the red dawn of day,
    Maryland!
Come with thy panoplied array,
    Maryland!
With Ringgold's spirit for the fray,
With Watson's blood at Monterey,
With fearless Lowe and dashing May,
    Maryland, my Maryland!
Come! for thy shield is bright and strong,
    Maryland!
Come! for thy dalliance does thee wrong,
    Maryland!
Come to thine own heroic throng,
Stalking with Liberty along,
And chant thy dauntless slogan-song,
    Maryland, my Maryland!
Dear Mother, burst thy tyrant's chain,
    Maryland!
Virginia should not call in vain,
    Maryland!
She meets her sisters on the plain,—
"Sic semper!" 'tis the proud refrain
That baffles minions back amain,
    Maryland, my Maryland!
I see the blush upon thy cheek,
    Maryland!
For thou wast never bravely meek,
    Maryland!
But lo! there surges forth a shriek
From hill to hill, from creek to creek,—

Potomac calls to Chesapeake,
   Maryland, my Maryland!
Thou wilt not yield the Vandal toll,
   Maryland!
Thou wilt not crook to his control,
   Maryland!
Better the fire upon thee roll,
Better the blade, the shot, the ball,
Than crucifixion of my soul,
   Maryland, my Maryland!
I hear the distant thunder-hum
   Maryland!
The old Line's bugle, fife, and drum,
   Maryland!
She is not dead, nor deaf, nor dumb;
Huzzah! She spurns the Northern scum!
She breathes! She burns! She'll come!
She'll come!
   Maryland, my Maryland!

The John Brown Song

The origins of what is more commonly known as "John Brown's Body" of "John Brown's Song" are obscure. The tune seems to have been adapted from an old Negro spiritual, "Say, Brothers, Will You Meet Us?" by William Steffe in 1852 and was used for several songs over the next few years. The words are attributed to one Thomas B. Bishop. The two were somehow combined shortly after the war began, reputedly by two Massachusetts men, Messers Gilmore and Greenleaf, and soon became a favorite Union march, possibly the most popular of the war, particularly in the early days. As with all genuine folk songs, there were many variations. In early 1862 the most enduring and powerful version was written, "The Battle Hymn of the Republic."

The John Brown Song
John Brown's body lies a-mouldering in the grave;
   John Brown's body lies a-mouldering in the grave;
   John Brown's body lies a-mouldering in the grave;
      His soul goes marching on!
Glory, halle—hallelujah! Glory, halle—hallelujah!
    Glory, halle—hallelujah!
        His soul is marching on!
He's gone to be a soldier in the army of the Lord!

He's gone to be a soldier in the army of the Lord!
He's gone to be a soldier in the army of the Lord!
His soul is marching on!
Chorus
Glory, halle—hallelujah! Glory, halle—hallelujah!
Glory, halle—hallelujah!
His soul is marching on!
John Brown's knapsack is strapped upon his back!
John Brown's knapsack is strapped upon his back!
John Brown's knapsack is strapped upon his back!
His soul is marching on!
Chorus
Glory, halle—hallelujah! Glory, halle—hallelujah!
Glory, halle—hallelujah!
His soul is marching on!
His pet lambs will meet him on the way;
His pet lambs will meet him on the way;
His pet lambs will meet him on the way;
As they go marching on!
Chorus
Glory, halle—hallelujah! Glory, halle—hallelujah!
Glory, halle—hallelujah!
As they go marching on!
They will hang Jeff Davis to a sour apple tree!
They will hang Jeff Davis to a sour apple tree!
They will hang Jeff Davis to a sour apple tree!
As they march along!
Chorus
Glory, halle—hallelujah! Glory, halle—hallelujah!
Glory, halle—hallelujah!
As they march along!
Now, three rousing cheers for the Union!
Now, three rousing cheers for the Union!
Now, three rousing cheers for the Union!
As we go marching on!
Glory, halle—hallelujah! Glory, halle—hallelujah!
Glory, halle—hallelujah!
Hip, hip, hip, Hurrah!

All Quiet Along the Potomac

Ethel Lynn Eliot Beers, a sensitive young woman from New York, was moved to poetry by the newspaper headline, "All Quiet Along the Potomac," which appeared frequently in the autumn of 1861, usually followed by a subhead dealing with some minor incident or other. One day the subhead read "A Picket Shot." The incongruity of the headline, which suggested nothing of importance, and the subhead, which reported a personal tragedy of devastating consequence, prompted Beers to write a sad poem, "The Picket Guard." By some accounts first published in an unidentifiable newspaper on 21 Oct 1861, the poem certainly appeared in *Harper's Weekly* for 30 Nov 1861, signed "E.B.", for "Ethelyn Beers." The poem shortly came to the attention of John H. Hewitt, a noted journalist, poet and musician, serving as an officer in the Confederate Army, who set it to music as "All Quiet Along the Potomac."

Hewitt credited the words to Lamar Fontaine of Texas, which the latter did not dispute. Indeed, Fontaine claimed to have written them in August of 1861 and to have circulated handwritten copies among his comrades at the front. When Mrs. Beers' claims were advanced, Fontaine argued that she must have obtained a copy from a Yankee who had looted the body of a dead Confederate. While Lamar's father, an Episcopal rector, swore that his son was telling the truth, the latter was a notorious liar: among other tales, he claimed that he had lived four years among the Comanche while a child, that he had served in the Crimea and that he had been wounded 67 times during the Civil War while taking part in 27 battles and 57 skirmishes. Mrs. Beers' authorship seems probable. The song became rather popular with the troops on both sides, dealing, as it did, with the pain and suffering caused by the war.

All Quiet Along the Potomac
"All quiet along the Potomac to-night!"
  Except here and there a stray picket
Is shot, as he walks on his beat, to and fro,
  By a rifleman hid in the thicket.
'Tis nothing! a private or two now and then
  Will not count in the news of a battle;
Not an officer lost! only one of the men
  Moaning out, all alone, the death rattle.
All quiet on the Potomac to-night!
  Where the soldiers lie peacefully dreaming;
And their tents in the rays of the clear autumn moon,
  And the light of their camp-fires are gleaming.
A tremulous sigh, as a gentle night-wind
  Through the forest leaves slowly is creeping;
While the stars up above, with their glittering eyes,
  Keep guard o'er the army sleeping.

There's only the sound of the lone sentry's tread,
　As he tramps from the rock to the fountain,
And thinks of the two on the low trundel bed,
　Far away, in the cot on the mountain.
His musket falls slack, his face, dark and grim,
　Grows gentle with memories tender,
As he mutters a prayer for the children asleep,
　And their mother—"may heaven defend her!"
The moon seems to shine forth as brightly as then—
　That night, when the love, yet unspoken,
Leaped up to his lips, and when low-murmured vows
　Were pledged ever to be unbroken.
Then drawing his sleeve roughly over his eyes,
　He dashes off the tears that are welling;
And gathers the gun closer up to his breast,
　As if to keep down his heart's swelling.
He passes the fountain, the blasted pine-tree,
　And his footstep is lagging and weary;
Yet onward he goes, through the broad belt of light,
　Towards the shades of the forest so dreary.
Hark! was it the night-wind that rustled the leaves?
　Was it the moonlight so wondrously flashing?
It looked like a rifle: "Ha! Mary, good-by!"
　And his life-blood is ebbing and splashing.
"All quiet along the Potomac to-night!"
　No sound save the rush of the river;
While soft falls the dew on the face of the dead,
　And the picket's off duty forever!

III

1862

I propose to move immediately upon your works.
—Ulysses Grant

We must this day conquer or perish.
—Albert Sidney Johnston

Come on! Come on! Do you want to live forever?
—Unknown Confederate Colonel

If we have lost today, we have yet preserved our honor.
—George B. McClellan

Fight, fight—be whipped if you must, but fight on.
—Edwin M. Stanton

The enemy may win a victory, but we must make it a victory that will ruin him.
—Edwin V. Sumner

It is well war is so terrible, we should get too fond of it.
—Robert E. Lee

1862

Both sides prepared for 1862 with enormous energy, for it was generally expected that it would be the decisive year. Great armies had been raised and each side believed it had the ability to win. The Union adopted a realistic strategy: to strangle the enemy with a naval blockade, to send armies down the Mississippi River to cut the Confederacy in two and to attempt to seize Richmond, capital of the rebellion. In a sense the Confederacy adopted no strategy at all, counting on winning by being able to avoid defeat, which required that Federal forces be beaten back wherever they appeared.

In the West, the new armies were concentrated in Missouri and Tennessee and along the Ohio River, while in the East they were concentrated in Virginia and Maryland and around Washington. And when the armies began to move in early 1862, the troops were still but half-trained, led by generals as ill-prepared as themselves. It began in the West, where Union Brig. Gen. Ulysses S. Grant conducted a successful mid-winter offensive. In cooperation with a small naval flotilla, his 20,000 men seized the critical Confederate positions at Forts Henry (6 February) and Donelson (16 February), with some 12,000 prisoners. This had the effect of clearing Kentucky and Central Tennessee of Confederate forces. Advancing southwards up the Tennessee River, Grant, with some 35,000 men, was surprised by Confederate Gen. Albert Sidney Johnston with some 40,000 men at Shiloh on 6 April. After a brutal two-day fight by the still largely green armies, Grant threw back the enemy, having lost 13,000 men while inflicting some 10,000 casualties, including Johnston himself, who fell at the head of his troops. Soon after, on 25 April, a Federal naval squadron under Flag Officer David Glasgow Farragut boldly swept up the Mississippi to seize New Orleans. This meant that the Union controlled both ends of the river, making it a logical avenue for an advance which would cut the Confederacy in two. It was an opportunity for which Grant immediately began to prepare.

The key to Confederate control of the Mississippi lay at Vicksburg, a well-fortified city high above the river. In the late summer and early autumn of 1862 Grant undertook several offensives in Northern Mississippi. A series of battles, raids and skirmishes resulted in which Confederate Maj. Gen. Earl Van Dorn demonstrated that an overland advance was unprofitable. Grant altered his strategy. In late December his able subordinate Maj. Gen. William Tecumseh Sherman advanced down the Mississippi, with the object of taking Vicksburg by storm. The effort failed. Rather than withdraw Sherman's 32,000 men back up river, Grant left them in position on the Mississippi in Northern Louisiana, just across from Vicksburg, supplying them by river and there they settled down for the winter. Meanwhile, great battles were being fought in the heartland of the Confederacy.

In the summer of 1862 Confederate armies under the general direction of Gen. Braxton Bragg undertook an invasion of Kentucky, primarily as a strategic diversion to draw Federal attention from the vulnerable line of the Mississippi. Considerable maneuvering resulted, as Union forces sought to pin Bragg down and destroy him. Union Maj. Gen. William S. Rosecrans, with 45,000 men, finally ran Bragg to earth at Murfreesboro, Tennessee, on 29 December. Bragg, who had about 35,000 men, attacked. A tough fight followed, which lasted on and off for three days (31 December 1862 to 2 January 1863) after which Bragg drew off southwards, each side having incurred about 12,000 casualties. The months of maneuvering had basically restored the situation as it was before Bragg's offensive.

Meanwhile, the armies in the East had not been idle. After Bull Run, there was a long lull in the East as the armies were made ready. Confederate forces in Virginia were commanded by Gen. Joseph E. Johnston and concentrated north of Richmond, with the intention of defending the city against an advance from Washington. Union forces concentrating about Washington were under Maj. Gen. George McClellan. A talented, energetic and brilliant planner and organizer, McClellan created the *Army of the Potomac*, but lacked the instincts and will to lead it into battle, despite the great confidence which he publicly and repeatedly expressed. As the spring of 1862 approached, anticipation of a Federal offensive rose. McClellan dithered, demanding yet more men and yet more equipment. Taking counsel of his fears, he argued that he was greatly outnumbered, when, in fact, overall Union forces available for offensive operations were about twice those of the Confederacy (150,000 to 75,000). After much prodding he made his move, in a brilliantly conceived amphibious operation. He placed some 112,000 men on the peninsula between the James and the

York Rivers on the coast of Virginia in early April, intending to advance on Richmond before the Confederate forces in Northern Virginia could be properly redeployed. Then he lost his nerve, frittering away a month in unnecessary siege operations.

McClellan thus gave Johnston time to shift his forces and turn what could have been a spectacular Union victory into a dismal and disappointing failure. While Brig. Gen. Thomas "Stonewall" Jackson covered his exposed rear by a brilliant campaign in the Shenandoah Valley, Johnston held McClellan away from Richmond, though two efforts to inflict a major defeat on the Union forces were frustrated by inexperience, a rather confused Confederate command structure and some remarkably hard fighting on the part of the Union troops. Wounded, Johnston was replaced by the very able Gen. Robert E. Lee on 1 June. While McClellan lapsed into inactivity not ten miles outside Richmond, Lee laid his plans. Then on 26 June, having recalled Jackson from the Valley, he undertook a brilliant series of successful, though costly, counter-attacks known as the "Seven Days Battles." By their end, McClellan's *Army of the Potomac* had been forced back into a fortified camp up against the James River, from where it could draw supplies. During much of this fighting McClellan had performed poorly, though his conduct of the retreat to the James was superb and he remained remarkably popular with the troops. Wars, however, are won neither by retreats nor by popularity.

Faced with apparent disaster in the Peninsular Campaign, Lincoln attempted to recover the situation with an advance by the forces remaining in the Washington area. On 26 June, even as Lee began his counter offensive, Lincoln ordered the creation of the Union *Army of Virginia*, placing it under Maj. Gen. John Pope, a mildly successful commander from the western theater who happened to be junior in rank to his subordinates.

Pope advanced south from the Washington area with 45,000 men on 14 July. Lee, alert to the threat to his rear, dispatched Jackson northwards with 24,000 men. Jackson dealt Union Maj. Gen. Nathaniel Banks, commanding Pope's leading army corps, a crushing blow at Cedar Mountain on 9 August. Pope fell back towards Bull Run, while being reinforced by sea from the Army of the Potomac. On 28 August, Lee, with some 55,000 men, boldly undertook an envelopment against Pope's 75,000. In the series of battles which followed (Groveton, Second Bull Run, Chantilly), Pope conducted Union forces so ineptly that by 1 September they had suffered 21 percent (c. 16,000) casualties as against the enemy's 19 percent (c. 9,200). Confederate leadership had again proven itself superior.

However, these Confederate victories had been won by forces on the strategic defensive. In order to secure genuine victory and independence from the Union, the Confederacy would have to demonstrate an ability to carry the war to the enemy. On 4 September 1862 Lee took the 55,000 men of the Army of Northern Virginia across the Potomac into Maryland. By 7 September he was concentrated about Frederick, in Western Maryland, from whence he could threaten both Washington, some 40 miles to the southeast, or Baltimore, some 50 miles to the east. Desperate, Lincoln re-appointed McClellan to the command of the *Army of the Potomac.* McClellan advanced cautiously westward with his 85,000 field troops. He missed an opportunity to cut Lee's army in two on 13 September, when he captured a copy of Lee's orders, but managed to keep his army well concentrated. A series of small battles resulted. Lee began to fall back. On the evening of 16 September he held an ambiguous position around Sharpsburg in Western Maryland. While the terrain tended to favor the defense, and Antietam Creek partially covered his front, he had his back to the Potomac. Moreover, some 13,000 of his available 40,000 men were several miles to the south of the Potomac, over which there was but one available crossing. Lee had placed himself in a trap. Confronted by an abler foe than McClellan, he would have paid dearly for his error. McClellan, however, was true to form. In the Battle of Antietam, fought on 17 September, he appears to have had no overall plan of attack, but merely threw in army corps after army corps, in ill-coordinated, poorly supervised and piecemeal attacks which did not take advantage of his superiority in numbers and which permitted Lee to shift his slender resources from one part of his front to another as the situation dictated. For all that, Union forces almost won a smashing victory, but Lee's situation was saved in a powerful counterattack delivered by his last arriving division. McClellan received some reinforcements during the night and, given Lee's precarious situation, could have renewed the fight on the next day with excellent chances of securing a crushing victory over his foe. Ever cautious, he failed to do so. The armies faced each other throughout 18 September. That night Lee slipped back across the Potomac to Virginia. The battle had been a remarkable defensive success for Lee. Nevertheless, he had been forced out of Maryland with nothing to show for his efforts save a considerable casualty list (c. 13,700). Union performance had been poor, with casualties high (c. 12,400), but a strategic success could be claimed, for the Army of Northern Virginia had been thrown back into the South. This success was sufficient to give Lincoln the opportunity to more clearly define Union war aims in the form of the Emancipation Proclamation.

After Antietam both armies withdrew to recuperate. The Army of Northern Virginia was heavily reinforced, underwent a major reorganization which saw the introduction of proper army corps, and was partially re-equipped. McClellan put the *Army of the Potomac* through much the same drill, while feuding by telegraph with his superiors in Washington, who wished him to advance at the earliest opportunity. There was some maneuvering on the part of both armies in late October, but nothing decisive resulted. Finally, thoroughly exasperated with McClellan's "slows," Lincoln replaced him with the reluctant Ambrose E. Burnside on 7 November. Burnside was apolitical, had a number of successes under his belt, and had not performed noticeably worse than anyone else. But he lacked confidence in himself and said so. Nevertheless, he almost immediately undertook an offensive, commencing a series of maneuvers which by 17 November saw his forces begin to concentrate on the north side of the Rappahannock River, across from Fredericksburg, on Lee's right flank. He planned to effect a crossing and then strike against Richmond in Lee's rear, but a shortage of pontoons delayed the crossing, giving Lee time to gather his own forces. Burnside got much of his 110,000-man army across on 11-12 December in the face of light resistance. The next day he ordered a series of frontal attacks against Lee's 75,000 well-entrenched troops. The result was a one-sided Confederate victory (some 12,000 U.S. casualties to about 5,000 C.S.). Burnside withdrew.

Thus ended 1862. For the Confederacy it had seemed a successful year. Despite some losses in the West, the Union armies had repeatedly been beaten back in the East. For the Union, the year seemed disastrous, for the victories in the West appeared small alongside the failures in the East. Yet the West was far more decisive a theater than most realized, and the performance of the Federal armies there had demonstrated that it was not the troops who were at fault but their leaders. The men on both sides had performed splendidly. The key to the outcome of the fighting in the East lay in the fact that the Confederate forces were better led than those of the Union. And so the armies went into winter quarters for the second time.

Incidents of War

A Valley Bivouac

Late in December of 1861 Thomas "Stonewall" Jackson undertook an expedition to destroy the Chesapeake and Ohio Canal. It was bitterly cold in the Shenandoah Valley that winter, and the troops crumbled mightily as they marched and camped in the ice and snow. One morning early in January, near the town of Bath, a group of Jackson's troops woke up to find themselves covered with snow, for it had snowed once again while they slept. As the men got up, shook out their snow-covered blankets, and started to get into the routine of the day, they cursed Jackson roundly for the miseries of their lives.

While this was going on, no one noticed one slug-a-bed curled up in his blanket under a nearby tree. Shortly, the man stirred, crawled out of his blanket and, shaking off the snow, stood up. The troops were shocked into silence, for it was Jackson himself and they braced themselves for a blast of general's ire. But the gallant Stonewall, who had ridden up in the night, made a smiling remark to a couple of the men, shook out his blanket and was soon away.

"Go to your right"

William F. Jenkins, a 17-year old private in the 12th Georgia, was severely wounded and left on the field during the Second Battle of Bull Run (29-30 August 1862). Soon after nightfall, two of his comrades came looking for him. By good fortune they located Jenkins, gave him what help they could, and then proceeded to carry him off to a field hospital. Making their way through the darkness they heard a challenge.

"Who goes there?"

"Two men of the 12th Georgia," they replied, "carrying a wounded comrade."

A Yankee sentry appeared, "Don't you know you're in the Union lines?"

"No," said the startled Rebels.

"Well you are," said the Yankee, adding "Go to your right." As the bluecoat faded back into the darkness, one of Jenkins' buddies called out, "Man, you've got a heart in you," and they continued on their way.

Butler Recruits a Black Brigade

Maj. Gen. Benjamin Butler, an amateur general of little ability in the field but much political influence, commanded the Union forces occupying New Orleans in 1862. Butler was one of the first senior officers to see the value of recruiting black troops for the Union. His account of how the first black regiments were mustered into his army is taken from *Butler's Book* (Boston, 1892).

...the rebel authorities in New Orleans had organized two regiments from the free Negroes, called "Native Guards, Colored." When [Maj. Gen. Mansfield] Lovell ran away with his troops these men stayed at home. The rebels had allowed the company officers to be commissioned from colored men—colonels, lieutenant colonels and majors, and the staff officers—they were white men.

I found out the names and residences of some twenty of these colored officers, and sent for them to call on me. They came, and a very intelligent-looking set of men they were. I asked them if they would like to be organized as part of the United States troops. They unanimously said they would. In all bodies of men there is always a spokesman, and while many of my guests were of a very light shade, that spokesman was a Negro nearly as dark as the ace of spades.

"General," he asked, "shall we be officers as we were before?"

"Yes; every one of you who is fit to be an officer shall be, and all the line officers shall be colored men."

"How soon do you want us to be ready?"

"How soon can you give me two regiments of a thousand men each?"

"In ten days."

"But," I said, "I want you to answer me one question. My officers, most of them, believe that Negroes won't fight."

"Oh, but we will," came from the whole of them.

"You seem to be an intelligent man," said I, to their spokesman; "answer me this question: I have found out that you know just as well what this war is about as I do, and if the United States succeed in it, it will put an end to slavery." They all looked in assent. "Then tell me why some Negroes have not in this war struck a good blow somewhere for their freedom? All over the South the men have been conscripted and driven away to the armies, leaving ten Negroes in some districts to one white man, and the colored men have simply gone on raising crops and taking care of their women and children."

The man's countenance lightened up. He said: "You are General here, and I don't like to answer that question."

"Answer it exactly according as the matter lies in your mind, and I pledge you on my honor, whatever the answer may be it shall harm no one of you."

"General, will you permit a question?"

"Yes."

"If we colored men had risen to make war on our masters, would not it have been our duty to ourselves, they being our enemies, to kill the enemy wherever we could find them? and all the white men would have been our enemies to be killed?"

"I don't know but what you are right," said I. "I think that would be a logical necessity of insurrection."

"If the colored men had begun such a war as that, General, which general of the United States army should we have called upon to help us fight our battles?"

That was unanswerable.

"Well," I said, "why do you think your men will fight?"

"General, we come of a fighting race. Our fathers were brought here slaves because they were captured in war, and in hand-to-hand fights, too. We are willing to fight. Pardon me, General, but the only cowardly blood we have got in our veins is white blood."

"Very well," I said, "recruit your men and let them be mustered into service at"—I mentioned a large public building—"in a fortnight from to-day, at ten o'clock in the morning. Report, and I will meet you there. I will give orders that the building be prepared."

On that morning I went there and saw such a sight as I never saw before: two thousand men ready to enlist as recruits, and not a man of them who had a white "biled shirt" on.

General Lew Wallace and the Great Sioux Uprising

In late 1862, the Santee band of the Sioux Indians of Minnesota, "unreasonably" resentful over the fact that white settlers had stolen 90 percent of their land, driven off most of the game, plundered their burial places and generally subjected them to abuse, went on the war path. Although the nation was just then engaged in the Civil War, the army reacted swiftly and overwhelming force was rapidly concentrated.

Among the troops ordered to proceed to Minnesota were the paroled prisoners-of-war being held at Camp Chase, near Columbus, Ohio, pending formal exchange. Since both the troops, and their commander, Maj. Gen. Lew Wallace, had enlisted to fight Rebels, not Indians, they were not inclined to depart for Minnesota. As a result, Wallace began a series of bureaucratic maneuvers designed to avoid this unpleasant duty.

To begin with, Wallace observed that conditions at Camp Chase were abominable, and that there were numerous sick and debilitated men in his charge. Permission was sought, and granted, to relocate the men to a more salubrious site in preparation for their eventual movement to Minnesota. This done, a matter which occupied several days, he then requested that the troops be paid before being transferred. Thus ensued several more days of paper-shuffling, culminating, when the local paymaster refused to issue the monies in question, in Wallace's arresting the fellow and seizing the funds at gunpoint. Now, of course, the troops had to be properly organized, outfitted and equipped, which caused several more days' delay.

Finally, of course, there were no more dodges available. The men would have to move. But Wallace had one more trick up his sleeve. He paraded the men and made a grandiloquent speech announcing that they were shortly to depart for Minnesota, where they would fight Indians, warning them not to try to desert, even though they had all that money in their pockets. That night he posted guards. Much to his surprise, the next morning he discovered that the guards had deserted. He again paraded the troops and once again warned them against desertion. That night he doubled the guard, only to find that they too deserted. He repeated this performance for two or three more nights, until virtually all the parolees were gone. Then he wired the War Department, explaining that most of his men had deserted, but recommended that no charges be made against them, as they would probably all shortly report to their original regiments.

Perhaps because Wallace proved to be correct, the War Department took no further action in the matter. In any case, neither Lew Wallace nor any of the parolees were involved in the disgraceful slaughter of the Santee which followed.

"The Angel of Marye's Heights"

On the night after the Battle of Fredericksburg (13 December 1862), thousands of Union troops lay dead and wounded on the cold ground before the Confederate lines on Marye's Heights. The piteous cries of the wounded could be heard throughout the night. Finally, as the new day dawned, Confederate Sgt. Richard R. Kirkland, a 19-year-old from South Carolina, could bear it no more. Kirkland asked permission to succor the wounded. His superiors demurred, but the young man pressed them and finally the brigade commander assented.

Carrying a number of canteens, Kirkland climbed over the low stone wall which ran along the crest of the heights and had formed the mainstay of the Confederate lines. No one fired on the young soldier as he went to a wounded Yankee and, kneeling, gave him a drink of water and a few words of comfort. For over an hour Kirkland went from man to man, giving them water and trying to make them more comfortable, as the amazed men of both armies looked on. He spread his overcoat to cover one man, and bundled up one that he found on the field to pillow the head of another man. In the end, as he walked back to his own lines, the watching Union troops cheered him for a gallant enemy.

Kirkland died at Chickamauga on 20 September 1863, but the memory of his brave and compassionate deed lives on.

Captain Newsham at Fort Donelson

During Grant's Henry and Donelson Campaign in early 1862, Capt. T. L. Newsham was Assistant Adjutant General on the staff of Brig. Gen. Charles F. Smith. During the heavy fighting at Fort Donelson on 15 February, Newsham's duties caused him to ride several times back and forth along the Union front. Since he was mounted on a splendid white horse, he very quickly attracted the attention of the enemy. Among those who spotted Newsham was Brig. Gen. Simon Bolivar Buckner, ablest of the three Confederate generals in the fort.

Buckner personally ordered several of the most experienced gunners in the garrison to let fly at the officer on the white horse, but Newsham never received so much as a scratch despite a considerable volume of ammunition being expended at him. Among the rounds aimed at Newsham were six shots from a six pounder, several more from a ten pounder, and at least one charge of grapeshot. Several of the rounds came close, including a couple which passed between his body and his horse's head, one which passed over the horse's back and the grapeshot, which passed between the horse's legs, leaving nought but a few scratches. The most unusual piece discharged at Newsham was a hand-crafted Turkish rifle of .75 caliber, of fine damascus steel, with inlaid bands of silver, gold and ivory, worth about $1,000. The owner of this piece, a Captain Naughton, claimed to have loosed eleven rounds at Newsham to no avail.

When Fort Donelson surrendered on the 16th, Newsham met Buckner outside his headquarters. Spotting the white horse, the general inquired as to whether Newsham was the same officer whom he had observed on the previous day. When Newsham replied in the affirmative, Buckner told him "Then you certainly bear a charmed life." As for Captain Naughton, he gave his rifle to Newsham.

Hardee and the Straggler

While Confederate Maj. Gen. William J. Hardee's corps was making a forced march in Mississippi during the Shiloh Campaign, the General came upon one of his men straggling far behind his regiment. Hardee ordered the man to press on so as to rejoin his comrades as quickly as possible. The soldier replied that he was trying, but that he was tired and hungry, not having had even half-rations for several days.

"That's hard," said Hardee, "but you must push forward, my good fellow, and join your command, or the provost guard will take you in hand."

Looking up at him, the soldier said, "Ain't you General Hardee?"

"Yes."

"Didn't you write Hardee's Tactics?"

"Yes."

"Well, General, I've studied them tactics and know 'em by heart," said the man. "You've got an order thar to double column at half distance, ain't you?"

Curious, the General said, "Well what has that order to do with your case?"

"I'm a good soldier, General, and obey all that is possible to be obeyed; but if you can show me an order in your tactics, or anybody else's tactics, to double distance on half rations, then I'll give in."

At that, Hardee let out a hearty laugh, allowed as how there were no tactics that applied in this case, and, spurring on his horse, rode off, leaving the soldier to make his way on his own terms.

Vidette Duty

During the Peninsular Campaign there was some skirmishing around Lee's

Mills, Virginia, in April of 1862. It is said that one particular morning, a Georgian and a Down-Mainer chanced to be on vidette opposite each other, each well ensconced behind a stout old tree. As the two ineffectively traded shots, they kept up a steady stream of conversation and became rather friendly. After a while the business grew tedious. Finally, the Georgian called out, "Give me a show," meaning that the other fellow should expose himself a bit and give him a chance for a hit. As was perfectly natural, the Bluecoat stuck his head out a little, and of, course, the Georgian let fly, but the ball went wide. "Too high," shouted out the Mainer, "Now give me a show."

The Georgian obligingly poked out his head and the Yankee squeezed one off. Again the ball went wide. "Too low," called out the Rebel, "My turn again." And so, in this fashion the two swapped a few more rounds. Then, by chance, the Yankee sent a ball into the tree, barely clearing the Rebel's ear.

"Cease fire," called out the Georgian.

"Cease it is," said his opponent.

"Look here," said one to the other, "we have carried on this business long enough for one day. S'pose we adjourn for rations?"

"Agreed," replied the other.

And so, after an exchange of good wishes, the two marched off in different directions, one allegedly whistling "Yankee Doodle" and the other "Dixie."

"What Did You Do?"

During one of his battles in the West, it is said that an officer rode furiously up to U.S. Grant as he stood with his staff. Touching his cap in salute, he addressed the general in a heavy German accent, "Dscheneral, I vants to make vun report; Schwartz's battery is tooken."

"How was that?" said Grant.

"Vell, you see, Dscheneral, die sczessionists come up in die front of us, und die sczessionists come up in die flank of us, und then die sczessionists come up in die rear of us, und Schwartz' battery vas took."

"Well, sir," inquired the General, "you of course spiked the guns?"

"Vat!," cried the officer, "schpike die guns, schpike die new guns! —no, it vould schpoil dem!"

With a sharp look, Grant asked, "What did you do?"

"Do? Vy, we took dem back again!"

The Kentuckians at Stones River

During the Battle of Stones River/Murfreesboro (31 December 1862 - 2 January 1863), as Maj. Gen. William S. Rosecrans' Union *Army of the Cumberland* battled Gen. Braxton Bragg's Confederate Army of Tennessee, there allegedly occurred an incident which could have only happened in a civil war.

The battle opened at dawn on 31 December, when Bragg's left, under Maj. Gen. William J. Hardee fell upon Rosecrans' right, under Maj. Gen. Alexander McCook. The Union troops put up a tough fight, but were forced back by Hardee's troops. After about two hours, the Union line began to stabilize. Bragg strengthened Hardee for one more try and at about 1:00 p.m. Hardee essayed another attack. As his troops advanced, his 3rd Kentucky found itself confronting the *23rd Kentucky*, a Union regiment recruited from men of the very same county. As if by mutual consent, these former friends and kin and neighbors ceased firing and are said to have begun to berate each other with fearsome curses and insults. This went on for some minutes in the midst of the great battle which raged about them.

Suddenly, someone on one side said something which caused someone on the other side to really get angry. Muskets were once more brought into play and the firing grew heated. Then the two regiments clashed in an intense hand-to-hand struggle with knives, clubbed rifles, fists, bayonets and pistols, as rough-and-tumble a fight as ever occurred anywhere. Gradually the Rebel Kentuckians began to gain the upper hand, but then, quite suddenly some of their erstwhile friends and neighbors managed to get athwart their flank and began pouring fire into their ranks. The 3rd Kentucky fell back, bringing with them not a few of their former friends and neighbors as prisoners. Just then the Union *9th Ohio* came into action, charging into the 3rd Kentucky in time to liberate most of the Union men while bagging many of the Rebel ones. Hardee's attack had been halted. Meanwhile, the Unionist Kentuckians discovered that a number of their Confederate counterparts had fortuitously brought whiskey in their canteens, rather than less potent stuff. The canteens in question began to pass from hand to hand. Soon, the two groups of Kentuckians, who had some minutes earlier been striving mightily to massacre each other, were renewing old friendships, inquiring about mutual associates, laughing, joking and talking together, getting into the spirit of the New Year as it were.

The Men

Robert E. Lee

Born on a plantation in Virginia, Robert Edward Lee (1807-1870) was the son of Revolutionary War cavalry hero Henry "Light Horse" Harry Lee— whose spendthrift ways resulted in the family living in genteel poverty for many years—and the nephew of two signers of the Declaration of Independence. Lee graduated from West Point 2nd in the class of 1829. An engineer, he served in garrison, on various civil and military engineering projects, and in Mexico with notable brilliance, being once wounded and receiving three brevets. Meanwhile he found time to marry Martha Washington's granddaughter by her first husband. Lee was superintendent of West Point from 1852 to 1855, at a time when his son and his nephew were cadets. He was then acting commander of the *2nd Cavalry* (renamed the *5th* in 1861) in Texas and Utah from 1857, on the "Mormon Expedition." In Washington on leave in 1859, Lee commanded the detachment of Marines which captured John Brown at Harper's Ferry.

General-in-Chief Lt. Gen. Winfield Scott apparently offered Lee command of the Federal armies on 18 April 1861. However, Lee would not serve against his state. He declined the offer and on 20 April resigned his commission, entering Virginia's service as commanding general of state forces. On 14 May he entered Confederate service as a brigadier general and was promoted full general one month later.

Lee's first wartime command was in West Virginia, where he displayed little talent as a field commander. He was shortly transferred to command Confederate forces on the Georgia and Carolina coasts, and was then called to serve as military advisor to Jefferson Davis in March of 1862. He helped plan Jackson's famed Valley Campaign and the Peninsular Campaign. Upon the wounding of Gen. Joseph E. Johnston, Lee was given command of Confederate forces defending Richmond on 1 June. From then on his career and reputation were inextricably bound up with the Army of Northern Virginia.

Almost from the moment he assumed command, Lee displayed remarkable skill as a tactician, beating back McClellan's *Army of the Potomac* from the gates of the city during the Seven Days Battles (26 June-2 July). He went on to lead the Army of Northern Virginia with considerable success during the balance of the Peninsular Campaign, and in the Second Bull Run, Antietam, Fredericksburg and Chancellorsville Campaigns, the last of which was his most brilliant tactical success. During the Gettysburg Campaign he did not perform up to his own standards, failing to properly coordinate the actions of his subordinates and possibly fighting an unnecessary battle. After Gettysburg he continued to lead the Army of Northern Virginia in the long, grinding defensive battles of the Campaigns of 1864 and 1865, during which his health deteriorated seriously. In February of 1865 he was made general-in-chief of all Confederate forces, much too late to influence the course of the war. His surrender at Appomattox on 9 April of that year is generally considered to mark the end of the war.

After the war Lee served as president of Washington College—now Washington and Lee University—until his death.

One of the finest soldiers in American history, Lee, who always managed to appear immaculately dressed, regardless of circumstances, looked every inch the great commander he was. Immensely loved by his troops, who called him "Marse Robert" and "Bobbie Lee," Lee was essentially a tactician and a good defensive strategist on a theater level. He failed to rise above local professional concerns and view the war as a whole, displaying little interest or understanding of the overall strategic situation, demonstrating a predilection for Virginia—and Virginians—to the exclusion of all other theaters. More seriously, he never realized that it was he who was the real soul of the Confederacy and not Jefferson Davis. Nevertheless, it is difficult to believe that the war would not have taken a different course had he been named general-in-chief sooner.

Nathaniel P. Banks

Born in Massachusetts, Nathaniel Prentiss Banks (1816-1894) rose from relatively humble origins to become one of the most influential men in the nation. He had little formal education, at an early age going to work in a cotton mill which his father managed. At 23 he was admitted to the bar. Banks built a successful law practice while attempting to engage in politics, making seven tries for a seat in the Massachusetts legislature before actually securing one. His political career took off from there. He was shortly elected speaker of the Massachusetts House of Representatives, presided over the state constitutional convention of 1853 and was elected to Congress. In 1856 Banks became Speaker of the House of Representatives on the 133rd ballot, and proved an effective voice for compromise in a period when sectionalism and slavery were becoming increasingly heated issues. Elected governor of Massachusetts in 1858, Banks resigned his seat early in 1861 to offer his services to Abraham Lincoln, who promptly named him a major general of volunteers. Banks proved himself an inept field commander. Sent to the Shenandoah Valley in late 1861, he was roughly handled by Stonewall Jackson. Given a corps in John Pope's *Army of Virginia*, he was again badly handled by Jackson at Cedar Mountain, in mid-1862.

After briefly commanding the defenses of Washington, he was transferred to command in Louisiana. Banks proved himself an able and—perhaps most importantly—an honest military governor and administrator, but once more bungled operations in the field, making costly and unnecessary assaults on Port Hudson in mid-1863 and embarking on the almost disastrous Red River Campaign in 1864. Relieved, Banks remained inactive until mustered out in August of 1865.

After the war Banks reentered politics, serving six terms in the House of Representatives—five as a Republican and one as a Democrat—at various times, while at other times serving again in the state legislature and as United States marshal for Massachusetts. Although his political services were considerable, Banks was one of the least successful amateur generals of the war.

Philip Kearny

The "most gallant officer in the United States Army," Philip Kearny (1815-1862) was born into one of the wealthiest and most prominent families in New York City. Shortly after graduation from Columbia in 1833, he was admitted to the bar and traveled widely. Inheriting a million dollars in 1836, he gave up the law to enter the army the following year, securing a direct commission in the *1st Dragoons* (now the *1st Cavalry*), commanded by his uncle, Col. Stephen W. Kearny. Kearny attended the French Army Cavalry School at Saumur in 1839 and got his first taste of combat with the *Chasseurs d'Afrique* in Algiers in 1840. Returning to the United States, he was shortly appointed an aide-de-camp to Maj. Gen. Alexander Macomb, the general-in-chief, and was retained in this position by the latter's successor, Winfield Scott. Kearny resigned early in April of 1846, but returned to active duty six weeks later, on the outbreak of the Mexican War. At his own expense Kearny recruited a troop of cavalry which Scott made his personal escort during the Mexico City Campaign. Kearny himself served with considerable distinction, losing his left arm at Churubusco, for which action he was breveted major.

After the war, he served for a time in California. Resigning his commission in 1851, Kearny traveled extensively, married, and settled in New Jersey. On the outbreak of the Italian War in 1859, Kearny joined Napoleon III's *Garde Imperial* and, according to tradition, took part in every cavalry charge at Magenta (4 June) and Solferino (24 June), holding the reins in his teeth, for which he became the first American to win the Cross of the Legion of Honor.

Still abroad when the Civil War broke out, Kearny immediately returned to the United States. Made a brigadier general of volunteers, he was given a brigade of New Jersey troops. Kearny served with great ability during the Peninsular Campaign, rising to command a division and securing promotion to major general. Commanding part of the rear guard during the Second Bull Run Campaign, he accidentally rode into the Confederate lines at Chantilly on the night of 1 September 1862. Challenged by some sentries, he attempted to escape but was killed instantly. A small, dashing looking man, Kearny was a superb officer with a genuine zest for combat, who was greatly mourned by both sides.

The "Kearny Patch"

Philip Kearny was responsible for the invention of one of the most enduring American military traditions, the unit patch. As the story has it while commanding the *3rd Division* of the *III Corps* during the Peninsular Campaign, Kearny came upon some officers loitering by the side of a road. He gave them a severe dressing down, and then, much to his embarrassment, discovered that they were not from his command. Shortly thereafter he ordered all the men in his division to sew a red diamond patch to their caps. Inspired by his idea, in the spring of 1863 Daniel Butterfield designed similar badges for the rest of the *Army of the Potomac,* and the practice soon spread to the rest of the Union Army.

The Italian Wars

Phil Kearny was not the only man in the Civil War who had served in the Italian Wars of Independence. Col. Philip St. George Cooke of the *2nd Dragoons* was in Italy in 1859-1860 as an official observer, later becoming a Union brigadier. The future Confederate Maj. Gen. James J. Pettigrew was a volunteer observer with the Sardinian Army at San Martino (24 June 1859). Two former French regular officers rose to brigadier generalships in the Union service, Alfred Napoleon Alexander Duffie, who served as a cavalry officer at Solferino, and Gustave P. Cluseret, who commanded the French volunteers fighting with Garibaldi and was wounded at the Volturno (1 October 1860), while Chatham R. Wheat, who later raised the famed "Louisiana Tigers" served with Garibaldi's English volunteer legion. Former Sardinian cavalryman Luigi di Cesnola, who served in the Italian War of 1848-1849, rose to command the *4th New York Cavalry* and briefly led a brigade in the *Army of the Potomac*, before becoming one of the founders of the Metropolitan Museum of Art. In the Spring of 1862 veteran Italian artilleryman Capt. Achille de Vecchi obtained a year's leave, during which he organized and commanded the *9th Massachusetts Battery*, which served with distinction in the *Army of the Potomac*.

An unusually distinguished veteran of the Italian Wars was Robert d'Orleans, the *duc de Chartres*, who had served as a 16-year old junior officer in the Piedmontese Nizza Light Cavalry Regiment in 1859, earning a decoration for gallantry from, of all people, Napoleon III. Together with his brother, the Comte de Paris, the Bourbon pretender to the throne of France and the Prince de Joinville, young Chartres served as an aide-de-camp to McClellan in 1862.

Perhaps the most interesting veteran of the Italian Wars to turn up in the Civil War was Frank Vizetelly, an artist/correspondent for *The Illustrated London News*, who had covered the 1859 war and the expediton of Garibaldi and "The Thousand" in 1860. On the outbreak of the Civil War he came to the United States, covering events from behind the Union lines in 1861-1862, and then slipping over to the other side for 1862-1865.

There was very nearly an even more impressive veteran of the Italian Wars in Union service, for Lincoln made a tentative offer of a commission to Giuseppe Garibaldi, which the latter tentatively accepted. But Garibaldi would serve only on condition of immediate emancipation, a move which Lincoln found politically inopportune early in the war. And in any case, Garibaldi had other fish to fry.

James Ewell Brown Stuart

"Jeb" Stuart (1833-1864) was born in Virginia and graduated from West Point 13th in the class of 1854. Most of his career was spent on the frontier, where he was wounded. From 1855 he was with the *1st Cavalry* (renamed the *4th* in 1861). He was in Kansas during the pre-statehood dispute over slavery and was with Robert E. Lee when John Brown was captured at Harper's Ferry in 1859.

Stuart resigned as a captain on 3 May 1861 and was made a lieutenant colonel by Virginia. He entered Confederate service soon after and was named colonel of the 1st Virginia Cavalry, with which he served in the Shenandoah Valley and during the Bull Run Campaign with great distinction. He was promoted brigadier general in September and further distinguished himself commanding a brigade of cavalry in various skirmishes through the winter of 1861-1862.

During the Peninsular Campaign Stuart demonstrated remarkable abilities in reconnaissance, raiding and screening, and once rode entirely around the *Army of the Potomac.* In July of 1862 he was given command of the Cavalry Division of the Army of Northern Virginia and made a major general. He led his command, later elevated to the status of a corps, thereafter until his death, serving with great skill in the Second Bull Run, Antietam and Fredericksburg. During the Chancellorsville Campaign, in May of 1863, he demonstrated some ability for higher command, when he temporarily led II Corps after Stonewall Jackson and Richard Ewell had both been wounded.

During the Gettysburg Campaign Stuart proved relatively ineffective. Taking advantage of some ambiguity in his orders he embarked on an unnecessary and unprofitable raid. This foray, undertaken primarily to restore his reputation after the unusual success of the Union cavalry at Brandy Station in June, effectively deprived Lee of the "eyes" of his army and had much to do with the disastrous failure which resulted. Nevertheless, Stuart performed well during the retreat, and in numerous skirmishes and engagements along the Rappahannock line in the winter of 1863-1864.

He led his corps ably during the Battles of the Wilderness and Spotsylvania in the Campaign of 1864, and was mortally wounded by Union cavalrymen at Yellow Tavern on 11 May, attempting to block Maj. Gen. Philip Sheridan's raid on Richmond. He died the next day, greatly mourned.

Heros von Borcke, Stuart's Prussian aide and himself one of the unique characters of the war, wrote that Stuart was "a stoutly built man, rather above average height, of a most frank and winning expression." One of the finest cavalrymen in American history, Stuart had a remarkable ability to gather information, screen operations and conduct raids, but he was overly sensitive about his reputation, and perhaps a bit too aggressive, with the result that he had to be issued careful instructions lest he go off on his own, which is precisely what happened in the Gettysburg Campaign. Stuart, who wore a beard to hide a receding chin, was the son-in-law of Brig. Gen.

Philip St. George Cooke, a fellow-Virginian who remained loyal to the Republic, despite the fact that his sons and son-in-law "went South."

Albert Sidney Johnston

Kentucky-born Albert Sydney Johnston (1803-1862), one of nine children, was educated at Transylvania College before entering West Point, from which he graduated in 1826. After a period of garrison duty, he served in the Black Hawk War, before resigning in 1834 to care for his ailing wife. When she died, in 1835, he briefly attempted to take up farming. In 1836 he enlisted as a private in the Army of the Republic of Texas, rising to brigadier general and army commander within a year, despite being seriously wounded in a duel with a jealous subordinate, an injury which left him slightly lame and subject to occasional numbness and pain in his right foot. The following year he was named Secretary of War of Texas. Resigning in 1840, Johnston settled down in Brazoria County. Johnston served briefly as colonel of the *1st Texas Volunteer Foot Rifles* and then as a staff officer during the Mexican War, and was shortly afterwards commissioned colonel in the United States cavalry. Serving in various posts, he was given the newly formed *2nd Cavalry* in 1855. In 1857 Johnston was made a brevet brigadier general and commanded the so-called "Mormon Expedition" and the garrison of Utah.

The outbreak of the Civil War found him commanding United States forces on the Pacific coast. He soon resigned his commission and was named a full general in the Confederate Regular Army on 31 August 1861, to rank from 30 May. He was shortly afterwards assigned to command all Confederate forces west of the Allegheny Mountains.

While Johnston strove to organize and equip his forces, they were involved in a number of small actions through the balance of 1861 most of which were inconclusive or reverses. Nevertheless, the situation in his department at the beginning of 1862 was satisfactory.

The loss of Forts Henry and Donelson in February radically altered this state of affairs. Concentrating forces from all over the West, Johnston prepared a counterstroke which he delivered at Shiloh on 6 April 1862. Johnston's attack completely surprised Ulysses S. Grant's forces, which nevertheless put up a stubborn fight. At about 2:30 p.m., while directing operations on his left flank, Johnston rode too far forward and was hit in the leg by a musket ball which severed the femoral artery. None of his staff officers having the presence of mind to apply a tourniquet, Johnston bled to death within minutes. The next day Grant, somewhat reinforced, went on to win the battle.

Johnston's death "at the moment of victory" rapidly became part of the legend of the "Lost Cause," the claim being advanced that had he lived, the battle would have been won. In fact, there is little in Johnston's career to justify the oft-stated conclusion that he was a brilliant commander. Indeed, the plans for the Confederate attack at Shiloh were extraordinarily poor: Johnston's corps attacked in successive waves, rather than each on an individual front, so that, had Grant's men been ready, the attackers would have suffered a devastating defeat. As it was, the Confederate forces became so intermingled, that command control was largely lost. At best Johnston was a capable organizer and administrator who never was tested in action.

Daniel Butterfield

Originally from New York, Daniel Butterfield (1831-1901) studied law and traveled extensively in his youth. At the outbreak of the war he was superintendent of the eastern operations for American Express, of which his father was a founder. He enlisted as first sergeant in, and was sub-sequently elected colonel, of the *12th New York Militia*, in which Dan Sickles and Francis Barlow also served. This was the first Federal outfit to set foot in Virginia.

He was in the Shenandoah Valley during the Bull Run Campaign and was subsequently promoted brigadier general of volunteers. Butterfield led a brigade in the Peninsular Campaign—subsequently being awarded a Medal of Honor for his services at Gaines' Mill, where he was wounded—and in the Second Bull Run Campaign. He later led a division, and subsequently *V Corps* at Fredericksburg, having risen to major general of volunteers.

Appointed chief-of-staff of the *Army of the Potomac* when Hooker assumed command, he continued in this post under Meade and was badly wounded at Gettysburg. After the battle he engaged in an undignified dispute with Meade as to whether the latter intended to abandon the fight on the night of 1 July, and was removed as chief-of-staff.

Butterfield subsequently served in the West, first as Hooker's chief-of-staff and later commanding a division in the *XX Corps* during the Atlanta Campaign until relieved due to ill-health.

At the end of the war he remained in the regular army as colonel of the *5th Infantry*, but resigned in 1869. He subsequently became a highly successful businessman, confidant of President Grant and world traveler.

His skills as an organizer were called upon many times, and he directed Sherman's funeral, the Washington Centennial celebrations and Dewey's triumphant return after the Spanish-American War. A good chief-of-staff, Butterfield performed his duties well, but he allowed his friendship with Hooker to color his relationship with Meade and his conduct after Gettysburg was frankly disloyal to his commanding officer.

Butterfield is responsible for two of the most enduring of American military customs. Based on an idea of Philip Kearny, he designed the badges which each corps in the *Army of the Potomac* wore for identification purposes, a system which was eventually extended to all Union armies, and he wrote "Taps".

David Glasgow Farragut

The nation's first admiral, David Glasgow Farragut (1801-1870), was born in Tennessee. The son of naval hero George Farragut (1755-1817), David G. Farragut was adopted by Commodore David Porter, father of the nation's second admiral, David Dixon Porter. Commissioned a midshipman at the age of nine, Farragut served with Porter during the War of 1812, and at the age of twelve was made master of the prize *Frolic*, thus becoming the youngest person ever to command a ship in the United States Navy, and was briefly a prisoner-of-war. After the war he rose steadily through the ranks, while serving in the Mediterranean, the West Indies, the South Atlantic and in the Mexican War. During his long career he established the Mare Island Navy Yard in California and acquired fluency in several languages.

A captain on the outbreak of the Civil War, Farragut was a resident of Norfolk, Virginia, and immediately removed to the North. Although he encountered some difficulties because of his southern background, in December of 1861 Secretary of the Navy Gideon Welles gave him command of the West Gulf Squadron with orders to maintain the blockade and capture New Orleans. Displaying considerable skill as an organizer, Farragut put together a powerful expeditionary force, and proceeded to take New Orleans by running his fleet up the Mississippi past the Forts Jackson and St. Philip, which had been subject to the attentions of a mortar flotilla under his adoptive brother Cdr. David Dixon Porter, on 24 April 1862, earning for himself the thanks of Congress and a promotion to rear admiral.

During the Summer of 1862, Farragut operated his oceanic fleet on the Mississippi, twice running the defenses of Vicksburg, but failing in his efforts to take the place by riverine power alone. Returning with his squadron to the Gulf, Farragut tightened the blockade, assisted in the army's operations on the lower Mississippi, most notably against Port Hudson, and tried to interest Washington in the capture of Mobile.

Finally given permission to take Mobile, Farragut boldly steamed into Mobile Bay 5 August 1864, uttering the famous line "Damn the torpedoes! Full steam ahead!" after the monitor *Tecumseh* sank after hitting a mine. Although the city itself did not fall, Farragut's operation effectively closed the port, for which Congress promoted him to vice admiral.

Soon after Mobile, ill-health put Farragut on the beach until early 1865, when he assumed command in the James River, in time to be present at the surrender of Richmond. After the war he was promoted to full admiral and died on active duty.

Farragut was an excellent administrator, fine seaman, and a bold tactician who cared little for his own safety, preferring to view the action from a perch in the rigging—where he was once joined by his cabin boy—than from the relative safety of the deck of his flagship, the sloop-of-war *Hartford.*

Henry Halleck

A native of New York, Henry Halleck (1815-1872) ran away from home rather than take up farming and was eventually adopted by his maternal grandfather, who saw to it that the brilliant and ambitious young fellow received an excellent education (Phi Beta Kappa, Union College). At West Point Halleck was assigned as an assistant professor even before graduating 3rd in the class of 1839. He entered the Engineers and helped design the harbor defenses of New York before touring French coast defenses in 1844. He wrote several important works, including *Report on the Means of National Defense* and *Elements of Military Art and Science* and translated Henry Jomini's *Political and Military Life of Napoleon from the French.* Halleck saw administrative service in California during the Mexican War, emerging with a brevet, and later served as inspector and engineer of lighthouses and on the fortification board for the Pacific Coast. He somehow also found time to help frame the Constitution of the State of California and study law. In 1854 he resigned from the army and founded a major law firm in California. Refusing a judgeship and a U.S. Senate seat, Halleck devoted himself to his profession, to writing, to business and to the state militia, becoming an authority on mining and international law and quite wealthy in the process.

At the outbreak of the war he was appointed a major general in the regular army at the suggestion of Winfield Scott.

Great things were expected of Halleck, but he proved an inept field commander. This fact took some time to become apparent as when he commanded in the West in 1862 his subordinates included Ulysses S. Grant and William S. Rosecrans. Appointed general-in-chief of the army in July of 1862, Halleck's great administrative abilities proved immensely valuable. Despite the fact that he acted more as a clerk-in-chief, he did much to promote a more efficient organization of the army and managed to keep the troops supplied and reinforcements forthcoming, but could have done far more to coordinate the activities of the Union armies. In early 1864 he was replaced by Grant and demoted to the status of chief-of-staff, a task which he performed to perfection. After the war he held various administrative posts until his death.

Had there never been a war, Halleck—whose pre-war army nickname "Old Brains," conferred in recognition of his great intellectual achievements, was eventually replaced by "Old Wooden Head"—might have remained a soldier of great promise, rather than a great disappointment.

Robert Smalls

Robert Smalls (1839-1915) was born into slavery in Beaufort, South Carolina, and, unusual for a slave, received a rudimentary education, and learned to read. In 1851 his master removed to Charleston, where young Smalls was permitted to work as a boatman for day wages. On the outbreak of the Civil War, Smalls, who by then was married and had two children, was impressed into the Confederate Navy. He was made steersman of the armed transport *Planter*, which carried goods and supplies to the various forts and installations in the vicinity of Charleston harbor. As about a dozen of the vessel's crew were fellow-slaves, Smalls soon began to plot an escape.

In the early hours of 13 May 1862 *Planter* was lying at her normal berth, near army headquarters on the Charleston waterfront. Although steam was up, the captain and the other white crew members were all ashore. Smuggling his wife and children aboard, Smalls took command of the ship. Quickly casting off, he steered her boldly for the harbor entrance. Since the little ship was a familiar sight, none of the troops on guard thought anything amiss as she steamed past in a rather leisurely fashion, Confederate flag proudly streaming behind and whistle tooting in her usual salute. As soon as the ship was out of range, Smalls ordered full speed and headed for the blockading Union warships. As one of the blockaders approached, Smalls hauled down the Confederate colors and hoisted a white flag.

Smalls' exploit made him a hero throughout the North, and a prosperous man as well, for as "captain" he received a sizable share of the prize money which was awarded him and his men. Lincoln promptly appointed him a pilot in the Navy. In this capacity he served on a number of vessels, being cited for courage under fire while serving on the ironclad *Keokuk* during the naval assault on Charleston in 14 April 1863. That December, Smalls was given a ship of his own, thus becoming the first black man to command a ship in the United States Navy.

After the war Smalls returned to his native Beaufort. He served as a Republican in both houses of the South Carolina legislature from 1868 through 1875, when he was elected to Congress. With the exception of the 1879-1881 term, Smalls served in the House of Representatives until 1887, making a reputation as an advocate of civil rights legislation. Thereafter he was United States Collector of the Port of Beaufort during Republican administrations from 1889 to 1913, and as delegate to the state constitutional convention of 1895, he fought a losing battle to preserve the remnants of civil rights for blacks in South Carolina.

Earl Van Dorn

Mississippian Earl Van Dorn (1820-1863) graduated from West Point in 1842. His initial service was on the Texas frontier, where he fought in a number of engagements with the Comanches, incurring four serious wounds in one skirmish. During the Mexican War he was wounded once again, earning two brevets in the process. Remaining in the army after the war, he served on the frontier, in garrison, and against the Seminoles. Transferring to the cavalry, by the eve of the Civil War he was a major in the *2nd Cavalry*, serving under Albert Sidney Johnston and Robert E. Lee.

Resigning upon the secession of Mississippi in January of 1861, he was made a brigadier general of the state militia, and shortly promoted to major general of the militia when Jefferson Davis resigned to become president of the Confederacy. Entering Confederate service as a colonel in March of 1861, Van Dorn served briefly as commander of the Mississippi River forts below New Orleans before being assigned to command the Department of Texas, where he performed the unusual feat of capturing the famed Union steamer *Star of the West*, object of the first shot of the war during her relief attempt at Sumter in January of 1861. Promoted brigadier general in July and major general in September, Van Dorn was shortly transferred from Texas to Virginia and given a division to command and, incidently, being entrusted with one of the first three Confederate battle flags. The following January he was assigned to command the Trans-Mississippi Department, which he did with little success, culminating in the Confederate reverse at Pea Ridge (7-8 March). Once again transferred, Van Dorn was given overall direction of the Army of Mississippi, entrusted with the defense of his home state and particularly Vicksburg, and also of the Army of Western Tennessee, which was supposed to defend the western portions of that state. Defeated at Corinth (3-4 October 1862), Van Dorn was superseded and assigned to command the cavalry of the Army of Mississippi, under John Pemberton. It was at this point that Van Dorn, hitherto not particularly successful, began to show some promise as a commander.

Van Dorn's cavalry proved extremely adept at interfering with the supply lines of Union Maj. Gen. Ulysses S. Grant, greatly impeding his efforts to capture Vicksburg, most notably by his capture of the Federal supply depot at Holly Springs in December of 1862 and the action at Thompson's Station the following March. As a result, Van Dorn was rapidly emerging as one of the war's better cavalrymen when, on 7 May 1863, an irate husband walked into his headquarters and gunned him down.

A small, handsome, elegant man, Van Dorn, like many Civil War commanders, proved a failure largely because he was promoted beyond his abilities. Starting out as an army commander, a post for which he lacked the administrative skill and strength of character, Van Dorn did not find his niche until the war was nearly two years old. Death overtook him just as he was beginning to develop as a cavalry commander.

Ambrose E. Burnside

Although born in Indiana, Ambrose E. Burnside (1824-1881) came from Southern stock, his father having been a slaveholder in South Carolina before moving northwards and freeing his bondsmen. After completing primary school, Burnside ran a tailor shop for a time until he secured an appointment to West Point through his father's political connections. Graduating in 1847, he served on occupation duty during the Mexican War and was subsequently on the frontier, where he was wounded in a skirmish with the Apaches. Resigning from the army in 1853, he went into the firearms business in Rhode Island, attempting to manufacture a breech-loading rifle of his own design. Although the venture was only moderately successful, Burnside became active in state politics, serving in

Congress and receiving an appointment as a major general of militia. A close friend of George B. McClellan, the latter secured for him an appointment as treasurer of the Illinois Central.

On the outbreak of the Civil War, Burnside organized the *1st Rhode Island,* which was among the first regiments to reach Washington. He commanded a brigade with some ability at Bull Run and was shortly made a brigadier general. Having attracted the eye of President Lincoln, in October of 1861 Burnside was entrusted with command of an expedition to the Carolina coasts. He carried out this operation with considerable success, earning a promotion to major general. From February through June of 1862 Burnside inflicted several defeats on the opposing forces, capturing New Bern and a number of other minor ports, establishing a firm grip on the coast of North Carolina. Recalled in early July, he joined the *Army of the Potomac* as a corps commander—it is generally believed he was offered, and refused, command of the army at this time. Although he did moderately well commanding his *IX Corps,* Burnside did poorly when entrusted with the Union left wing at Antietam, although the Union failure to destroy Lee at this battle was more directly McClellan's failure to exercise close control of the battle than Burnside's poor handling of his part of it. Again offered command of the *Army of the Potomac,* Burnside attempted to refuse, but was pressured into accepting by most of the other corps commanders, who did not want Joseph Hooker to get the job.

Burnside's modest opinion of his abilities was well founded and his tenure in command of the army was disastrous, culminating in an unnecessary and bloody reverse at Fredericksburg in December of 1862. Although allowed to remain in command, his fate was sealed by the humiliating "Mud March" the following January, when he persevered in an attempt to flank the Army of Northern Virginia despite extraordinarily heavy rains which made it virtually impossible for the army to move. Burnside now demanded that Lincoln relieve seven generals or find a new army commander. The President removed Burnside, replacing him with Hooker.

Shortly afterwards Burnside was given a departmental command in the Ohio Valley. He did well in this post, taking strong measures against Copperhead activity—including the shadowy "Knights of the Golden Circle" and even capturing the elusive Confederate raider John Hunt Morgan. That autumn, Burnside took to the field with considerable success in order to defend Knoxville from Confederate Lt. Gen. James Longstreet. In consequence, he was restored to command of the *IX Corps.*

During the opening stages of Grant's Overland Campaign in the Spring of 1864, Burnside's corps operated in conjunction with, but not under the command of, Maj. Gen. George Meade's *Army of the Potomac*. Burnside performed his duties well, even after the corps was brought under Meade's direct command. It was Burnside who planned the operation which subsequently became known as the "Battle of the Crater" (30 July 1864). The disastrous outcome of the operation was primarily due to interference on the part of Grant and Meade—24 hours before the action was to begin they replaced a specially-trained black division with an untrained white one—but Burnside was relieved of command. Kept idle for the rest of the war, he resigned from the service on 15 April 1865.

After the war Burnside grew prosperous in railroading, served three terms as governor of Rhode Island and represented his state in the Senate from 1874 to his death.

A big, genial, impressive looking man with enormous "Burnsides"—hence "side burns"—Burnside was by no means an incapable commander. A good administrator and satisfactory organizer, he was fairly successful as a corps commander, at his best with modest forces. Perhaps no one understood his abilities and limitations better than he did.

Carl Schurz

A native of Rhenish Prussia, Carl Schurz (1829-1906) was educated at the universities in Cologne and Bonn. In 1848 he abandoned his doctoral studies and served the German Revolution as a junior officer. Upon the defeat of the revolution he fled, first to Switzerland and then to France. Expelled from France, he lived briefly in England and then migrated to the United States in 1852. He began a career as an orator and politician with a strong anti-slavery message, settling in Wisconsin.

At the start of the war he was minister to Spain, but resigned in 1862 to urge immediate emancipation of the slaves. Lincoln demurred, but made Schurz a brigadier general of volunteers, a political move designed to enhance German-American support for the war. Schurz led a division with some ability in the Second Bull Run Campaign. Made a major general in March of 1863, his division performed poorly as part of *XI Corps* at Chancellorsville that spring. At Gettysburg he briefly commanded the corps, but neither it, nor his division performed with brilliance, though he did manage to hold the line on Cemetery Hill on 2 July. Later that year Schurz went West with his division, where it again did poorly at Chattanooga. Relieved, he spent the next year in administrative posts and stumping the country for Lincoln's reelection. Later he served ably as chief-of-staff to Maj. Gen. Henry W. Slocum's *Army of Georgia*. After the war Schurz became one of the most prominent political leaders in the country, championing a variety of progressive causes, and one of the few steadfast spokesmen for black civil rights in print, on the podium and in the Senate. His political influence was enormous, particularly wherever there were large numbers of German-Americans, and there are probably more monuments to his memory in more different places than any other Civil War figure of comparable rank.

The Women

Clara Barton

For many people the war was a liberating and maturing experience. Under the pressures of the conflict, many men and women who were of little note rose far above the ordinary. One such was Clara Barton (1821-1912), a native of Massachusetts. Nothing in the first forty years of her life suggests anything but the ordinary. Trained as a teacher, Clarissa Harlowe Barton was working as a clerk in the Patent Office when the war broke out. Appalled at the lack of facilities for the troops, she began, voluntarily and unofficially, to minister to the casualties in the field. Often arriving while the fighting was still going on, Barton was frequently under fire—a wounded man was once killed in her arms—and her skirts were several times pierced by bullets. She developed and supervised a network of volunteer nurses and welfare workers. By the end of the war she was Superintendent of Nurses to the *Army of the James* and charged with compiling a master list of missing troops, which helped identify numerous unknown dead. After the war Barton went on to found the American Red Cross, served once more in the field during the war with Spain, wrote and lectured.

Lincoln

"In the Matter of Nathaniel Gordon"

Although the importation of slaves into the United States was banned in 1808, the trade was too lucrative to be halted entirely. As a result, an unknown number of Africans were brought into the United States as slaves right down to the end of the Civil War. To be sure, efforts were made to suppress this illicit trade, and under an act of 1820 engaging in the slave trade was classed as piracy, punishable by death. But, as with the drug trade in contemporary society, parochial interests and corruption made such laws difficult to enforce. Although by treaty, Britain's Royal Navy was charged with enforcing the international ban on the slave trade, British seamen were loath to intercept vessels wearing the American flag due to the often testy relations between the two nations. Thus, all that a slaver had to do was run up the "Stars and Stripes" to be secure against search and seizure. The United States Navy did, of course, have its own anti-slavery patrol, but this was more of a token force than a determined effort. Hampering American efforts to stop the slave trade was the fact that a significant proportion of the nation was devoted to the "peculiar institution." As a result, even when slavers were caught "red handed" they were rarely brought to trial, and never convicted. That is, until 1861, with the Civil War well underway.

The first—and only—person convicted under the 1820 act was Nathaniel Gordon, caught by the naval blockade while trying to run a cargo of slaves into the Confederacy in late 1861. Gordon was given the maximum sentence. Appeals followed, but at each level the sentence was confirmed, even by pro-slavery Chief Justice Roger B. Taney. As a last resort, Gordon's lawyers penned an appeal to Lincoln for executive clemency. The President responded:

> ...if this man had been guilty of the worst murder that can be conceived of, I might perhaps, have pardoned him. You know the weakness of my nature, always open to appeals of repentance or of grief; and with such a touching letter, and such recommendations, I could not resist. But

any man who would go to Africa and snatch from a mother her children, to sell them into interminable bondage, merely for the sake of pecuniary gain, shall never receive pardon from me.

On 21 February 1862 Nathaniel Gordon became the first, and only, person in American history to be hanged as a slave trader. The importation of slaves into the United States did not cease until the Civil War was over.

Incident at the Navy Yard Hospital

The suffering caused by the war grieved Lincoln greatly. He often visited the more than forty military hospitals in the vicinity of Washington to speak with the wounded and offer what comfort he could. One such occasion was on 27 September 1862, little more than a week after Antietam.

It was a Saturday, and the president set out early, intending to visit as many hospitals as possible. Beginning with that at Georgetown University, he visited hospital after hospital until, towards evening, he arrived at the Navy Yard. As the president passed among the wounded men, he chanced to come upon a badly wounded Confederate, "little more than a child." Lincoln knelt by the boy's bedside, exchanged a few words with him and said a silent prayer. Then Lincoln passed on to sit with other men. After a time the tired president took his leave, and left the hospital.

As Lincoln was entering his carriage one of the nurses came out and said that the dying Confederate boy had asked to see him again. Though tired and drained, the president left his carriage and returned to the boy's side.

"What can I do for you?" asked Lincoln.

In a barely audible voice the boy replied, "I am so lonely and friendless, Mr. Lincoln, and I am hoping that you can tell me what my mother would want me to say and do now."

Kneeling once more at the soldier's bedside, Lincoln said, "Yes, my boy, I know exactly what your mother would want you to say and do. And I am glad that you sent for me to come back to you. Now, as I kneel here, please repeat the words after me." Then, slowly, the dying soldier repeated the words which his only friend uttered in a soft, weary voice:

Now I lay me down to sleep,
I pray the Lord my soul to keep.
If I should die before I wake,
I pray the Lord my soul to take.
And this I ask for Jesus' sake.

The Units

The 1st Minnesota

Generally regarded as the first regiment to be accepted for Federal service, the *1st Minnesota* was offered by Alexander Ramsay on 14 April 1861, even before Lincoln's first call for volunteers had gone out, and was promptly accepted by Secretary of War Simon Cameron. Two weeks later, on 29 April, the *1st Minnesota* mustered in for three years service under Col. Willis A. Gorman. After a brief period of training, the regiment "took the cars" to Washington, reaching the capital on 26 June, thereby making what would be the longest journey of any regiment to join the Eastern armies. This regiment, which for a long time wore a distinctive black uniform with red shirt and black hat, was the only Minnesota outfit in the East during the war and fought in every battle of what would become the Army of the Potomac, from First Bull Run to Appomattox.

At First Bull Run, the *1st Minnesota* was a brigade in Col. Samuel P. Heintzelman's *3rd Division*, which formed the Federal right, and sustained the heaviest casualties of any Union regiment in the battle, 180 men. During the battle the regiment refused to leave the field until being ordered to do so three times. The following October, the regiment formed the rear guard after the badly managed skirmish at Ball's Bluff. Early in 1862 the 1st *Minnesota* was briefly in the Shenandoah Valley, but was shortly transferred back to the *Army of the Potomac*, where it was brigaded with *II Corps*, with which it served to the end of the war.

The *1st Minnesota* served all through the Peninsular Campaign, fighting at Yorktown, Seven Pines, Savage's Station, White Oak Swamp and Malvern Hill with great courage and determination. Heavily engaged at Second Bull Run the regiment again demonstrated its tenacity at Antietam, when, during an attack on the Confederate center, its supports having given way, it nevertheless refused to fall back until nearly overwhelmed in a storm of Rebel fire. Though lightly engaged at Fredericksburg and Chancellorsville, the *1st Minnesota* numbered a little less than 400 men at the start of the Gettysburg Campaign. Despite this, Gettysburg was the regiment's finest hour.

On 2 July the *1st Minnesota*, with but eight companies (262 men) present, undertook a desperate counter-attack against an advancing Confederate brigade, some 1,500 men. The audacious blow, delivered at close quarters with great elan halted the enemy, helping to stabilize the Union lines. The desperate and heroic attack against extraordinary odds—of which *II Corps* commander Maj. Gen. Winfield Scott Hancock said "There is no more gallant deed recorded in history."—cost the regiment 215 of the 262 men engaged (82.1 percent), including Col. William Colville, Jr., who had been released from arrest to lead the regiment in that critical moment, the highest loss for a single action in the battle and in the war. Although reduced to a veritable corporal's guard, the regiment remained in action, the hundred or so unengaged men helping to hold the line of Cemetery Ridge the next day.

The *1st Minnesota* continued to serve with the *Army of the Potomac* until the following April. At that time the surviving three-years men were discharged. But the regiment was not discharged, as it had a number of unexpired men in the ranks. From these, and from men who reenlisted and new recruits, two full companies were organized and the *1st Minnesota* fought through to the end of the war, from the Wilderness to Appomattox, mustering out in July of 1865.

Though it never again equaled the gallantry which it had earlier displayed—a matter due as much to the changing nature of the war as to any lack of intestinal fortitude—the regiment served to the end of the war. The *1st Minnesota* ranks 23rd on the list of Union regiments having the highest proportion of men killed in action during the war, suffering 187 combat deaths of the 1,242 men who were carried on the rolls, a telling commentary on its combativeness.

The 1st Minnesota Alumni

Four of the officers of the *1st Minnesota* became generals. Col. Willis A. Gorman was given a brigade command in July of 1861, and a brigadier's commission that September, rising to acting division commander by late 1862, after which he performed occupation duties in Arkansas until mustering out in the Spring of 1864.

Col. Napoleon Jackson Tecumseh Dana—blessed with such a militant appellation, he had no choice but to be a soldier—led the regiment from October of 1861 to the Spring of 1862, when he was made a brigadier general, after which he commanded various brigades until wounded at

Antietam. Shortly promoted a major general, Dana held a variety of administrative and command positions but saw no further combat.

Col. Alfred Sully took over the *1st Minnesota* from Dana in March of 1862, temporarily left it to command a brigade in the Peninsular Campaign, but was back with it at Antietam, after which he was made a brigadier general. Sully served as a brigade commander until after Chancellorsville, when the old Indian fighter was made a major general and sent to command in the Dakotas, and served out his career in the Regular Army on the frontier.

Lt. Col. Stephen Miller, who had been in temporary command at Ball's Bluff, was also promoted to brigadier general after serving as colonel of the *7th Minnesota* in the Sioux uprising, and in 1864 was elected Governor of Minnesota. Two other officers, Col. William Colville, Jr., and Col. Charles P. Adams were made brigadier generals by brevet at the end of the war.

Perhaps the most colorful veteran of the *1st Minnesota* was German-born Al Sieber, who enlisted as a private in March of 1862 and served through the war, taking a severe wound in Colville's gallant charge at Gettysburg. After the war Sieber became a noted Indian agent and fighter, and scout, being wounded 29 times while serving under Philip St. George Crook, Oliver O. Howard and Nelson A. Miles, not giving up the ghost until 1907, when he was crushed to death in a construction accident.

The Confederate Regular Army

On 6 March 1861 the Confederate Congress enacted legislation providing for the creation of a regular army for the Confederacy and authorizing Jefferson Davis to raise as many as 3,000 men in order to support the South Carolina state troops investing Ft. Sumter at Charleston. Recruitment for this force was never seriously undertaken and it never amounted to much, as most Southerners preferred their state volunteer regiments in the "Provisional Army of the Confederate States," the equivalent of the Union's "Volunteer Army."

Despite this, Davis persisted in maintaining the fiction that there existed a regular establishment, in order to lay the foundation for the postwar period. Davis believed that after the war the Confederacy would require a regular force of about 10,000 men, including a half-dozen infantry regiments, a cavalry regiment, an artillery corps, an engineer corps, and various staff departments. At the start of the war six general officers were commissioned in the regular service, as were many members of the various staff corps, usually before passing into the Provisional Army. In addition, several regiments were actually activated.

Altogether seven infantry regiments, five cavalry regiments and a battery of light artillery were actually raised in the regular army in addition to small bodies of specialized troops plus four provisional regiments and two battalions of engineers. These formations were mostly activated through the conversion of existing state units or the merger of small contingents from several states. There is considerable confusion in tracing the activities and history of these organizations. Changes in designation were common, and some units are sometimes referred to as battalions and at others as regiments. Enumeration was erratic, so that a perusal of the *Official Records* reveals mention of eleven regiments and two battalions of cavalry plus seven regiments and five battalions of infantry, which were in reality all the same five cavalry regiments and seven infantry regiments in various manifestations, guises and redesignation. In the end, it seems likely that perhaps 750 of the men enrolled in the regular establishment during the war were officers, including the six senior-most men in the Confederate Army: Samuel Cooper, Albert Sidney Johnston, Robert E. Lee, Joseph E. Johnston, Pierre G.T. Beauregard and Braxton Bragg, who ranked as generals, the only grade above colonel. Probably no more than 1,000 men were in organized formations at any one time and only about 5,000 were ever enrolled, of whom fully 1,279 deserted. Only one regular outfit was with the Army of Northern Virginia, the 1st Provisional Engineer Regiment, serving from its organization in the Spring of 1864 to Appomattox. Only two Regular Army formations achieved any distinction. The 5th Confederate Regiment, a sort of "foreign legion" composed of men of many different nationalities, but mostly Irish, fought under Gen. John B. Hood in Tennessee in 1864. The 8th Confederate Battalion, raised from Yankee prisoners of war and colloquially known as the "Galvanized Yankees," performed yeoman service in covering the escape of the Confederate government through North Carolina in the period after the fall of Richmond, holding Salisbury for a day against a Union cavalry division.

The Pennsylvania Bucktail Regiments

Three of the bravest and most effective regiments in the Union Army bore the collective nickname "Bucktails." When Lincoln made his first call for volunteers in April of 1861, the response in Pennsylvania was so enthusiastic that the state's quota was rapidly oversubscribed by over 30 per cent. For political reasons, then-Secretary of War Simon Cameron refused to accept the additional men into Federal service. Rather than turn them away, Gov. Andrew G. Curtain had the great foresight to convince the state legislature to foot the bill to enroll, equip, train and maintain them as state troops. Thus was born the *Pennsylvania Reserve Corps*, comprising thirteen fine infantry regiments, which were eventually mustered into Federal service as the *30th* through *42nd Pennsylvania Volunteers*. The entire corps formed a division in *V Corps* which proved one of the toughest formations in the *Army of the Potomac* until mustered out in early 1864. It was, however, the *13th Pennsylvania Reserves*—the *1st Pennsylvania Rifles* or the *42nd Pennsylvania Volunteers*—which became famous as the *"Pennsylvania Bucktails."*

The *13th Pennsylvania Reserves* was recruited as a rifle regiment from among the hardy lumbermen and backwoodsmen of the wild northern part of the state—one company white-watered down to the regimental rendezvous. Before a man would even be considered for service he had to produce a bucktail in proof of his marksmanship. The regiment's nickname, "Bucktails," derived from the habit the men had of fastening this trophy to their hats. Initially armed with a variety of rifles, each man providing his own favorite shooting iron, the regiment was equipped with Sharps breechloading rifles in time for Gettysburg, and later carried Spencer repeating rifles. Although formally attached to the *Pennsylvania Reserve Division*, the *13th* frequently served in a more or less independent role, as skirmishers and sharpshooters. Indeed, for some months in early 1862 it did not even serve intact. During the Peninsular Campaign, four companies served in the Shenandoah Valley under Col. Thomas L. Kane, later a brigadier general, fighting at Harrisonburg and Cross Keys, while the rest of the regiment fought with the *Army of the Potomac* from Mechanicsville to Malvern Hill. The regiment was reunited in time for Second Bull Run, under Col. Hugh W. McNeil, who was killed at Antietam.

Heavily engaged at Fredericksburg, where it suffered 161 casualties, the regiment, along with the *Pennsylvania Reserve Division*, was shortly afterwards transferred to the defenses of Washington. During the opening phases of the Gettysburg Campaign two of the division's three brigades volunteered for field service. The *Pennsylvania Reserves* rendered excellent service at Gettysburg, and the "Bucktails" were rather seriously engaged around Little Round Top, where Col. Charles F. Taylor was killed. The regiment went on to serve in the Mine Run and Bristoe Station Campaigns, and in Grant's Overland Campaign in the Spring of 1864, until mustered out on 11 June. In not quite three years of Federal service, the *13th Pennsylvania Reserves* suffered 609 casualties, 52.2 percent of the

1,165 men who served, including 162 battle deaths. A number of men who reenlisted and all those who, having joined the regiment after it had mustered in, still had time left on their enlistments, were transferred to the *190th Pennsylvania*, and thus many of the "Bucktails" continued to serve to the end of the war. Meanwhile, additional "Bucktail" regiments had taken the field.

Impressed by the fighting qualities of the *13th Pennsylvania Reserves*, in July of 1862 Secretary of War Edwin M. Stanton authorized Maj. Roy Stone, one of the regiment's veterans, to recruit a "Bucktail" brigade. Acting with commendable speed and efficiency, Stone shortly recruited two full regiments. The *149th Pennsylvania* mustered in at Harrisburg at the end of August, with Stone as colonel, and the *150th* mustered in a few days later under Col. Langhorne Wister. For some time the two regiments served as part of the garrison of Washington, where *Company K* of the *150th* was detailed to provide a bodyguard for the president, which service it performed to the end of the war. In February of 1863 the regiments were grouped with the *143rd Pennsylvania* as a brigade in *I Corps*, with Stone in command. But lightly engaged at Chancellorsville, the regiments were heavily involved in Gettysburg where they helped open the wall on 1 July and so lost their colonels and lieutenant-colonels there. The *149th* suffered 336 casualties of 450 men engaged (74.7 percent), the *150th* had 264 out of 400 (66.0 percent), and the 143rd 253 of 465 (54.4 percent). The two "Bucktail" regiments served in all the subsequent campaigns of the *Army of the Potomac* until Petersburg, by which time they were in two different divisions of *V Corps*.

In February of 1865 they were transferred to prisoner-of-war guard duty, in which capacity they served until mustered out. Although the two new "Bucktail" regiments never equaled the original in fighting skill, they amassed quite creditable records. Of 1,454 men who served in the *149th*, fully 613 (42.2 percent) became casualties, as did 431 of the 1,008 (42.8 percent) in the *150th*. The "Bucktails" proved themselves to be among the finest fighting regiments in the Union Army.

War and Society

Blacks in the Ranks

Black men were involved in some of the earliest actions of the Civil War. Indeed, Nicholas Biddle, a black freeman from Pottsville, Pennsylvania, was widely regarded as the first casualty by Rebel action. Biddle was injured by a brick-bat on 18 April 1861 when the *27th Pennsylvania*, in which he was serving as an officer's orderly, was attacked by a Baltimore mob, one day before the more-widely publicized attack on the *6th Massachusetts*. And, indeed, when Lincoln issued his call for volunteers, black men immediately offered themselves for service. Black volunteer companies were rapidly organized in New York, Boston and Cleveland; a battalion was offered in Washington. However, public sentiment was by no means favorable. Moreover, such a move might have had an explosive effect on the wavering loyalties of the slaveholding Border States. As a result, all such offers of service were rejected.

Though Frederick Douglass and other black leaders tried to keep the issue alive, little progress was realized for more than a year. Only gradually, as casualties mounted and as the issue of emancipation came to the fore, did the hostility towards blacks in the ranks ease. In July of 1862, Congress authorized the President to raise black troops and formal authority to raise black regiments was granted by the War Department on 25 August 1862. But even before that black men had begun to don the uniform of the Republic.

The first black unit raised for Federal service was the *1st South Carolina Volunteers*, organized by Brig. Gen. David Hunter on the Carolina sea islands beginning on 7 May 1862. Political considerations soon caused the regiment to be disbanded, though *Company A* continued in existence informally until the regiment was reactivated that November, by which time other black regiments had already mustered in. Meanwhile, the Navy had been enlisting blacks for over a year; as early as August of 1861 black men were serving as gunners on Union warships. The first properly authorized black unit in Federal service was the *1st Kansas Colored Volunteers* (later the *79th U.S. Colored Troops*), which began organizing in July of 1862, although it was not officially completed for service until January of 1863 by which time it had already been in action.

The first full black regiment to be mustered in was the *1st Louisiana Native Guards*, authorized by Maj. Gen. Benjamin Butler, on 27 September 1862, an outfit which had actually been raised for Confederate service in 1861 by the free black men of the state. Additional regiments of this corps were on duty by the end of the year.

The Emancipation Proclamation removed all formal obstacles to black recruitment, though the racism of individual commanders and political leaders often impeded efforts to raise troops in particular areas.

The first black military organization to enter combat was the *1st Kansas Colored Volunteers*, at Island Mounds, Missouri, on 29 October 1862. Black troops participated in an increasing number of actions. Over the next eight months they served with particular distinction at the Siege of Port Hudson (27 May-9 July 1863) and the Battle of Milliken's Bend (6-8 June 1863), where black recruits beat off an assault by superior numbers of Confederate veterans. However, public recognition was long in coming, until the black *54th Massachusetts* lost over 25 percent of its strength in the attempt to storm Fort Wagner, on Morris Island, S.C., on 18 July 1863.

Black troops served well, despite considerable discrimination and mistreatment. Until nearly the end of the war the pay for black enlisted men was $10.00 a month, regardless of rank, from which $3.00 were deducted as a clothing allowance, leaving but $7.00, little more than half what white private soldiers earned—the *54th Massachusetts* refused to accept any pay until the inequity was rectified. Moreover, black troops often found themselves doing more than their fair share of fatigue duties. They were involved in about 5 percent of the combat actions of the war, about 450 engagements, including some of the most sanguinary, such as Olustee (20 February 1864). Indeed, statistically black combat casualties were 35 percent higher than white, partially because of a Confederate penchant for massacring blacks captured in arms. About two dozen black men—both army and navy—were awarded the Medal of Honor. During the last two years of the war black troops served in every theater, and were particularly important in the Mississippi Valley, where they constituted a significant proportion of Federal forces.

Altogether 178,975 black men were recruited for the armies, of whom 2,751 were killed in action, mortally wounded, or murdered by Confederate troops. Black troops amounted to roughly 12 percent of total Union manpower at the end of the war, by which time the "black iron hand" of the Federal armies amounted to 120 infantry regiments, seven cavalry regiments, a dozen heavy artillery regiments and ten batteries of light artillery, for a total of 140 regiments. It was the largest black army that had ever been seen.

The Ways of War

The Cavalry

In both armies the cavalry began the war looking to play a glorious role in the grand tradition of the eighteenth century and the Napoleonic Age, as the arm of shock, bringing about a decisive decision on the battlefield. But even in Napoleonic times the boot-to-boot charge with lance and saber was beginning to become a risky venture, and notably so against seasoned troops. By the Civil War the rifled musket had made the cavalry charge not merely risky, but frankly obsolete unless the circumstances were particularly favorable, such as against very green troops. As a result, the cavalry spent much of the war looking for a role. And in the end, it found an excellent one.

As it developed during the war, the role of the cavalry came to encompass a considerable variety of activities. The missions of the mounted arm included conducting reconnaissance, establishing and maintaining contact with enemy forces, screening the movements of friendly forces and raiding against enemy lines of communication. Any serious fighting was best done dismounted, using carbines and serving as light infantry, though the saber and the pistol and even the shotgun, were useful in mounted skirmishes.

The cavalryman's favorite role was raiding, for it gave him a chance to run free, causing as much destruction as possible and avoiding the monotonous burdens of patrol duty. Moreover, raids tended to catch the attention of the public, already inclined to be overly fond of the troopers. However, while raids sometimes could have a useful effect on the course of a campaign, they were distinctly less important than reconnoitering and screening before the army. These were missions which never ended, for the need to seek out information on the enemy, and to deny it to him, never ceased. Thus, unlike the infantry and the artillery, which relatively speaking had plenty of time to spare between campaigns, the cavalry worked most of the time. Not in combat, but in patrolling, scouting and serving on picket. These were boring, grueling tasks which placed a heavy burden on the troopers and an even greater strain on their mounts. Casualties among the horses were always higher than those among their riders and a regiment could easily run through two or three issues of horses in a year.

The organization of the cavalry was very similar on both sides. A Union regiment consisted of a headquarters and twelve companies, which could be organized into three battalions of four companies or six squadrons of two companies as the situation dictated. At regimental headquarters the officers included a colonel, a lieutenant colonel, three majors, three lieutenants serving respectively as regimental adjutant, quartermaster and commissary and a surgeon with his assistant. The headquarters staff included a sergeant-major, three sergeants serving respectively as quartermaster, commissary and saddler, a farrier (blacksmith) and two hospital stewards. Each company had a captain, a first and second lieutenant, a first sergeant, a quartermaster sergeant, a commissary sergeant, five other sergeants, eight corporals, two teamsters, a wagoner, two farriers, a saddler, two musicians and about 70 troopers.

A Confederate cavalry regiment normally consisted of a headquarters and ten companies. On paper, at least, the headquarters staff was virtually identical to that of the Federal regiment, though with only two majors. Each company was supposed to have a captain, three lieutenants, five sergeants, four corporals, a farrier and his assistant and about 85 troopers. On paper then, the Union cavalry regiment had about 1200 men, while the Confederate one ran to only about 900. In practice, however, the number was far less, due to casualties and a lack of replacements. At Gettysburg, for example, Union regiments averaged a little more than 360 men and Confederate ones about 280.

In both armies several regiments formed a brigade. Federal brigades had from three to six regiments and Confederate ones normally about five, but occasionally as few as two. In rare instances a battery of horse artillery was attached to a brigade, but this was more normally found at a higher level. In both armies the usual cavalry division was composed of two or three brigades, and a division of, say, 3,600 troopers with two batteries. All of this usually occupied about four miles of road. J.E.B. Stuart's Cavalry Division in the Army of Northern Virginia eventually grew to six brigades plus a large contingent of horse artillery. This proved rather clumsy and soon after Gettysburg the division was reorganized as a corps.

The cavalry of the *Army of the Potomac* had been formed into a corps of three divisions and a sizeable contingent of horse artillery by Maj. Gen. Joseph Hooker in February of 1863, a move marking the beginning of the maturation of the Federal cavalry, which until then had been significantly inferior to that of the Army of Northern Virginia.

Since the Regular Army had six regiments of cavalry at the start of the Civil War (the *1st* and *2nd Dragoons*, the *Regiment of Mounted Rifles* and the *1st, 2nd* and the newly raised *3rd Cavalry*, which were respectively redesignated the *1st* through *6th Cavalry* in August of 1861, with devastating effects on morale) it might have been expected that the Union cavalry would have been more effective, at least at the onset of the war, than was that of the Confederacy. However, this was not the case, for the regular regiments had important duties to perform on the frontier. There was also a relative shortage of good riding stock and a relative lack of riding skills in the comparatively urban North. More importantly, the Union was tardy in forming brigades and divisions of cavalry, which left the mounted forces without centralized direction.

It was the Southern cavalry which first developed as an efficient combat arm. And the South benefitted from the fact that some of her sons were among the finest cavalrymen ever known, such as Turner Ashby, who died early, Nathan Bedford Forrest, a gifted amateur in the West who was perhaps the only Confederate cavalryman who really understood that war meant damaging the enemy more than securing personal glory, the youthful Joseph Wheeler, another "Westerner," and famed J.E.B. Stuart, who served with the Army of Northern Virginia. With such leadership, the Confederate cavalry developed an early and significant edge over that of the Union, an advantage which it maintained for much of the war.

Eventually, of course, excellent cavalrymen began to emerge in the Union ranks, men such as John Buford and Elon Farnesworth, who died soon after attaining high rank; Alfred Pleasanton, who started in the East and ended up in the Trans-Mississippi; Benjamin Grierson and James H. Wilson, who distinguished themselves in the West; and Judson Kilpatrick, George A. Custer and Philip Sheridan, who distinguished themselves with the *Army of the Potomac.*

By the time of Vicksburg and Gettysburg the Federal cavalry had matured to the point of being able to stand up and trade blows successfully with that of the Confederacy. This was due partially to the creation of distinct cavalry corps, which put all the troopers in an army under one central direction for operational purposes, and partially due to the introduction of the Sharps carbine, which gave the Union troopers a considerable advantage in firepower.

The first indication of this maturity in the West was Benjamin H. Grierson's raid from La Grange, Tennessee, to Baton Rouge, Louisiana, a seventeen day, 800 mile expedition which wrecked havoc with the Confederate rear-area in April of 1863, during the opening phases of Grant's final drive on Vicksburg. In the East the change was signaled by Brandy Station (9 June 1863), at which the Yankee troopers surprised J.E.B. Stuart's cavaliers and then, in the long, involved action which followed, pretty much gave as good as they got. Then came all the little cavalry skirmishes along the Blue Ridge and South Mountain chains in the early phases of the Gettysburg Campaign, in which the Yankees came off the better more often than not. This newfound skill and determination became particularly evident when, during this same campaign, Stuart, in order to restore the luster to his bruised reputation, took most of his men off on a raid into Maryland and Pennsylvania, disappearing from Lee's sight for over a week. Though Maj. Gen. Alfred Pleasanton, commanding the *Cavalry Corps* of the *Army of the Potomac*, was neither as brilliant nor as spectacular a trooper as was Stuart, he did his job, keeping his three divisions close in hand, screening before the advance of the army and seeking out the enemy. As a result, Lee was taken totally by surprise when Henry Heth ran into Union cavalrymen on the Chambersburg Pike northwest of Gettysburg on the morning of 1 July. Stuart tried to set things aright with his attack against Union communications along the Hanover road on the afternoon of 3 July, but his troopers were outfought and outridden in a crazy melee fought on foot and horse. The old edge had gone, and gone forever.

Ballooning

The ancient dream of flight was not achieved until 5 June 1783, when the Montgolfier brothers launched a hot air balloon, with the first manned ascent taking place on 21 November. The military potential of the balloon was recognized quite early. In 1793 the armies of Revolutionary France began to make use of balloons for observation and reconnaissance. Military use of balloons grew as the years went by. In 1849 the city of Venice became the first to be subject to what is generally considered a twentieth century horror, aerial bombardment. By mid-century, ballooning had become relatively commonplace, with commercial and sporting applications as well as military. As a result, on the outbreak of the Civil War a number of people came forward to offer their services as "aeronauts."

Maj. Hartman Bache, a grandson of Benjamin Franklin, was among the first to talk the War Department into considering the use of balloons. Availing himself of the services of John Wise, a balloon "manufacturer" from Lancaster, Pennsylvania, Bache procured a varnished raw silk balloon for $850. This reached Washington in July of 1861, shortly before First Bull Run. Entrusted to the care of Maj. Albert J. Myer, the Chief Signal

Officer, the balloon proved less than useful—Myer tried to tow it fully
inflated into a position from which he could observe Confederate movements during the battle. As a result, he missed the battle entirely, and the
thing tore in the bargain. Sent back to Washington, the balloon was
repaired, but broke its tether one day and had to be brought down by rifle
fire, thus technically becoming the first victim of anti-aircraft fire. Although he was hardly to blame for Myer's lack of experience, Wise received
no further orders from the War Department. Not that there was a shortage
of prospective suppliers.

Even before Bull Run, Brig. Gen. Benjamin Butler, commanding at
Fortress Monroe on the Virginia coast, had been approached by John
LaMountain with a proposal to use balloons for reconnaissance. A native
of Troy, New York, LaMountain, was a former seaman who had gained
some fame as a prewar aeronaut. Among his achievements was a flight of
1,100 miles eastwards from St. Louis in only 24 hours. On 31 July
LaMountain went aloft from the fortress and provided valuable information on Confederate dispositions in the vicinity. This was only the beginning, and he made several more ascents over the next few months, even
using the armed transport *Fanny* to tow his balloon into position, technically making her the first aircraft carrier in history. Among his other
achievements were the first nighttime reconnaissance flights, during which
he estimated Confederate numbers by counting campfires, a trick which
the wily Rebels quickly caught on to and promptly imposed history's first
"black out." However, there were those who questioned the value of
LaMountain's work, charging that much of the information which he
supplied was unreliable, a matter which is difficult to determine more than
a century after the fact. In any event the army parted ways with him in early
'62.

The most important Civil War aeronaut was "Professor" Thaddeus
Lowe. Only 29 at the start of the war, Lowe had already established a
reputation as an inventive and daring balloonist, with a number of long-
range voyages to his credit and several transatlantic attempts as well. On
June 1861 he lofted his *Enterprise* 500 feet above the Capitol building to
demonstrate the capabilities of balloons, telegraphing a message to Lincoln
in which he described the view. This convinced the president of the
potential usefulness of balloons. As a result, the United States Balloon
Corps was set up, with Lowe at its head despite some bureaucratic opposition. The bureaucrats were right in a number of ways. The balloons had
limited mobility. When deflated they could be moved with relative ease,
but could not be lofted at need, as the larger ones required several hours to

inflate, while inflated balloons could be towed behind wagons, but only at very low speed. A further disadvantage was that generating sufficient hot air to inflate a balloon was a long and difficult process. This latter problem was resolved when Lowe invented a portable gas generator which permitted the use of more efficient, if more dangerous, hydrogen.

Despite the drawbacks, balloons had their uses, as was soon demonstrated in the Peninsular Campaign. The U.S.B.C. used seven balloons during the campaign with considerable success, the largest being the 32,000 cubic feet *Intrepid*, which had an envelop of 1,200 yards of silk and cost $1,500.00. Hundreds of ascents were made, including several by McClellan himself. In addition to using wagon-mobile balloon equipages, Lowe made extensive use of the barge tender *George Washington Parke Custis*—named after Robert E. Lee's father-in-law—which was fully equipped to service and launch balloons, thus also technically being even more qualified to be termed the first aircraft carrier. As always, experience proved the best teacher. It was quickly found that free balloons were too unreliable and dangerous. Nor was great altitude of particular value. Although a tethered balloon could easily reach 1,500 feet, with a view in excess of 50 miles, 300 feet was militarily far more useful, at which the view was 15 miles. Dawn was the best time for reconnaissance, as the observer could locate enemy positions and estimate manpower on the basis of breakfast campfires. Balloons proved useful for engineers interested in mapping terrain, observing fixed defenses, locating bridging sites in anticipation of advances, and similar work. In addition, balloons were of some use in helping to spot artillery fire, a feat which Lowe accomplished for the first time on 24 September 1861, when he directed mortar fire against some Confederate patrols in the environs of Washington, communicating with the gunners by telegraph. The presence of balloons with the *Army of the Potomac* caused the Confederates to somewhat modify their activity in camp, so they also had a nuisance value. Although the Confederates often fired on balloons, they never managed to bring one down. Indeed, there was greater danger in being part of the ground crew, since fire directed at the balloon often landed among them. Amazingly, although Lowe's balloons used hydrogen, none ever seem to have accidentally gone up in flames.

The Confederacy also developed an interest in ballooning, though their efforts were hampered by a lack of resources. Despite romantic tales, the few Confederate balloons which did see service were not made from silk dresses. There would have been far too many small panels and an excessive number of seams which even the best varnishing would have proven difficult to make leak proof. The Southern aeronautical effort was under the command of Capt. Edward Porter Alexander, the Chief of Ordnance of the Army of Northern Virginia, and former associate of Union Maj. Albert J. Myer in the creation of the Signal Corps. The balloons were first built by Dr. Edward Cheves of Savannah, an old experimenter.

The first Southern aeronaut, however, was Lt. John R. Bryan, whose enthusiasm for the service appears to have declined in direct proportion to the number of ascents he made. During the Peninsular Campaign two balloons were used at Richmond, which had a municipal gas works. They were inflated at the gas works and towed to their observation position by locomotive, a far more effective mode of transport than wagons. An attempt was also made to use river boats to tow balloons around. This was abandoned when the armed tug C.S.S. *Teaser* ran aground and its precious cargo fell into Yankee hands on 4 July 1862. The crew of one of the Rebel balloons had an exciting afternoon once when they became the object of the attentions of three rounds from a 3" rifle which Union Capt. Thomas W. Osborn of *D Battery, 1st New York Light Artillery* had rigged for high angle fire. The Rebel aerostatists were, however, able to avoid gaining the dubious distinction of becoming the first fliers to be shot down in flames.

During the Seven Days, the Confederates captured three of Lowe's inflating mechanisms, but made no use of them. In addition to operations at Richmond, at least one balloon was employed at Charleston in the spring of 1863, under the direction of Charles Crevor, but it caught an unfortunate wind one day and drifted off never to be seen again.

The use of balloons was most extensive in early and mid-1862. Many Union commanders were very enthusiastic about them. McClellan, Fitz John Porter, Irvin McDowell and Benjamin Butler all made ascents. But the numerous problems attendant upon the use of balloons limited their effectiveness. In addition, there was considerable bureaucratic in-fighting over administrative control of the U.S.B.C. At various times it was under the authority of the Corps of Topographical Engineers, the Quartermaster Corps and the Corps of Engineers, while it battled with the Military-Telegraph Corps over control of telegraph apparatus and with the Signal Corps over control of signals. This squabbling did much to impair the efficiency of the balloon corps. Nevertheless, by the spring of 1863 over 3,000 ascents had been made, mostly in the Eastern Theater, although one balloon did see service in the West. Then in May of 1863, Maj. Gen. Joseph Hooker cut Lowe's salary, reduced his staff, interfered with his operations and subordinated him to the Corps of Engineers. Frustrated, Lowe, who, it must be said was not easy to get along with and was careless about his bookkeeping, resigned on 8 May. Without him the U.S.B.C. rapidly declined and it was disbanded in June of 1863, by which time the Confederates had long since abandoned the use of balloons for lack of resources.

Machine Guns

By the mid-nineteenth century technology had progressed to the point where the dream of a self-loading, continuous firing gun was finally within reach. By the time of the Civil War several inventors were working on machine guns and they made serious efforts to get the armies to adopt their devilish devices, with little success. Five of these weapons are of particular interest.

Ager Union Repeating Gun: The Ager was a crew served, crank operated, hopper fed piece firing pre-capped .58 caliber metallic cartridges at about 120 rounds per minute. Lincoln witnessed a test firing in June of 1861 and immediately dubbed it the "coffee mill" gun, a nickname which stuck. He also bought 10 of them that October at $1,300 each and McClellan acquired another 50 in December at about $735 apiece. Altogether 63 were made, including the demonstration models. There is some rather unreliable evidence that the Ager gun was first used in action by the *28th Pennsylvania* while on picket along the Potomac in January or February of 1862. This same regiment definitely used one in action on 28 March 1862 in a skirmish at Middleburg, Virginia, when, according to observers, some Confederate cavalry was cut to pieces at 800 yards. Despite this, the regiment's commander, Col. John W. Geary—who later proved a capable division commander—soon returned the pieces in his charge with the comment that they were "inefficient and unsafe to their operators." Some use was made of the Ager gun during the Peninsular Campaign. The *56th New York* employed a battery of the wheeled guns at Yorktown in April of '62 and several—possibly the same battery—were used at Gaines' Mill (27 June). While there was some satisfaction over the resultant destructive effects on the enemy, this was not sufficient to justify wider use of the weapon. Nevertheless, since the pieces were on hand, they were occasionally used through to the end of the war, notably by the navy on the Mississippi and during the protracted investment of Petersburg. The Confederacy acquired several Ager guns, two being taken by Brig. Gen. Isaac R. Trimble's North Carolina Brigade at Gaines' Mill after a hard fight, and about a dozen by Stonewall Jackson when he seized Harper's Ferry in September of 1862, but there is no record of their being put to any use. Although the Ager gun had some value, it was a clumsy device, and dangerous to use, being prone to misfires. In addition, the breech seal was not very good and fragments of cartridge casing were often scattered about. William Tecumseh Sherman was slightly wounded in this fashion in early 1863.

Bellinghurst-Requia Battery Gun: This piece was invented by Requia, a man but vaguely known, and promoted by Bellinghurst, who came from New York, but is also little known. Their device was essentially a somewhat modernized version of the late medieval *ribauld*. It had 25 breech loading barrels laid alongside each other at a slightly divergent angle to provide some "spread" to the bullets. The bullets, standard musket rounds, were fixed so as to project from a rod-like clip which had a powder train running along its length which could be set off by a single percussion cap. Upon firing, the spent clip was discarded and another put in its place. With practice, a crew of three could get off seven volleys in a minute—175 rounds. The principal flaws were that the powder train was exposed to the weather, burned irregularly in the best of circumstances and could misfire. As a result, the piece, which was mounted on a light artillery-like carriage, saw only limited use by Union forces in the defense of covered positions, such as bridges, hence its name "covered bridge gun".

Gatling Machine Gun: The first version of Dr. Richard Gatling's machine gun was used by Union forces on an experimental basis. A crew served weapon, it had a good rate of fire, initially about 250 rounds per minute using paper wrapped .58 caliber musket cartridges, which were gravity fed from a hopper, while a crank operated the firing mechanism, rotating the six barrels to avoid overheating. With the introduction of metallic cartridges the rate of fire could be increased to 600 rounds per minute. However, the device had a number of flaws, not least of which was that Gatling found his Southern origins an obstacle to securing a proper hearing. In addition, the piece was heavy, being mounted on a light artillery-type carriage. There were also some technical flaws, the most notable being a difficulty in aligning the barrels to the chamber. The early model resolved this by making the diameter of the base of the barrels greater than that of the .58 caliber chambers, and tapering the bore towards the muzzle, which meant that the rounds had poor velocity and accuracy. These bugs might have been worked out, but Gatling's factory burned down after only a few pieces had been produced. By the time Gatling got back into production it was 1864 and interest in machine guns, never very great, had declined. Nevertheless, he was able to demonstrate a somewhat more advanced model to Maj. Gen. Benjamin Butler. Impressed, Butler prodded Massachusetts into buying a dozen at $1000 apiece and these were used with limited success during his operations against Petersburg. In early 1865 Gatling demonstrated a much improved version which caught the attention of the Army, but it was not approved for use until the following year. Of all the "machine guns" devised during the Civil War, Gatling's— even his early model—was unquestionably the best.

Vandenberg Volley Gun: The Vandenberg was similar to the Bellinghurst gun, in that all the rounds were set off simultaneously by a single percussion cap, but it could also be set to fire in volleys, with only a portion of the barrels discharging simultaneously. The Vandenberg gun, which came in several models, had 85 to 451 bores in one massive barrel. A case containing cartridges and cap was loaded by means of a single breech block, thus greatly resembling the French *mitrailleuse*, which proved such a disappointment in the Franco-Prussian War. The weapon, which was as massive as a field gun, did not get beyond the demonstration stage.

Williams Rapid-Fire Gun: Invented by one R.S. Williams of Kentucky and initially built at Richmond's Tredegar Iron Works, the Williams gun was actually a rapid firing light artillery piece. It had a four-foot long barrel mounted on a light wheeled carriage. The piece came in two models, a 1.57" caliber which had one pound rounds, and a 2" caliber with 1.25 pound rounds, with a choice of solid shot or buckshot available. It had a colt-like revolving mechanism operated by a crank and fed by hopper, with a rate of fire of up to 60 rounds per minute—the sustainable rate was 20—to an extreme range of 2000 yards, and was operated by a three-man crew: one dropped the cartridges into the hopper, one fed percussion caps to the firing mechanism, and one turned the crank to chamber and discharge the round. The Williams gun was first used in action by Brig. Gen. George Picket's Virginia Brigade at Seven Pines on 31 May 1862. The effects were impressive, and the South ordered seven batteries of six pieces each. By the end of the 1863 about 46 had been produced—20 by Tredegar and four by Samson and Pae at Richmond, a dozen at Lynchburg and six more at Mobile. Four pieces saw some service with Sterling Price in the Trans-Mississippi Department, a battery was with the Army of Tennessee for a time, attached to the 4th Kentucky Cavalry, and several were used during the trench warfare around Petersburg, but most saw little action. Despite the initially high hopes for the piece, it was not a success. Due to metallurgical problems, the breech mechanism heated up rapidly, expanded easily and jammed with excessive frequency.

Despite several promising devices, machine guns played an insignificant role in the Civil War. Part of the reason for the poor reception of these early machine guns was bureaucratic obstructionism. Union Chief of Ordnance

Brig. Gen. James W. Ripley, for example, was notoriously hostile to new ideas, and even impeded the introduction of breech loading and repeating rifles. But there were also technical problems. All of the weapons were unreliable and excessively delicate. In addition, their production required considerable technical sophistication, which was seriously lacking in the Confederacy. In passing, it should be noted that none of the weapons in question was a true "machine gun." Two were volley guns or mitrailleuses, discharging a large number of rounds simultaneously, and the others were crank operated rapid-fire guns, whereas a machine gun maintains a sustained volume of fire by means of a mechanism which uses the recoil or gas blowby of each round to eject the spent cartridge and load and fire a fresh one. Despite this technicality, had any of the three most promising weapons, the Williams, the Ager, or particularly the Gatling, been perfected and procured in substantial numbers the war would have been even bloodier than was actually the case.

The Ships

C.S.S. *Arkansas*

One of the most dramatic careers of any vessel in the war was that of the Confederate ironclad ram *Arkansas*, which had an operational life of little more than seven weeks.

Arkansas, a casemate ironclad designed by John Shipley, was one of two ships laid down at Memphis in October of 1861. By the following spring, Union movements on the upper Mississippi so threatened the security of Memphis that, while her sistership *Tennessee* was burned on the stocks, the incomplete *Arkansas* was towed some 200 miles downstream to the mouth of the Yazoo River, and then 75 miles up the Yazoo to Yazoo City, in the heart of the delta country of Mississippi. There the ship was completed in remarkably primitive conditions. Making matters worse, a barge hauling most of her armor from Memphis sank en route and could not be salvaged until divers were brought in from the East Coast. The director of construction, Lt. Isaac N. Brown, C.S.N., found himself constantly at odds with local civil and military leaders, many of whom had little regard for his project or his problems. In the end, Brown had to secure the intervention of Jefferson Davis to get enough men together to form a crew. As a result of such delays, *Arkansas* was not completed until July of 1862: if she had been completed as scheduled she would have proven a serious obstacle to David Farragut's ascent of the Mississippi with a squadron of wooden vessels on 26-29 June.

Arkansas was 165 feet long, with a beam of 35 feet and a draught of 11 to 12 feet. She carried ten guns and had a crew of about 200 men. The ship was armored with railroad iron and her casemates had vertical sides, save at the ends where they sloped at perhaps 50 degrees. Like most Confederate ironclads, she was rather under-engined, though she apparently could do about 10 knots downstream. She did, however, have twin screws, which made her rather more maneuverable than the norm.

Under the command of Lt. Henry K. Stevens, *Arkansas* sortied on the morning of 15 July, intending to make for Vicksburg. As she steamed down the Yazoo, she encountered three Union vessels on reconnaissance, the ram *Queen of the West*, the lightly armored gunboat *Tyler* and the ironclad *Carondelet*. A hot fight ensued. The two lighter Union vessels were soon forced to flee, but *Arkansas* and *Carondelet* continued to slug it out for a time as they steamed downstream. Then both vessels ran aground. *Carondelet* was stuck fast, but *Arkansas* was able to free herself in a short time. Keeping his mission in mind, Stevens wisely chose to ignore the helpless *Carondelet* and, stoking up the boilers, laid on all steam in pursuit of the lighter Union vessels.

The chase took *Arkansas* into the Mississippi and right into the Union riverine and oceanic fleets, 30 of the most powerful warships in the world, all lying quietly at anchor, uncharacteristically unprepared for action. Steven's gamble paid off, for he arrived virtually with the vessels he was pursuing and the fleet was not ready to receive him. He plunged on ahead, right through the Union armada, firing as he went, mostly for effect, though he did inflict some injury to several vessels. Although the unprepared fleet began to fire back almost immediately, *Arkansas* was able to get away, somewhat damaged. Several vessels took up the pursuit, but Stevens was able to gain the security of the Confederate batteries at Vicksburg. Although she had taken some damage and suffered a number of casualties in her run through the Union fleet, *Arkansas* was now in position to alter the strategic situation on the Mississippi, for she threatened to sever Union river communications, and potentially bottle up David G. Farragut's ocean-going vessels in the river. In addition, she was a powerful reinforcement to the defenses of Vicksburg.

Realizing the danger which *Arkansas* posed, Farragut acted swiftly, knowing that she would need time to effect repairs. That very night he ran the fleet past Vicksburg once again, concentrating part of his fire on *Arkansas* as she lay alongside the river bank. Although the damage inflicted by the fleet was relatively light, repairs took rather a long time. Not until 3 August was *Arkansas* again ready for "sea." By that time she was desperately needed to support an attempt to retake Baton Rouge from the Yankees.

Arkansas sortied on 4 August, without the Yankees learning of it. Things went well at first and, unpursued, she steamed steadily down river. But the next day her engines began to give trouble and she had to anchor in order to effect repairs. On the morning of 6 August she raised steam again and was making good progress when her engines once more gave out, virtually within sight of Baton Rouge. As nothing could be done to get her going again, and with a Federal squadron led by the powerful ironclad *Essex* approaching, *Arkansas* was abandoned and burned. Union domination of the "Father of the Waters" was never thereafter threatened by Confederate warships.

U.S.S. Monitor and C.S.S. Virginia

Ironclad warships began to come into vogue shortly before the outbreak of the Civil War, with France and Britain having several in service and other powers striving to catch up. As a result, both the Union and Confederate navies very early began to consider acquiring such for their own use.

It was Confederate Secretary of the Navy Stephen R. Mallory who made the first move. Since the Union retained virtually the entire prewar navy, the South would always be hopelessly behind in conventional warships. By quickly beginning to build ironclads, the Confederacy might gain an immediate advantage over the Union, permitting it to break the blockade. Under Mallory's prodding, the Confederate Congress appropriated $2,000,000 for ironclads. Mallory immediately authorized the reconstruction as an ironclad of the hulk of the frigate U.S.S. *Merrimack*.

Merrimack, one of the most powerful conventional warships in the world when completed in 1855, had been burned and sunk at the Gosport Navy Yard when Union forces evacuated the place on 20-21 April. There were many technical problems to overcome in order to realize the completion of this project. Although the precious drydock had survived intact, most of the facilities at the Gosport yard had been severely damaged or destroyed. In addition, the South had slender iron working facilities—only the Tredegar Iron Works in Richmond were capable of producing armor plate—and little in the way of a steam engine industry. Nevertheless, Mallory acted with commendable speed. Within a short time he had collected an effective team to oversee the work, consisting of John Porter, an experienced naval architect, William Williamson, a naval engineer and John Brooke, a former officer in the United States Navy and an inventive ordnance specialist.

The sunken hulk of the frigate was raised on 30 May and work began at once. The vessel was cut down almost to the waterline, while her engine—which had been none too good before the ship was torched and had now been subject to five weeks immersion— was refitted and lowered deeper into the hull. Eschewing traditional superstructure and rigging, a sloping casemate structure was built just above the waterline, and a broad flat deck extended outwards from this, overhanging the hull. There were may delays in converting the vessel. Not only did Tredegar take until February of 1862 to produce the 723 tons of armor required, but a shortage of suitable flatcars hampered its delivery date. The ship was finally ready for service in March of 1862.

As completed, the newly rechristened C.S.S. *Virginia* was 275 feet long and had a 38.5 feet beam. She drew 22 feet, was top-heavy, not very maneuverable and slow: as a 4,600-ton frigate her engines were barely sufficient to propel her along at nearly nine knots; as an ironclad the vessel displaced over a thousand tons more and she could barely make 7.5 knots. *Virginia's* casemate was built up with 30" of pine, covered by 4" of oak, over which were laid two layers of 2" iron plates, all at a 35 degree angle to help deflect shells. In addition, there were 1" iron plates extending below the waterline under the overhang to protect the hull; this was supposed to extend nearly two feet, but as completed was barely 6" deep. The ship had ten guns: a 7" muzzle loading rifle on a pivot at the fore and the after end of the casemate, plus three 9" Dalghren smoothbores and one 6" rifled muzzle loader along either side. She also had a 1,500 pound cast iron ram fixed to her bow.

Finding a crew for *Virginia* was difficult. No officer was appointed to command her, so that Lt. Catesby ap Rogers Jones, was technically in command. The other officers were all mostly Old Navy men as well. But there was a shortage of common seamen in the South. About 80 old salts were released from regiments in the Norfolk-Suffolk area, but most of the ship's crew of about 300 were landsmen. On 8 March *Virginia* was ready for her trials, which would also be her first operational sortie, with Cdr. Franklin Buchanan, commanding the James River defenses, aboard and acting as captain. Buchanan was an Old Navy veteran who had resigned in anticipation of the secession of his native Maryland, only to try to withdraw it when Maryland remained loyal!

Accompanied by a couple of small gunboats, *Virginia* steamed slowly into Hampton Roads at about 1:00 p.m on that Saturday, making slowly for the nearest of the blockading Union warships, two old sailing vessels, the 50-gun frigate *Congress* and the 24-gun sloop-of-war *Cumberland.* Fire was opened at about 2:00. In the ensuing engagement, *Cumberland* was rammed, *Virginia's* iron beak wrenching loose in the process, while *Congress* was run aground and set on fire. *Cumberland* went down at about 3:30, with her guns still firing and flags still flying. Meanwhile, *Virginia* continued to pound *Congress*, killing McKean Buchanan, brother to Franklin, who was himself wounded in the exchange. At about 4:30 *Congress* struck, but some infantry regiments on the shore nearby kept up such a heavy fire on *Virginia*, that Lt. Catesby ap Rogers Jones, who had assumed command from Buchanan, resumed firing on the helpless vessel. By this time three powerful steam frigates attempted to intervene but ran aground. *Virginia* tried to approach U.S.S. *Minnesota*, a sister of the old *Merrimack*, but the tide was ebbing and she could not get close. It being about 5:00 p.m., Jones decided to retire. In some three hours of combat, *Virginia* had suffered superficial damage, including a leak when her ram had been wrenched off, which reduced her already low speed still further. About a score of her crew had been injured in the engagement, in which hundreds of Union seamen had become casualties. *Virginia* steamed slowly back up the Elizabeth River.

At dawn the next morning the little Confederate flotilla sortied once again, making for Old Point Comfort, where *Minnesota* was still firmly aground. Lying near the grounded warship was an odd looking raft-like object with a boxy projection. It was the Union's first ironclad, U.S.S. *Monitor*.

With recent developments in Europe in mind, and some information about Confederate intentions, Union Secretary of the Navy Gideon Welles proposed the construction of ironclads in May of 1861. In August the Navy advertised for proposals and 17 were received. A board appointed to examine the proposals deemed two likely prospects and construction of these was authorized. One was an ironclad steam frigate, which became U.S.S. *New Ironsides*, one of the most successful ships of the war, and the other was an ironclad gunboat, U.S.S. *Galena*, which was to prove unsuccessful.

The designer of *Galena*, Cornelius Bushnell, asked John Ericsson, the distinguished naval architect and inventor—among other things, he had perfected the screw propeller—to review his proposal and perhaps give him some advice. Ericsson approved Bushnell's plan, and then showed him a dusty model of a peculiar looking ironclad vessel, which he claimed to have once offered to French Emperor Napoleon III; no record of such an offer has ever been found in French archives. This vessel was to be built entirely of iron, with a very low freeboard and virtually no superstructure, save for a large revolving turret with two 11" guns.

Ericsson, who had a long-standing feud with the Navy Department, had not bothered to submit his design for consideration, but Bushnell immediately recognized its revolutionary nature. He pulled some strings and got Ericsson some introductions which led, after much acrimony, to a $275,000 money-back guarantee contract to build the vessel. Ericsson did it in 124 days; the ship was laid down at a slip on what is now Monitor Street in Greenpoint, Brooklyn, on 25 October 1861, was launched on 30

January 1862, and commissioned on 26 February. U.S.S. *Monitor* was completed on time and under budget, though not to specifications, Ericsson ignoring a clause which required that she be rigged as a sailing vessel.

The new ship was unique. Displacing a little less than a thousand tons, she looked like a 172 long, 416" wide raft on which was perched a 20 wide and 9 high turret. The only other features were two 6 tall smokestacks, two 46" air intakes and a pilot house which jutted about the same height above the deck forward. The ship was heavily armored, with nine 1" layers of plate on the gun port covers and eight on the turret sides. The hull was plated with 2" to 4.5" and the decks had 1". Although designed for eight knots, she could make only about six, and had barely 14 inches of freeboard, so that she was awash in anything but a flat calm. *Monitor* had only two guns, huge 11" smoothbores. She had a crew of 58 officers and men under Lt. John L. Worden, U.S.N.

After a few trials in New York harbor, *Monitor* steamed for Hampton Roads on 6 March 1862. She arrived there on the night of the 8th, just in time to see *Congress* blow up spectacularly. Taking station to protect *Minnesota* she awaited the morrow.

There is little to say about the celebrated *Monitor-Merrimack* duel. It began at about 9:00 a.m. and for two hours the two ships, neither of which was very speedy nor very maneuverable, fired on each other and circled around, with little effect. Each attempted to ram, and *Monitor* once managed to deliver a glancing blow to her adversary, with little effect. At about 11:00 *Monitor* broke off the action for a time in order to bring more ammunition up from her magazine into the turret. About half an hour later she returned to the fray. Soon afterwards a lucky shot struck *Monitor* in the pilot house, temporarily blinding Worden. His second-in-command, Lt. Samuel D. Greene, was in the turret at the time, and the ship drifted off into the shallows, temporarily out of action, before he could assume command.

Seeing the foe drifting away, *Virginia* turned her attention on the nearby *Minnesota*, opening a devastating fire which set her ablaze and sank one of the tugs trying to get her off the shoals. With his ship burning about him, Capt. G.J. Van Brunt let loose a full broadside at the Confederate vessel, 23 guns of 8", 9" and 10" caliber. Every round struck *Virginia* square, and every one bounced off. Just as it seemed *Virginia* was about to make an end to the wounded frigate, *Monitor* returned to the fray. They again circled each other, firing away with little effect. Finally, riding high as her coal was depleted, *Virginia* broke off the action, shortly after noon and steamed away. The battle was over.

In about three hours of pounding each other, both ships had taken some damage. *Monitor's* pilot house had been badly battered, while some of *Virginia's* armor had been severely strained by her opponent's 11" balls. Casualties had been few, even Worden recovered within a few weeks. Tactically it had been a draw. But it need not have been so, for *Monitor* was using reduced charges in her 11" guns. Later experimentation would demonstrate that charges twice the size of those used were possible, and it is probable that had such been used at Hampton Roads that morning *Virginia* would have suffered grievously. As it was, both sides came away claiming the honors of the day. There was never a rematch, and, indeed, neither vessel ever fought again, both coming to sad ends; *Virginia* was blown up on 9 May, after an operational life of but two months, when the Confederates evacuated the Norfolk area, and *Monitor* foundered in a gale on 31 December 1862 off Cape Hatteras, where her hull was recently rediscovered and is now the object of intense study.

Although tactically a draw, the first battle between ironclads had important strategic consequences. *Virginia* was, after all, unable to break the Yankee hold on Hampton Roads, which permitted the Peninsular Campaign to go on and furthered the blockade of the South. And, of course, the engagement was decisive for the introduction of the iron warship.

Army Life

The Medal of Honor

The awarding of decorations for military service and valor did not take root in the United States for a very long time, largely because the practice smacked of aristocracy and seemed incompatible with republican institutions. A medal for distinguished service was authorized during the Revolutionary War, but only three were awarded—to the men who arrested Maj. John Andre, Benedict Arnold's accomplice—before it lapsed, to be revived in the twentieth century as the Purple Heart. To be sure, from time to time Congress did single out particular individuals for a special reward, such as a vote of the "Thanks of Congress," the award of a "sword of honor," or a brevet promotion. Shortly before the War with Mexico, Congress authorized the "Certificate of Merit," a formal diploma awarded to men who distinguished themselves in action, which came with a $2.00 a month pay increase. However none of these involved modifications to the uniform, which is the essence of a military decoration, signaling that the wearer is a person of particular courage and skill. Thus, when the Civil War began, the nation had no systematic way of rewarding valorous conduct. The need for such was recognized quite early in the war.

The lead in creating a decoration for heroism was taken by the Navy. At the request of the secretary of the navy, on 21 December 1861 Congress authorized the award of a "Medal of Honor" to enlisted men of the Navy and Marine Corps who displayed conspicuous courage. After some delay the War Department secured similar authorization on 12 July 1862, which was extended to include officers on 3 March 1863.

Surprisingly, no action was taken under these measures for a quite some time. Not until 25 March 1863 were the first Army Medals of Honor awarded, to the six survivors of the Andrews' Raid, the so-called "Great Locomotive Chase." The Navy was even more tardy than the Army, and did not award its first Medal of Honor until early the following month.

Aside from the Certificate of Merit, which slowly fell into disuse, the Medal of Honor—which also brought $2.00 a month in extra pay—was the nation's sole decoration. Moreover, the conditions under which it could be awarded were rather vaguely defined. In essence, the Medal of Honor could be awarded for heroism in battle, which was clear enough, but also for "distinguished soldierly conduct." And in the Navy it could be awarded for heroism not connected with combat, such as rescues at sea. As a result, the Medal of Honor was granted for deeds which would today merit a considerably lesser decoration.

Nearly 2,400 Medals of Honor were awarded during the Civil War, many on the most dubious pretexts—the entire *27th Maine* received it on one occasion—and often as a result of political pull. In 1916 a review board was convened which disallowed hundreds of such questionable awards, including that to Dr. Mary Walker, which was restored in 1977. As a result, the official awards of the Medal of Honor for the Civil War are:

Personnel	Awards	Awards Ratio/1000	Enlisted Battle Deaths
Army	1,199	0.59	12.6
Navy	310	3.67	146.0
USMC	17	2.53	114.9
Dr. Walker	1		
TOTAL	1,527		

Some idea of the manner in which the Medal of Honor was awarded during the Civil War can be gained by considering the Gettysburg Campaign. From the time the armies left the Rappahannock lines on 9 June, through 26 July 1863, when they returned, there were some 65 awards of the Medal of Honor. Nearly 60 of these were for deeds performed during the battle itself, the highest number of awards for a single engagement in history. The reasons for some of the awards are frankly enigmatic. Thus, 2nd Lt. James K. Durhen, of Company E, *17th West Virginia*, received one for his conduct at the Battle of Winchester (14 June), during which he "led his command over the stone wall, where he was wounded." Many awards went to men who captured Confederate battle flags, fifteen for this reason to men who were on Cemetery Ridge on 3 July, the record being held by the *19th Massachusetts*, which received four, followed by the *14th Connecticut*, with three. Several went to men who saved the colors from the enemy, and many to soldiers who rescued wounded comrades from imminent capture. A great many were awarded for the defense of the artillery, particularly on 2 July. Thus, 2nd Lt. Edward M. Knox, who held his *15th New York Battery* in position until he was down to one gun, which he helped drag to safety despite being severely wounded, and Bugler Charles W. Reed, of the *9th Massachusetts Battery*, who prevented the capture of the wounded battery commander, and Capt. John B. Frasset of *Company F, 23rd Pennsylvania,* who led his regiment to the relief of a beleaguered battery, retaking it from the Rebels, all received one. A number of officers received the Medal of Honor for refusing to leave the field despite severe wounds, most notably Lt. Col. H.S. Huidekoper of the *150th Pennsylvania,* on 1 July. Six men received the Medal of Honor for one incident, when, on 2 July, Sgt. John W. Hart and five other volunteers of the *6th Pennsylvania Reserves* braved intense fire to storm a log cabin which was sheltering five Rebel snipers near the Devil's Den, capturing them all.

Some of the awards are poignant, such as that to Pvt. Jefferson Coates of *Company H, 7th Wisconsin,* who, on 1 July, displayed "unsurpassed courage in battle, during which he had both eyes shot out." Several awards were for consistent distinguished conduct under fire, most notably that to Sgt. Harvey M. Munsell of *Company A, 99th Pennsylvania,* who received his for "gallant and courageous conduct as color bearer," a feat which he performed through 13 separate engagements during the war, and those to Col. Joshua Chamberlain of the *20th Maine* who helped defend Little Round Top and to Brig. Gen. Alexander Webb, who held "the Angle."

The people who did not receive a Medal of Honor are almost as interesting as those who did. Lt. Alonzo H. Cushing of *Battery A, 4th Artillery,* who, on 3 July, died defending Cemetery Ridge literally to the last round, did not receive one, though his sergeant, Frederick Fuger, who survived, did. Neither Brig. Gen. Strong Vincent nor Col. Patrick H. O'Rorke of the *140th New York,* who both fell at the head of their troops during the defense of Little Round Top, received one. This was because very few of the awards were made posthumously. Indeed, remarkably few of the awards were made at the time. Most were granted many years later—the last Civil War awards were made during World War I—and were frequently the result of considerable politicking on the part of the awardee and his regimental veterans organization. This was one reason why Maj. Gen. Daniel Sickles received a Medal of Honor for his less than sterling performance commanding *III Corps* on 2 July, while neither Maj. Gen. John F. Reynolds nor Maj. Gen. Winfield Scott Hancock did for their unusually heroic and valuable services. Reynolds died during the battle, and Hancock in 1886, before Medal of Honor collecting became a fad.

1862

War and the Muses

The Battle Hymn of the Republic

Julia Ward Howe (1819-1910), the daughter of a wealthy New York banker and mother of six, was noted as an abolitionist, women's rights advocate, writer, poetess and reformer. As an editor, with her husband Samuel G. Howe of the abolitionist journal *Commonwealth*, she had several books to her credit before the Civil War. After the war she wrote several more books, became prominent in the international peace movement, and was the first woman elected to the American Academy of Arts and Letters. Despite all of this noteworthy activity, Mrs. Howe is today best remembered for "The Battle Hymn of the Republic."

In December of 1861 Mrs. Howe paid a visit to the *Army of the Potomac* in the company of Governor John A. Andrew of Massachusetts and several other friends. One evening, as their carriage passed among the camp fires of the army, a regiment marched by singing "The John Brown Song." It was an inspiring scene, but the nonsensical words of the song seemed wrong.

That night, as Mrs. Howe lay asleep in her bed at the Willard Hotel, some words came to her which somehow seemed more fitting. She got up and jotted them down in the dark. The next day she revised them and thus was born "The Battle Hymn of the Republic." The song first appeared in print in the February 1862 issue of *The Atlantic Monthly*, for which Mrs. Howe was paid $4.00, a goodly sum at the time. It rapidly became one of the most popular, and certainly the most enduring, of all Civil War songs.

The Battle Hymn of the Republic
Mine eyes have seen the glory of the coming of the Lord:
He is trampling out the vintage where the grapes of wrath are stored;
He hath loosed the fateful lightning of His terrible swift sword:
His truth is marching on.
I have seen Him in the watch-fires of a hundred circling camps;
The have builded him an alter in the evening dews and damps;

I have read His righteous sentence by the dim and flaring lamps:
        His day is marching on.
I have read a fiery gospel writ in burnished rows of steel:
"As ye deal with my contemners, so with you my grace shall deal;
Let the Hero, born of woman, crush the serpent with his heel,
        Since God is marching on."
He has sounded forth the trumpet that shall never call retreat;
He is sifting out the hearts of men before His judgement-seat:
Oh! be swift, my soul, to answer him! be jubilant my feet!
        Our God is marching on!
In the beauty of the lilies Christ was born across the sea,
With a glory in his bosom that transfigures you and me;
As he died to make men holy, let us die to make men free,
        While God goes marching on.

The Battle-Cry of Freedom

George F. Root wrote a number of important songs during the Civil War, including "Tramp, Tramp, Tramp" and "Just before the Battle, Mother," both of which became quite popular. But his most lasting effort was certainly "The Battle-Cry of Freedom." Written in 1861, the song did not catch on until the following year, by which time it had been popularized by two of the most notable singing groups in the nation, the Lombard Brothers and the Hutchinson Family. The song soon became a favorite among the troops, who often sang on the march and in camp. It is said that Confederate troops during the Seven Days and after Fredericksburg despaired of victory when they heard it being sung by the Yankees despite their recent defeats.

The Battle Cry of Freedom
Yes, We'll rally round the flag,
   Boys, we'll rally once again,
   Shouting the battle cry of Freedom,
   We will rally from the hillside, we'll gather from the plain,
   Shouting the battle-cry of Freedom.
Chorus: The Union forever,
   Hurray! boys, Hurrah!
   Down with the traitor, up with the star;
   While we rally round the flag boys, rally once again,
   Shouting the battle-cry of Freedom.
We are springing to the call of our brothers gone before,
   Shouting the battle-cry of Freedom;
And we'll fill the vacant ranks with a million freemen more,

Shouting the battle cry of Freedom.—Chorus
We will welcome to our numbers the loyal, true and brave,
Shouting the battle-cry of Freedom;
And altho' they may be poor, not a man shall be a slave,
Shouting the battle-cry of Freedom.—Chorus
So we're springing to the call from the East and the West,
Shouting the battle cry of Freedom;
And we'll hurl the rebel crew from the land we love the best,
Shouting the battle cry of Freedom.—Chorus

Barbara Fritchie

One of the most famous Civil War poems, "Barbara Fritchie," is based on an incident which occurred during the Antietam Campaign in September of 1862. The poem itself recounts the tale as legend has it. For it is indeed a legend. However the truth, as recounted by several eye-witnesses, is in its way, even more interesting. As Stonewall Jackson's men were passing through Frederick, Maryland, on 6 September, Mrs. Mary A. Quantrill, the loyalist in-law of the notorious Confederate border-ruffian William C. Quantrill, was standing by her gate with her little daughter, both boldly waving Union flags. At first the troops were annoyed at this, but as Mrs. Quantrill and her daughter persisted, irritation turned to admiration, and a Confederate officer—not Jackson, who passed down another street—saluted, saying "To you, madam, not your flag." Barbara Fritchie, already a fixture of town folklore for having once met George Washington, got attached to the story; her daughter even supplied her with a flag which was pointed out as "the" flag. The tale spread, eventually reaching John Greenleaf Whittier, who wrote the poem in good faith.

Barbara Fritchie

Up from the meadows rich with corn,
Clear in the cool September morn,
The clustered spires Frederick stand
Green-walled by the hills of Maryland.
Round about them orchards sweep,
Apple and peach trees fruited deep,
Fair as the garden of the Lord
To the eyes of the famished rebel Horde,
On that pleasant morn of early that fall
When Lee marched over the mountain-wall;
Over the mountains winding down,
Horse and foot, into Frederick town.
Forty flags with their silver stars,

Forty flags with their crimson bars,
Flapped in the morning wind: the sun
Of noon looked down, and saw not one.
Up rose old Barbara Fritchie then,
Bowed with her fourscore years and ten;
In her attic window the staff she set,
To show that one heart was loyal yet.
Up the street came the rebel tread,
Stonewall Jackson riding ahead.
Under his slouched hat left and right
He glanced; the old flag met his sight.
"Halt!"—the dust brown ranks stood fast.
"Fire!"—out blazed the rifle blast.
It shivered the window, pane and sash;
It rent the banner with seam and gash.
Quick, as it fell, from the broken staff
Dame Barbara snatched the silken scarf.
She leaned out the window-sill
And shook it forth with a royal will.
"Shoot if you must, this old gray head,
But spare your country's flag," she said.
A shade of sadness, a blush of shame,
Over the face of the leader came;
The nobler nature within him stirred
To life at that woman's deed and word:
"Who touches a hair of yon gray head
Dies like a dog! March on!" he said.
All day long through Frederick street
Sounded the tread of marching feet:
All day long that flag tree tost
Over the heads of the rebel host.
Ever its torn folds rose and fell
On the loyal winds that loved it well;
And through the hill-gaps sunset light
Shone over it with a warm good-night.
Barbara Fritchie's work is o'er,
And the Rebel rides on his raids no more.
Honor to her! and let a tear
Fall, for her sake, on Stonewall's bier.
Over Barbara Fritchie's grave,
Flag of Freedom and Union, wave!
Peace and order and beauty draw
Round thy symbol of light and law;

And ever the stars look down
On thy stars below Frederick town!

Stonewall Jackson's Way

No other commander in the war inspired as much song and poetry as did
the "Gallant Stonewall." Indeed, so numerous are the pieces dedicated to
him that Bruce Catton once remarked "A volume could be compiled of
poetic tributes to the great Stonewall." One of the best, and certainly the
liveliest, was written by Dr. John W. Palmer, wandering adventurer, journalist, and, at the last, Confederate officer.

Stonewall Jackson's Way

Come, stack arms, men! Pile on the rails,
    Stir up the camp-fire bright;
No matter if the canteen fails,
    We'll make a roaring night.
Here the Shenandoah brawls along,
There burly Blue Ridge echoes strong,
To swell the brigade's rousing song
    Of "Stonewall Jackson's way."
We see him now—the old slouched hat
    Cocked o'er his eyes askew,
The shrewd, dry smile, the speech so pat,
    So calm, so blunt, so true.
The "Blue-Light Elder" knows 'em well;
Says he, "That's Banks—he's fond of shell;
Lord save his soul! we'll give him—well,
    That's Stonewall Jackson's way."
Silence! ground arms! kneel all! caps off!
    Old Blue-Light's going to pray.
Strangle the fool that dares to scoff!
    Attention! it's his way.
Appealing from his native sod,
In *forma pauperis* to God—
"Lay bare thine arm, stretch forth thy rod!
    Amen!" That's Stonewall's way."
He's in the saddle now. Fall in!
    Steady! the whole brigade!
Hill's at the ford, cut off—we'll win
    His way out, ball and blade!
What matter if our shoes are worn?
What matter if our feet are torn?

"Quick -step! we're with him before dawn!"
    That's "Stonewall Jackson's way."
The sun's bright lances rout the mists
    Of morning and by George!
Here's Longstreet struggling in the lists,
    Hemmed in an ugly gorge.
Pope and his Yankees, whipped before,
"Bayonets and grape!" near Stonewall roar;
Ah! maiden, wait and watch and yearn
For news of Stonewall's band!
Ah! widow, read with eyes that burn
    That ring upon thy hand.
Ah! wife, sew on, pray on, hope on!
Thy life shall be forlorn.
The foe had better ne'er been born
    That gets in "Stonewall Jackson's way."

Tenting Tonight

Although written early in the war by Walter Kittredge, of New Hampshire, a popular singer of the day, "Tenting Tonight" was too overtly defeatist and pessimistic to find a publisher. But Kittredge sang it when he joined the army, and it soon became immensely popular with the troops on both sides.

Tenting Tonight
We're tenting tonight on the old camp ground,
Give us a song to cheer our weary hearts,
A song of home, and the friends we love so dear.

Chorus:
    Many are the hearts that are weary tonight,
    Wishing for the war to cease;
    Many are the hearts looking for the right
    To see the dawn of peace.
    Tenting tonight, tenting tonight,
    Tenting on the old camp ground.

We've been tenting tonight on the old camp ground,
Thinking of days gone by, of the loved ones at home
That gave us the hand, and the tear that said "good-bye!"—Chorus

We are tired of war on the old camp ground,

1862

Many are dead and gone, of the brave and true
Who've left their homes, others have been wounded long.—Chorus

We've been fighting today on the old camp ground,
Many are lying near; some are dead
And some are dying, many are in tears.

Last Chorus: Many are the hearts that are weary tonight,
            Wishing for the war to cease;
            Many are the hearts looking for the right,
            To see the dawn of peace.
            Dying tonight, dying tonight,
            Dying on the old camp ground.

IV

1863

An ever kind Providence will bless us with great success.
—Thomas J. Jackson

You have no idea what a horrible sight a battlefield is.
—Robert E. Lee

I consider it an honor to die for my country.
—Paul Jones Semmes

The last full measure of devotion.
—Abraham Lincoln

The North is fighting for Union, for that
insures emancipation.
—Henry Ward Beecher

The mother suffered, and the wife and the child, and the
musing comrade suffered.
—Walt Whitman

1863

By the beginning of 1863 both sides were fully prepared for war, their armies skilled and trained in the hardest of schools, their enthusiasm still high. For the Union, the year opened with a telling political, diplomatic, and propaganda blow, the implementation of the Emancipation Proclamation. But hard fighting would be needed to settle issues. For several months there was much fighting, but all of it on a small scale, guerrilla operations, raids, and the ever-tightening Union naval blockade. When it began, it began in the West, where Ulysses S. Grant was still trying to secure control of the Mississippi by taking Vicksburg.

Beginning in March, Grant made three attempts to turn the Vicksburg position by means of the many swamps and bayous in the area. Each attempt failed, less by force of arms than by the forces of nature. In the spring Grant tried a different approach. Aided by the river fleet under Rear Adm. David Dixon Porter, which successfully ran past the Vicksburg batteries, Grant embarked the bulk of his army, crossed the Mississippi south of the city and advanced eastward, out of supply, with over 40,000 men. This maneuver befuddled Lt. Gen. John Pemberton, commanding the Confederate forces, who wasted precious days trying to sever Grant's non-existent line-of-supply. Meanwhile, Grant secured control of central Mississippi, defeating a Rebel relief column under Gen. Joseph E. Johnston. Grant then turned back on Pemberton. Under orders from Confederate President Jefferson Davis to hold Vicksburg at all costs, Pemberton fell back on the heavily fortified city, permitting Grant to bottle him up there on 18 May 1863, with some 30,000 of the South's finest troops. Grant now laid formal siege to the place. After that it was just a matter of time. Vicksburg surrendered on 4 July. It was a date on which the Union had much to celebrate, for success had crowned its arms in the East as well.

Early in 1863 Lincoln had appointed Maj. Gen. Joseph Hooker to command the *Army of the Potomac*. When Hooker took command the *Army of the Potomac* was in terrible shape. Morale was low, equipment deteriorating, organization clumsy. He undertook the re-equipment of the army, made some changes in its organization, and introduced a rational leave policy for the first time. Morale soared, and desertion was greatly reduced. Having proven himself an even abler administrator than McClellan had been, Hooker went on to demonstrate that he was an even bolder planner. He devised a brilliant scheme to crush Lee and the Army of Northern Virginia. In early April he concentrated some 110,000 men along the Rappahannock in the vicinity of the old Fredericksburg battlefield. He undertook a number of diversionary attacks designed to pin Lee's forces and attentions to the lower Rappahannock. Then he struck, sending the bulk of his forces westward, to cross the Rappahannock on 29 April. Soon he had 75,000 men in Lee's rear, near Chancellorsville, with another 40,000 in front of Lee at Fredericksburg. Lee was suddenly in a seemingly untenable position: his 60,000 men were more or less trapped by two strong Union forces. In a desperate situation, Lee calmly took desperate measures. Leaving a small rear-guard behind, he began to shift forces to confront Hooker on the afternoon of 1 May. The situation remained desperate, for a determined Federal advance would have forced Lee either to accept battle on highly unfavorable terms or retreat, abandoning the Rappahannock line, one of the best defensive positions in Virginia. At this critical juncture, Hooker lost his nerve and pulled back into defensive positions. Then Lee struck boldly, almost desperately. With perhaps 45,000 men in hand, he once more divided his forces, sending Maj. Gen. Thomas "Stonewall" Jackson to turn right flank on 2 May. When Jackson fell on Hooker's right flank it fell back in disorder. Jackson pressed forward after nightfall, but was mortally wounded by one of his own men in the confusion, halting the Confederate drive. Lee's position was still precarious, indeed, his army was now divided into three segments, each of which was greatly inferior to the Federal forces confronting it. A determined stand by Hooker could easily have turned Lee's masterful holding action into a disastrous defeat. That stand was never made. Taking counsel of his fears, Hooker began to pull back on the afternoon of 3 May. The Battle of Chancellorsville was a spectacular victory for the Confederacy. Though the cost had been high, an apparently unbeatable Federal offensive had been stopped. The situation in the Eastern Theater had been restored. And now Lee decided it was once again time to carry the war into the North.

In early June Lee led the Army of Northern Virginia into the Shenandoah Valley, marched it northwards, and debouched into Pennsylvania, as Hooker slowly got the *Army of the Potomac* on the road after him. By 28 June, Confederate forces were foraging over a broad swathe of central

Pennsylvania while the *Army of the Potomac*, under a new commander, Maj. Gen. George Meade, began to close up and march towards him. At this critical moment, Lee's "eyes," his cavalry, failed him, for J.E.B. Stuart had gone off on raid, leaving Lee without effective reconnaissance. And thus, it was only when Maj. Gen. Harry Heth's division ran into some Union cavalrymen at Gettysburg on the morning of 1 July, that Lee knew the *Army of the Potomac* was near at hand. The battle which erupted among the verdant hills and rich fields and sparkling brooks about Gettysburg lasted three days. On the first, Lee crushed the Union forces north and west of the town, driving them back onto Cemetery Ridge. The next day Lt. Gen. James Longstreet's I Corps smashed the Union left wing, south and west of the ridge. And on the 3rd, Lee essayed a massive blow against the center of the Union line, hurling some 12,000 men across nearly a mile of open ground. The slaughter was great and, though some, a gallant few, ascended the crest of Cemetery Ridge, it was a forlorn hope and the shattered regiments drifted back painfully to Lee's lines. On the fourth day Lee waited, hoping Meade would strike back. But Meade, having seen the fate of Lee's attack, and innately cautious, held back. On 5 July Lee slipped away. By the end of the month the armies were back on the Rappahannock. Gettysburg was a blow from which the Confederacy never recovered.

While the high dramas of Chancellorsville, Vicksburg, and Gettysburg were unfolding, the war in the heartland was also reaching a climax.

After months of preparation, in late June Union Maj. Gen. William S. Rosecrans undertook a series of brilliant operations in central Tennessee, driving Confederate Gen. Braxton Bragg back nearly a hundred miles by clever maneuver, finally securing Chattanooga in early September after a virtually bloodless campaign. But then the tables were turned. In a well managed movement, Confederate Lt. Gen. James Longstreet's corps was shifted from Virginia to Tennessee and used to strengthen Bragg's Army of Tennessee for a counterblow. On 19 September, Bragg fell on Rosecrans' widely dispersed army and, in the two day Battle of Chickamauga, threw it back on Chattanooga after a terrible defeat. The Union command reacted swiftly. U.S. Grant was summoned from the Mississippi Valley, Rosecrans was replaced by Maj. Gen. George Thomas, and the Union forces strengthened by the victors of Vicksburg. And on 25 November Thomas led a massive breakout culminating in the storming of seemingly impregnable Missionary Ridge. Within hours, Bragg's Army of Tennessee was streaming rearward. Thus ended the last major operation of 1863.

It had been a year of triumph for the Union, and one of tragedy for the Confederacy.

Incidents of War

Reunion

There are many tales of long-lost kinfolk who encountered each other as a result of the war. In one instance a wounded man in blue found, upon being brought to a hospital, that he had been laid down next to his brother, who wore gray. During the battle of Gettysburg, a Union colonel captured his Confederate nephew. But of all such stories, the strangest is one recounted by Frank Moore in his classic *Anecdotes, Poetry, and Incidents of the War* (New York, 1866).

Nine or ten years ago, a citizen of one of the towns in the eastern part of Massachusetts was unjustly suspected of a crime which the statute cannot easily reach, but which deservedly brings upon him the guilty of it the indignation of upright men. There were circumstances which gave color to the suspicion, and the unfortunate gentleman suffered the misery of loss of friends, business and reputation. His sensitive nature could not face these trials, and he fell into a condition of body and mind which alarmed his family. At length, having invested his property where it could be easily managed by his wife, he suddenly disappeared, leaving her a comfortable home and the care of two boys, ten and twelve years old. The first fear that he had sought a violent death was partly dispelled by the orderly arrangement of his affairs, and the discovery that a daguerreotype of the family group was missing from the parlor table. Not much effort was made to trace the fugitive. When, afterwards, facts were developed which established his innocence of the crime charged, it was found impossible to communicate with him; and as the publication of the story in the columns of several widely-circulated journals failed to recall him, he was generally supposed to be dead.

At the outbreak of the present civil war, his eldest son, now a young man, was induced by a friend, a captain in a Western regiment, to enlist in his company. He carried himself well through campaigns into Missouri and Tennessee, and after the capture of Fort Donelson was rewarded with a First Lieutenant's commission. At the battles of Murfreesboro' he was wounded in the left arm, but so slightly that he was still able to take charge of a squad of wounded prisoners. While performing this duty, he became aware that one of them, a middle-aged man, with a full, heavy beard was looking at him with fixed attention. The day after the fight, as the officer was passing, the soldier gave the military salute, and said:

"A word with you, if you please, sir. You remind me of an old friend. Are you from New England?"

"I am."

"From Massachusetts?"

"Yes."

"And your name?"

The young lieutenant told his name, and why he came to serve in a Western regiment.

"I thought so," said the other, and turning away, he was silent. Although his curiosity was much excited by the soldier's manner, the officer forbore to question him, and withdrew. But in the afternoon he took occasion to renew the conversation, and expressed the interest awakened in him by the incident of the morning.

"I knew your father," said the prisoner. "Is he well?"

"We have not seen him for several years. We think he is dead."

Then followed such an explanation of the circumstances of his disappearance as the young man could give. He had never known the precise nature of the charges against his father, but was able to make it quite clear that his innocence had been established.

"I knew your mother, also," continued the soldier. "I was in love with her when she married your father."

"I have a letter dated from her, dated ten days ago. My brother is a nine months' man at New Orleans."

After a little desultory conversation the soldier took from under his coat a leather wallet and disclosed a daguerreotype case.

"Will you oblige me," he said, "by looking at this alone in your tent?" Agitated almost beyond control, the young officer took the case and hurried away. He had seen the picture before! It represented a man and a woman, sitting side by side, with a boy at the knee of each.

The romantic story moved the commander of the division to grant the youth a furlough; and both father and son reached home soon after.

The Medal of Honor Regiment

All 864 members of the *27th Maine* were awarded the Medal of Honor during the Gettysburg Campaign. The veteran regiment was nearly at the expiration of its enlistment when the crisis of the Gettysburg Campaign erupted. As an inducement to encourage the regiment to stay with the colors a bit longer, Lincoln authorized the award of the Medal of Honor to any man in the regiment who extended his enlistment until the danger was passed. Such an award was in keeping with the original purpose of the Medal of Honor, at that time the nation's only decoration, designed essentially to reward distinguished soldierly conduct. Only 311 men of the regiment volunteered. Moreover, the campaign unfolded so rapidly that they saw no action. Within a short time they were mustered out with the rest of their regiment. As it turned out, there was no official list of the 311 volunteers, so the War Department couldn't figure out which of the men of the *27th Maine* deserved a medal and which did not. The wheels of Army bureaucracy began to turn. In the end it was decided to award the Medal of Honor to each of the 864 men originally in the regiment, whether they had volunteered to extend their enlistments or not. Years later, in 1916, a board was convened to review the suitability of all prior awards. The result was that the 864 given to the men of the *27th Maine* comprised the bulk of the 911 awards which were disallowed and rescinded.

Above and Beyond the Call of Duty

The courage, discipline, and devotion of the Confederate soldier in battle has never been in doubt. But the nobler qualities of the men in gray were probably never put to a sterner test than on 30 June 1863, during the Gettysburg Campaign. As reported by Lt. Col. Arthur Fremantle, a British observer on the scene, a considerable store of whiskey was discovered in Chambersburg, a small town not far from Gettysburg, in south central Pennsylvania. As one of the reasons for the invasion of Pennsylvania was to lay in supplies for the army, a great deal of this whisky was gathered up along with less exciting items like victuals and shoes. But not all of the fire water could be taken. Since leaving so much alcohol lying around might create a problem, a contingent of Texas troops from Brig. Gen. Jerome B. Robertson's brigade were assigned to destroy it. The temptation was great, for the men had been marching for weeks with little opportunity to relax. Nevertheless, as Fremantle put it, "they did their duty like good soldiers," in the face of a threat to their courage, discipline, and devotion as great as any ever posed by Yankees shot, shell, and ball.

A Sort of Sentinel

While the fighting qualities of Johnny Reb were beyond question, he was generally a little less than soldierly about the soldiering side of war. The informal and individualistic Rebels generally ignored what would today be called the "Mickey Mouse" of military life, including respect for rank. Nothing less than a full general—and then possibly only Robert E. Lee—was likely to be held in awe by the average Southern soldier. An incident which occurred in the Army of Northern Virginia illustrates both points quite neatly. The form given here was pieced together from several different versions.

In mid-1863 the 11th Mississippi was transferred to the Army of Northern Virginia, becoming part of Maj. Gen. Henry Heth's division, just in time for Gettysburg and all the hard campaigns which followed it. In the same division there was an Alabama regiment—the 13th Alabama seems to be meant—the colonel of which was a stickler for the minutia of military life. One day this colonel was making the rounds of the division's lines in his capacity as field officer of the day. As he walked from post to post he came upon a rifleman of the 11th Mississippi sitting on the ground, quietly cleaning his weapon, which he had taken to pieces. The stunned colonel said, "Don't you know that a sentinel, while on duty, should always keep on his feet?"

Without looking up, the Mississippian replied, "That's the way we used to do it when the war first began; but that's played out long ago."

Wondering if the man was, indeed, the sentry, the colonel asked, "Are you the sentinel here?"

Continuing at his task, the man replied "Well, I'm a sort of a sentinel."

"Well," shouted the now very angry colonel, "I'm a sort of officer of the day."

Still not looking, the man replied "Well, if you'll hold on 'til I sort of git my gun together, I'll give you a sort of salute."

A Busy Day at the Oakridge Seminary

For many years during the mid-nineteenth century Miss Carrie Shead ran the Oakridge Seminary, a school for young ladies in the family home on the Chambersburg Pike, just west of the little town of Gettysburg, in southern central Pennsylvania. On the afternoon of 1 July the Battle of Gettysburg engulfed her home as Union forces began to fall back from

Seminary Ridge, just to the west. Miss Shead—who had four brothers fighting for the Union, two of whom died in the war—declared school over for the day and, with her assistants and her students, turned the place into an improvised hospital. During the morning's fighting about 75 wounded were brought to the house. Then, with the pressure against the Union forces northwest of the town becoming irresistible, the tide of battle swept past the house. As the tired troops retreated on Gettysburg, some took shelter in the Shead house. One such was Col. Charles Wheelock of the *97th New York.*

Wheelock ran into the house, closely followed by several Confederate soldiers intent on taking him prisoner. He fled down into the cellar, but the Rebels—and Miss Shead—followed him. A Confederate sergeant demanded that Wheelock give up his sword. The latter refused. An argument ensued in which both Miss Shead and her aged father became involved. Then, before the sergeant could take the sword by main force, a second group of Rebels came down the stairs, herding some Yankee prisoners. Some confusion ensued. After a moment, however, the sergeant renewed his demand for Wheelock's sword. But it was gone, taken, Wheelock said, by one of the other Confederate soldiers. The sergeant went off angrily, deprived of his precious souvenir. Wheelock was later herded out of the house with several other prisoners.

Miss Shead and her little flock tended the wounded for the duration of the battle and for several days thereafter, until the army's field hospitals relieved them of the task. Remarkably, although under fire for much of the first day of the battle, neither Miss Shead nor any of her charges was injured, despite the fact that the house was hit more than 60 times. But the end of the battle and the departure of the wounded were not the end of Miss Shead's adventures. On 9 July Col. Wheelock, having escaped his captors during their retreat, turned up at the Shead house to pay his compliments to Miss Carrie and to recover his sword, which she had hidden under her skirt. Nor was that all.

The Shead house had been crowded that first day of July. Aside from Col. Wheelock, Pvt. Asa Hardman of the *3rd Indiana Cavalry* had also taken refuge there, after fighting all morning along Seminary Ridge. He too was taken prisoner, but was unable to elude his captors. Eventually exchanged, Hardman also paid a return visit to the Sheads, so that he could marry Carrie's sister Louisa.

The Old Hero of Gettysburg

In 1863 there lived in the little town of Gettysburg one John Burns. Burns, about 70, was no stranger to war, for he had served in the War of 1812, against Mexico, and as an Indian fighter. Nevertheless, although a staunch Union man, he planned to sit this one out. Until, that is, the war came to him, for that June, Robert E. Lee brought his splendid Army of Northern Virginia into southern Pennsylvania. As the Rebel troops spread out over the countryside, they foraged with a will. Around the 20th, a Confederate foraging party seized Burns' cows. Then, on the 1st of July Union and Confederate forces clashed northwest of the town. Burns sat in his rocking chair all morning listening to the fighting. Finally, he decided he had to get into it himself.

Burns took his old state militia musket down off the wall. His wife asked what he was doing.

"Ah," replied Burns, "I thought some of the boys might want the old gun, and I am getting it ready for them." Then he headed for the door.

"Where are you going?"

Saying, "Oh, I'm going out to see what is going on," Burns slipped out of the house, and headed towards the sound of the fighting.

Around noon the men of the Union *I Corps* were holding back strong Confederate forces along the line on McPherson's Ridge. Suddenly Maj. Edward P. Halstead, of the corps staff, saw an elderly gentleman walking towards the ridge with a musket on his shoulder and a powder horn in his pocket. "Which way are the Rebels?" the old man asked, "Where are our troops?" Halstead told him that they were just ahead and that he would soon find them.

Within minutes the elderly gentleman took his place in the line alongside the men of the *150th Pennsylvania*, most young enough to be his grandsons. At first the youngsters were amused by the little man who wore a blue, swallow-tail coat with smooth brass buttons, and joked with him a bit. Seeing the ancient flintlock musket he carried they offered him a rifle. He waved it away, as he did also when given a cartridge box, saying "I'm not used to them new-fangled things." Then he had at the Rebels.

The fighting was hot, and Burns seems to have accounted for at least three of the foe, as he fought first with the *150th Pennsylvania*, and then, when the *Iron Brigade* came up with the *7th Wisconsin* and the *24th Michigan*, who convinced him to try one of the "new-fangled" muskets, which proved to his liking. Burns later had high praise for the boys alongside whom he had fought, telling Lt. Frank Haskell—who later wrote an excellent account of the battle— "They fit terribly. The Rebs couldn't make anything of them fellers." The troops returned the compliment. While with the *24th Michigan*, Burns, who already had two slight wounds, was hit again, taking a bullet in the belt buckle which left him unable to continue, though not seriously hurt. As Confederate pressure increased, the Union troops were forced back, abandoning their wounded, including John Burns. When the Rebels came up he told them a tale about having blundered into the fighting while on an errand to fetch help for his ailing wife. The ruse succeeded, for the Rebels took pity on the old fellow and carried him to his home, where he recovered in a few days.

After the battle the old man became a popular figure. Lincoln met with him when he visited Gettysburg on the occasion of his famous address, and the two attended church together, an unusual activity for the crusty old Burns, who had hitherto been considered something of a crank. Later a special Act of Congress granted him a pension of $8.00 a month. He died in 1872, full of years and honor.

The Jackson Cotton Works

On 15 May 1863, having just taken Jackson, Mississippi, U.S. Grant and William T. Sherman took a stroll about town. They chanced upon a cotton mill, busily at work, oblivious to the fact that a battle had been fought for the town and that it was now occupied by Union troops. Moreover, no one paid the least bit of attention to the pair when they entered the place. A great many women were tending various machines which were turning out tent cloth by the mile, with "C.S.A." neatly woven into each bolt. The two generals toured the installation for a bit. Then Grant turned to Sherman, saying "I think they have done work enough." He ordered all work to cease and told the women that they could take as much cloth as they wished. Then he had the place burned down. As an incident of war, it was a minor one and soon forgotten. Forgotten that is, until one day many years later.

Years later, when Grant was president, a Southern gentleman turned up in Washington and requested a meeting. The man stated that he had been the owner of the cotton mill in Jackson which Grant had put to the torch. Claiming that the place was private property, he asked Grant to give him a statement testifying to the fact that it had been burned at Grant's orders, for he wished to lay a claim for recompense on the Congress. Grant demurred, the laconic "I declined" which appears in his memoirs perhaps concealing somewhat stronger sentiments on the matter.

"Girls! We Must Do Something!"

During a lull in the Mississippi Campaign a young Confederate soldier decided to spend a night at the home of a local family with whom he had occasion in the past to spend some pleasant evenings, though whether it was because they laid a heavy table or because they had two charming young daughters cannot be determined. By chance, his habits had become known to the Yankees, for the family home lay within Federal lines, and on this night they decided to capture him. Not long after the lights in the house had gone out, a Union patrol began hammering on the front door, demanding entry. As the master of the house tried to stall the Bluecoats, his nightgowned daughters rushed to the young man's bed to wake him. Alas, though he was up in an instant, there could be no escape, for the patrol was already rumbling through the house, and there was neither a window nor a door which would permit easy flight. Just ahead of the pushy Yankees the mistress of the house came rushing into the young man's room, shouting "Girls! We must do something—the Yankees are already in the passage!" Suddenly, even as the Yankees were opening the door, the two daughters of the South leaped into the bed, to lie one on each side of the young fellow, concealing him between them. Never was there such turmoil as when the Bluecoats entered the bedroom, for the young ladies screamed and carried on for their lost modesty, clutching the bed clothes close about themselves as the Yankees searched every corner of the room, peered into closets, and probed under the bed itself, but not once, not even for an instant, thinking to look in the bed. Finally, the search having proven fruitless, the Yankees left and the young man was safe.

Share and Share Alike

During the Mine Run Campaign the Army of Northern Virginia and the *Army of the Potomac* confronted each other across the little creek of that name for several days (28 November-1 December), in anticipation of a battle which would not take place. On one bitterly cold morning the videttes of both armies were ignoring each other, as was by then in the war traditional, lest someone get hurt. It was boring duty, with time dragging ever onwards. Suddenly a sheep strayed into view and walked slowly along the creek, on the Confederate side. In an instant, one of the Rebel videttes took a bead, fired, and felled the animal. Dropping his rifle, the man advanced to claim his prize. As he did, a Yankee picket from just across the creek called out, "Divide is the word, or you are a dead Johnny," covering the man with his rifle as he did.

Seeing the irrefutable logic of the Yankee's argument, the Rebel assented and soon fell to skinning and cleaning the poor sheep, as dozens of other videttes, both Blue and Gray, looked on. Soon completing his work, the Rebel took half the carcass and retreated to his post. In an instant, the Yankee put down his rifle and crossed the creek to claim his half of the unfortunate animal, then retraced his steps, to be greeted by the cheers of his comrades, anticipating a share in the booty. Both men then resumed the work at hand, keeping an eye on each other's lines, in case those in higher authority might decide to resume the war.

The Men

George G. Meade

Although his family had its roots in Pennsylvania, George G. Meade (1815-1872) was born in Cadiz, Spain, where his father had mercantile interests. He graduated from West Point 19th in the class of 1835, but resigned from the army the following year to practice civil engineering. In 1842 he reentered the army as a lieutenant of Topographical Engineers and was thereafter employed almost continuously in a variety of navigational engineering projects, including lighthouse construction, coastal surveys, and port development, save for a tour of duty in Mexico, where he won a brevet. In 1861 Meade was named a brigadier general of volunteers at the urging of Governor Andrew G. Curtin of Pennsylvania and given a brigade of Pennsylvania troops. He led his brigade ably in the Peninsular Campaign, where on one occasion he was wounded twice, and at Second Bull Run. He was then given a division under Hooker in *I Corps*, leading it at Antietam and Fredericksburg. At the end of 1862 he was made a major general and given *V Corps*, which he led at Chancellorsville. Hooker's manifest inability to lead the *Army of the Potomac* in the early days of the Gettysburg Campaign saw Meade appointed to its command on 28 June, after Maj. Gens. John Reynolds, John Sedgwick, and Henry W. Slocum, all senior to Meade, indicated a willingness to serve under him.

Meade assumed command of the *Army of the Potomac* at a critical time, with Lee's Army of Northern Virginia on the march in central Pennsylvania. Within two days of taking over, he had to confront Lee in the Battle of Gettysburg, which, under the circumstances, he did with considerable success, inflicting a serious defeat on the best general and army in the Confederacy. His movements thereafter have been criticized, but the balance of opinion seems to agree that his caution was well-founded. For the balance of 1863 he showed a good deal of ability during the series of maneuvers known as the Bristoe (9 October-9 November) and Mine Run Campaigns (26 November-2 December). In early 1864, when Lt. Gen. Ulysses S. Grant assumed command of the Union forces, Meade offered his resignation if the latter wanted it. Grant declined and Meade continued to lead the *Army of the Potomac* to the end of the war, maintaining a delicate, but friendly relationship with Grant.

After the war Meade was made a regular major general and served in a variety of administrative posts until his death. A modest, unassuming man, Meade could display considerable anger if confronted by stupidity or ineptitude. By no means a brilliant soldier, Meade nevertheless understood his mission, was careful of his troops, was open to advice, and was willing to fight to the utmost when necessary, precisely the qualities which earned him the command of the *Army of the Potomac*, in which he served ably if not spectacularly. As a soldier Lee summed him up well when he remarked "Meade will commit no blunder...."

Brother Against Brother

George G. Meade was an almost perfect example of how the Civil War divided some families. Two of his sisters married Southerners and were ardent secessionists, their husbands serving in the Confederate forces. The husbands of his other three sisters all served the Republic, and his brother was a captain in the U.S. Navy. Meade's son served on his staff at Gettysburg. Mrs. Meade's sister was married to Henry A. Wise, who had signed John Brown's death warrant while Governor of Virginia, and during the war served as a Confederate brigadier general.

James Longstreet

A native of South Carolina, James Longstreet (1821-1904) graduated West Point 54th out of 62 in the class of 1842. He served in the infantry against the Seminoles, with distinction in Mexico (one wound, two brevets), on the frontier, and in garrison until resigning on 1 June 1861 as a paymaster major. He immediately sought appointment in Confederate service and was made a brigadier general, leading a brigade at Bull Run the following month. That October he was promoted major general and given a division, which he led with distinction in the opening phases of the Peninsular Campaign in early 1862. Longstreet performed poorly when given a higher command shortly thereafter, but redeemed himself during the Seven Days Battles and was ever after in Lee's confidence, commanding what would become the I Corps of the Army of Northern Virginia. He led his corps—designated a "wing" until late in '62—with considerable ability during the Second Bull Run and Antietam Campaigns, and was promoted lieutenant general in time for Fredericksburg. In the spring of 1863 he briefly took the corps on a expedition along the Carolina coasts, returning to Virginia in time for the Gettysburg Campaign. Throughout the Confederate invasion of Pennsylvania, Longstreet maintained serious reservations over the wisdom of the daring offensive.

During the Battle of Gettysburg, Longstreet's I Corps bore the brunt of the fighting, particularly on 2 and 3 July. Longstreet was notably dissatisfied with Lee's offensive plans for both days, and his doubts have tended to be confirmed in retrospect. After Gettysburg, Longstreet took his corps west in September of 1863 to support Braxton Bragg's operations in Tennessee and he was largely responsible for the Confederate victory at Chickamauga, but did poorly around Knoxville on his own. Returning to Virginia in early 1864, he was seriously wounded by his own men at the Wilderness in May, not returning to duty until October. He then led his corps in all the succeeding battles of the Army of Northern Virginia from Petersburg to Appomattox, where he was the only general officer to urge continued resistance if the terms offered by Grant were dishonorable.

After the war Longstreet settled in New Orleans, where he became a Republican and a supporter of Reconstruction, once commanding black militiamen against a rioting white mob. These stands compounded the difficulties Longstreet was beginning to have with his erstwhile comrades-in-arms. After the death of Lee his reputation was besmirched by Jubal Early and William Nelson Pendleton, who attempted to place all blame for the reverse at Gettysburg on him, despite the fact that he had retained Lee's confidence to the end. Longstreet was afterwards made minister to Turkey by President Grant, who became a close friend, wrote his memoirs, and served in a variety of other government posts. In 1896 the widowed Longstreet married Helen Dortch, a beautiful young woman over 40 years his junior who survived until 1962, the last Confederate general's wife to die. Nicknamed "Old Pete" by the troops and "Old War Horse" by Lee, before the war Longstreet had been a merry, affable man, but had become reserved and "cheerless" after three of his daughters died of scarlet fever in Richmond in the winter of 1861-1862. An excellent corps commander, with a good eye for ground and a fine tactical sense, he had little talent for independent command. As a soldier, his reputation has been long in recovering from the attacks of his enemies.

Joseph Hooker

A native of Massachusetts, Hooker (1814-1879) was educated in local schools and graduated from West Point 29th in the class of 1837. He served with great distinction in the Mexican War, winning three brevets.

Subsequently on the Pacific Coast, he resigned from the army in 1853 after a two year leave of absence, and took up farming in northern California, at which he was unsuccessful, while becoming active in the militia. Hooker attempted to reenter the army in 1858 but his application was ignored and his fortunes steadily declined. He returned to the army on the outbreak of the Civil War, being made a brigadier general of volunteers in August of 1861.

Hooker commanded a brigade in the defenses of Washington, and later a division in the *Army of the Potomac* during the Peninsular Campaign, serving in *III Corps*, during which he earned the nickname "Fighting Joe Hooker" as a result of a telegraphic error in a newspaper story. In the Peninsula, during the Second Bull Run Campaign, and at Antietam, Hooker displayed considerable talents as a soldier, rising to the command of *I Corps*. At Fredericksburg he was given overall direction of several corps comprising the Federal center. His severe criticism of Maj. Gen. Ambrose E. Burnside's conduct of this battle precipitated the latter's relief, whereupon his connections with Secretary of the Treasury Salmon P. Chase and several other cabinet members secured him command of the *Army of the Potomac* in Burnside's stead early in 1863. Hooker proved an able and popular administrator. Operationally, however, he left much to be desired.

Hooker developed a brilliant plan for the Chancellorsville Campaign but totally bungled its execution. His confusion during the early days of the Gettysburg Campaign led to his removal on 28 June 1863. Subsequently he commanded a pair of corps sent West the following September, serving with some distinction in the operations around Chattanooga. Nevertheless, he was relieved "at his own request" later that year because he preferred not to serve under an officer to whom he was senior. Hooker saw no further combat service and retired from the Regular Army as a major general in 1868.

Hooker was an excellent example of an officer promoted beyond his abilities. Fairly good as a corps commander, he was inept and confused when given an army.

Charles Bruner

Charles Bruner was one of numberless ordinary people caught up in the cauldron of war. A native of Northampton County, Pennsylvania, he chanced to be in Wisconsin at the start of the war. When the *23rd Wisconsin* was organized in 1862 he enlisted, the only Pennsylvanian in the regiment. During his war service he had a distinguished career, rising to captain.

Bruner first attracted attention at Port Gibson (1 May 1863), the opening battle of Grant's final Vicksburg Campaign. Leading about 50 men of his regiment, Bruner was among the first men to enter the Confederate fort. As they attacked, the color sergeant was hit. Seizing the colors, Bruner led his men forward, planting the flag on the ramparts despite heavy enemy fire. Two weeks later, at Champion Hill (16 May), Bruner's regiment showed signs of breaking as it attempted to assault a Confederate entrenchment. Taking the colors in hand, Bruner cried out "Boys, follow! Don't flinch from your duty!" and led the men forward again, to take and hold the enemy position. On the very next day, Bruner's regiment was again in action, at the Battle of the Big Black River.

At the Big Black, a short but heated affair, Bruner's *Company B, 23rd Wisconsin,* was given orders to support the planting of a cannon so that a troublesome Confederate battery could be brought under fire. The piece was emplaced and soon hotly engaged, with most of its crew and their infantry supports put out of action. Bruner rallied the men in time to beat off a determined enemy attack in hand-to-hand combat, during which he was several times on the verge of capture. There followed the siege of Vicksburg and occupation duty, and, in 1864, more campaigning with the *XVII Corps.*

Although Bruner served through to the end of the war, he was never afterwards called upon to display the heroic qualities which he had so well demonstrated in the Vicksburg Campaign. Altogether he fought in over a dozen major battles, personally capturing three enemy battle flags, yet does not seem to have ever been wounded. A singular record.

Braxton Bragg

A native of North Carolina, Braxton Bragg (1817-1876) graduated from West Point in the class of 1837. He served in the artillery against the Seminoles, on the frontier, and in Mexico, where he particularly distinguished himself, winning three brevets. Bragg left the Old Army as a lieutenant colonel in 1856 to become a planter in Louisiana. At the start of the war Jefferson Davis is believed to have briefly contemplated making Bragg secretary of war, but instead appointed him a brigadier general and sent him to command on the Gulf coast in 1861. Later that year he was made a major general and given a corps, which he led at Shiloh. On the basis of his not particularly spectacular performance at Shiloh, Davis, a personal friend, made him a full general in the Regular Army and gave him command of the Army of Tennessee in June of 1862. Bragg's career was thereafter inextricably bound up with that of his command.

Bragg launched an invasion of Kentucky in August of 1862 only to be defeated in the Battle of Perryville (8 October). He later saw a potential victory slip through his grasp at Murfreesboro, Tennessee (31 December 1862-2 January 1863). Forced to retreat into southwestern Tennessee by Union Maj. Gen. William S. Rosecrans' Tullahoma Operation in July of 1863, Bragg restored Confederate fortunes in the theater by his smashing victory at Chickamauga (18-19 September 1863), but was unable to eject the *Army of the Cumberland* from Chattanooga. On 25 November reinforced Union forces delivered a crushing blow against the Army of Tennessee at Missionary Ridge, after which, Bragg resigned his command in favor of Gen. Joseph E. Johnston.

Jefferson Davis then appointed Bragg to serve as a sort of chief of staff, advising the president on military matters and strategy. Bragg was largely ineffective in this post, though the fault lay elsewhere: Davis preferred to keep his own counsels. When Lee was made general-in-chief, Bragg was given a division during Joe Johnston's Carolina Campaign in early 1865, which he led with some skill during the closing weeks of the war.

Although by no means an incompetent organizer or planner, Bragg lacked the intellectual and emotional flexibility necessary to be a good commander, and often took counsel of his fears. In addition, he had serious defects of character which caused him to quarrel with his subordinates, who consequently had little confidence in his abilities. Allan Nevins summed up the man well when he said "Bragg wore failure as a habit."

Ulysses S. Grant

Born in a small town in Ohio, Hiram Ulysses Grant (1822-1885) became Ulysses Simpson Grant due to an error on a letter of recommendation to West Point, which he entered in 1839. Although an indifferent, rather indolent student, he did moderately well at the academy, graduating in 1843. Although he was a fine horseman, he was commissioned a brevet 2nd lieutenant in the *4th Infantry* as there were no openings in the cavalry. He spent the next four years on garrison duty with his regiment, and followed it to Texas in 1845. During the Mexican War Grant, who believed the struggle to be unjust, served under two commanders who would greatly influence his own military style, Zachary Taylor and Winfield Scott. Grant distinguished himself as a regimental quartermaster under Taylor in Northern Mexico and as a combat officer at Vera Cruz, Molino del Rey, and Chapultepec, during Scott's brilliant Mexico City Campaign, winning two brevets. After the war, he was assigned to duty on the Pacific Coast, during which he was rumored to have developed an unusual fondness for the bottle, a charge which, though apparently exaggerated, would plague him for the rest of his life. In mid-1854 Grant resigned his commission. Grant was unsuccessful in civilian life, being variously a farmer, realtor, peddler, political candidate, and civil servant, before going to work for his two brothers as a clerk in their leather goods store in Galena, Illinois. At the age of 38, U.S. Grant was an undoubted failure with a wife and two children to support. Then the Civil War broke out.

On the start of the war Grant served as an informal drill instructor for several volunteer companies in the Galena area, while trying to secure a commission in the volunteer army. Plagued by rumors of drunkenness, he got nowhere for several months. Finally, in June of 1861 Representative Elihu B. Washburn, mindful of the importance of patronage, convinced Gov. Richard Yates of Illinois to make Grant colonel of the *21st Illinois.* Grant did such a good job whipping the regiment into shape, that, again with the help of Washburn, he was made a brigadier general of volunteers in August, with his commission pre-dated to May. Grant was soon sent to Cairo, Illinois, where he headed the District of Southern Missouri, an amorphous command embracing southern Illinois, western Kentucky, and southeastern Missouri. Much of the balance of the year was spent in administrative and logistical preparations, but Grant did essay one offensive move, the brief Belmont Campaign, in November. Although the operation was a failure, it was an important educational experience. By the beginning of 1862 Grant, under the overall authority of Maj. Gen. Henry Halleck, was ready for some serious campaigning.

Grant first came to public notice as a result of his campaign against Forts Henry and Donelson on the Tennessee River in Kentucky in February of 1862, during which he captured an entire Confederate Army, earning the nickname "Unconditional Surrender" and a major generalcy in the bargain. This operation permitted the Union to overrun much of central and western Tennessee, so that by the beginning of April, Grant's army had reached Pittsburgh Landing, within a few miles of the Alabama and Mississippi state lines. There he suffered a near-disaster in Gen. Albert Sidney Johnston's surprise attack on 6 April. Nevertheless, the Battle of Shiloh turned into a Union victory on 7 April. Grant's next objective was Vicksburg, which dominated the Mississippi River.

Grant made five unsuccessful attempts on Vicksburg over the next year.

A direct approach was frustrated by Confederate cavalrymen such as Nathan Bedford Forrest and Earl Van Dorn, who interdicted his supply lines, creating insurmountable logistical problems. Efforts to secure a passage through the many bayous and marshes were blocked by a combination of natural obstacles and minor Confederate victories. Finally, on 30 April 1863 he landed his army on the east bank of the Mississippi, some 50 miles downstream from Vicksburg. Once ashore, he cut his communications and launched his forces inland. Skillful maneuvering and a couple of hard-fought battles over the next two weeks divided the forces of Confederate Lt. Gen. John Pemberton and Gen. Joseph Johnston, and drove the former into the defenses of the town on 18 May. After two ill-advised attempts to storm the place, Grant settled down to a formal siege. Vicksburg surrendered on 4 July. After Vicksburg Grant engaged in operations to secure control of central Mississippi and then led his army to the relief of Chattanooga in November. In March of 1864 Grant was called east by President Lincoln, promoted to lieutenant general, and made general-in-chief. On 4 May 1864 Grant began what he believed would be a decisive campaign against Robert E. Lee and the Army of Northern Virginia.

Grant's strategy was simple, to maintain continuous pressure on Lee so that the latter would be forced to give battle under the most unfavorable terms possible, in the hope of defeating Lee in the field by forcing his army to fight for its lines of communication. Grant realized that only a sustained offensive could end the war. The result was his Overland Campaign, which in a period of little more than two months drove Lee from the Rappahannock to the gates of Richmond, in a series of devastating battles and hard marches. Grant failed to secure the destruction of the Army of Northern Virginia in the open, through a combination of Lee's tactical skills and the enormous defensive abilities of the Confederate soldier. The result was a protracted investment of Richmond and Petersburg which lasted through the winter of 1864-1865. As this pinned Lee and his fine army to Virginia, Grant's alter-ego, William T. Sherman, was able to grind his way through the vitals of the Confederacy virtually unhindered. Thus, when Grant resumed offensive operations in the spring, the result was never in doubt.

After the war Grant, a political novice, was elected president, serving for two terms, 1869-1877. Although personally honest, his administration was the most corrupt in American history until the Harding and Reagan years. Upon leaving the White House he made a triumphal world tour. In 1880 he rejected an offer to run for the Presidency again and in the following year went into the banking business in New York, only to go broke three years later when his partners defrauded him. In an effort to recoup his finances, he began to write his memoirs, which he completed just a few days before his death from cancer.

Grant's abilities as a soldier have been the subject of some controversy. Certainly the most consistently successful Union commander, he has often been accused of engaging in pure attrition warfare, a charge which seems unjust. To be sure, his operations against Lee in 1864-1865 were enormously costly, but no more so than the combined losses of the successive Union offensives in the East from Bull Run to Chancellorsville, which had even less result. On the other hand, his efforts against Vicksburg demonstrated considerable flexibility, creativity, and economy and he conceived of the Union grand strategy for the final year of the war, including Sherman's devastating "March to the Sea." As with a number of other commanders, Grant's reputation had grown with the years.

William S. Rosecrans

A native of Ohio, William Starke Rosecrans (1819-1898) had a haphazard education, but nevertheless managed to graduate fifth in the West Point Class of 1838, entering the prestigious Corps of Engineers. His military service, entirely administrative, ended in 1854, when he resigned to go into business. Although he attempted several professions, civil engineering, architecture, refining, his civilian career was not a success. Rosecrans reentered the service at the start of the war as a colonel, initially as an aide-de-camp to newly appointed Maj. Gen. George B. McClellan, and shortly thereafter as commander of the *23rd Ohio*. He was, however, almost immediately appointed a brigadier general in the Regular Army and led a brigade with some distinction in western Virginia (Rich Mountain, 11 July 1861), helping to drive Robert E. Lee out of the area. He later led a division with skill at Corinth (22-30 May 1862) and then the *Army of the Mississippi* at Iuka (19 September 1862) and Corinth (3 - 4 October 1862), by which time he had been promoted major general. Given command of the *Army of the Cumberland* on 27 October 1862, Rosecrans led it at Murfreesboro (31 December 1862-2 January 1863), and, after a long period of relative inactivity, in the brilliantly conceived and executed Tullahoma Operation (23 June-3 July 1863), and in the initially successful but ultimately disastrous Chickamauga Campaign (August-September 1863) until relieved on 19 October for letting himself be blockaded in Chattanooga.

During 1864 Rosecrans commanded the *Department of Missouri*, but was effectively unemployed thereafter, eventually resigning from the service in 1867, after over two years of inactivity. In subsequent years Rosecrans served briefly as Minister to Mexico (1868), Representative from California (1881-1885), and Register of the Treasury (1885-1893). An excellent organizer and brilliant planner, the devoutly Roman Catholic Rosecrans—his brother was a bishop—was meticulous about logistical matters and well-liked by his troops. In battle, however, he was slow to react and unlucky, which led William M. Lamers to aptly title his biography of Rosecrans *The Edge of Glory.*

Abner Doubleday

Doubleday (1819-1893) came from a family prominent in upstate New York; his grandfather was a Revolutionary War veteran and his father had served in Congress. Young Doubleday served as a civil engineer for two years before entering West Point, from which he graduated in 1842, 24th in a class which also included Richard H. Anderson, Lafayette McLaws, and James Longstreet. Doubleday served in the artillery in Mexico and against the Seminoles, but had an otherwise uneventful career until April of 1861, when he was part of the tiny garrison of Ft. Sumter; on 12 April Doubleday fired the first Union shot of the war.

Doubleday served in the Shenandoah Valley against Stonewall Jackson during the latter's brilliant campaign in 1862, and at Second Bull Run, by which time he was a brigadier general of volunteers. Doubleday commanded a division in *I Corps* at Antietam, Fredericksburg, and Chancellorsville, and led it into the Gettysburg Campaign. On 1 July he assumed temporary command of *I Corps* on the death of Maj. Gen. John Reynolds and attempted to hold the Army of Northern Virginia north and west of the town. After the retreat to Cemetery Hill, Doubleday returned to his division—Meade having reservations about his ability to lead a corps—which he led ably in the defense of Cemetery Ridge on 3 July. He was shortly relieved of command and did not serve again in the field, holding a variety of administrative posts in Washington. At the war's end he was named a major general of volunteers and colonel of the new *35th Infantry,* in which rank he retired from the Regular Army in 1873.

As a commander Doubleday, who had two brothers in blue, had a deliberate manner which earned him the nickname "Old Forty-eight Hours". Although his performance was satisfactory, it was by no means brilliant, and Meade's decision to relieve him of *I Corps* was probably correct. There is little beyond tradition to identify Doubleday with the invention of baseball—the rules of which he is alleged to have written in 1839, at the age of 19, when he was a cadet at West Point—as a primitive form of the game was known as early as the Revolution.

John F. Reynolds

A native of Lancaster, Pennsylvania, John Fulton Reynolds (1820-1863) was one of nine children. He graduated 26th in the West Point class of 1841. Reynolds had a varied career in the Old Army, serving against the Seminoles, on the frontier, in Mexico (two brevets), on exploration and survey duty in the West. After participating in the "Mormon War" he served for a time as Commandant of Cadets at West Point in 1860. On the outbreak of the war Reynolds was named lieutenant colonel of the newly activated regular *14th Infantry Regiment,* but was promoted brigadier general of volunteers in August of 1861.

Reynolds for a time commanded a brigade in the defenses of Washington. He was captured during the Peninsular Campaign, but exchanged in August of 1862. He was then given commanded of the famed *Pennsylvania Reserves* in *III Corps.* He led his division ably during the Second Bull Run Campaign, and was shortly thereafter assigned to command the militia called out in Pennsylvania during the Antietam Campaign. After Antietam Reynolds was promoted major general of volunteers and given *I Corps,* which he led at Fredericksburg and Chancellorsville. He is believed to have refused the command of the *Army of the Potomac* in favor of George G. Meade, who was his junior.

Meade made Reynolds commander of one wing of the army, and at Gettysburg his prompt and effective action on the morning of 1 July was important in determining that the ensuing action would be the decisive clash of the Pennsylvania Campaign. He fell as he rode the lines, shot by a Rebel marksman; his body was taken to his hometown, not 50 miles away, where it was interred on the 4th of July. Reynolds was not only a fine general, with an instinct for doing what was right in the midst of battle, but he looked like one, standing six-foot, with dark hair and eyes, and a frame which wore a uniform well. His brother, William Reynolds, had a distinguished career in the navy, rising to rear admiral.

Richard S. Ewell

"Dick" Ewell (1817-1872), a native of Georgetown in the District of Columbia, graduated from West Point 13th in the class of 1840 and entered the dragoons. Save for a tour in Mexico (one brevet) his entire service was against Indians in the southwest. He resigned from the Old Army as a captain on 7 May 1861 and promptly entered Confederate service as a colonel and was put in command of a cavalry training camp. In June of 1861 Ewell was promoted to brigadier general and commanded a brigade at Bull Run. He spent the balance of the year helping to organize and train his brigade. Promoted to major general in early 1862, he commanded a division under Thomas "Stonewall" Jackson in the Shenandoah Valley, and later in the Peninsula and during the Second Bull Run Campaign, where he lost a leg in the Battle of Groveton (28 August 1862). His recovery was long delayed, but during it Ewell—who had a reputation as a misogynist—fell in love with his young nurse and surprised everyone by marrying her. He returned to duty in May of 1863.

Upon returning to the Army of Northern Virginia, Ewell was promoted to lieutenant general and given command of the late Stonewall Jackson's II Corps. His wooden leg prevented him from mounting, so he had to be lifted into the saddle and strapped there during the invasion of Pennsylvania. It was his corps which spread out over much of the central portion of the state in the last week of June of 1863. At Gettysburg Ewell performed poorly. He ought to have been more aggressive on the first day, and badly mismanaged his attacks against the Union northern flank on Culp's Hill on the second and third days, most notably by failing to coordinate them with Longstreet's attacks further south, thus possibly costing Lee the battle. After Gettysburg he was again wounded late in 1863, but returned to duty in time to lead his corps in the opening phases of the Campaign of 1864. At Spotsylvania Ewell had a bad fall from his horse which rendered him unfit for further field service and he was assigned to command the defenses of Richmond. He was captured during the retreat to Appomattox. After the war he lived in retirement.

Ewell was an inspiring leader, though he hardly looked the part, being bald, with a prominent nose, bulging eyes, and a pronounced lisp. After he lost his leg, about which he was not the least bit self-conscious, he got about on crutches, in a traveling carriage, or, when in action, tied to his horse. Despite his many redeeming qualities, Ewell was unsuited to the command of a corps. Effective when closely controlled, he could not adjust to the freedom which Lee's general instructions gave him. As a result, he was hesitant and relied heavily on the advice of his subordinates.

Harry Heth

A native Virginian, Harry Heth (1825-1899) entered West Point after being refused an appointment to Annapolis. He graduated in 1847 at the bottom of his class. Heth served in Mexico, on the frontier, and in garrison, rising to captain before resigning in April of 1861 to enter Confederate service in the same rank. He was shortly afterwards commissioned colonel of the 45th Virginia and served in West Virginia in late 1861. Early the following year he was promoted to brigadier general and given an administrative post in western Virginia. Heth was soon sent west, and commanded a division during Braxton Bragg's Kentucky Campaign in 1862. Early in 1863 he was transferred to the Army of Northern Virginia at the request of Robert E. Lee and was given a brigade in A.P. Hill's division.

Heth lead his brigade during the Chancellorsville Campaign, where he assumed command of the division when Hill was wounded. He retained command of the division when Hill became corps commander, and led it into the Gettysburg Campaign. On the morning of 1 July skirmishers from his division opened the ball at Gettysburg. Heth handled his forces badly, losing heavily and being himself severely wounded, though able to return to duty within a few days. After Gettysburg he led his division with some ability in all subsequent campaigns of the Army of Northern Virginia, from the Wilderness to Appomattox.

In the post-war years Heth entered the insurance business, was a surveyor, and served in the Office of Indian Affairs. Said to have been the only person in the Army of Northern Virginia whom Lee addressed by his first name, Heth had some skill as a division commander, but had to be closely supervised. During the Gettysburg Campaign he twice blundered into engagements, at Gettysburg itself on 1 July and at Falling Waters, on 14 July, when he was supposed to be covering the retreat.

Daniel E. Sickles

A native of New York City and educated at New York University, Daniel Edgar Sickles (1819-1914) read law, was admitted to the bar, and almost immediately jumped into politics, becoming a prominent leader of the Tammany machine at an early age. By the time he was 28 Sickles was corporation counsel of the City of New York, a post which he shortly resigned to become secretary of the American legation in London. Sickles then served some years as a state senator and in 1857 was elected to the

House of Representatives. In 1859 he shot and killed his wife's lover, Philip Barton Key (son of Francis Scott Key, author of "The Star Spangled Banner") within sight of the White House. His defense, conducted by Edwin M. Stanton, who later became Lincoln's secretary of war, was based on "temporary insanity," and he was the first person ever acquitted on those grounds. He subsequently created a further sensation by forgiving his wife her indiscretion. At the outbreak of the war he raised the *Excelsior Brigade* in New York and became colonel of the *20th New York.*

In September of 1861 Sickles was made a brigadier-general of volunteers and led a brigade of *III Corps* with commendable aggressiveness during the Peninsular Campaign. Given the division, he led it at Antietam and Fredericksburg. When Maj. Gen. Joseph Hooker assumed command of *The Army of the Potomac,* he gave Sickles, a close friend, his old *III Corps.* Sickles led the corps at Chancellorsville, missing an opportunity to frustrate "Stonewall" Jackson's famed flank attack. At Gettysburg on 2 July his aggressiveness and lack of respect for Major General George Meade led him to deploy his corps too far forward, and over too wide a front, with the result that it was shattered by Lt. Gen. James Longstreet's attack, Sickles himself losing his right leg; whatever his shortcomings as a commander, his courage that day was undoubted and he calmly puffed on cigars as he was carried to the rear, still exhorting his men to fight on. He was the last non-West Point corps commander in the *Army of the Potomac.*

Sickles held no further field command, but performed various administrative functions for the balance of the war, while engaging in a disreputable smear campaign against Meade. After the war he served on occupation duty in the Carolinas until 1869, when he retired from the army as a regular major general. He served for some time as minister to Spain, where he became the friend of Queen Isabella II; as he was a notorious womanizer and she was noted for her affairs, the possibility that they were more than friends is strong. The balance of his long life was spent in various political, civic, and business pursuits—including a well-orchestrated campaign which resulted in an award of the Medal of Honor for his conduct on 2 July 1863. As a member of the House he introduced the legislation which established the Gettysburg Battlefield Memorial Park on 12 February 1895, where he does not, however, have a monument, for in 1912 he was removed from the chairmanship of the New York State Monuments Commission for peculation. Sickles' political connections and his undoubted aggressiveness and courage in battle secured him a command for which he was unsuited. Fairly effective when leading a division under close supervision, he ought never to have been entrusted with a corps.

1863

Winfield Scott Hancock

A native of Pennsylvania, Winfield Scott Hancock (1824-1886) graduated from West Point 18th in the class of 1844. He served on the frontier, in Mexico (one brevet), against the Seminoles, in Kansas, and in the Mormon War. The outbreak of the Civil War found him post quartermaster at Los Angeles, where he presided at a famous dinner for several officers who had resigned to "go South." In September of 1861 Hancock was appointed a brigadier general of volunteers and given a brigade in *IV Corps* which he led with considerable ability throughout the Peninsular Campaign. He was given a division in *II Corps* in time for Antietam, and was shortly thereafter promoted to major general, leading his division at Fredericksburg and Chancellorsville, where he particularly distinguished himself in covering the retreat of the *Army of the Potomac*. Given command of *II Corps* in mid-May of 1863, he led it into the Gettysburg Campaign.

Hancock's performance during the Battle of Gettysburg was remarkable. On the first day, Meade, a close personal friend, assigned him to direct the battle until he could himself reach the field. Hancock is largely responsible for preventing the defeat which the Army of Northern Virginia had inflicted upon *I Corps* and *XI Corps* earlier on 1 July from turning into a disaster. On 2 July Hancock commanded much of the left wing, endeavoring to salvage something from the disastrous situation which resulted when *III Corps* was virtually destroyed. It was on 3 July, however, that he proved particularly capable, commanding most of the forces on Cemetery Ridge and, by a brilliant display of courage and leadership, helped break Pickett's Charge, during which he was wounded. After Gettysburg, Hancock resumed command of his corps, leading it in most of the engagements of the Campaign of 1864. In November his Gettysburg wound reopened, which apparently made him quite irritable, with the result that he had to relinquish command; no other Federal officer commanded a corps for a longer period during the war. He thereafter held various administrative commands and was head of the Veterans Reserve Corps, a special body of reenlisted veterans, until the end of the war.

After the war Hancock, a regular major general, served in a variety of posts. In 1880 he ran for president as a Democrat, only to be beaten by James A. Garfield by less than 10,000 popular votes, though the electoral vote was 214 to 155. After the election, Hancock returned to active service and died in command of the Department of the East, at Governor's Island, New York. One of the finest soldiers of the war, Hancock had an imposing presence, the fiercest vocabulary in the Union Army, and a talent for inspiring men under fire.

George E. Pickett

Born in Richmond, George E. Pickett (1825-1875) graduated from West Point at the bottom of the class of 1846. An infantryman, he served in Mexico (one brevet) and on the frontier. While on garrison duty in Washington Territory in the period 1856-1861 he provoked a crisis with Great Britain when he occupied a disputed island in the Straits of Juan de Fuca. He resigned as a captain in late June of 1861 and was almost immediately commissioned a colonel in Confederate service. For several months Pickett commanded the defenses along the lower Rappahannock, and was then named a brigadier general in February of 1862.

During the Peninsular Campaign Pickett led a brigade with considerable panache until wounded at Gaines's Mill. He returned to command in time for the Antietam Campaign, after which he was promoted to major general, and given a division in Longstreet's I Corps. He led his division at Fredericksburg, in operations on the Virginia and Carolina coasts, and then during the Gettysburg Campaign. On 3 July, three brigades from his division formed the right half of the Confederate assault against Cemetery Ridge which has ever after borne his name—Pickett's Charge—which was bloodily repulsed; his performance during this action was not praiseworthy, for he took a post too far in the rear to influence events, and was, indeed, the only officer ranking in the division as lieutenant colonel or higher who was neither killed nor wounded during the attack. After Gettysburg, Pickett conducted operations against Federal enclaves on the Virginia and North Carolina coasts. Recalled to the Army of Northern Virginia during the Campaign of 1864, he led his division in all the subsequent battles for Richmond, surrendering at Appomattox.

After the war Pickett declined an offer of command from the Khedive of Egypt and a U.S. marshalship from President U.S. Grant to enter the insurance business, in which he prospered. Pickett was married three times, twice before the war—once to an Indian princess who died in childbirth—and again shortly after Gettysburg, to a teenaged girl who would survive him by 50 years. An able division commander, Pickett, who wore his hair in "long, perfumed ringlets that fell to his shoulders," has had the misfortune to have his name associated with a disastrous attack over which he had little control .

Lafayette McLaws

Born in Augusta, Georgia, Lafayette McLaws (1821-1897) graduated from West Point 48th in the class of 1842, along with James Longstreet. He served in the infantry in Mexico, in garrison, on the frontier and on the "Mormon Expedition," rising to captain before resigning from the army on 10 May 1861. McLaws entered Confederate service as a major, was soon commissioned colonel of the 10th Georgia and shortly afterwards made a brigadier general. He served with a brigade in the opening stages of the Peninsular Campaign. McLaws was sufficiently effective in this role to shortly merit promotion to major general and be given a division under "Stonewall" Jackson. He led this division in the Shenandoah Valley and during the later stages of the Peninsular Campaign. McLaws and his division were shortly thereafter transferred to Longstreet's corps, and served in the Antietam and Fredericksburg Campaigns in the autumn of 1862. McLaws particularly distinguished himself in the defense of Marye's Heights during the Chancellorsville Campaign in May of '63, when his division held back an entire corps. At Gettysburg his division performed well on 2 July.

During Longstreet's operations in the west in late 1863, McLaws was relieved by his commander for lack of cooperation, but he was subsequently cleared of all charges. His relations with Longstreet were stormy thereafter and he was sent to an administrative command in the Carolinas, and later directed the defense of Savannah. After the war McLaws was in the insurance business, and served as collector of internal revenue and postmaster at Savannah.

Although he had no talent for independent command, McLaws was an excellent division commander when given a clear objective and closely supervised by his superiors. A big bear of a man, he was also a man of considerable character; despite his personal differences with Longstreet he supported the latter when Jubal Early and John C. Pendleton tried to smear his reputation after the war.

The Women

Annie E. Jones

At the start of the Civil War Annie E. Jones (c. 1840-?), a patriotic young woman from Massachusetts, ran away from home to enlist as a nurse. Reaching Washington she found that she was disqualified from such service as a result of the stringent regulations established by the formidable Dorothea Dix, head of nursing services for the Union armies: to wit, Annie was too young, too pretty, and too unmarried. Seeking about for another way to serve the troops, Miss Jones began visiting the various encampments in the vicinity of the capitol, "more out of curiosity" than anything else. She soon established a close "friendship" with some of Maj. Gen. Franz Sigel's staff officers. It was a pleasant existence. Her "friends" gave her free run of the camps and supplied her with all the necessities of life, including a tent, rations, and horses, and even provided a military escort as she roamed around the countryside, often wearing a major's uniform. Miss Jones served as a "guest" of various officers. Brig. Gen. Julius Stahel "looked after" her for a time, and she was later taken up by Maj. Gen. Judson Kilpatrick. In mid-1863 she became the "friend and companion" to the handsome, gallant young Brig. Gen. George Armstrong Custer. This was a bad move, for Custer was Kilpatrick's subordinate in the *3rd Cavalry Division*, and the latter was sufficiently annoyed that within a week he issued an order "prohibiting all females from accompanying the war," which, considering his habits, amounted to cutting off his nose to spite his face. Annie went, but not for long. A few weeks later she returned to Custer's headquarters late one night "in an army ambulance with escort." Rather than turn her away into the cold darkness, the kindhearted Custer allowed her to stay. Kilpatrick soon learned of this and accused Miss Jones of espionage, which resulted in her being jailed in the Old Capitol Prison and soon after at the Barnstable House of Correction in Massachusetts. Outraged at this injustice, Annie appealed to Lincoln.

The number of ranking officers involved made the case a sensitive one, and Lincoln ordered an investigation. The officers involved were questioned. Most claimed no connection with Annie. Some suggested that she was a nurse or a scout or a spy; a few allowed as how she might have been plying another profession "among the troops." Miss Jones was brought to Washington and interviewed by Lincoln himself. She adamantly denied that she had been anything but "a companion to various commanding officers." Though admitting that she had engaged in "relations" with a guard at the Old Capitol, for which reason she had been sent to Massachusetts, she angrily noted that William P. Wood, the prison superintendent, had sent her off to Barnstable in the company of one Mary Johnson, a "common prostitute." The investigation satisfied Lincoln that there was no basis to the charge of espionage, but Annie remained incarcerated.

In the spring of 1864 Miss Jones wrote a letter to Representative Fernando Wood, a former mayor of New York City and noted Copperhead. She asked Wood, a complete stranger, to help her out, saying that she was in dire need of money, clothing, and books. Wood took up a collection among his friends, kicked in a sawbuck himself and sent her $50.00. In addition, he asked Secretary of War Edwin M. Stanton if Miss Jones might be released in his custody. Stanton granted the request on 3 July 1864, providing Wood "exercise sufficient influence to keep her away from the Army" and promptly forgot about the matter. Much to his surprise, the following March he received a communication from the Adjutant General of Massachusetts asking that the War Department pay for Miss Jones' continued upkeep. Upon inquiry, Stanton learned that Governor John A. Andrew of Massachusetts had refused to release Annie, fearing that Wood might make use of her to discredit the conduct of the war and the president in the 1864 election. The election had come and gone, and Annie had been forgotten. As the war was by then virtually over, Stanton ordered her release conditional on her remaining north of the Susquehanna. Miss Jones wrote to the secretary to thank him and requested permission to go to New Orleans to teach freedmen. And, indeed, there was an "Annie Jones" on the payroll of the Freedman's Bureau in Mississippi in 1866, which may not be the same woman. With that, Annie E. Jones vanishes from history. Or almost does. For in 1879, John D. Sabine, an official of the Adjutant General's Office, requested a copy of Annie's file for an unspecified "friend in Boston," a request which was denied on the grounds that it was not "advisable or conducive to the public interest." The enigmatic request and reply alike only whetted the appetite for more information about Miss Jones's fate, information which is, alas, not forthcoming.

Lincoln

The Signing of the Emancipation Proclamation

At noon on 1 January 1863 Secretary of State William H. Seward and his son Frederick brought the text of the proposed Emancipation Proclamation to Lincoln's office. Lincoln took the document, unrolled it, and laid it on a table. Picking up a pen, he dipped it in ink and prepared to sign. But then he paused, removed his hand from the paper, and put down the pen. For a moment Lincoln merely sat there. Then he again picked up the pen, reinked it, and held it once more over the page, only to hesitate yet again. He laid down his pen for a second time.

Looking up, Lincoln saw that Seward was puzzled by his apparent reluctance to sign. The president smiled and said, "I have been shaking hands since nine o'clock this morning and my right arm is nearly paralyzed. If my name ever goes down into history it will be for this act, and my whole soul is in it. If my hand trembles when I sign the Proclamation, all who examine the document hereafter will say, 'He hesitated.'"

Then Lincoln turned to the table once more, took up the pen again, reinked it, and with a firm hand slowly signed his name across the bottom. When he finished, he looked up, smiled, and said, "That will do."

In the Matter of Franklin W. Smith

Having concluded that Franklin W. Smith, a Boston contractor, had defrauded the service of certain monies, a Navy court martial sentenced him to a prison term. The record of the court martial was passed on to Lincoln for review. The president read it carefully, and then returned it with the following endorsement:

> *Whereas*, Franklin W. Smith, had transactions with the United States Navy Department to a million and a quarter of dollars, and had the chance to steal a quarter of a million; and *whereas*, he was charged with

stealing only ten thousand dollars, and from the final version of the testimony it is only claimed that he stole one hundred dollars, I don't believe he stole anything at all.

Therefore, the records of the court-martial, together with the finding and sentence, are disapproved, declared null and void, and the defendant is fully discharged.

"A. Lincoln"

"Who, Me?"

One day a certain Judge Baldwin, a highly respected elderly gentleman from California, called upon Maj. Gen. Henry Halleck in Washington. He asked the general-in-chief, whom he had known some years earlier, when the latter was active in California politics, for permission to pass through the Union lines in Virginia in order to visit his brother, who resided behind the Confederate lines. Since both the judge and his brother were noted Union men, Baldwin thought there would be no difficulty in securing a pass. As a result, he was quite surprised when Halleck said, "We have been deceived too often, and I regret that I can't grant it." The determined Judge Baldwin decided to go over Halleck's head, and appealed to Secretary of War Edwin M. Stanton. Unfortunately, Stanton was even briefer with Baldwin than Halleck had been, turning him down with a minimum of ceremony. This so annoyed the good judge that he decided there was nothing to it but to go over Stanton's head, to the president himself. In short order he secured an interview with Lincoln. Meeting the president, Baldwin briefly stated his case.

"Have you," asked the president, "applied to General Halleck?"

"I did," replied the Judge, "and met with a flat refusal."

"Then," said the president, "you must see Stanton."

"I have, and with the same result," replied the judge.

"Well, then," said the president, smiling, "I can do nothing, for you must know that I have very little influence with this administration."

The Gettysburg Address

On the cool afternoon of Thursday, November 19, 1863, a little more than four months after the Battle of Gettysburg, President Abraham Lincoln delivered what is perhaps the most well known speech in American history, a model of the oratorical art and a brilliant summary of the purpose of the war and the meaning of America. The occasion was the dedication of a portion of Cemetery Hill as a National Cemetery. Although the distinguished politician and orator Edward Everett was to be the principal speaker of the day, at the last minute Lincoln had been asked to say a few words.

Contrary to widely accepted tradition, Lincoln wrote the first draft of the address at the White House, not on a train. Nor did he write it on the back of an envelope. He began it on a piece of White House stationery. As originally composed, it had but eight sentences. He subsequently added a ninth, in pencil, which ran over on to another piece of paper. This was the version he brought with him to Gettysburg on 18 November.

That night, both Lincoln and Everett were guests at the home of David Wills, a local Republican Party official. At some point during the night Lincoln revised his speech, writing a second draft on two fresh sheets of paper, and adding the final tenth sentence.

The ceremonies occupied much of the next day, which was rather overcast. The 70-year-old Everett spoke at great length, and his 13,000 word address was well-received. When he was finished a patriotic ode was pronounced by a large chorus. Then Lincoln was introduced. The president delivered his few words standing, holding the text of the speech in his left hand, and referring to it only occasionally as he spoke slowly in his somewhat nasal, mid-western accent:

> Four score and seven years ago our fathers brought forth, upon this continent, a new nation, conceived in Liberty, and dedicated to the proposition that all men are created equal.
>
> Now we are engaged in a great civil war, testing whether that nation, or any nation, so conceived, and so dedicated, can long endure. We are met here on a great battlefield of that war. We have come to dedicate a portion of it as a final resting place for those who here gave their lives that that nation might live. It is altogether fitting and proper that we should do this.
>
> But in a larger sense we can not dedicate—we can not consecrate—we can not hallow—this ground. The brave men, living and dead, who struggled here, have consecrated it, far above our poor power to add or detract. The world will little note, nor long remember, what we say here, but can never forget what they did here. It is for us, the living, rather to be dedicated here to the unfinished work which they have, thus far, so nobly carried on. It is rather for us to be here dedicated to the great task remaining before us—that from these honored dead we take increased devotion to that cause for which they gave the last full measure of devotion—that we here highly resolve that these dead shall not have died in vain; that this nation shall have a new birth of freedom; and that this gov-

ernment of the people, by the people, and for the people, shall not perish from the earth.

Contrary to tradition, applause interrupted Lincoln five times during his brief address. At the end the crowd gave what one observer called "tremendous applause" and three cheers. Despite Lincoln's belief that the address was a "flat failure," its oratorical merit was recognized immediately. Everett put it best when he said "...there was more in your twenty lines than in my twenty pages." History, and popular sentiment, have proven him right.

What Did Lincoln Say?

Lincoln afterwards made several holographic copies of his address, as gifts for various people. There are slight differences in the text of several of these copies. Some scholars believe that these later drafts reflect the form of the address as Lincoln delivered it, or as he remembered delivering it, rather than the original text as he wrote it, which does survive. As a result, the precise words delivered by the president on that November afternoon are somewhat in doubt. But the differences among the several versions are not significant, as the spirit of the speech remains unaltered. It is indeed a masterful effort. Only 18 words have three or more syllables, while over 50 percent of them have four letters or less. Yet in less than 250 words, Lincoln was able to express the fundamental question at issue.

The President and the Paymaster

An army paymaster once sought to meet the president. Having an acquaintance who knew Lincoln, he prevailed upon the man to make the necessary arrangements. At the opportune moment, the paymaster was taken over to the White House by his friend and introduced to the president.

Knowing that nearly everyone who met Lincoln usually offered some unwanted advice, the paymaster merely shook his hand, saying with a smile, "I have no official business with you, Mr. President, I only called to pay my compliments."

"I understand," replied the president, "and from the complaints of the soldiers, I think that is all you do pay."

The Units

The Orphan Brigade

One of the most distinguished organizations in the Confederate Army was the 1st Kentucky Brigade, more commonly known as the "Orphan Brigade." For much of 1861 Kentucky, a slave state with strong Unionist sympathies, was trying to maintain a precarious neutrality. This was a situation which did not satisfy many Kentuckians. As a result, there was a great deal of informal recruiting by both Unionist and Secessionist elements. Since the state government frowned upon such activities, the troops so raised had to be organized and trained illicitly, and frequently outside the state. Unionist Kentucky volunteers concentrated in Ohio, while their Secessionist brethren went south into Tennessee. It was in these circumstances that the famed "Orphan Brigade" was born. Originally composed of four regiments (the 3rd, 4th, 5th, and 6th Kentucky), with two batteries and a troop of cavalry under Capt. John Hunt Morgan, who later achieved fame as a partisan of considerable ability, the brigade, commanded by Brig. Gen. Simon Bolivar Buckner, was about 4,000 strong when it returned to its native Kentucky in the autumn of 1861. It did not remain there long. When U.S. Grant's Henry-Donelson Campaign threw the "front" in the West back some hundreds of miles in February of 1862 Confederate troops abandoned Kentucky. The 1st Kentucky Brigade, by then under Brig. Gen. John C. Breckinridge, would not return to its native state for the duration of the war, thereby earning its nickname, the "Orphan Brigade." Despite this—or perhaps because of it—the Orphan Brigade went on to become one of the most notable units in the Confederate Army, amassing a combat record second to no other comparable formation.

The Orphan Brigade fought at Shiloh, Corinth, Vicksburg, and Baton Rouge in 1862, at Stone's River at the turn of 1862-1863, at Jackson and Chickamauga and Missionary Ridge in 1863, all through the Atlanta Campaign and during the "March to the Sea" in 1864. In early 1865 the brigade, a mere fragment of its former self, was mounted as cavalry.

The Orphan Brigade was a tough opponent in combat, and was always in the hottest part of the fight. Because of its elan and steadiness, it was frequently given the toughest assignments in the Army of Tennessee, and often served as a rear guard. As a result, casualties were usually high. It lost two commanders in combat. Brig. Gen. Roger W. Hanson was mortally wounded at Stone's River/Murfreesboro—where the brigade had over 400 casualties—and Brig. Gen. Benjamin H. Helm—who was married to Mrs. Lincoln's half-sister—was mortally wounded at Chickamauga. Cut off from its natural recruiting grounds, the brigade's strength dwindled from 4,000 to about 500 due to combat losses and disease. Despite hard service, far from home, desertions were few, morale remained high, and the brigade never lost its zest for combat.

Among the last Confederate units in the East to surrender, at Washington, Georgia, in early May of 1865, the Orphan Brigade truly deserved the judgment of both Joseph E. Johnston and John B. Hood that it was the "best brigade in the Army of Tennessee."

The Iron Brigade

The only brigade in the *Army of the Potomac* to be composed entirely of regiments from the West, the *Iron Brigade* amassed one of the most notable combat records of any Federal organization of comparable size in the war. When formed, near Washington in the autumn of 1861, the brigade comprised some 2,400 men of the *19th Indiana* and the *2nd, 6th,* and *7th Wisconsin Infantry Regiments* under the command of Brig. Gen. Rufus King. Early in 1862 the brigade was incorporated in *I Corps*, becoming the *1st Brigade* of the *1st Division.* In May of 1862 the brigade passed to the command of Brig. Gen. John Gibbon, a tough Regular who quickly brought it to a high degree of training and discipline. So pleased was Gibbon with his command that he provided each man with a black felt hat, which caused it to be nicknamed the "Black Hat Brigade." The brigade saw no action until the Second Bull Run Campaign, losing 751 men, 33 percent of its strength, at Groveton (28 August 1862) and forming part of the rear guard. At South Mountain (14 September 1862) it lost another 318 men, 25 percent of its strength, in an heroic action which led Maj. Gen. Joseph Hooker, commanding *I Corps*, to refer to it as his "iron brigade," a name which quickly caught on. Three days later at Antietam the brigade, by then little more than 800 strong, lost yet another 348 men (42 percent). After Antietam Gibbon was given a division, and the brigade passed to Brig. Gen. Soloman Meredith, the politically connected former colonel of the *19th Indiana.* Although the brigade's strength had risen to a little more than 800 men again, it received some badly needed reinforcements in the form of the new *24th Michigan*, more than doubling its numbers while preserving its Western character. But lightly engaged during Fredericksburg and Chancellorsville, the brigade, already among the most famous outfits in the war, gained its greatest glory at Gettysburg.

The 1,883 men of the *Iron Brigade* were among the first Union infantrymen to go into action at Gettysburg, marching up as the Confederate forces began to lap at the flanks of the Federal position along McPherson's Ridge. With one Rebel brigade working around the right and a second pressing its attack in the front and working around the left of the thin Union line, Maj. Gen. John F. Reynolds ordered up the newly arrived Wisconsonites, Michiganders, and Indianans of the *Iron Brigade*, instructing them to " ...drive those fellows out of those woods."

The veterans of the *2nd Wisconsin* came up first, in their distinctive big black hats, loading their muskets at the run. Shrugging off Confederate volleys, they plunged into the woods. Hitherto, many of the Confederate troops had believed they were engaged against militia, and now they were disabused of this illusion. As the *2nd Wisconsin* attacked, some of the Rebel's shouted "Thar come the black hats! 'Taint no militia! It's the *Army of the Potomac!*" as they fell back from the Federal left under their attack. The *Iron Brigade* fought through the rest of the day, along McPherson's Ridge, where it was joined by Old John Burns, back to Seminary Ridge, and thence through Gettysburg to Cemetery Ridge, always in the thickest of the action, helping to solidify the Union lines by nightfall. The price was high, fully 1,212 (65%) of the troops becoming casualties, with losses in the *24th Michigan* in excess of 70% and those of the *2nd Wisconsin* nearly as great. Gettysburg was the brigade's finest day, for the losses incurred virtually destroyed it. To flesh out its depleted ranks several Eastern regiments were added, destroying the Western character of the brigade. Although the *Iron Brigade* continued on the rolls of the *Army of the Potomac* until the end of the war, and rendered good service on many a field, it was but a shadow of its former self.

The *Iron Brigade* had made its name in little more than 300 days, during which it had been heavily engaged on only about five days. Losing over 2,600 men, some 75% of the approximately 3,500 which it had brought into action, the brigade had gained an impressive combat reputation.

The 54th Massachusetts Volunteers

In January of 1863 Massachusetts was authorized to recruit two regiments of black troops, the first to be raised in the North. Some of the most prominent men in America went out recruiting, including Frederick Douglass, fugitive slave, author, and lecturer, John M. Langston, a self-educated black Virginia attorney, and Dr. Martin R. Delany, one of the first black physicians in the nation, stumped the country to encourage blacks to enlist, as did the noted abolitionists Wendell Philips and William Lloyd Garrison, the poet Ralph Waldo Emerson, and the distinguished scientist Louis Agassiz. When the *54th Massachusetts* was accepted for service in May it was composed of free black men from all over the country, perhaps the only regiment, black or white, in the army to be recruited on such a broad basis, having men from eight states and even a few from Canada. Command was offered to 25-year-old Col. Robert Gould Shaw, a seasoned veteran and the son of a prominent white abolitionist; Lewis Douglass, son of the famed black leader was the regimental sergeant major. By May the regiment was ready. The *54th* made a triumphant parade through Boston, following a route which took them over the site of the Boston Massacre, where Crispus Attucks had fallen, passed beneath a balcony on which stood William Lloyd Garrison, with "his hand resting on a bust of John Brown," and then took ship for the South Carolina coast. A period of garrison duty followed, broken by several foraging raids into Confederate-held territory, a duty which Shaw found distasteful, calling it "plundering." Then, in early July, it was decided that a joint army-navy effort should be made to reduce the forts and batteries on Morris Island, which helped guard the ship channel into Charleston harbor. The Confederate position was a strong one, held by some 1,400 men and well-fortified from landward, as well as seaward assault. An attack on 11 July by white troops had come close to success but was beaten off with serious losses, over 100 Federals being killed or wounded to only a dozen Confederates. The position was subjected to a heavy naval bombardment over the next few days and then, on 18 July, a new assault was made, by some 6,000 infantry, including the *54th Massachusetts*, which had been "blooded" in a skirmish on the 16th, on which occasion it had suffered 46 casualties.

Col. Shaw accepted the honor of leading the assault at the head of his own regiment and five white ones. Promptly at 7:45 p.m. on 18 July he led his regiment forward. The attack was pressed with great courage and daring, across some 1600 yards of hard sand, between the sea and some rough ground. The troops gained the crest of the fortifications, but could do no more in the face of withering enemy fire. The recently married Shaw, who led the attack with a cigar clenched in his teeth, fell with a bullet in his heart. All around men went down. The attack was halted, then beaten back. A second effort by four fresh white regiments was equally unsuccessful. The survivors fell back. Casualties had been enormous, 1,515 men, over a quarter of those engaged, and most of the senior officers had been killed. The *54th* suffered 272 casualties out of about 650 engaged, 41.85%, the highest loss in a single engagement of any black regiment in the war; casualties among officers had been particularly heavy, and as the regiment fell back it was commanded by a captain. Confederate losses were but 174.

The attack on Fort Wagner was a failure. But for the *54th Massachusetts* it proved a moral triumph. Col. Shaw was posthumously awarded a Medal of Honor, as was 23-year-old Pvt. William H. Carney, who saved the national colors when the color bearers were hit, planted them on the parapet, and then brought them away safely, though himself seriously wounded. The regiment's steadiness and grim determination caught the public's attention, convincing even the most skeptical that black troops would fight. Even some of the enemy could not but comment favorably, and Confederate Lt. Iredell Jones wrote, "The Negroes fought gallantly and were led by as brave a colonel as ever lived." But other Confederates looked askance at the Union's daring experiment. Attempting to insult the gallant Shaw, the Rebels buried him "with his niggers"; after the war Shaw's father would halt efforts to return the body to the family, saying "We can imagine no holier place than that in which he is, among his brave and devoted followers, nor wish him any better company." More ominously, some of the black prisoners were murdered and some enslaved, setting a precedent which would recur on numerous occasions, and which served to fuel the determination of black troops.

The *54th Massachusetts* spent most of its war in the Charleston area, fighting at Honey Hill (30 November 1864), in the heavy skirmishing about Pocotaligo (December 1864-January 1865), as well as in several other small battles, and was also present at Olustee in Florida (20 February 1864), one of the bloodiest small actions of the war. While it performed well in all its engagements, and indeed brilliantly as part of the rear-guard at Olustee, the *54th Massachusetts* was fated to serve under a series of less than talented generals; none of the actions in which the regiment took part were well-planned or even well-advised. The regiment ended the war on occupation duty in Charleston and was mustered out in September of 1865 after a victory parade in Boston. It's most important service to the nation had not been to triumph in battle, but rather to demonstrate the mettle of black troops.

War and Society

The Erlanger Loan

At no time during the war were the finances of the Confederacy on a firm basis. A particular problem was that of securing foreign credit, without which precious war materials could not be purchased abroad. The Confederacy had some success selling treasury bonds in Europe, but the need was enormous. Knowing of the South's interest in securing foreign funds, in late 1862 the French firm of Émile Erlanger et Compagnie suggested to John Slidell, the Confederate commissioner to France, that the South make a major bond issue on the European market. This would not only secure funds, but would also stir European interest in a Confederate victory. Slidell thought the idea had merit and entered into negotiations with Erlanger, which suggested an issue of $24,000,000, about *fr* 100,000,000 or £5,000,000. As a result of Slidell's endorsement, on 29 January 1863 the Confederate Congress authorized Erlanger to issue $14,550,000—*fr* 60,000,000 or £3,000,000—in bonds. These bonds were to yield 7 percent interest annually, payable in gold "or its equivalent." The principal security for the loan was to be some 500,000 bales of cotton held by the Confederate government. The bonds could be redeemed in cotton at any time, at the rate of six pence per pound, which was quite attractive in early 1863, as cotton was then selling at about 24 pence a pound, provided one could carry the stuff away through the Union blockade. Those willing to wait a little longer could redeem them in gold six months after the conclusion of a treaty of peace between the United States and the Confederacy or receive payment in gold on maturity at 20 years from date of issue. As part of the deal Erlanger was to guarantee to the Confederacy a return of $77.00 per $100 par, with the difference between this and sale price being his profits, on top of which he would receive a 5 percent surcharge. Thus, the Confederacy could expect a yield of $72 per $100 valuation of bonds issued.

The bonds went on sale on 19 March 1863 in Paris, London, Frankfurt, and Amsterdam. As the South had successfully weathered the enormous Federal onslaught of 1862, belief in its eventual victory was strong in some

European circles and the issue was an immediate success. Indeed, it was actually oversubscribed by about 300 percent by the end of the day, and completely sold out at 90 percent of par within two days, for a profit to Erlanger of about $2,550,000 and a yield to the Confederate treasury of some $10,000,000. Trading was brisk over the next few days and within two weeks the bonds were selling at 95.5 percent of par. But this euphoria did not last long. In subsequent trading the price fell steadily, a development which panicked the Confederate commissioners. To restore their confidence, Erlanger offered to bolster the value of the bonds by using the Confederate funds in his possession—i.e., the Confederacy's $10,000,000—to secretly purchase bonds whenever the price fell below 90 percent of par, thus creating the impression that the issue was popular. No financial geniuses, Slidell and his colleagues acceded to this proposal, which, in effect, turned the proceeds of the issue over to Erlanger for speculative purposes. As a result, most of the funds which had been realized by the issue were expended by Erlanger in supporting the par value of the bonds. Meanwhile, of course, Erlanger continued to take in his 5 percent.

Erlanger knew a good thing when he saw it, and he was soon playing both sides against the Confederacy, forcing the value of the issue down by press manipulation—European newspapers of the day were notoriously bribable—and rumors, in which he was ably, if unknowingly, assisted by American agents. When the price fell, Erlanger purchased bonds at the reduced rate using the Confederacy's money, thereby boosting the price, and thus being able to resell at a profit. This made the Confederate bonds rather volatile, which attracted speculators. The clever scheme went on for some months, but even Erlanger couldn't keep it up forever in the face of the realities of war. After Vicksburg and Gettysburg the price of the bonds fell to 65 percent of par, and by December of '63 they were down to 37 percent.

Undaunted, Erlanger, who had meanwhile begun to court Slidell's daughter, approached the Confederacy with a proposal to float another loan, for *fr* 125,000,000, on essentially the same terms. Although initially interested, the Congress turned him down, even after he married Miss Slidell, in favor of trying for a £15,000,000 issue by a consortium of European bankers. As this was in January of 1865 the matter was by then mostly of academic interest only.

Altogether, the Confederacy realized only about $2,600,000 from the bond issue, most of which was expended on arms procurement in Britain and France. Of course, the South had been the victim of a gigantic scam. On the other hand, the issue did bring in hard cash which the Confederacy would not otherwise have had. The real victims, of course, were the European investors. People in Europe had sunk some $60,000,000 into the Confederacy, mostly in treasury bonds but also, of course, in the Erlanger issue. For nearly twenty years after the war representatives of the bond holders, and several European powers, attempted to get the United States to honor the terms of the loan, which was, after all, "payable six months after the conclusion of a treaty of peace between the Confederate States of America and the United States of America." Needless to say, they got nowhere.

The South Shall Rise Again.

On 24 November 1987, Sotheby's, the London auction house, sold a lot of 75,000 Confederate treasury bonds for $625,000 to a group of antique bond dealers in Texas and California, which plans to resell the lot in wholesale batches to antique dealers at a profit of some $2,000,000. As the bonds will eventually reach the retail market, their ultimate resale price will undoubtedly be several times that figure. So the bonds which the Confederacy issued are finally yielding a profit to someone, aside, that is, from Émile Erlanger.

The Ways of War

Infantry Weapons of the Civil War

Small arms fire accounted for 91.3 percent of the combat casualties in the Civil War, artillery being responsible for but 7.5 percent, while less than 0.1 percent were due to edged weapons, and the rest to land mines, hand grenades, and other causes. A great variety of small arms were used during the war, particularly in the early period, due largely to a lack of adequate stocks and a shortage of industrial plants. At the start of the war there were perhaps 500,000 muskets of various types in arsenals and armories around the country, 80 percent of which were obsolete smooth bores. As a result all sorts of weapons were procured abroad, a great many of which were of marginal quality. As late as mid-1863 Union small arms were still not standardized, with many regiments carrying odd weapons and some even being equipped with two or three different types; at the time of Gettysburg over 100 different models of rifles, muskets, carbines, and the like were still officially being borne by the troops. Confederate units were in even worse shape, often carrying a great variety of weapons, many of them captured from the Union. The pieces included in the accompanying table and notes cover over 80 percent of the long arms used in the Union and Confederate infantry and cavalry by the middle of the war.

Weapon	Load	Cal	Range	Weight	R/F	Note
Enfield 1855 Carbine	ML	.577"	350 yds	8.0pds	3	A
Enfield 1855 Rifle	ML	.577	450	9.2	3	B
Sharps 1848 Carbine	BL	.52	350	7.0	9	C
Sharps 1848 Rifle	BL	.52	450	8.0	9	D
Spencer 1860 Carbine	BL	.52	450	8.3	20	E
U.S. 1835 Musket	ML	.69	150	11.0	3	F
U.S. 1842 Musket	ML	.69	150	11.0	3	G
U.S. 1855 Rifle	ML	.58	400	10.12	3	H
U.S. 1861 Rifle	ML	.58	450	9.75	3	I

Weapon is the official designation of the piece in question. *Load,* refers to whether the piece is muzzle-loading (*ML*) or breech-loading (*BL*). *Cal* is the caliber, or diameter, of the bullet, expressed in inches; most of these rounds ran a half-ounce or better. *Range* is the normal effective range of the piece, in yards; most of these weapons could inflict lethal damage at up to four times that range, though accuracy was greatly reduced. *Weight* is for the weapon with bayonet—save for the Sharps and the Spencer, which had none—in pounds. *R/F* is the number of rounds per minute which could be sustained in combat, given a trained soldier and a clean weapon. *Note* refers to the lettered comments which appear below.

A. The cavalry version of the British Enfield 1855 Rifle, which was immensely popular with Confederate cavalrymen, when they weren't exercising a penchant for carrying shotguns.

B. The standard British infantry rifle between 1855 and 1867, nearly 500,000 of these were procured for the Union and over 100,000 for the Confederacy in the early years of the war. Both the rifle and the carbine were subsequently manufactured in the South, along with a special "officer's" model of particularly fine quality. The Enfields were good, serviceable weapons, very popular with the troops, particularly in the South.

C. The first breech loading shoulder arm to be issued to U.S. troops, the Sharps was a cavalryman's weapon. Over 80,000 were procured during the war, and the Confederacy even began manufacturing them. The Sharps was loaded by a lever which doubled as the trigger guard. Pushing this forward dropped the breech block. The soldier would insert into the breech a linen-wrapped cartridge, and close the block once more. Doing this would cut open the cartridge. The hammer had to be manually cocked. Firing was initially by means of percussion tape—similar to that used in child's cap pistol—but this was later replaced by percussion caps on a rotating disk. Very popular with the troops, at Gettysburg most of the Union cavalrymen carried this.

D. The infantry version of the Sharps Carbine, only about 10,000 were issued, mostly to units designated as "sharpshooters," which term does not, however, derive from the name of the rifle.

E. The Spencer Repeating Carbine was the first regularly issued repeating firearm in the world. Beginning in 1863 Union cavalry regiments were issued it and by the end of the war it was the only long arm borne by Union cavalrymen and had begun to appear in substantial numbers among the infantry; perhaps 100,000 were issued, and thousands more purchased by individual regiments or by various states for their own troops, along with about 12,000 of the longer infantry version. The Spencer had a tubular magazine with seven self-contained copper cased, rim fire cartridges. The magazine passed through the butt. As in the Sharps, pushing forward on the trigger guard lowered the breech block, ejecting the spent shell upwards. By pulling back on the lever, the block closed and a spring in the magazine inserted a fresh round. The weapon was manually cocked, and a good man could easily get off twenty shots in a minute, changing the magazine as he went. Each man was issued ten spare magazines, which he carried in a special case, giving him a total of 77 rounds. Altogether the Union issued over a dozen different types of breechloading rifles and carbines in small numbers during the war. Only the Sharps and Spencer were issued in any numbers. Other breechloaders were: the Colt 1855 Revolving Rifle, the Henry 1860 Repeating Rifle, the Maynard Carbine, and the Joslyn Carbine, about 10,000 of each being issued, many by individual states; the Starr and Galleger Carbines, upwards of 25,000 each being issued; and the Burnside Carbine, of which 55,000 were issued.

F. The last flintlock to be issued by the United States, this was an obsolete weapon in 1861. In many respects it was virtually unchanged from the weapons which Washington's men had carried. Numbers of these—and even older pieces such as the 1812 musket—were used in the early days of the war and some remained in service with Confederate militia units well into the struggle.

G. This was a modification of the 1835 flintlock musket, converted to percussion cap, or manufactured to the new specifications. Many units on both sides carried this with them in the early period of the war and some Confederate regiments still bore it at Gettysburg, by which time it had virtually disappeared from the Union forces, except for militia units, such as those called into service in Pennsylvania during that same campaign. It could be loaded with simple ball ammunition, or with "buck-and-ball," special cartridges which included some buckshot in addition to the musket ball. Troops would sometimes make up special cartridges entirely of buckshot, which could be particularly devastating at close range.

H. The first U.S. minie rifle, about 100,000 of these were produced in two slightly different versions before the war. Many remained in Confederate service long after Gettysburg and it was also used by some Federal militia regiments.

I. The famed "Springfield Rifle," over 900,000 of these were produced in three slightly differing versions during the war, some 150,000 of which found their way into the Confederate Army, mostly through capture. It was essentially an improved version of the 1855 rifle and was very popular with the troops of both armies. The Springfield was the last muzzle-loading weapon produced for the U.S.

All of these weapons were made of high grade cast iron, with hardwood stocks, black walnut generally being considered the best for this purpose. The barrel was cast as a solid piece and then bored out to the desired caliber. Lock mechanisms, triggers, and other fittings were produced individually. While technically mass produced with interchangeable parts, following the technology introduced by Eli Whitney—whose invention of the cotton gin had done much to strengthen slavery, thereby helping to bring about the war—in practice there was wide variation even among pieces produced in the same plant. As a result, the final assembly of the piece was always done by hand, with much filing sometimes required. This was one reason why breechloaders were unusually expensive, for it was difficult to secure a tight seal on the breech mechanism with contemporary production methods.

Loading the Rifled Musket.

All of the muzzle loading weapons used during the Civil War were handled in much the same way.

Holding his musket with his left hand, the soldier removed the ramrod from its slot beneath the barrel and swabbed out the tube to cleanse it of sparks, lest it flare while he was loading it. Then, placing the ramrod also in his left hand, he reached into his cartridge pouch for one of the paper-wrapped cartridges which it contained. Biting off the end, he carefully poured the powder down the barrel, tapping the butt lightly on the ground as he did so. He then dropped the bullet into the barrel, shoved the paper in after it as a wadding, and tamped everything down with the ramrod, which he then replaced in its slot. Resuming the piece, he cocked the hammer. He then took a percussion cap from a second pouch and placed it on a little nipple which connected with the chamber by a tiny touch hole. (With the old flintlock he actually had to put powder in the touch hole.) He was now ready to fire.

There was much that could go wrong. It was extremely difficult to load these weapons in any but a standing position. In addition, in the heat of battle a man might spill some of the powder or drop the ball or the percussion cap, and might not even be aware of what had happened, and so reload, thinking he had fired properly. Double or triple loaded muskets were not uncommon. Of about 24,000 rifles and muskets salvaged intact from the field after the Battle of Gettysburg, about 6,000 were either unloaded or contained one round, about 12,000 had double charges, and about 6,000 more contained a least three rounds, with the record being 23. These, of course, were the ones which had not exploded in some soldier's face. A man might even forget to remove the ramrod from the barrel, with the result that he fired it off, and was then unable to reload. Not for nothing did the troops universally prefer breech loaders, when they could get them. Curiously, at the onset of the war the United States War Department had turned down a proposal to equip the entire army with breech loaders, citing the expense—about $30.00 to $50.00 apiece as against $20.00—and claiming that breech loaders would only encourage the waste of ammunition. Whether anyone thought to consult the troops is unlikely.

Generally, the troops on both sides carried between 40 and 60 rounds, which came in packets of 20. The standard ammunition pouch had two tin trays, each of twenty rounds, one above the other, so if he had more than 40 rounds a soldier had to carry the extra ones in his knapsack or haversack. When the upper tray of his ammunition pouch was empty, he had to remove it and place it under the lower tray, which made carrying one's ammunition loose in a sack popular. Percussion caps were carried in a smaller pouch. It was not uncommon for extra ammunition to be distributed on the eve of battle, and, of course, one could always take it from the dead. Since both sides had mostly the same weapons, using captured ammunition was common.

Military Medicine in the Civil War

As with almost everything else in the Civil War, medical care for the troops had to be improvised. And the process of developing an efficient system for the care of the sick and wounded was slow, difficult, and literally painful. To begin with, the practice of medicine in the United States was primitive even by the standards of the times. The intellectual and humanitarian currents which had already begun to establish medicine on a scientific basis in Europe had barely affected the United States. Medical education was poor, most physicians and surgeons being educated largely through service as apprentices. The few formal medical schools were not much better; Harvard, which may have been best in the country, is said to have owned neither a microscope nor a stethoscope until after the war. There was little state supervision over the profession and little organization within it. Fads and fashions and frauds were common. Nevertheless, most medical personnel—all save a handful male—were honest, dedicated, and hard working.

The physicians of the age did their best and were actually fairly good at treating some problems. But, with the existence of bacteria being barely known in Europe and not even rumored in America, there was no scientific basis for an understanding of the nature of various conditions and as a result no systematic basis for treatment. Thus, *miasmotic* fevers were caused by "various atmospheric influences, such as products of vegetable or animal decomposition . . . ." Surgery was the most advanced branch of medicine at the time, which was fortunate, for the primary method of treating most wounds was to cut. Knowledge of anatomy was adequate, and the surgeon's tools were well developed. Anesthetics, in the form of chloroform and morphine were available and some surgeons made excellent use of them, but others used them to excess, with the result that there were some problems with addiction in the post-war period. Unfortunately, many surgeons eschewed anesthetics, believing that pain was medically useful. Antisepsis was unheard of, with the result that, however skilled the surgeon, recovery hinged pretty much on whether a patient could avoid serious infection, a matter complicated by the belief that bandages should be kept moist. Worse yet, it was customary to launder bandages and reuse them; due to a bandage shortage in the South non-reusable cotton lint was often employed to dress wounds and it is believed that the sepsis rate was somewhat lower as a result. The pharmacopeia was still largely filled with folk medicines, some of which—calomel, arrowroot, acacia, camphor, belladonna, mustard, assafoetida—had limited applications, and some of which—mercury, strychnine, ammonia, potassium arsenate, lead acetate, turpentine—were outright dangerous. Nevertheless, some progress had been made. It was understood that an adequate and balanced diet had something to do with health; a notion had arisen of the relationship between cleanliness and health; and many genuine medicines had been discovered, mostly on a hit or miss basis, such as quinine, iodine, and opium.

Disease was the biggest killer, not the enemy. Union records show that of 359,528 deaths recorded among the troops, only 67,058 men were killed in action, 18.65 percent. There were also 43,012 who died of wounds, for a further 11.96 percent, giving a total of 110,070 battle-related deaths, 30.6 percent of total deaths. Disease accounted for 224,586 deaths, fully 62.57 percent. The balance, 24,972, or 6.9 percent, was due to all other causes, including homicides (520), executions (267), drownings (4,944), accidents (4,114), and so forth, with a large number of unknowns (12,121). Disease caused nearly 50 percent more deaths than battle. The greatest losses from disease, however, came in the earlier part of the war, particularly in the first two years, when everyone was learning to soldier. One serious problem was that since large numbers of Union troops, and most Confederate troops, were of rural origins, many of them had not been subject to various illnesses which, though rather mild in children, can create serious problems for adults. In addition, during the early period of the war camp sanitation was often abysmal; food was usually of poor quality, inadequate supply, and unpalatable preparation; clothing and tentage were frequently shoddy and insufficient. In time the armies learned, though only the Union had the resources to adequately cope with the problem. During the Mexican War the average annual death rate from disease had been about 10.2 percent of strength. In the Civil War, which began little more than a dozen years later, this had declined to 6.2 percent, at least for the Union forces. Under Dr. Samuel Preston Moore, the Medical Department of the Confederacy tried its best, but despite great efforts could not really cope with a persistent shortage of resources, including surgeons, medicines, and other supplies. Although the Confederate medical service came under fierce Congressional criticism, the problems which plagued it were not readily resolvable given the military and economic situation of the South. Although records are inadequate, it appears that Confederate deaths from disease and wounds were relatively higher than Union ones. However, even at the end of the war a Union soldier was still more likely to succumb to disease than to bullets; the odds had just changed somewhat in favor of the latter. Not until well into the twentieth century would man's ability to kill men outstrip nature's.

At the beginning of the war physicians volunteered along with everyone else. While a surprising number signed up to fight rather than to heal, most became volunteer surgeons, serving either as commissioned officers or under contract. Commissioned surgeons usually ranked as majors or captains, while contract surgeons held the temporary rank of lieutenant. Some of these surgeons were inept, some were unsuited to the military persuasion, and some could not take the pressure—nurses frequently observed that doctors were often drunk on duty—but most did their jobs as well as they could. In the field they worked under appalling conditions, often in barns and hayricks. The firearms of the period fired low velocity, relatively heavy bullets which smashed bone with great effectiveness, making any surgical procedures difficult. Nevertheless, the surgeons tried, with varying degrees of success.

Many military surgeons showed great courage and devotion. At Gettysburg, for example, two Union surgeons, Lt. Col. Theodore Heard and Maj. Thomas H. Bache, remained with the wounded as the I Corps fell back through the town on 1 July. For three days they tended the wounded, Union and Confederate alike, alongside their Rebel counterparts. On 2 July Maj. Augustus M. Clark, Acting Chief Surgeon of the Union V Corps was wounded while directing the corps field hospital. And on 4 July several Confederate surgeons elected to stay with the many thousands of wounded who had to be abandoned when the Army of Northern Virginia retreated from the field, among them Dr. Simon Baruch, father of Bernard Baruch, the financier and statesman.

In both armies medical services were initially organized on a regimental basis. Each Union regiment had a surgeon, two assistant surgeons, and a hospital steward, while Confederate ones made do with only a surgeon and an assistant surgeon. These men would set up a regimental hospital as needed to treat the sick and wounded. This proved inadequate. Some regiments might be more severely injured than others and not have available sufficient medical personnel to take care of everyone. Things began to change rapidly. As early as Shiloh, a tent field hospital was established by pooling regimental resources so that the wounded could be treated as close to the battle line as possible. When Dr. Jonathan Letterman became Medical Director of the *Army of the Potomac* in mid-1862, not long before Antietam, he began to institute significant changes. While each regiment continued to have its medical detachment, regimental aid stations were no longer organized. Instead, all medical personnel in each brigade established a single field hospital. This worked better, but was still not satisfactory, so Letterman instituted divisional field hospitals. Functioning under the chief surgeon of the divisions, each hospital had a surgeon, two assistant surgeons, three medical officers with three assistants, plus various stewards and nurses. These hospitals had four medical wagons and fourteen transport wagons, permitting the establishment of a 22-tent field hospital, complete with cooking and laundry facilities. These worked very well. They ensured that in action all available medical personnel would actually be tending the wounded. In addition, they greatly facilitated the complex supply arrangements needed by medical units—a single medicine wagon carried copious amounts of 76 different medicines, a supply of 18 different items used in making dressings, various numbers of 17 different medical instruments, and dozens of other items from bed pans to razors and from matches to pill boxes, plus a supply of food staples and the tools for their preparation.

There were at first no arrangements for the collection of the wounded. If they could not get themselves to the rear they would remain on the field until someone took pity on them. One result of this was men would often leave the firing line to carry wounded comrades to safety. While considered a comradely thing to do, the practice was not conducive to military efficiency, and the faint-hearted could use it as an excuse to get away from the action. Letterman organized the Ambulance Corps, a disciplined body of men whose sole task it was to recover the wounded and bring them back to the field hospitals. Each regiment, brigade, and division had its Ambulance Corps detachment, all under the control of the Medical Director of the corps. In an infantry regiment, the ambulance detachment comprised a sergeant, nine privates, and three ambulance wagons with drivers, supplemented by the band in those regiments which had one. Letterman also decided that it was better to avoid moving the wounded as much as possible. As a result, he established regular hospitals to treat the worst of the wounded in place rather than evacuate them great distances. Largely as a result of these arrangements, a wounded man had a fair chance of survival; of the wounded who received medical assistance only 13.3 percent died, despite the inadequacies of the medical science of the day. Letterman's system worked so well that it was soon extended to all the Union forces, though it took an Act of Congress to overcome the resistance from arch-conservatives in the Medical Department.

The scandalous medical situation which prevailed at the start of the war sparked considerable public interest in the problem, not least of all among the women. In both North and South women joined various volunteer nursing organizations and many thousands were formally enrolled as army nurses. A number of women such as Clara Barton, Anna M. Holstein, and Anna Etheridge, even went into the field to succor the troops, often under fire. In addition, women were prominent in setting up new hospitals all over the country.

Several organizations were set up to render aid to the soldiers when their government failed them. In Richmond, for example, the Association for the Relief of Maimed Soldiers was formed to help provide artificial limbs to amputees. Two of the groups in the North, the United States Sanitary Commission, headed by the architect Frederick Law Olmstead, himself physically unfit for military service, and the Christian Sanitary Commission, began to wield considerable political clout. Using it unashamedly, and with the enthusiastic support of the men in the field, they virtually took over the direction of medical affairs from the Medical Department. The War Department also began to implement changes, the most notable of which was the appointment of Dr. Joseph K. Barnes, a career army surgeon, as "Acting Surgeon General" and "Medical Inspector" in early 1863. Barnes began a thorough reform of the Medical Department, greatly improving services to the sick and wounded. By the end of the war the Medical Corps had evolved to the point where military hospitals had a capacity of 136,894 beds, or roughly one for every eight men in the army. It was, however, the common people of America, both North and South, who, with help from a few particularly devoted surgeons like Letterman,

Barnes, and Moore, were largely responsible for the many changes which affected the practice of medicine in the field, and the health and safety of the troops.

The Ships

U.S.S. Hartford

Although several other ships are more famous, no vessel which served in the Civil War had a more distinguished or varied career than did the steam sloop-of-war *Hartford*. Built at the Boston naval shipyard and launched on 22 November 1858, *Hartford* displaced 2,550 tons. She was 225 feet overall, with a beam of 44 feet and a draught of a bit more than 17 feet. As built, *Hartford* carried a main battery of 20 nine inch Dahlgren smooth bores, which were later supplemented with two 20-pounder Parrott guns and a pair of 12-pounders, making her among the most powerful warships of her class in the world. However, like most American warships of the day, she was rather slow; her underpowered engines could yield only about 9.5 knots and she could do little better under sail. *Hartford's* brief pre-war career was spent as flagship of the East Indian Squadron. At the outbreak of the war she was called home, landing at Philadelphia in December of 1861. On 28 January 1862 *Hartford* sailed for the Gulf of Mexico wearing the broad pennant of Capt. David G. Farragut, recently named commander of the West Gulf Blockading Squadron. *Hartford* was to be associated with Farragut for her entire wartime career.

Hartford's first combat service during the war came in April, when Farragut ran up the Mississippi to take New Orleans, during which she was under fire from the Confederate river forts, avoided being rammed by the novel ironclad C.S.S. *Manassas*, dodged a fire raft, and was briefly aground. Working free, she proceeded up river to New Orleans, which was captured on 29 April 1862. For more than a year, *Hartford* engaged in riverine and coastal activities, several times running the Confederate water batteries at Vicksburg, bombarding Port Hudson, assisting Grant's assault across the Mississippi in the spring of 1863, patrolling, and in general serving as a ship-of-all-work, while she continued as Farragut's flagship.

In 5 August 1864 *Hartford* led a fleet of four monitors and fourteen other warships into Mobile Bay, boldly running the shore batteries to engage the small Confederate squadron defending the harbor. It was a desperate three hour fight, during which Farragut, as usual in his favorite place during action, up in the rigging where he could see what was going on, uttered the famous line "Damn the torpedoes! Full speed ahead!" During the engagement, *Hartford* was one of several Federal vessels to ram the ironclad C.S.S. *Tennessee.* Although rather seriously strained by her effort, *Hartford* remained as flagship of the West Gulf Squadron until the end of the year, when she was taken in hand for repairs at the Brooklyn Navy Yard, work which was still in progress when the war ended.

After the war *Hartford* continued in the Navy for many years. Upon being retired, the Navy found itself unable to decide what to do with her. As a result, the old ship was merely ignored. In 1956 *Hartford,* or what was left of her, sank at her berth. Some feeble efforts were made to salvage her, but she was a constructive total loss. Adding insult to injury, no comparable warship has ever borne the name *Hartford,* a sad end to so noble a vessel.

Submarines

Technically the submarine was not among the many innovations in weaponry which appeared during the Civil War, but the war did lead to some important progress in its development. Interest in a vessel which could move under the sea is probably as old as seafaring itself. Nor were inventors slow in trying their hands at creating such. Although Leonardo da Vinci's design for an undersea ship existed on paper only, by the eighteenth century a number of people had actually built and tested submarines, often with fatal results. One of the earliest successful underwater vessels was David Bushnell's *American Turtle.* Extensively tested during the American Revolution, the man-powered vessel worked well, but was unsuccessful in several attempts to fasten an explosive charge against the hulls of blockading British warships and the project was abandoned; nevertheless, *American Turtle,* piloted by Sgt. Ezra Lee of Connecticut, was indirectly responsible for the destruction of a British schooner off New London in 1777. A generation later Robert Fulton designed and built a practical submarine which he named *Nautilus,* and offered it to the Royal Navy, which turned him down on the reasonable grounds that such an invention was more of a threat than a benefit to British sea power. Napoleon proved no more receptive to the idea, for different reasons, and Fulton turned his talents to designing a practical steamboat, which proved more profitable. By the outbreak of the Civil War submarines had become almost as familiar a notion as space travel is today, with successful experimental vessels being designed in France and Russia. The importance of the Civil War in the history of the submarine is that it was the first time that a government became seriously interested in their development. In consequence, several submarines were built, with the Confederacy being particularly active because the submarine held out the promise of breaking the blockade.

The Confederate effort to design and develop a successful submarine began as a private venture. The principals were Robert R. Barrow, a businessman, and two marine engineers, Baxter Watson and James McClintock. Barrow's brother-in-law, Horace L. Hunley, provided the initial funding for what was generally considered a profit making enterprise; the object was not to build a submarine in order to break the blockade for the greater glory of the Confederacy, but to enable blockade runners to reap greater profits. Nevertheless, their efforts were remarkable.

The first submarine designed by Watson and McClintock was named *Pioneer*. She was built in New Orleans late in 1861, out of iron plates, a roughly cylindrical vessel about 19 feet long. Not a true submersible, *Pioneer* had a snorkel-like arrangement which enabled her to operate below the surface, but not actually completely under water. She made a successful dive in Lake Pontchartrain early the following year, and managed to sink a barge by attaching an explosive charge. Unfortunately, a second test-dive proved less successful: the crew of four drowned. The vessel was salvaged, but was not fully repaired by the time the United States Navy steamed up the Mississippi to capture New Orleans that April. As a result, the hulk was towed out into the lake and scuttled; some years after the war *Pioneer* was accidentally rediscovered and now rests in a museum.

Undaunted, Messers Hunley, Barrow, Baxter, and McClintock removed to Mobile and set up shop again, this time aided by William A. Alexander, a British machinist. Their first effort, *American Diver*, was a failure, which unfortunately sank several times with considerable loss of life. This convinced them that they needed to rework their basic concept. After a good deal of work they built a new vessel, a genuinely submersible one, *H.L. Hunley*, fittingly named after the fellow who was putting up the cash.

Made from an old boiler, *Hunley* was the most successful submarine design of the war. She was roughly cigar-shaped, 25 feet long, five feet in the beam and had a depth of hold of 3.5 feet. The vessel had iron ballast fastened along her bottom which could be released to raise ship, hand worked ballast pumps, and a hand cranked propeller. The crew numbered eight to nine men, of whom six or seven provided the motive power, while one steered, and one conned and controlled ballast. When water was let into the ballast tanks by means of sea cocks, the vessel would begin to submerge, and she had diving planes to control the angle of descent. The vessel was conned through viewports in two small hatches which jutted above her deck; she could make four knots with these viewports just above the water. As designed, *Hunley* was supposed to tow explosive charges at the end of a 200 foot line, submerging to pass under Union warships, in order to bring the "torpedo" against their hulls.

Hunley was extensively tested in Mobile Bay. A number of dives were made and a barge was sunk. Despite the fact that one crew drowned during these tests, the vessel was considered a success. In late 1863 *Hunley* was sent to Charleston by rail and readied for service. At Charleston, she proved less successful. All but one member of her crew was lost when the wash from a passing ship flooded through an open hatch. Despite this misfortune, Gen. Pierre G.T. Beauregard, commanding the Charleston defenses, was impressed, not least because of the success of another experimental vessel, a smaller semi-submersible torpedo boat named *David*.

David was financed by the citizens of South Carolina, and was not a true submarine. She was cigar-shaped, about 20 feet long, and five feet in diameter, with a 60 pound spar torpedo extending from her bow. Since she was designed to operate awash, *David* had a small steam engine and could make a fair speed, perhaps eight knots.

On 5 October 1863 *David* made an attack on the broadside ironclad U.S.S. *New Ironsides*. Approaching with her deck just awash, *David* was not detected until she was very close to the Union warship, at a point where the ironclad's guns could not bear. Though Union sailors and Marines directed a lot of small arms fire at her—to which her crew replied with a couple of shotgun blasts—*David* was able to ram her torpedo into the ship's side with serious effects, causing sufficient damage to require repairs in port. However, the blast threw an enormous amount of water in the air, and as this splashed down, some of it poured into the vessel's smoke stack, causing her boiler to go out. Within minutes, *David* was wallowing about virtually in the midst of the Union blockading squadron. Most of crew abandoned ship, but two men managed to restart her boiler and got her away amidst a hail of Yankee fire. Despite this mishap, the vessel was considered a success and efforts were taken in hand to build more. Eventually eight were built at Charleston, but none were ever used. Meanwhile, *Hunley* continued to have development problems, which was particularly unfortunate for her crews: most of two additional crews drowned in training, including Horace L. Hunley himself. Although she was eventually able to make completely successful dives, once remaining submerged for 155 minutes, the risks of using her as a submarine were considered too great. As a result, *Hunley* was recast as a spar torpedo boat, similar to *David.*

Shortly before 9:00 p.m. on 17 February 1864, Lt. George E. Dixon of the 21st Alabama took *Hunley* on her first "war patrol." Dixon approached the Union screw sloop *Housatonic* as she was standing off Charleston harbor on blockade duty. As in the case of *David* and *New Ironsides, Hunley* was not detected until she was too close for the ship's guns to bear. Despite receiving some small arms fire, Dixon was able to ram *Hunley's* spar torpedo into the ship's side. There was a tremendous explosion as *Housatonic* blew up and sank, remarkably with a loss of only five men. Unfortunately, *Hunley* went down as well, with all hands—for the sixth time—, though whether from the explosion or the vortex made by the sinking *Housatonic* cannot be determined. Years later both vessels were found lying virtually side-by-side.

The unfortunate experience with *Hunley* wrote finish to further experiments with submarines, and with semi-submersible torpedo boats as well. Despite this, the basic concept and design of *H.L. Hunley* was actually rather sound. However, the poor technical resources of the Confederacy, the limited time available for perfecting the design, and the lack of an effective weapon system were all factors in determining the eventual failure of the effort to create the world's first practical submarine warship.

U.S.S. Alligator

Since the Union had far greater naval resources than did the Confederacy, it had less interest—and much less need—in developing a submersible warship. As with Confederate efforts, the first experiments were conducted by private interests, but the Federal government became involved in the process much earlier than the Confederate government. Despite this Union efforts were even less successful than were the Confederate ones. Union efforts to build a submarine were inextricably linked to Brutus de Villeroi. Villeroi had considerable experience in submarine design, having conducted numerous experiments in his native France: in 1835 he spent two hours under water in a vessel of his own design, in an experiment witnessed by seven-year old Jules Verne. Villeroi was in the United States at the beginning of the war, working on a number of ideas. He built and tested an experimental submarine in the Delaware River in the spring of 1861, which ran aground north of Philadelphia on 16 May. That September he offered Lincoln his 35 foot submarine, which had been refitted and somewhat redesigned. As was the case with a number of technical innovations—machine guns, balloons—Lincoln was impressed. He ordered the Navy to conduct tests, and was impressed even more. As a result, the Navy ordered a submarine. This vessel, named *Alligator*, caused a great deal of dispute between the designer and the builder and the Navy over many technical questions. As completed, she emerged with a kind of oared propulsion system, despite the fact that Villeroi's original design was screw driven. *Alligator* made an exploratory cruise in Hampton Roads in mid-1862, which proved somewhat satisfactory, but she was shortly thereafter lost while under tow off Cape Hatteras. This ended Union interest in submarines.

War and the Muses

When This Cruel War Is Over

On both sides the heroic and romantic airs which prevailed in the early part of the war gradually gave way to more somber, sadder, and even defeatist songs as the fighting dragged on and the casualty lists grew ever longer. The most popular song during 1863 was probably *When This Cruel War Is Over*, which remained popular through to the end of the war.

When This Cruel War Is Over
Dearest Love, do you remember
    When we last did meet,
How you told me that you loved me,
    Kneeling at your feet?
O, how proud you stood before me
    In your suit of blue
When you vowed to me and country
    Ever to be true.
Chorus—Weeping, sad and lonely,
    Hopes and fears, how vain;
Yet Praying
    When this cruel war is over,
Praying that we meet again.

When the summer breeze is sighing
    Mournfully along,
Or when the autumn leaves are falling,
    Sadly breathes this song.
Oft in dreams I see thee lying
    On the battle-plain,
Lonely, wounded, even dying,
    Calling, but in vain.
Chorus—Weeping, sad &c.

If amid the din of battle,
  Nobly you should fall,
Far away from those who love you,
  None to hear you call,
Who would whisper words of comfort?
  Who would soothe your pain?
Ah, the many cruel fancies
  Ever in my brain!
Chorus—Weeping, sad, &c.

But our country called you, darling,
  Angels cheer your way!
While our nation's sons are fighting,
  We can only pray.
Nobly strike for God and liberty,
  Let all nations see
How we love the starry banner,
  Emblem of the free!
Chorus—Weeping, sad and lonely,
  Hopes and fears, how vain;
Yet Praying
  When this cruel war is over,
Praying that we meet again.

Cavalry Crossing a Ford

Arguably the greatest American poet Walt Whitman (1819-1892), served with great devotion as a journalist and nurse during the war. Said to be one of only three men who never despaired of the Union cause—the others being Lincoln and Grant—Whitman penned numerous poems on war themes. His "Cavalry Crossing a Ford" is a fine word picture of a commonplace incident of the war.

Cavalry Crossing a Ford
A line in long array where they wind betwixt green islands,
They take a serpentine course, their arms flash in the sun
  —hark to the musical clank,
Behold the silvery river, in it the splashing horses
  loitering stop to drink,
Behold the brown-faced men, each group, each person a
  picture, the negligent rest on the saddles,

Some emerge on the opposite bank, others are just entering
  the ford—while
Scarlet and blue and snowy white,
The guidon flags flutter gaily in the wind.

Only a Soldier's Grave

Among the most moving poems to emerge out of the South was that by
Mississippian S.A. Jones, whose "Only a Soldier's Grave" rather effectively
expresses both pride in the cause and sadness over the cost.

Only a Soldier's Grave

Only a soldier's grave! Pass by,
For soldiers, like other mortals, die.
Parents he had—they are far away;
No sister weeps o'er the soldier's clay;
No brother comes, with tearful eye:
It's only a soldier's grave—pass by.
True, he was loving, and young, and brave,
Though no glowing epitaph honors his grave;
No proud recital of virtues known,
Of griefs endured, or triumphs won;
No tablet of marble, or obelisk high;—
Only a soldier's grave:—pass by
Yet bravely he wielded his sword in fight,
And he gave his life in the cause of right!
When his hope was high, and his youthful dream
As warm as the sunlight on yonder stream;
His heart unvexed by sorrow or sigh;—
Yet, 'tis only a soldier's grave:—pass by.
Yet, should we mark it—the soldier's grave,
Some one may seek him in hope to save!
Some of the dear ones, far away,
Would bear him home to his native clay:
'Twere sad, indeed, should they wander nigh,
Find not the hillock, and pass him by.

V
1864

All that has gone before is mere skirmishing.
—William Tecumseh Sherman

General Grant will not retreat.
—Robert E. Lee

I intend to fight it out on this line if it takes all summer.
—Ulysses S. Grant

Damn the torpedoes! Full speed ahead!
—David Glasgow Farragut

If we must die, let us die like men.
—Patrick R. Cleburne

1864

*T*he onset of 1864 boded ill for the Confederacy. Though the heartland of the South had yet to feel the tread of Union troops, and though strong Confederate armies under able commanders were still in the field, militarily the decision on the Civil War had been reached in 1863, the year of Vicksburg, Gettysburg, and Missionary Ridge, and the initiative had passed decisively to the Union. The material war had also been lost, as the logistical situation of the South began to become increasingly desperate. And the war had been lost diplomatically as well, for hope of securing foreign recognition—and perhaps intervention—had long since faded. But the South could yet win politically. War-weariness and defeatism were widespread in the North and 1864 was an election year. If the Confederate armies could hold back the increasingly stronger Federal forces until November, political disaffection in the North might eject the Lincoln administration from Washington, bringing in its place one inclined to a compromise peace. It was perhaps a slender reed upon which to lean, but by 1864 the South had few other options.

In March of 1864 Lincoln called the most consistently successful Union commander to the East. Promoted to lieutenant general—the first since George Washington—Ulysses S. Grant was made general-in-chief. In his methodical fashion Grant began to shape Union strategy for the coming year. There would be two grand offensives. In the East the *Army of the Potomac* would hit Robert E. Lee and his Army of Northern Virginia with a series of hammer blows and maneuvers designed to pin it down so that it could be destroyed. Meanwhile, in the West, Maj. Gen. William T. Sherman would conduct an offensive from southeastern Tennessee into Georgia, smashing Gen. Joseph Johnston's Army of Tennessee, capturing Atlanta, and cutting the Confederacy in two yet again by marching to the sea. And that is essentially what happened.

The *Army of the Potomac* moved first. Under Maj. Gen. George G. Meade it crossed the Rappahannock on 3 May 1864, 120,000 strong to try to conclude with Gen. Robert E. Lee's Army of Northern Virginia, little more than half its strength. The Battle of the Wilderness (5-6 May) followed. Grant maneuvered to turn Lee's right in the dense growth below the Rappahannock. Lee blocked the effort and a bloody stalemate resulted after the Union had suffered perhaps 15,000 casualties and the Confederacy some 10,000. At this point the military situation seemed a repetition of former Federal offensives; the Yankees, having come South, had been stopped by the Rebels and could now be expected to fall back, lick their wounds, and make ready for another try. But Grant changed the rules. On the evening of 7 May he pulled the *Army of the Potomac* out of the lines and marched it south, once again maneuvering to turn Lee's right. It was stunningly simple; Grant had come south to fight and he intended to stay in the field until a decision was reached. As they began to move out, the blue-clad veterans cheered.

Thus began a bloody series of engagements which, though often tactical reverses for Grant, were strategic defeats for Lee, who was forced to fight repeated costly defensive actions. The Wilderness was followed by Spotsylvania Courthouse (8-19 May), the North Anna River (23-26 May), and Cold Harbor (3 June). Each time the Rebels gave better than they received, but each time Grant pressed them closer to Richmond. And finally, aided by a movement of the *Army of the James* from the Virginia coast, Grant arrived before Richmond in mid-June. It had been a bloody campaign. Union casualties were perhaps 50,000 and Confederate ones have been estimated at between 20,000 and 40,000. Grant had failed in his principal objective, to destroy the Army of Northern Virginia in the field. But he had succeeded in pinning it down. With his back up against Richmond Lee lost his ability to maneuver. Although the defensive abilities of the Army of Northern Virginia remained high, it was no longer able to deliver the lightning-like surprise attacks which characterized its performance earlier in the war.

For strategic and logistical reasons Grant shifted front, bringing the *Army of the Potomac* south of the James River to invest Petersburg, a small city about 20 miles south of Richmond. This maneuver permitted him to keep his back to the sea, while positioning him to threaten Lee's lines of supply, which ran southwest from the town. Then he began the "siege" of Petersburg, a protracted investment of the place punctuated by occasional offensive maneuvers which would last until the following spring. Meanwhile, the war went on in the West.

By the spring of 1864 William Tecumseh Sherman had concentrated some 100,000 men in the vicinity of Chattanooga. On 6 May he undertook an offensive against Atlanta, about 100 miles to the southeast. The defense of Atlanta was entrusted to Confederate Gen. Joseph E. Johnston and the Army of Tennessee, about 50,000 strong. What followed was a protracted duel between two talented commanders. Sherman and Johnston marched and fought in a series of maneuvers and battles. On balance, Sherman won, but so did Johnston, for Sherman required two months to reach the vicinity of Atlanta. Wary of his opponent's superior numbers, Johnston had kept his forces in motion, preferring maneuver to battle, thereby preserving his army, which was Sherman's principal objective. Johnston had conducted a brilliant campaign, but it was not viewed as such in Richmond. Personally disliking the little general anyway, on 17 July Jefferson Davis replaced Johnston with John B. Hood, "a man who will fight."

Hood did fight, but Sherman won all the battles. There were four major engagements around Atlanta between 20 July and 31 August, and Sherman won them all, while slowly tightening a noose around the city. Fearing that he would become bottled up in Atlanta, Hood evacuated it on 1 September putting much of it to the torch as he retreated to the southwest. A few days later Sherman ejected the remaining inhabitants and burned down what was left. For about a month things were quiet. Hood was desperately trying to rebuild his army, while Sherman was having serious logistical problems, his long line of supply back into Tennessee being under constant danger from Confederate cavalry and partisans. Finally, early in October, Hood marched north.

Having rebuilt the Army of Tennessee to about 40,000 men, Hood intended to avoid Sherman's main body and operate against his lines of supply. He was surprisingly successful and by mid-October was within striking distance of Chattanooga. Sherman tried to pin Hood down, but the latter proved elusive. Finally, with Grant's permission, he abandoned the chase. Rather than worry about his lines of supply, he ignored them altogether and marched on Savannah. Curiously, at about the same time Hood had decided to give up the game in favor of an invasion of Tennessee and Kentucky. Thus, by the end of October both armies were actually marching away from each other.

Hood's offensive was a disaster. A series of spectacular marches resulted in pyrrhic victories at Spring Hill (29 November) and Franklin (30 November). Then Union Maj. Gen. George Thomas held him before Nashville (2 December) and later shattered his army in a devastating offensive (15-16 December). And as the remnants of the Army of Tennessee drifted southward, Sherman's armies were preparing to take Savannah.

Sherman launched his "March to the Sea" on 12 November. Abandoning his lines of supply, he took 62,000 men and 20 days rations and set out to "make Georgia squeal." Sherman advanced on a broad front, with each army corps driving eastward on a parallel line of advance while his considerable cavalry covered the flanks and scouted ahead. An enormous amount of damage was inflicted upon the Georgia countryside, Sherman's men concentrated on military objectives. The host of camp followers, refugees, fugitive slaves, and deserters from both armies which traveled in his wake was less discriminating. There was little fighting. Savannah fell on 21 December and the Confederacy had been cut in two yet again.

Militarily 1864 was a disaster for the Confederacy. Worse, it was a political disaster, for the failure of Southern arms helped re-elect Lincoln in November. With that there was no longer any hope for an end to the war on terms favorable to the South. But the Union success in the field had not been total. And so the war would last another winter, one of unmitigated misery throughout the South.

1864

Incidents of War

Close Order Drill

While passing through Georgia on some military business, a Confederate general chanced to stop for a time in a small country village. The news of his presence soon reached the ears of the captain of the local home guard company. Since the captain was proud of the skill with which his little command executed the various evolutions in the drill book, he decided to put on a show for the general. He had the company fall in outside of the general's quarters and began to put the men through their paces. Within a few minutes the captain's shouted orders and his company's prompt and military response had attracted the general's attention, and he came outside to watch.

The guardsmen were doing quite nicely until their commander decided to attempt some complex counter-march maneuver at the double-quick. Within seconds the neat formation which the men had hitherto maintained disintegrated and the company was left in what one observer described as a "solid circle." In his most stentorian tone the frustrated captain cried out "Halt!" and, with some embarrassment, surveyed the mess into which he had gotten his men. The general looked on with renewed interest as the captain seemed to sink deep in thought. Then, suddenly, the man's face brightened, and he called out "Company, disentangle to the front, march!"

Within seconds the company was back in proper formation. The general came over, and the officer, who had expected a withering blast of major general's proportions, received instead the general's compliments on having issued the best command he had ever heard given.

The Canadian Front

The Confederate efforts to "bring the war home" to the North by means of raids from Canada form an obscure chapter in the history of the Civil War. As a strategy it wasn't likely to win the war, but it could have caused

271

significant problems for the Union, possibly easing pressure on the Confederacy and perhaps even exacerbating American relations with Britain. At least three operations were actually put into effect, and two of them involved the U.S.S. *Michigan*, a lightly armed gunboat and the only Federal warship on the Great Lakes.

The first attempt was engineered by Capt. John Wilkinson. C.S.N., who had had a long career in the United States Navy before the war. The plan was really quite simple. A cargo of cotton would be run through the blockade to provide financing for the operation. These funds would be used to procure arms—including two 9-pounder cannon—and various other equipment which would be shipped to Montreal in crates labeled "machinery." Meanwhile Wilkinson would concentrate his men at Montreal, recruiting additional personnel from among the many escaped Confederate prisoners-of-war living in Canada. When all was in readiness, the "machinery" would be loaded aboard a lake steamer and the men would take passage in various guises. Once "at sea" Wilkinson and his men would seize the ship, break out their weapons, and steam for Sandusky, where *Michigan* was normally to be found. Timing their arrival for dawn, the raiders would stage a collision with the Union vessel, permitting them to board and capture her. They would then commission her in the Confederate Navy and head for Johnson's Island, where about 3,000 Confederate troops, mostly officers, were being held as prisoners-of-war. Using the ship's guns, Wilkinson would effect the release of the prisoners, and then proceed to terrorize Union lake traffic. There were some fuzzy aspects of Wilkinson's plan, notably what was to be done with all those thousands of prisoners, many ill and debilitated, so many hundreds of miles from the Confederacy. Nevertheless, had he succeeded, Wilkinson would have caused enormous disruption to Northern commerce, and delivered a blow to Yankee morale and a boost to that of the Rebels.

Initially the operation went smoothly. In January of 1864 the fast steamer *Robert E. Lee* sailed from Wilmington, North Carolina, with a load of cotton, successfully eluded the Union blockade, and made for Halifax. Wilkinson was soon busily procuring the arms and equipment he needed and moving his men to their rendezvous at Montreal. However, Union intelligence, apparently warned by Canadian authorities, got wind of the scheme. *Michigan* was alerted to the danger, the garrison at Johnson's Island was increased, and other precautions taken. As a result, Wilkinson dispersed his men. Making his way back to the Confederacy, he was for a time commander of the famed ironclad *Albemarle* and several other vessels.

Although Wilkinson's scheme failed, it was sufficiently reasonable to be adopted virtually whole for a second attempt on *Michigan.*

In August of 1864 John Beall, a Confederate naval officer, began recruiting a crew from among the Confederate escapees in Canada. On 19 September Beall and his men seized the lake steamer *Philo Parsons* and set course for Sandusky. Beall's plan called for Confederate agents ashore to distract the attention of the crew of the Union warship, thereby making it easier for him to seize the ship. However, the attempt to distract the crew was unsuccessful and Beall had no choice but to abort the operation. Steaming back to Canada aboard *Philo Parsons*, Beall chanced to encounter the American steamer *Island Queen*, which he seized and scuttled, the only naval casualty of the war on the Great Lakes. While Beall could have attempted to use *Philo Parsons* a while longer, he was in a precarious situation, for both American and Canadian authorities were looking for him. As a result, shortly after his encounter with *Island Queen*, he ran his ship aground and abandoned it, making his escape overland.

The final Confederate effort to bring the war home to the North occurred in October of 1864. Lt. Bennett H. Young, a Kentuckian resident in Canada due to the exigencies of the war, secured permission from Richmond to undertake a raid on the town of St. Albans, Vermont, with the intention of diverting Union forces from the armies in order to secure the Canadian border. Disguised as hunters, Young and his band, about 25 escaped Confederate prisoners-of-war, drifted into St. Albans in small groups over several days in October of 1864. Then, at about 3:00 p.m. on 19 October, the raiders struck.

Divided into several groups, some of Young's men arrested the townsfolk, concentrating them on the village common, while others gathered up the available horses, and a third group cleaned out the three local banks of some $20,000 in cash. A few of the townsfolk objected to the proceedings, and some firing resulted, which caused one of the raiders to be killed and two of the locals to be wounded. Meanwhile, some people fleeing the town alerted folks in the surrounding areas, who, aided by two Union veterans on leave, organized a posse and gave chase. Young and his men fled towards the border, breaking up into several groups in order to elude pursuit. Despite this, the posse managed to grab about a dozen of the raiders, only to discover that they had strayed into Canada. The Canadian authorities took charge of the prisoners, rounded up the rest of the band, and incarcerated the lot. The Federal government immediately demanded extradition on the grounds that Young and his men were criminals, but the

Canadian courts ruled that they had been acting as soldiers under orders. As a result, Young and his men were interned under bond.

The Confederate efforts to strike at the United States from Canada demonstrated considerable daring and ingenuity. Had they been successful, they would have caused considerable difficulties for the Union. But it is highly unlikely that they would have significantly altered the outcome of the war. Indeed, the effort were very much a confession of failure and of the inability of the Confederacy to develop a strategy which could bring the war to a successful conclusion.

Grant Has an Inquisitive Visitor

In the simpler times during which the Civil War was fought army camps were frequently crowded with visitors, who would often importune high officers for favors or try to pump them for information. Dealing with such people was sometimes difficult.

One day, during his Overland Campaign, Lt. Gen. U.S. Grant was sitting quietly before his tent puffing on one of his inevitable cigars and chatting with a staff officer. A civilian who chanced to be in the camp came up and attempted to engage the General in conversation.

"General," the man asked, "If you flank Lee, and get between him and Richmond, will you not 'uncover' Washington and leave it prey to the enemy?"

Calmly letting forth a cloud of smoke, Grant replied, "Yes, I reckon so."

The visitor pressed on, "General, do you think Lee can detach sufficient force from his army to reinforce Beauregard and overwhelm Butler?"

"Not a doubt of it," replied the General.

Yet again, the visitor posed a question, "General, is there not a danger that Johnston may come up and reinforce Lee, so that the latter will swing around and cut your communications and seize your supplies?"

Grant extracted the cigar from his mouth, studied it for a moment, flicked the ash off the tip with his little finger, and said, "Very likely."

The stunned stranger could take no more. Believing that Grant and all the Union forces in Virginia were on the verge of destruction he took his leave, heading for Washington, to be the first with the terrible news.

And Grant and his aide had a quiet laugh together.

"I Know You!"

Confederate President Jefferson Davis went riding on an almost daily basis,

unescorted, as was his wont, despite criticism for showing "little pru-
dence." One day as he was engaged in this equestrian exercise, he chanced
upon a soldier from a North Carolina regiment.

The man looked up and waved him to a stop. When Davis had done so,
the man asked, very politely, "Sir, mister, be'ent you Jefferson Davis?"

Perhaps expecting some difficulties, Davis replied rather sternly, "Sir,
that is my name."

The soldier chuckled, "I thought so, you look so much like a postage
stamp."

Grant and the Sentry

One day late in 1864 Grant was out alone, walking along a dock at City
Point, Virginia, with the inevitable cigar in his mouth. A black sentry
approached him and attempted to gain his attention, but the general was
deep in thought and failed to notice the man. The soldier touched the
general on the arm, saying "No smoking on the dock, sir."

Looking up, Grant said, "Are these your orders?"

In a firm but polite voice, showing not the least bit of intimidation
about giving orders to the army's only lieutenant general, the sentry
replied, "Yes, sir."

Taking the cigar from his mouth, Grant looked at it, said "Very good
orders," and threw it into the water.

The sentry rendered a proper salute and the general walked on.

The Men

George H. Thomas

A native Virginian, George H. Thomas (1816-1870) graduated 12th in the West Point Class of 1840, entering the artillery. He fought the Seminoles, served on the frontier and in garrison, won two brevets in Mexico, and taught at West Point. During the Secession Crisis he was recuperating from an arrow wound in the face. Expected to "go South" with his native Virginia, Thomas remained loyal to the Union and by August of 1861 had risen from major to brigadier general. His career during the Civil War was a brilliant one.

Thomas served in the Shenandoah Valley in 1861 and then went to Kentucky (Mill Springs, 19-20 January 1862). Appointed a major general in April of '62, he commanded divisions and later corps in all the principal battles in Tennessee. At Chickamauga the heroic stand of his troops earned him the nickname "The Rock of Chickamauga" and subsequently command of the *Army of the Cumberland* when Grant assumed direction of affairs in Central Tennessee. His troops again distinguished themselves at Missionary Ridge and Thomas thereafter became one of the principal Federal commanders, serving under Sherman during the Atlanta Campaign (Peach Tree Creek, 20 July '64). When Confederate Gen. John B. Hood invaded Tennessee in an effort to draw Sherman away from central Georgia, Thomas stopped him cold at Nashville and then smashed his army (15-16 December '63), despite unfamiliar, mistrustful subordinates. After the war Thomas continued in the service, dying in San Francisco, where he was commanding general for the West Coast.

A big, deliberate man of considerable ability, Thomas' Virginia background probably retarded his rise to independent command. Nevertheless, he was one of the most successful Union commanders, surpassing all but Sherman and Grant in this regard.

John Gibbon

A native Philadelphian, John Gibbon (1827-1896) was raised in North Carolina from boyhood. Graduating from West Point 20th in the Class of 1847, along with Ambrose P. Hill and Ambrose E. Burnside, he served in Mexico and against the Seminoles, before putting in five years as an artillery instructor and quartermaster at West Point. During this period he wrote *The Artillerist's Manual,* which, while not officially adopted by the War Department, was widely used as a handbook by both sides during the war. Although his three brothers all entered Confederate service, Gibbon remained loyal to his oath at the outbreak of the Civil War, which found him at an isolated post in Utah. He served in various artillery posts for a time, then, since promotions in the artillery were slow, transferred to the volunteers and was almost immediately commissioned a brigadier general. In the spring of 1862 Gibbon assumed command of what would become the famed *Iron Brigade* in *I Corps,* giving it the black hats which earned it its other nickname, "*The Black Hat Brigade,*" and leading it during the Second Bull Run and Antietam Campaigns. Later that year he was given a division, which he led at Fredericksburg, suffering a severe wound. In the spring of 1863 he returned to duty as a division commander in Maj. Gen. Winfield Scott Hancock's *II Corps,* serving at Chancellorsville. During the Gettysburg Campaign Gibbon took over the corps when Hancock was assigned higher command, and demonstrated great ability in a critical situation; it was on this front that the "High Tide" of the Confederacy washed. Again severely wounded, he was placed on administrative duty until the following spring, when he resumed command of his old division. Gibbon fought in all the battles of the *Army of the Potomac* from the Wilderness to Petersburg, earning a major generalcy in the process. In early 1865 he was given the *XXIV Corps* in the *Army of the James,* which he led until Appomattox, when he was named one of the three commissioners to receive the surrender of the Army of Northern Virginia.

After the war Gibbon became a colonel in the regular army. Commanding the *7th Infantry,* he saw service on the frontier for the next 30 years, becoming a noted Indian fighter and retiring as a brigadier general in the Regular Army. Gibbon wrote his memoirs, *Personal Recollections of the Civil War,* in 1885, an interesting book which did not see print until 1928. He was one of the ablest division commanders of the war.

John B. Hood

A native of Kentucky, John B. Hood (1831-1893) graduated from West Point 44th in the class of 1853. Commissioned initially in the infantry, he later transferred to the cavalry. Hood served in garrison and on the frontier, where he was wounded, before resigning from the army as a first lieutenant in April of 1861, immediately entering Confederate service in the same rank. Hood held a variety of minor commands, including the 4th Texas with some distinction until the Peninsular Campaign, when he was named brigadier general and given a brigade of Texans which he led with skill and verve at Gaines' Mill and thereafter in the Second Bull Run and Antietam Campaigns. In October of 1862 Hood was named major general and given a division in Longstreet's I Corps, leading it ably at Fredericksburg and in the Carolinas.

At Gettysburg, Hood's division made the principal Confederate attack on 2 July which almost destroyed the *Army of the Potomac*, during which his left arm was crippled. Recovering quickly, Hood went west with Longstreet's corps later in 1863, briefly commanding it and several divisions of the Army of Tennessee at Chickamauga, where he lost his right leg. Remaining in the West, he was given a corps in the Army of Tennessee by Joe Johnston and promoted lieutenant general. He led his corps with commendable aggressiveness in the opening stages of the Atlanta Campaign, during which Johnston's clever maneuvering kept Federal gains to a minimum, but proved bad for Confederate morale. In July Hood was made an acting general, superseding Johnston in command, an action dictated by Jefferson Davis' dissatisfaction over Johnston's refusal to fight. Hood fought, but Sherman won, securing Atlanta and ultimately launching his famed "March to the Sea." In a desperate move, Hood launched his army into Tennessee, hoping to divert Sherman's attention from Georgia. Hood's invasion of Tennessee proved a disaster, with a Pyrrhic victory at Franklin followed by a devastating defeat in front of Nashville at the hands of George Thomas, Hood earning the distinction of being the only Civil War commander to lose virtually his entire army in action. Relieved at his own request, Hood reverted to his permanent rank but saw no further service. After the war he became a merchant in New Orleans, married and had eleven children in ten years, and wrote his memoirs. The yellow fever epidemic of 1878 caused a financial crisis which wiped out his fortune and, in the following year carried off him, his wife, and one of their children. A big, aggressive man who loved combat, Hood was not a subtle commander and had an unfortunate tendency to blame his subordinates for his own errors. Confederate Senator Louis T. Wigfall of South Carolina observed, with perhaps as much accuracy as acid, that Hood "had a fine career before him until [Jefferson] Davis undertook to make of him what the good Lord had not done—to make a great general of him."

John Sedgwick

A native of rural Connecticut, John Sedgwick (1813-1864) graduated from West Point in 1837, 24th in a class which included Braxton Bragg, Jubal Early, Joseph Hooker, and John C. Pemberton. He served against the Seminoles, in the relocation of the Cherokees to Oklahoma ("The Trail of Tears"), in Mexico (two brevets), on the frontier, and in garrison. Early in 1861 Sedgwick became colonel of the *1st Cavalry* (shortly renamed the *4th*) upon the resignation of the colonel and lieutenant colonel, Robert E. Lee and William J. Hardee. He was soon afterwards named a brigadier general of volunteers, serving as inspector general of the defenses of Washington and then as a brigade commander in the *Army of the Potomac.*

Sedgwick commanded a division during the Peninsular Campaign until wounded and was promoted major general. At Antietam he led his division with great courage and was wounded three times. Returning to duty within 90 days he commanded various corps until being given *VI Corps* in February of 1863. He led his corps at Chancellorsville, performing his duties with considerable skill and courage. Although he outranked Meade, he gallantly offered to serve under the latter when he was appointed commander of the *Army of the Potomac.* Sedgwick's corps was but lightly engaged at Gettysburg. He led it with distinction at the Wilderness and Spotsylvania in the spring of 1864, where he was killed instantly by a sharpshooter while choosing sites for his artillery. A tough disciplinarian, he was nevertheless a friendly and generous commander, and reputedly the most well-liked higher officer in the entire army, for which he was nicknamed "Uncle John."

Fitzhugh Lee

"Fitz" Lee (1835-1905) was born on a plantation in Virginia. At West Point he was almost dismissed for misconduct, but managed to convince the superintendent, his uncle Robert E. Lee, to permit him to remain. He graduated in 1856, 45th in his class, and was commissioned in the cavalry. Lee served on the frontier, being severely wounded while fighting Indians. When Virginia seceded he was tactical officer at West Point. He resigned his commission as a first lieutenant on 21 May 1861, almost immediately entering Confederate service in the same grade, and shortly was named lieutenant colonel of the 1st Virginia Cavalry.

During the Peninsular Campaign Lee at first served on Richard Ewell's staff and later on that of Joseph E. Johnston, during which he accompanied J.E.B. Stuart on his famous "Ride around the Union army." He was made a brigadier general in July of 1862 and commanded a cavalry brigade at South Mountain and Antietam and on various raids and reconnaissances in late 1862 and in early 1863. His brigade covered the flank march of Lt. Gen. Thomas "Stonewall" Jackson's II Corps during the Chancellorsville Campaign and he served ably during the Gettysburg Campaign which followed, being promoted major general shortly afterwards. During the Overland Campaign of 1864 Lee led a division with particular distinction at Spotsylvania and during Jubal Early's operations in the Shenandoah Valley. In January of 1865 he assumed command of the Cavalry Corps when Wade Hampton was ordered to the Carolinas. He led his uncle's cavalry thereafter until Appomattox. After the war Lee took up farming and writing, producing a biography of his famous uncle and several other historical works. He served as governor of Virginia from 1885 to 1889, and as U.S. Consul in Havanna from 1896 to the outbreak of the Spanish-American War in 1898, during which he was commissioned a major general of volunteers and given a corps which performed occupation duties. Lee retired from the army in 1902 as a regular brigadier general.

Leonidas Polk

Born in North Carolina, Leonidas Polk (1806-1864) caught religion while a cadet at West Point. Shortly after graduating from the Military Academy in 1827 he resigned from the army to enter the Virginia Theological Seminary. In 1830 he was ordained in the Episcopal Church. Polk rose rapidly through the hierarchy, becoming Missionary Bishop of the Southwest in 1836 and Bishop of Louisiana in 1841, a post which he occupied until the outbreak of the war. Upon the secession of Louisiana, Polk traded in his vestments for a uniform. In June of 1861 his close friend Jefferson Davis appointed him a major general in the Provisional Army and assigned him to command in the Upper Mississippi Valley, a post in which he was superseded by his friend and West Point roommate Gen. Albert Sidney Johnston some months later. On 7 November 1861 Polk had the satisfaction of defeating an effort by the obscure Union Brig. Gen. Ulysses S.

Grant to occupy Belmont, Missouri. Polk was soon after given a corps in the Army of Tennessee.

Polk led his corps with some ability at Shiloh and all the subsequent actions of the Army of Tennessee until Chickamauga, earning a promotion to lieutenant general for distinguished service at Perryville in October of 1862. Although this promotion was based upon the recommendation of Gen. Braxton Bragg, then commanding the Army of Tennessee, Polk's relations with the latter—who rarely got along with anyone—were poor and deteriorated steadily. Matters between the two men reached a crisis after Chickamauga, when Bragg demanded that Polk be subject to a court martial for failure to obey orders. Jefferson Davis, who was friendly with both men, prevented this, but, to avoid further trouble, transferred Polk to command the Department of Alabama, Mississippi, and East Louisiana.

Polk did poorly in his new command. During Sherman's Meridian Campaign (February-March 1864), he dispersed his forces over too wide an area, failed to make the most effective use of his best troops, Nathan Bedford Forrest's cavalry, and generally lost control of the situation. In May he was ordered to take the bulk of his troops to reinforce Gen. Joseph Johnston and the Army of Tennessee as they prepared to confront Sherman's drive on Atlanta. While on reconnaissance at Pine Mountain, Georgia, on 14 June 1864, Polk was killed by an artillery shell.

A big, handsome man, Polk was a fair but unspectacular corps commander, and certainly lacked the capacity for independent command. It is difficult to avoid the conclusion that his rise was primarily the result of his friendship with Jefferson Davis.

Wade Hampton

Born into a family of wealthy planters in South Carolina, Wade Hampton (1818-1902) was the grandson and principal heir of Maj. Gen. Wade Hampton (c. 1751-1835), a hero of the Revolutionary War and the War of 1812. Young Hampton graduated from South Carolina College at the age of 18. Reputedly the largest landowner in the South, Hampton owned some 3,500 slaves. He spent most of his life managing his extensive holdings in South Carolina and the Mississippi Valley. Hampton also was active in state politics, serving for many years in the legislature. Although he had doubts about the economic utility of slavery and opposed secession, he nevertheless supported his state when it seceded in late 1860.

In 1861 Hampton organized a mixed regiment which he raised at his own expense, the Hampton Legion, which afterwards split into separate infantry, cavalry, and artillery elements. Commissioned a colonel, he led his regiment during the First Bull Run Campaign, in which he was wounded, and commanded an infantry brigade in the Peninsular Campaign, during which he was promoted to brigadier general and once again wounded. In mid-1862 Hampton was given a cavalry brigade and was shortly after also made second-in-command of Maj. Gen. J.E.B. Stuart's cavalry division. He participated in most of the operations of the division through 1864.

Hampton was seriously wounded during the Gettysburg Campaign and was soon after promoted major general. Upon the death of Stuart in May of 1864, Hampton succeeded to command of the cavalry, leading it for the balance of the campaign of 1864, by the end of which many of his troopers were fighting as infantry due to a shortage of mounts. Early in 1865 he went to South Carolina with part of his forces to collect horses, and while there was promoted lieutenant general. He helped cover the retreat of Gen. Joseph Johnston's army in the closing weeks of the war and briefly considered attempting to escape westward and continue resistance, but instead surrendered and was paroled.

After the war Hampton gradually rebuilt his fortune and supported the mild Reconstruction program of President Andrew Johnson, seeking a fusion of black and white interests. During Radical Reconstruction, Hampton devoted himself to his private affairs and campaigned for an end to Reconstruction. When this occurred he served two terms as governor of his native state, 1876-1879, during which period he gained the confidence of both blacks and whites by evenhanded administration and an opposition to violence. From 1879 he served in the United States Senate, retaining his seat until 1891, when a radical racist faction took control of state politics. In later life he served as United States Commissioner for Pacific Railways. A physically imposing man, Hampton was one of the best amateur officers of the war, and one of the few high ranking southern leaders who in post-war years attempted to build a better society.

Gouverneur K. Warren

Born at Cold Spring, New York, Gouverneur K. Warren (1830-1882) was named after Gouverneur Kemble, noted literateur and artillery designer who established the West Point Foundry there in 1818. Warren graduated from nearby West Point second in the class of 1850. His Old Army service was in the Corps of Topographical Engineers and as an instructor of mathematics at the academy.

At the start of the war he became lieutenant colonel of the *5th New York*, seeing action at Big Bethel in June of 1861. He soon became colonel of the regiment and led it in the Peninsular Campaign, where he acquired a wound and a brigade in *V Corps*, which he led with distinction at Second Bull Run and Antietam. Warren was promoted brigadier general of volunteers in September of 1862 and led his brigade at Fredericksburg. That spring he joined the staff of the *Army of the Potomac*, rising to major general in May and becoming Chief of Engineers in June. At Gettysburg the most important of his many services was his improvised defense of Little Round Top on the afternoon of 2 July. After Gettysburg Warren assumed command of *II Corps* during the convalescence of Maj. Gen. Winfield Scott Hancock. During the Mine Run Campaign, it was Warren who first detected the Confederate concentration which would have made George Meade's proposed attack a disaster. The following spring he was given *V Corps*.

Warren commanded *V Corps* with distinction through all the battles of the Campaign of 1864 up to Five Forks, when he was relieved by Maj. Gen. Philip Sheridan, with the consent of Lt. Gen. U.S. Grant. Though no reason was given for this at the time, Warren's relief appears to have been due to a personality clash with Sheridan, who later stated that Warren had been lethargic in his movements during the battle. This effectively ruined Warren's career. Thereafter he held various administrative posts. Remaining in the army after the war, Warren did not rise to lieutenant colonel of engineers until 1879, when, after years of effort, a court of inquiry exonerated him, concluding that there had been no grounds for his relief. Aside from the published verdict of the court, and his belated promotion, Warren received nothing. A good man, and a fine general, he deserved better for his distinguished and honorable services to the Republic.

James B. McPherson

James B. McPherson (1828-1864) was born on a farm in Ohio. When he was 13 his blacksmith father was declared mentally incompetent and young McPherson had to seek employment as a store clerk in order to help support his family. Finding him a bright lad, his employer helped him through Norwalk Academy and he secured an appointment to West Point in 1849. McPherson, who was rather older than the average cadet, graduated first in the class of 1853 and entered the Corps of Engineers. After teaching engineering for a time at the Military Academy, he spent several years working on improvements to navigation, harbor development, and coastal fortifications. When the war came he continued in this duty for some time, and was not promoted to captain until August of 1861. This was an unauspicious start for what would be one of the most spectacular careers in the Union Army; within 14 months he would rank as a major general of volunteers.

McPherson held a variety of posts during the war, serving in both command and staff positions with equal ability. In November of 1861 he was jumped to lieutenant colonel, appointed an *aide de camp* to Maj. Gen. Henry Halleck, commanding the Department of Missouri. The following February he was named chief engineer in Maj. Gen. Ulysses S. Grant's *Army of the Tennessee*, serving with distinction at Henry and Donelson, Shiloh, and Corinth. In May he was appointed colonel, and almost immediately afterwards brigadier general of volunteers and given a brigade of engineers in the *Army of the Tennessee*. He led his brigade through early October, when he was promoted major general of volunteers and given a division in *XIII Corps*. On 18 December 1862 McPherson was given *XVII Corps*.

McPherson led *XVII Corps* with great skill, courage, and success for some 14 months, during the Vicksburg Campaign and the operations which followed it in central Mississippi, meanwhile earning the praises of his superiors, U.S. Grant and W.T. Sherman, and a coveted promotion to brigadier general in the Regular Army. In March of 1864 McPherson assumed command of the *Army of the Tennessee*, leading it in Sherman's army group during the Atlanta Campaign. Though he was criticized somewhat for excessive caution, it was McPherson's corps on which Sherman most frequently relied when executing his numerous flank marches. On 22 July 1864, McPherson chanced to be at Sherman's headquarters when Confederate Gen. John B. Hood delivered a massive blow against Federal forces before Atlanta. Endeavoring to reach his troops, McPherson and his orderly blundered into a band of Confederates and he was shot as he tried to escape. It is said that Sherman cried when he saw McPherson's body.

One of the finest tactical commanders in the Union Army, McPherson was held in high esteem by both Grant and Sherman, the latter once remarking that if the war lasted long enough McPherson would emerge as the finest commander of all. At the time of his death McPherson was engaged to a young woman from Baltimore, but had been forced to postpone their wedding because Sherman could not spare him from the army.

Patrick R. Cleburne

Patrick R. Cleburne (1828-1864) was one of only two foreign-born officers to attain a major generalcy in the Confederate Army, the other being Camille Armand Jules Marie, the Prince de Polignac. Born near Cork, Ireland, he was the son of a prominent Protestant physician. Educated as a apothecary, in 1846 Cleburne failed the language examinations for licensing and promptly enlisted in the 41st Foot (The Welch Regiment). Three years later he bought himself out and went to the United States. Over the next few years Cleburne resided variously at New Orleans, Cincinnati, and finally Helena, Arkansas, where he became a partner in a pharmacy. He read law and soon became a fairly successful attorney. On the eve of the war Cleburne helped organize a volunteer company. Although he enlisted as a private, he was shortly elected captain. With his company he helped seize the Little Rock Arsenal from its minuscule Federal garrison upon the secession of Arkansas. The "Yell Rifles" were shortly thereafter incorporated in the 15th Arkansas, and Cleburne soon became its colonel. He served under Maj. Gen. William J. Hardee in Kentucky in the fall of 1861, and, although he saw no action, his experience and ability earned him a brigadier generalcy in March of 1862.

The first occasion on which Cleburne was under fire was at Shiloh in April of 1862, when he commanded a brigade in Hardee's III Corps, on the Confederate left. His performance was extraordinary: on the first day he stemmed a potential rout among the Confederate troops after a Federal counterattack and led his men to the banks of the Tennessee River, while on the second he once more averted a rout and helped cover the retirement of the army with his depleted brigade. At the Battle of Richmond, Kentucky, (29-30 August 1862) he commanded a small division, but was seriously wounded. He shortly thereafter received the thanks of the Confederate Congress. Returning to duty, he led a brigade at Perryville the following October. Two months later he was commissioned a major general.

Cleburne commanded a division in the subsequent campaigns of the Army of Tennessee with great courage and skill. He served with distinction at Murfreesboro at the turn of the new year, led his division ably at Chickamauga, and won a second vote of thanks from Congress for saving the army's trains after Chattanooga in November of 1863.

On 2 January 1864 Cleburne stirred up a hornet's nest. He prepared a letter to the Congress, which he read to the regimental commanders and general officers of the Army of Tennessee. In it he recommended that the

Confederacy organize black regiments for service against the Union. He believed that if promised their freedom blacks would fight for the South. This idea apparently had been maturing in his mind for some time, for he had already privately ascertained the views of most of the senior officers of his division, who seem to have supported his proposal. Observing that if the Confederacy did not use its black manpower in this fashion, the Union surely would, Cleburne expressed a willingness to give up command of his own fine division to organize, train, and ultimately lead a division of blacks into action. Cleburne was the first army officer to publicly express a notion which had already been aired by several newspapers. The idea was too revolutionary and Cleburne found himself the target of considerable abuse. Aspersions were cast upon his loyalty and he was greatly maligned in the press. Yet by his statement Cleburne showed himself more firmly devoted to the cause of Southern independence than his critics; if the war was being fought to establish a Southern nation, any measure which furthered that objective was legitimate. But, and this was what upset his critics, if the war was being fought to preserve slavery, the very measure he proposed would be impossible. It is probable that Cleburne's statement cost him a promotion to lieutenant general, for which he was certainly well-qualified.

Cleburne led his division with great skill through the Atlanta Campaign, finding the time, meanwhile, to organize a contingent of sharpshooters who proved of considerable value in harassing Union outposts. He met his death at the Battle of Franklin, on 30 November 1864, during John B. Hood's ill-advised frontal assault across two miles of open ground against well entrenched Union infantry. He died as he had lived, in the forefront of the fighting; when his horse was shot out from under him, he mounted another, which was also killed, whereupon he put his kepi at the point of his sword and led his men forward on foot, falling within 50 yards of the Federal lines. His death was a serious blow to the Confederacy ad he was greatly mourned.

Nicknamed "The Stonewall Jackson of the West," Cleburne was a bold, aggressive commander with a good feel for doing what was right. As a man he was intelligent, agreeable, and affable. He clearly merited high rank, which was denied him both because of his foreign birth and because of his political naivete concerning the purpose of the war.

William J. Hardee

Georgian William Joseph Hardee (1815-1873) graduated from West Point in 1838 and was commissioned in the *2nd Dragoons* (now the *2nd Cavalry*).

He served against the Seminoles and in 1840 was sent to France to study cavalry tactics at Saumur. Returning in 1842, he spent two years on the frontier. Hardee's rise up the promotion ladder was rather remarkable: by 1844, only six years out of West Point, he was already a captain. During the Mexican War he served under Brig. Gen. Zachary Taylor at Monterey and later under Maj. Gen. Winfield Scott in the Mexico City Campaign, winning two brevets. In 1855 he was promoted to major and assigned to the newly organized *2nd Cavalry* (now the *5th*), the most prestigious regiment in the army at the time. That same year he published *Rifle and Light Infantry Tactics*, better known as *Hardee's Tactics*, which became the standard textbook for regular and militia officers in the coming years. In 1856 Hardee was promoted to lieutenant colonel and named Commandant of Cadets at West Point, a post which he held until January of 1861, when he resigned upon the secession of Georgia. Briefly in the service of his native state, Hardee was soon commissioned a colonel in the Confederate Army, was made a brigadier general in June, and a major general the following October.

Hardee's first war service was in Arkansas, where he raised a brigade in late 1861. Early the following year he brought his command across the Mississippi to serve under Gen. Albert Sidney Johnston. Johnston gave Hardee a corps, which he led with some distinction at Shiloh (6-7 April 1862), and during Braxton Bragg's invasion of Kentucky, where his performance at Perryville (8 October) earned him a lieutenant generalcy. Hardee led a corps or wing in all the operations of the Army of Tennessee from Murfreesboro to Missionary Ridge, and then during the Atlanta Campaign in 1864. A masterful rearguardsman, Hardee was made commander of the Department of South Carolina in September of 1864. Bereft of troops, he could do little to hamper Sherman's operations during the "March to the Sea" and the Carolina Campaign, successively abandoning Savannah, Charleston, and Columbia. In the final weeks of the war he brought his command to the support of Gen. Joseph E. Johnston, with whom he surrendered in late April.

After the war Hardee lived quietly in Alabama, engaging in farming. Not a brilliant commander, Hardee was good at whatever he did, well-meriting his nickname "Old Reliable." He was one of the few officers whose Old Army reputation as an academic soldier was confirmed in the field.

William Tecumseh Sherman

Ohio-born William Tecumseh Sherman (1820-1891) lost his father at an early age. As the family was large—eleven children—and poor, the children were distributed among various relatives and friends, Tecumseh—the "William" was added so that he could have a "Christian" name at baptism—being allocated to Sen. Thomas Ewing, whose daughter he later married and whose three sons all became brigadier generals during the Civil War. Ewing secured young Sherman—who was nicknamed "Cump" because his siblings found Tecumseh difficult—an appointment to West Point, from which he graduated 6th in the class of 1840, entering the infantry. Sherman's first 13 years in the army were unusually uneventful, and although he won a brevet "for meritorious service in California" during the Mexican War, he saw no action. In 1853 he resigned from the army to become a banker in San Francisco. While Sherman did well in his new profession, the parent bank failed in 1857. Sherman essayed a legal career at Leavenworth, Kansas, in partnership with two of his foster-brothers, but proved an unsuccessful attorney. In 1859 he considered reentering the army, but instead accepted the superintendency of the Louisiana State Seminary of Learning and Military Academy—afterwards L.S.U.—in which post he was serving at the time of the state's secession. Rather than accept responsibility for military supplies seized by the secessionist government, Sherman resigned in January of 1861. Family influence shortly secured for him the presidency of a street railway in St. Louis, in which position he was serving at the outbreak of the war.

In May of 1861 Sherman was appointed colonel of the newly authorized *13th Infantry* in the Regular Army, and was shortly assigned to command a brigade in Brig. Gen. Daniel Tyler's *1st Division* at Washington. Sherman's brigade did well at First Bull Run—the division had the heaviest losses of any Union unit engaged—and as a result on 7 August he was named a brigadier general of volunteers, the seventh to be appointed in the war. He was shortly sent to Kentucky to assist Maj. Gen. Robert Anderson in holding the state for the Union. When Anderson fell ill, Sherman assumed command. His fiery temper, impatience with amateur soldiers, and dislike of newspaper correspondents quickly got the better of him. After a couple of outbursts he acquired a reputation for mental instability and was relieved of command. Soon afterwards the influence of his powerful relatives the Ewings prompted Maj. Gen. Henry Halleck to give Sherman a command under Ulysses S. Grant, with whose career his was ever after closely linked. It was Sherman's division which bore the brunt of the Confederate assault at Shiloh on 6 April 1862. Despite the fact that he had been surprised, his subsequent performance was such as to merit a promotion to major general at the beginning of May.

After Shiloh Sherman played a crucial role in Grant's operations in the Mississippi Valley in 1862-1863. He commanded in the unsuccessful assault on Chickasaw Bluffs at the end of '62, took part in capture of Arkansas Post early the following year, participated in Grant's several efforts to get around Vicksburg, and was finally at the fall of the Confederate river bastion on 4 July 1863 as commander of *XV Corps.* That autumn Sherman and his corps took part in the relief of Chattanooga. When Grant was promoted general-in-chief and transferred to the East, Sherman took command of the Western Theater, with Atlanta as his objective. There followed a protracted duel with Confederate Gen. Joseph Johnston, as the two wily commanders each sought to out-maneuver the other and a series of major battles against Gen. John B. Hood which culminated in the fall of Atlanta on 1 September 1864. After Atlanta Sherman directed the "March to the Sea," cutting a swathe through Georgia some 50 miles wide and taking Savannah in late December. Sherman subsequently marched northwards through the Carolinas and accepted Johnston's surrender 26 April 1865.

After the war Sherman was promoted to lieutenant general when Grant received a fourth star, and to full general when Grant entered the White House. Sherman's tenure as general-in-chief was a rather stormy one, as he continuously clashed with bureaucrats and political leaders. Among his accomplishments was the creation of what would become the Command and General Staff College at Fort Leavenworth. In 1884 Sherman retired and was immediately bombarded with requests to run for president, which he refused: "If nominated I will not run, if elected, I will not serve."

Sherman, a tall, sinewy red-head with a lean face and piercing eyes, was a brilliant strategist, years ahead of his time in understanding the nature of war in the industrial age, with an unusual ability to reduce complex military problems to their essentials. A master of maneuver, as a tactical commander he was no better than average.

The Women

Dr. Mary E. Walker

Mary E. Walker (1832-1919) was one of the few women physicians in the United States at the time of the war. A native of New York, she attended Syracuse University and, upon graduation, entered the medical profession, no mean feat given the attitudes of the time, while becoming active in the women's rights movement. A woman of great energy, in her early years she wore "bloomers," the pantaloon-style garb of the radical feminists of the age.

When the Civil War broke out Dr. Walker applied for a surgeon's position, much to the shock of the Medical Department, which rejected her with considerable verbosity. Not one to be discouraged, she stayed in Washington, serving as a nurse in various camps and in a hospital for Indiana troops, while renewing her application from time to time and buttonholing politicians to plead her case. Meanwhile, she was instrumental in establishing an organization which aided needy women who came to Washington to visit wounded kinfolk.

Dr. Walker met with considerable abuse over her persistent demands to be made a surgeon, but also earned considerable respect for her many good works. Meanwhile she abandoned bloomers and adopted a modified version of male attire, with a calf-length skirt worn over trousers, keeping her hair relatively long and curled so that anyone could know that she was a woman. In September of 1863 Maj. Gen. George Thomas appointed her an assistant surgeon in the *Army of the Cumberland*, and she was assigned to the *52nd Ohio*, near Chattanooga, a position in which she served well, wearing a somewhat modified version of the standard surgeon's uniform.

Dr. Walker's work as a physician and surgeon appears to have been satisfactory. However, she served in this capacity for but a short time. In April of 1864 she was captured by Confederate troops, having remained behind to tend Confederate wounded upon a Union retirement. Charged with being a spy and arrested, her male attire constituting the principal evidence against her, Dr. Walker spent four months in various prisons, subject to much abuse for her "unladylike" occupation and attire, until she was exchanged for a Confederate surgeon in August.

Returning to duty, Dr. Walker was officially commissioned as a contract surgeon by the Medical Department in October of 1864, thus ranking as a first lieutenant; only one other woman would achieve this distinction in the war, Dr. Sarah E. Clapp. She was shortly thereafter appointed Superintendent of a military prison for women in Louisville, in which post she spent the balance of the war. In June of 1865 Dr. Walker was discharged from the service and President Johnson awarded her a Medal of Honor, which she wore for the rest of her life.

After the war Dr. Walker remained active in the women's rights movement, and was a crusader against immorality, alcohol and tobacco and for clothing and election reform, while bombarding various political figures for various favors, including pension benefits and a civil service post. Among her more unusual positions was that there was no need for a women's suffrage act, as women already had the vote as American citizens. In 1897 she was instrumental in the establishment of a women's colony, which failed to thrive.

Dr. Walker had an abrasive personality, which did little to further her goals. She became increasingly eccentric, and eventually adopted complete male dress, including wing collars, bow ties, top hats, and canes. In her old age her manner caused her to become increasingly isolated from her family, her friends, and her associates in the women's movement.

When, in 1916, a review board included Dr. Walker's Medal of Honor among the 911 awards to be rescinded as inappropriate to the nature of the decoration, Dr. Walker is said to have replied "Over my dead body," and proceeded to picket the Capitol building for restoration of her rights. In May of 1977 President Jimmy Carter rescinded the recension, and thus Dr. Walker remains the only woman ever to have won a Medal of Honor.

Elizabeth Van Lew and Mary Bowser

One of the strangest stories of the Civil War involves two women, Elizabeth Van Lew and Mary Bowser. Elizabeth Van Lew's parents were of Northern origins. Her father had removed to Richmond, become a merchant, and, at his death, left his wife and daughter a spacious home and a small fortune. Years before the war, as was the custom among prosperous Southern families, the Van Lews had purchased a young black child, Mary Bowser, to serve as a companion and playmate for their daughter. The two girls grew up together and a strong friendship was formed, a not uncommon development. In time, Mary, who was some years younger than Van Lew, was given her freedom and sent off to a private school for women in Philadelphia. When the war broke out Elizabeth, who was then about 40, an ardent Unionist, decided that the best way she could serve the cause was as a spy. She asked Mary to return to Richmond in order to assist her and the latter eagerly complied. Soon the two women had become critical players in a complex espionage ring, one which included Miss Van Lew's mother, several other patriotic Richmond women, and a considerable number of other people, male and female, black and white, slave and free.

Elizabeth Van Lew, who was quite plain looking, had a reputation as an eccentric and abolitionist. Capitalizing on this, she behaved with increasing peculiarity, which provided excellent cover for the serious work in which she involved herself, while earning her the nickname "Crazy Bet." She soon had a number of agents supplying her with all sorts of valuable information, such as Samuel Ruth, the Northern-born superintendent of the Richmond, Fredericksburg, and Potomac Railroad. Mary Bowser was a decided asset in this important, if dangerous work. Since a slave was virtually invisible and was thus able to go anywhere, this polished, well-educated freedwoman assumed the guise of an ignorant housemaid. Thus attired, she several times passed through Confederate lines to carry information to Union commanders, particularly during the 1864-1865 operations around Richmond and Petersburg, when both U.S. Grant and Benjamin Butler benefitted from the information she supplied. In this fashion the pair of patriotic and brave women rendered enormous services to the Union, passing along information about troop movements, providing details of fortifications, and while, on the pretext of providing "Christian charity" to the Union officers incarcerated in the notorious Libby Prison, facilitating the escape of a number of prisoners-of-war. By some accounts, their greatest achievement was to secure access to the inner-most counsels of the Confederacy, to obtain information directly from Jefferson Davis' desk.

The matter is unclear, for the story seems to have grown in the telling, but apparently late in the war the Davis' were looking for a new housemaid. Moving quickly, Elizabeth Van Lew arranged for Mary Bowser to secure the position. It was a superb situation in which to secure information. The supposedly illiterate slave was given virtually free run of the Davis' quarters, including the president's office. As she went about her duties, dusting, polishing the silver, cleaning the windows, Mary Bowser was able to read, and even make copies of, some of the most sensitive military documents in the Confederacy. On other occasions she was called upon to serve at lunch or dinner meetings at which Davis met with his political and military advisors to discuss the war. All of this information was passed on to Van Lew. She, in turn, passed it on to a baker who came to the Van Lew place each day to obtain eggs and milk. He supposedly would bake the memoranda into loaves of bread, which were then smuggled across the Confederate lines and into the hands of the appropriate Union officials.

Elizabeth Van Lew ultimately came under some suspicion of espionage, but her eccentric manner misled officials into thinking that she was harmless. The two women conducted their activities with complete immunity until the end of the war, rendering inestimable service to the Republic. After the war, however, neither Elizabeth Van Lew nor Mary Bowser prospered. "Crazy Bet" was ostracized by her neighbors and, having spent virtually her entire fortune in the Union cause, sank slowly into poverty. In 1869 the then-President U.S. Grant—whose table during the last months of the war was supposedly graced by flowers from Elizabeth's garden—made her postmistress of Richmond. She held this job until Grant left office, in 1877, and was thereafter supported by an annuity provided by some of the officers whom she had helped escape from prison, dying around the turn of the century. Meanwhile, Mary Bowser, her friend and associate, had gone North and her later life is unknown. It was a poor reward for such important services.

Lincoln

"...*Ain't of Much More Account*"

Shortly after word of the crushing defeat inflicted on Confederate Gen. John B. Hood at the Battle of Nashville (15-16 December 1864) by Union Maj. Gen. George H. Thomas reached Washington, Joseph Medill, editor of the Chicago *Tribune,* and one of Lincoln's close friends, asked the president, "There isn't much left of Hood's army, is there?"

"Well, no, Medill," replied Lincoln, "I think Hood's army is about in the fix of Bill Sykes' dog, down in Sangamon County. Did you ever hear of it?"

Sensing one of the president's famous tales in the offing, Medill replied "Never," and settled back to listen.

"Well," said Lincoln, "Bill Sykes had a long, yaller dog, that was forever getting into the neighbors meathouses and chicken-coops. They had tried to kill it a hundred times, but the dog was always too smart for them. Finally one of them got a bladder of a 'coon and filled it up with powder, tying the neck around a piece of punk. When he saw the dog coming, he fired this punk, split open a hot biscuit and put the bladder in, then buttered it all nicely and threw it out. The dog swallowed it at a gulp. Pretty soon there was an explosion. The head of the dog lit on the porch, the fore legs caught astraddle the fence, the hind legs fell in the ditch, and the rest of the dog lay around loose. Pretty soon Bill Sykes came along, and the neighbor said 'Bill, I guess there ain't much of that dog of your'n left.'

"'Well, no,' said Bill, 'I see plenty of pieces, but I guess that dog, as a *dog*, ain't of much more account.'

"Just so, Medill, there may be fragments of Hood's army around, but I guess that dog, as a *dog*, ain't of much more account."

Lincoln is also said to have told this story with reference to the army of Lt. Gen. John Pemberton, taken at Vicksburg on 4 July 1863.

1864

The President Under Fire

During Confederate Lt. Gen. Jubal A. Early's "raid" on Washington in July of 1864, Lincoln expressed a desire to observe the action, remarking that as commander-in-chief, he thought he had a right to watch a battle fought by his own troops. Though Maj. Gen. Horatio Wright, commanding the reinforcements from the *Army of the Potomac*, replied "There is nothing in the Constitution authorizing the constitutional commander-in-chief to expose himself to the enemy's fire where he could do no good," the president went to the front anyway. In fact, he went twice.

On 11 July Lincoln paid a visit to the fortifications to observe Early's skirmishers in action against the defenses. Descending on Ft. Stevens, little more than four miles from the White House, with the Secretary of War and several other dignitaries, the president climbed the parapet to get a good look at the action. His "host" was a nervous young colonel of artillery. Certain that the Rebels had spotted the president's tall frame, if only from the volume of fire which appeared to be directed towards him, the young officer several times politely suggested that Lincoln consider moving to a less exposed location, but the president was so engrossed in the scene that he ignored the man, even when a nearby soldier went down with a ball in his thigh.

The desperate young officer turned to one of the civilians standing about, E.L. Chittenden, present on a newspaper assignment, and asked for advice. Chittenden replied, "What would you do with me in like circumstances?"

"I would civily ask you to take a position where you were not exposed."

"And if I refused to obey?"

"I would send a sergeant and a file of men and make you obey."

"Then treat the president just as you would me or any civilian."

"I dare not; he is my superior officer, I have taken an oath to obey his orders."

"He has given you no orders," observed Chittenden. "Follow my advice and you will not regret it."

"I will," replied the officer. "I may as well die for one thing as for another. If he were shot, I should hold myself responsible."

The colonel walked up to the president as he stood looking over the parapet. In a forceful manner he said, "Mr. President, you are standing within range of 500 Rebel rifles. Please come down to a safer place. If you do not, it will be my duty to call a file of men and make you."

Lincoln looked at the man, "And you would do right, my boy!" and, coming down from the parapet, said, "You are in command of this fort, I should be the last man to set an example of disobedience," as the relieved young officer showed him to a safer vantage point.

The next day, the president again decided to visit the fort. As he stood looking out over the parapet, a man standing nearby was hit. At that young Capt. Oliver Wendell Holmes, Jr.—later the famous Supreme Court Justice—cried out, "Get down, you fool, or you'll be killed." The president complied, but smilingly remarked, "Well, Captain, I see you have already learned how to address a civilian."

The Units

Hood's Texas Brigade

One of the most notable combat records of the war was that of Hood's Texas Brigade. The outfit which would eventually be known by the name of Kentuckian John B. Hood was organized in Virginia on 12 November 1861 as the "Texas Brigade," comprising the 1st, 4th, and 5th Texas Infantry, and the 18th Georgia, all under the command of Col. Louis T. Wigfall, and was shortly incorporated into what would become the Army of Northern Virginia. Soon afterwards, Wigfall was elected to the Confederate Senate, and Col. John B. Hood of the 4th Texas was made a brigadier general and given the command. The brigade first went into action at Eltham's Landing, Virginia, on 7 May 1862, and went on to fight in every battle of the Army of Northern Virginia, finding the time to get over the Appalachians and into the Western Theater for a while in the fall of 1863. Hood led the brigade for less than six months, through the Peninsular Campaign, during part of which the infantry of Hampton's Legion was attached. The brigade particularly distinguished itself during the Seven Days, when it routed Union troops from a seemingly impregnable position at Gaines' Mill (27 June 1862). Largely on the basis of his performance in command of the Texas Brigade, Hood was given the division in the summer of 1862 and Col. Jerome Bonaparte Robertson of the 5th Texas was promoted to brigadier and given the brigade. At about the same time, the 3rd Arkansas replaced the 18th Georgia, leaving the brigade organization as it would remain for the balance of the war.

Under Robertson, the Texas Brigade—which included a number of Mexican-Americans—fought brilliantly at Second Bull Run and notably so at Antietam, where it lost nearly 75 percent of its strength: the 1st Texas lost 82.3 percent of its 226 men present, the highest loss in a single engagement of any Confederate regiment in the entire war. Service at Fredericksburg and Chancellorsville followed, and the brigade was again heavily engaged on the second day at Gettysburg, in the fighting around the Devil's Den, where Robertson was wounded for a third time. By the time Robertson returned to command, the brigade was heading west to operate with Longstreet's Corps in Tennessee and Kentucky, fighting at Chickamauga, Chattanooga, and Knoxville. While in the West, Robertson ran afoul of Longstreet and was relieved, being replaced by a new officer from Texas, Brig. Gen. John Gregg.

Brought East under Gregg after Knoxville, the brigade was again in the thick of things during Grant's Overland Campaign in 1864. It distinguished itself in the Wilderness on 6 May 1864, on which occasion there occurred the famous "General Lee to the rear" incident, when the general attempted to lead an attack, only to have the troops refuse to go forward until he removed himself from the scene. Shortly after this the brigade made an unsupported attack which cost nearly 60 percent of its 711 officers and men, effectively breaking it as a combat force, though morale remained so high Jefferson Davis hesitated to disband it. Gregg was killed in October, during the Petersburg Campaign. Though the brigade survived under various officers until the Army of Northern Virginia surrendered at Appomattox, it was but a shadow of its former self, only 617 men being present of the approximately 5,300 who had enlisted in 1861, a loss of over 85 percent, one of the highest of the war.

Hood's Texas Brigade was noted not only for its fighting qualities, but also for some of the unusual characters in the ranks, including one man who was a veteran of the Alamo and San Jacinto, on the Mexican side. Perhaps the most colorful was Capt. Ulysses Paxton, the "Fighting Preacher" of the 5th Texas, who was wont to spout scripture in the midst of battle.

The Hampton Legion

In the late eighteenth and early nineteenth centuries a type of military organization known as the "legion" enjoyed a degree of popularity. A legion was what would today be called a combined arms combat team. Usually consisting of a battalion of infantry, some cavalry, and a battery or two, legions were supposed to serve in various specialized roles, such as advanced guard and rear guard. Several legions were organized at the outbreak of the Civil War, mostly in the South. The most famous of these was the Hampton Legion.

The Hampton Legion was formed in South Carolina in the spring of 1861 by Wade Hampton, one of the richest men in the country and probably the largest slaveholder. Since Hampton footed the bills, including the cost of six very expensive British-made Blakely field pieces, he was commissioned as the legion's first colonel. As organized, the legion had six infantry companies, four cavalry companies, and a battery of artillery, for a total of nearly 1,200 picked men, selected from some 2,500 who had volunteered.

As the legion was still organizing—it took time to get the Blakelys through the blockade—in July of 1861, Hampton took the infantry battalion off to Northern Virginia to join the Confederate forces concentrating to meet the anticipated Federal attack. The infantry of the legion, who numbered about 600, were attached to Brig. Gen. Pierre G.T. Beauregard's Army of the Potomac—the original incarnation of the Army of Northern Virginia—and played an important role at First Bull Run, earning considerable praise, while suffering 121 casualties, including Hampton, who was wounded. When the artillery and cavalry contingents arrived shortly after Bull Run, the entire legion began to serve together and in November of 1861 was brigaded as part of Maj. Gen. James Longstreet's division.

The Hampton Legion served under Longstreet during the initial phases of the Peninsular Campaign, by which time Hampton himself had been promoted to brigadier general. Despite good fighting qualities, operational experience during the campaign demonstrated that the legion concept was unsound. As a result, the legion was broken up. The infantry became a separate battalion in Hood's Texas Brigade, while the cavalry became part of the 5th Virginia Cavalry Regiment, and the battery became Capt. James F. Hart's South Carolina Horse Artillery Battery. The fighting qualities of the component parts of the legion do not seem to have suffered from this operation.

The infantry of the legion, commanded by Lt. Col. Martin W. Gary, served with Hood's Texans during the Seven Days, at Second Bull Run, and at Antietam, impressing the tough Texans with their "grit...staying quality and...dash." After Antietam the battalion was incorporated into Brig. Gen. Micah Jenkins' brigade of Maj. Gen. George Pickett's division. It served in this command at Fredericksburg, but missed Chancellorsville because Longstreet's I Corps was temporarily absent on the Carolina coasts, and Gettysburg because Jenkins' brigade was left behind in Virginia. But the battalion—which was always know as "Hampton's Legion"—saw hot service at Chickamauga and Knoxville when I Corps went west in the autumn of 1863. Returning to Virginia, the battalion was converted to mounted infantry in the spring of 1864. Thus mounted, the legion served in all the subsequent actions of the Army of Northern Virginia until the end of the war, being among the last units to leave Richmond when the city was evacuated.

Capt. James F. Hart's South Carolina Horse Artillery Battery served mostly with the horse artillery of J.E.B. Stuart's cavalry from the Peninsula to the end of the war, although it missed Chancellorsville, and ended its service under a lieutenant.

The 5th Virginia Cavalry had been organized in the spring of 1861. It saw its first serious combat service during the Peninsular Campaign, during which it incorporated the cavalry elements of the Hampton Legion. As part of J.E.B. Stuart's cavalry command, the regiment fought from the Peninsula to Appomattox. Initially under Col. Thomas L. Rosser, when that officer became a brigadier general in late 1863, the regiment passed to Col. Henry Clay Pate, who was killed in action at Yellow Tavern, to be replaced by Col. Rueben B. Boston, the last properly appointed regimental commander, who was himself killed in action on 7 April 1865, helping to cover the retreat of the Army of Northern Virginia from Appomattox.

For a "morprodite" outfit, the Hampton Legion amassed a combat record matched by few organizations of comparable size in the war.

The Legions

A number of legions were raised in the early months of the war, mostly for Confederate service. Like the Hampton Legion, these were eventually broken up into their component parts. Several of the legions achieved some distinction in the war, notably Cobb's Legion and Phillip's Legion in Confederate service, and the Union's *Purnell Legion.*

Cobb's Legion was raised in Georgia in June of 1861 by Representative Thomas R.R. Cobb, an ardent slavocrat. Originally ten companies of 100 men each—three of cavalry, six of infantry, and one of artillery—, it left its gunners behind when it went to Virginia. Although Cobb was initially an inept commander, he later became rather skilled at his trade. The legion fought as a unit at Antietam, where it took heavy losses, and Fredericksburg, where Cobb was mortally wounded. Shortly before Chancellorsville, the legion was broken up into two battalions, one of cavalry and one of infantry, which were soon afterwards both expanded to regiments. The two regiments rapidly gained a reputation for tenacity. The infantry served with Longstreet's I Corps right through to Appomattox. The cavalry served with the cavalry of the Army of Northern Virginia until it was transferred to Georgia in the early part of 1865.

Phillip's Legion, was raised by William Phillips, a wealthy Georgian, who recruited 1,000 volunteers in June of 1861 to form a battalion each of infantry, cavalry, and artillery in the state service. The legion was accepted for Confederate service in September of 1861, shortly afterwards losing its artillery batteries, which were dispersed among the various Confederate armies. The legion performed garrison and security duties in West Virginia, South Carolina, and Virginia until late in 1862, when it fought at Fredericksburg, with the infantry and cavalry components serving separately, although still technically part of the same organization. This expedient was also used at Chancellorsville, and shortly afterwards the separation was made formal, with the cavalry being attached to J.E.B. Stuart's command and the infantry to Lafayette McLaws' division of Longstreet's I Corps, both meanwhile being recruited to more or less regimental strength. Thereafter, the experience of the legion was very much like that of Cobb's legion.

Purnell's Maryland Legion was raised by William H. Purnell, the postmaster of Baltimore, in November and December of 1861 and consisted of nine companies of infantry, two of cavalry, and two of light artillery. Most of the legion's service was on garrison and security duty in Maryland, but it did take the field at Antietam, and in 1864 served with the *Army of the Potomac*, from the Wilderness to Petersburg, mustering out in October, by which time it had lost 43 men killed in action. *Company A* of the cavalry served with the *Army of the Potomac* from Gettysburg until discharge.

War and Society

The Great Gold Hoax

On the morning of 18 May 1864 some New Yorkers were stunned when *The Journal of Commerce* and *The World* revealed that U.S. Grant's newly launched offensive against Robert E. Lee had ended in a bloody disaster. Reading on, they learned that President Lincoln had proclaimed a day of "fasting, humiliation, and prayer" and had called for the drafting of an additional 400,000 men. The devastating news set shock waves through the stock exchange and gold shot up by 10 percent. But then cooler heads prevailed. No such news had appeared in the city's five other dailies. Perhaps it was all a hoax.

Meanwhile, news of the panic had reached Washington. At the urging of Secretary of State William Seward and Secretary of War Edwin M. Stanton, who believed the incident was part of a conspiracy to discredit the administration, Lincoln ordered the seizure of the two offending papers, along with that of the Independent Telegraph Company, which had carried the dispatch. Although Maj. Gen. John A. Dix, commanding in New York, believed that the two papers were themselves probably the victims of a hoax, he sent his troops to occupy their offices, which caused an uproar throughout the journalistic community. As it turned out, Dix was right. A massive hoax had been perpetrated. The other papers in the city had picked up the story, which arrived on Associated Press "flimsies." However, the night editor at one of them, smelling a rat, had made a quick inquiry of the A.P. When the A.P. denied any knowledge of the dispatch, he had killed the story and alerted the other papers. But by the time *The Journal of Commerce* and *The World* received the word the morning edition had already gone out.

The object of the hoax was not to inflict injury on the administration but rather to boost the price of gold so that the perpetrators could make a killing, and, perhaps, to tweak the noses of the journalistic establishment. The perpetrator was Joseph Howard, Jr. (1833-1908), a prominent, imaginative journalist.

The war made Howard's reputation. He first gained the public's eye with a fabricated account of Lincoln's arrival in Washington in February of 1861, wearing "a Scotch cap and a military cloak." He covered most of the early battles in the East for *The New-York Times*, where his vivid, often creative reporting earned him a by-line, an unusual distinction in those days. He was resourceful and imaginative in seeking out stories and preventing his rivals from doing the same. For a time he cultivated the friendship of Mrs. Lincoln, gaining some valuable tidbits on policy matters. On one occasion, having gotten to the only open telegraph line ahead of his rivals, he padded a dispatch with lengthy portions of *The Bible* to monopolize the line; the cost was considerable, but his paper gladly paid it for the privilege of getting a scoop. When the press was barred from the funeral of Maj. Gen. Philip Kearny, Howard managed to infiltrate the rites in the guise of a Roman Catholic priest. By early 1864 he had secured the post of city editor at *The Brooklyn Eagle*. Most newspapermen would have considered this a plum, but Howard found it unsatisfactory. Efforts to secure employment at some of the more prestigious papers proved fruitless, for Howard had acquired a bad odor in some journalistic circles for creative reporting. Bored and annoyed, he hit upon the idea of having a little fun at the expense of the journalistic establishment and making a profit at the same time. With the aid of Francis A. Mallison, an *Eagle* reporter, Howard invested heavily in gold in the early spring of 1864. He then procured some A.P. telegraph "flimsies" and forged the bogus dispatch. It was a clever scheme, and actually did work. But in the end Howard outsmarted himself.

Shortly before 18 May Howard had spoken of making a killing in gold to several people. Two days after the bogus story broke he was arrested. Not wanting to take the rap alone, Howard implicated Mallison. Lincoln ordered the two incarcerated without trial in Fort Lafayette, a harbor defense installation on a reef in The Narrows, where they languished for almost three months, until the Rev. Henry Ward Beecher interceded for their release. Of course *The World* and *The Journal of Commerce* were returned to their owners, but the outcry which their seizure provoked echoed for some time; Governor Horatio Seymour of New York, a strong foe of the administration, even attempted to have General Dix indicted.

Neither Howard nor his accomplice were brought to trial for the hoax, nor did his career suffer as a result of it. After the war Howard worked on various papers, had a widely syndicated column in the 1880s, and served for a time as president of the New York Press Club. His sometimes outrageous approach to journalism earned him a widespread reputation, and he became the model for a number of fictional journalists, including

Jules Verne's Alcide Jolivet in *Michael Strogoff* and his Claudius Bombarnac in *The Special Correspondent*.

Black Combatants in the Confederate Army

Although the Confederacy never put black troops in the field, an unknown number of blacks did fight for the South. Though evidence is fragmentary, blacks helped man coast defense installations in Mobile Bay through to the end of the war, and were active in home guard units which performed security duties in many areas. A number of black men were involved in regular combat well. Free blacks were willing to serve because the South was, after all, their home. Others found volunteering more convenient than waiting to be conscripted for labor service, where they would be brigaded with slaves. But slaves also fought for the Confederacy. Aristocratic Southern officers from the planter class frequently went to war with their personal servants, who were often devoted companions from childhood. The bonds of loyalty forged over a lifetime were strong, and stronger still the bonds of blood which often linked master and slave. As a result, it was not unknown for the black orderlies of Confederate officers to engage in combat. In addition, slaves sometimes took up arms to defend popular masters from the depredations of Union troops or Confederate deserters. As one slave put it, "We would rather fight for our own white folks than for strangers." Unfortunately, while there exist general references to such activity, only a few such individuals can be specifically identified.

Old Dick: a freeman, Old Dick had served in the Mexican War as a musician in South Carolina's *Palmetto Regiment*. When the Civil War broke out he enlisted as a drummer in the 18th Virginia. At First Bull Run he picked up a musket, joined the firing line, and was credited with the capture of several Union prisoners, including Col. Alfred M. Wood of the *14th New York*. He served with his regiment for some time thereafter. Though apparently well-regarded by his comrades in arms, away from his regiment he was subject to the normal abuses which were inflicted upon blacks, and was once even arrested for being armed.

Jacques Esclavon: described as a 40-year old mulatto, Esclavon joined Ragsdale's Texas Cavalry Battalion in September of 1864 and served as a combatant through to the end of the war.

Levin Graham: a black servant, took up a musket and allegedly "killed four of the Yankees" in an action in late 1861.

Gabriel Grappe: enlisted in September of 1862 in the 6th Louisiana

Cavalry, a regiment which appears to have had as many as eight men of mixed background, all free volunteers.

Tom and Overton: two black camp servants, picked up some arms at Brandy Station in June of 1863, mounted a couple of stray horses, and took part in several charges.

Jean Baptiste Pierre-August: a freeman, he joined the 29th Louisiana in the spring of 1862. Captured at Vicksburg he was later exchanged and returned to his regiment. Although apparently a combatant prior to Vicksburg, he later served as a cook.

Lufray Pierre-August: with the 16th Louisiana in the Army of Tennessee in 1862, being discharged at Murfreesboro in early December, because he was "colored." It is unclear what degree of kinship he shared with Jean Baptiste Pierre-August.

Peter Vertrees: Kentuckian of about 21, he served throughout the war in the 6th Kentucky Infantry as cook and bodyguard to his half-uncle, John Luther Vertrees, being several times engaged in combat at his side. In 1986 he became the first black honored by the Sons of Confederate Veterans.

Mention should also be made of the unknown number of legally black individuals who had "passed" successfully into white society in the South and who, when the war came, enlisted in the ranks. A few of these men can also be identified, notably Charles Lutz, who fought with the 8th Louisiana, a regiment in which there seems to have been several men of mixed parentage.

The obvious prominence of blacks from Louisiana is not surprising, given that the state was probably the most racially tolerant in the country—the whole country, not just the South—and free men of color enjoyed a considerable measure of status, partially as a result of the state's French heritage.

The Ways of War

Moving Troops by Rail

When the Civil War broke out railroads were among the most technologically sophisticated devices in the world, and had already proven of some value in military operations, most recently during the Italian War of 1859, when the French had surprised everyone by moving several army corps to ports of embarkation by rail. In 1860 there were 31,000 miles of railroads in the United States, about 30 percent in what would become the Confederacy. This was by no means a unified system. Most of the railroads were small and there were frequently no through connections between different lines even in major cities. There was a great deal of variation in rolling stock and no standardized track gauge. Many lines did not even have iron rails, but used wooden rails with iron straps fastened to them. Wrecks were common. But their numerous shortcomings were insignificant when compared with the advantages which railroads conferred on armies. As a result, railroads played an important part in the war from the very beginning. Indeed, one of the most famous incidents in the early days of the war, the attack on the *6th Massachusetts* by a secessionist mob in Baltimore on 19 April 1861, occurred because the regiment had to change trains.

The first important operational use of railroads took place in mid-July of 1861, when Confederate Brig. Gen. Joseph E. Johnston moved his 12,000 man army from the Shenandoah Valley to unite with Brig. Gen. Pierre G.T. Beauregard's 20,000 men in time to fight the First Battle of Bull Run. Thereafter the use of railroads became increasingly common, particularly for logistical support and administrative movement, but occasionally for operational purposes as well.

It took a little time for the armies to learn how to use railroads effectively. Early in the war a number of large scale troop movements, which ought to have been made by rail were made on foot, often with serious effects on the course of operations. Nevertheless, with practice came experience and by 1863 railroading had become part of the military art. It was in September of that year that there took place the most spectacular use of railroads in the war. Over a period of nine days the major part of Confederate Lt. Gen. James Longstreet's corps was transferred by rail over a circuitous route involving 16 different lines—there were altogether 112 in the Confederacy—and some 900 miles of track from Northern Virginia to central Tennessee, despite the fact that by this time the Confederacy's lack of heavy industry was causing serious problems on Southern railroads. It was a brilliantly conceived and executed strategic movement which permitted the Confederacy to reinforce Gen. Braxton Bragg's Army of Tennessee so that it could smash Union Maj. Gen. William S. Rosecrans' *Army of the Cumberland* at Chickamauga on 19-20 September. Confederate success was short-lived, however, for within days the Union *XI* and *XII Corps* were likewise en route by rail from Northern Virginia to Central Tennessee. In this operation an even greater number of men moved with considerably more speed and efficiency over an even longer route, if only because of the superior physical resources of the Union railroads.

Infantry

The infantry was the easiest of all the arms to move by rail, making fewest demands on resources. To move 1,000 men—on paper a full regiment—with all their equipment, stores, transport, and animals, required approximately 40 wagons and two or three locomotives.

Type of Car	Number
Passenger	16 - 18
Box	5 - 7
Flat	6
Horse	12

The figures given are for a comfortable, orderly movement, without crowding the troops. In a pinch, the troops could be crammed into as few as a dozen passenger cars, or, for that matter, into any of the other types of wagon. Similarly, many of the regiment's 200 or so horses and mules, 30 to 50 tons of stores, and most of its transport wagons could be left behind, so that as few as 20 cars of various types might be required. Fully equipped troops could board a train in a matter of minutes, but it required about 20 minutes to load the animals, wagons, and supplies. Ignoring their baggage, infantry could detrain with great speed and could go into action almost immediately.

Cavalry

Cavalry was rather difficult to move by rail and required considerable resources. The rail transport of 420 men with all their animals, equipment, and impedimenta—on paper four companies—required some 40 to 50 cars plus two or three locomotives.

Type of Car	Number
Passenger	7 - 8
Box	2 - 5
Horse	30 - 40

Unlike the infantry, cavalry could not readily be crowded onto fewer wagons. At best, by crowding the men and cutting stores to a minimum, one could reduce the rolling stock requirements by perhaps 20 percent. A battalion of cavalry required about a half hour to entrain or detrain. Cavalry could not always immediately go into action upon detraining, particularly if the horses had been long in the cars.

Artillery

Artillery was the most difficult arm to transport by rail, though, of course, its combat power more than compensated for this. A full six gun battery required, for its 150 or so men and 115 animals, plus pieces, stores, equipment, and baggage, from 23 to 38 wagons, plus two or three locomotives, depending upon the type of artillery pieces.

Type of Car	Number
Passenger	3
Box	1
Flat	12 - 20
Horse	8 - 15

The rolling stock requirements for the artillery could not be reduced much without unduly complicating loading and unloading, though the troops could ride with the guns and horses, thus eliminating the passenger wagons. Artillery was difficult to load onto a train—at least a half hour for a battery, the time increasing with the caliber of the pieces—and required special equipment to be done with any degree of speed. Detraining was equally difficult and, as with cavalry, the artillery could not always go immediately into action upon detraining.

Civil War Rolling Stock

The lack of standardization in American railroading in the mid-nineteenth century extended even to rolling stock. Due to the lack of standard gauge, rolling stock from one line might not be able to operate on the tracks of another. Moreover, the capacity of rolling stock from different lines might vary greatly. Nevertheless, it is possible to get some idea of the capacity of various types of rolling stock, keeping in mind the considerable degree of variation prevalent at the time.

Type of Car	Passengers	Cargo Capacity Tons - Cubic Yards
Passenger	56	
Box	10 - 15	50 - 55
Flat	8 - 12	15 - 23
Horse	15 - 20	

Passenger cars were fitted with seats—sleepers existed but were rare until after the war—and in a pinch could hold 80 men, though some staff officers seemed to think 100 was possible. The critical limitation on the utility of the other types of wagons lay not so much in their tonnage capacity as in their cubic volume; a single 3" rifled cannon with its caisson and limbers weighed considerably less than eight tons, but required more than one flat car for efficient transport.

The better locomotives of the period were able to haul about 50 loaded freight wagons—a gross weight of some 800 tons—"on the flat" at 15 miles per hour. More practically, considering variations in terrain and the condition of trackage, Civil War trains averaged 16 to 22 wagons—some 250 to 300 tons—at 15 to 20 miles an hour, though in the Confederacy the average speed was about half this due to track and equipment problems. Still, moving troops at eight miles an hour over the Confederacy's poor railroads was superior to moving them at four miles an hour by foot over the Confederacy's poor roads.

Railroads and Logistics

Although railroads proved immensely useful for the movement of troops, their most particular value lay in the movement of supplies. Indeed, only water transport was more efficient. As a general rule of thumb, and omitting consideration of construction and upkeep, the cost of wagon transport during the Civil War was at least ten times that of rail transport, which in turn was three times more expensive than water transport.

Consider the needs of an army of 50,000 men, of whom 15 percent are cavalrymen and 5 percent artillerymen, with about 100 guns. Such an army would require a minimum of 10,000 horses and mules, even if traveling lean, as Sherman's men did during the "March to the Sea." The ration requirements can now be calculated.

This army would need about 75 tons of food each day to give every man a ration of about three pounds. Since rations came in barrels and heavy cases an additional 15 tons has to be added to account for packaging. In addition, a further 125 pounds would be required each day to feed the animals, at 18 to 25 pounds of fodder and feed per head: horses can't eat grass and haul howitzers. Thus, the net daily ration requirements come to 215 tons.

The standard army wagon at the time of the Civil War had a lifting capacity of 1.5 tons. As each pair of wagons required three men and twelve mules, lifting 215 tons required about 145 wagons, 220 men and 870 mules. These, in turn, must be fed, for a total of about 10 additional tons of rations, or about seven more wagon loads, and the additional animals and men for these would require yet another wagon load. So to lift one day's rations some 153 wagons, about 230 men and 918 mules were needed. Such a column would, if moving along one road—and given the road net which prevailed in much of the country at the time of the Civil War there was very often only one road—would extend nearly a mile and a half. Now this assumes that the army is operating within 10 miles of its supply base, sufficient distance for the wagons to make one round trip each day. If the army is operating 20 miles from its supply base—a two day round trip—transport requirements increase to 312 wagons, 468 men, and 1,872 mules. In practical terms, an army can be supplied by animal transport at no more than 50 miles from its base, a five day round trip of 100 miles. At that distance, some 1520 wagons, nearly 2,300 men, and over 9,000 animals would be needed just to transport food and fodder for the men and horses who are actually combatants; the transport troops and animals have yet to be fed. Nor do any of these figures include the numbers of men and horses necessary as escorts. And we have yet to consider ammunition, the demand for which was never as constant as that for rations, but could rise to enormous levels at times of major battles. Now consider the effects of all this traffic on the execrable roads of the day, and the effects of the season on road movement. There had to be a better way, and there was, the railroad.

Wartime experience demonstrated that armies of enormous size could be sustained even over the low speed, single track lines which prevailed in the Confederacy. To lift 215 tons of rations by rail required only about 17 box cars plus a locomotive and a couple of tenders, with a crew of a half dozen men. One such train could maintain an army of 50,000 men in rations at 50 miles with more efficiency than could a wagon train operating at 10 miles. To be sure, tracks and rolling stock would require protection from partisans, but wagon trains were even more vulnerable to such attacks and could not carry their own protectors. In the end, the railroad was vital to the Union victory, providing the logistical capacity to sustain the armies in the field. But the railroad was also the principal sustainer of the Confederate forces. It is by no means a coincidence that Robert E. Lee abandoned Richmond on 3 April 1865, the day after Union forces had cut the South Side Railroad, which had been the life line of his brave Army of Northern Virginia.

Serving the Guns

Artillerymen were the most professionally expert soldiers in either army, due partially to the technical demands of their trade, and also to the care which both armies took with their training. The artillery was organized into batteries. In the Confederate Army these were usually of four guns. Union batteries were of six guns for most of the war, but in 1864 Lt. Gen. U.S. Grant decided—with some cause—that the *Army of the Potomac* was over-gunned and reduced many batteries to four pieces. Allowing for this difference, there was great similarity in artillery organization and practice between the two armies.

A battery was divided into sections, each under a lieutenant. A section had two complete artillery equipments, including gun, two limbers, and a caisson. There was, in addition, a spare limber and caisson with extra ammunition. The battery itself had one additional ammunition caisson with limber for each gun or howitzer, plus a traveling forge, and a battery wagon with tentage and supplies. Altogether, with a captain, four lieutenants, two staff sergeants, six sergeants, a dozen corporals, six artificers, two buglers, 52 teamsters, and 70 cannoneers, a battery officially had 155 men. In practice, however, Union batteries averaged about 105 men, Confederate ones about 90. The number of horses depended upon the type of guns. Heavier pieces, Napoleons or 20-pounder Parrotts, required six horses, so a battery of six such had about 115 horses, while a lighter battery ran a dozen less. All pieces in Union batteries were usually of the same type, but many Confederate batteries had two or even three different types, a matter which ought to have been resolved by a proper redistribution of the available pieces from time to time. On paper Union batteries were organized into regiments, of which the Regular Army had five, plus one or more for each state, but they were never deployed as such. Some Southern states followed a similar procedure, but there were cases of permanent battalions being formed which actually served together. Operationally, both armies formed groups of four or five batteries for tactical control, called brigades in the Federal service and battalions in the Confederacy.

Normally guns were deployed 14 yards apart, which, with each piece occupying two yards, gave the battery an 82 yard front, with a depth of almost 50 yards. Given time, the gunners, and available infantry supports, would often strengthen their position by building log and earth breastworks. But batteries frequently went into action without advanced preparation, moving directly from the march. A trained crew could unlimber and fire their first round in 30 seconds. A full battery could do so in about a minute. The working of the guns was actually in the hands of the senior non-commissioned officers, the lieutenants and the battery commander being responsible for target selection. Most pieces could be fired two or three times a minute. This, however, depended upon the skill of the crew and the tactical situation, and when hotly pressed it was not unheard of for a gun to fire four canisters in a minute. Since most of the guns used during the war were muzzle loaders, the basic procedure was fairly standard. Assuming a piece already has just fired:

> The gun crew moves into action as the piece recoils from its previous shot. As the ventman covers the touch hole with his padded thumb, the tube is sponged out to ensure that no live embers are left over from the last shot. Meanwhile, the loader selects the appropriate type of round from the available supply, which are pre-packed into bundles consisting of a projectile, a wooden wad, and a cloth-wrapped powder charge all loosely bound together. This charge is placed in the tube and rammed home. Under the direction of the gunnery sergeant the crew relays the piece, pushing it into position to fire. The sergeant adjusts the aim, using a screw mechanism and main force, while the ventman shoves a priming wire down the touchhole, piercing the powder bag. As everyone steps clear of the rear of the piece, the trigger mechanism, a friction primer, is set and the gunnery sergeant awaits the command to fire. When it comes, he gives the lanyard a sharp pull, which sets off the friction primer and discharges the piece. Lacking a recoil mechanism, the gun leaps back several feet as the projectile roars on its way in great burst of fire, smoke, and noise. The crew begins to move into action for the next round.

Generally a battery carried about 100 rounds of ammunition per gun. About three-quarters of the supply was usually evenly divided between solid shot and shrapnel, while the balance was split between canister and shell. Army supply columns usually carried about as many more additional rounds, though occasionally more, as during the Gettysburg Campaign, when the Union artillery brought along some 20 additional rounds per piece, so that there were about 220 rounds available per gun, some 10 percent-15 percent more than Lee's pieces had. In action a battery could run through its basic supply of ammunition in less than an hour, though it could stretch that limit by deliberately firing slowly, which greatly increased accuracy. This was, of course, a luxury of which a hotly engaged battery might not be able to avail itself.

If they had to, gunners could get out of a fight quickly. A single gun could be limbered up and begin moving in about a minute, while an entire battery required but three minutes. This, of course, assumed that casualties were minimal. The guns themselves were virtually indestructible, though their carriages were highly vulnerable to enemy artillery fire. If a battery lost too many men and horses, it began to have problems. A gun could sustain fire for some time with as few as three men, though nine was the norm. Loss of horses was often more of a problem than loss of men, however, for the horses were invariably killed or wounded in greater numbers than were the men. Two horses could move a light gun, though with difficulty. A heavier piece, a Napoleon or 20-pounder, required at least four. And in either case, it meant abandoning the spare caisson. As a result, the biggest cause of lost artillery pieces was casualties among the horses. At Gettysburg fewer than a dozen pieces changed hands undamaged, a remarkable tribute to the dedication and courage of artillerymen.

Artillery Ammunition

There were several types of artillery ammunition in use, each designed for a particular task. Smooth bore pieces fired mostly spherical projectiles, while rifled guns fired cylindro-conoidal projectiles looking like nothing less than an artillery shell.

Canister. Canister, a type of "case shot," consisted of a light tin can filled with musket balls or slugs packed in dry sawdust. For a 12-pounder Napoleon, the can was a bit larger than a standard 46 ounce juice can, contained 76 balls, and weighed a bit more than 12 pounds. When fired, the can disintegrated, scattering the bullets like a great shotgun blast. Ineffective at more than 400 yards, canister could be devastating at close ranges. Canister was best used with smooth bore artillery, for the great number of balls could damage the lands and grooves of a rifled gun. Canister was sometimes mistakenly referred to as "grape shot."

Grape Shot. Grape was another form of case shot. It consisted of a number of large iron or lead balls—for a Napoleon there were nine—packed between two light metal plates or into a lightly reinforced canvas bag. When fired the package would disintegrate, and the balls would smash anything before them. Since the balls were larger than those used in canister, grape shot was effective at longer ranges, up to about a thousand yards. However, it was going out of fashion by the Civil War, since it was unsuited to rifled guns, and was anyway being replaced by shrapnel. It was rarely used on the battlefield after 1862.

Shell. Sometimes called "Explosive Shell", this was a light, hollow cast iron sphere or "shell" filled with explosives. For a Napoleon, the standard shell weighed about 9.75 pounds, seven ounces of which was explosive charge. When set off by a fuze, fragments of the casing would be scattered and, if detonated against the ground pieces of wood and rock and other debris would be scattered in all directions. A variety of fuzes were available. Spherical shell could be set off by percussion fuzes, which worked mechanically upon impact. Explosive shell for rifled cannon had a fulminate detonator in their tips which would go off on impact. Both of these had to hit something in order to go off. Since detonation of a shell above the heads of massed troops would give the maximum results, time fuzes were also used. The typical time fuze was a color coded paper wad which plugged into the shell: black burned for four seconds, red for six, green eight, and yellow ten, though each fuze was two inches long. In addition, the gunner would cut the fuze to obtain a shorter burning period. If he cut it right, and if it burned at the prescribed rate, and if the gun was properly trained, the fuze would set the shell off above, and just in front of the target, so that the shell fragments would be thrown downwards, scattering right into the assembled troops. This did not always happen. Nevertheless, at anything but extreme ranges, shell was more effective than solid shot against troops, though its effectiveness was reduced at under 800 yards. In general, Union manufacturing standards were higher than those prevailing in the Confederacy, so that Union shells and fuzes were more reliable.

Shot. Often called "Solid Shot" or "Round Shot," was a cylindrical or cylindro-conoidal slug of iron or steel used to smash things, such as walls, earthworks, and troops. Upon hitting the ground, cylindrical (i.e. "round") shot would often bounce several times, and could cut great swathes through large formations, a practice which could not be done with cylindro-conoidal shot. Shot was the ammunition of preference when firing at long ranges or against "hard" targets.

Shrapnel. Invented by Henry Shrapnel, a British general, this was more correctly, but less clearly, called "case shot" or "spherical case shot." Shrapnel was essentially a combination of canister and explosive shell. A hollow, cast iron projectile was filled with lead bullets packed in sulphur and provided with a bursting charge which could be set off by a percussion or time fuze, thus scattering the balls. Since it could be used at the same ranges as grape shot, and had the advantage of an explosive charge as well, it rapidly replaced the latter. Essentially a variant of explosive shell, shrapnel suffered from the same drawbacks as shell did.

Rifled Artillery Ammunition. There were two classes of rifled artillery ammunition which could be any of the types noted above. Parrott guns and 3" rifles used a round which was essentially a scaled up minie ball, with an expanding base to catch the lands and grooves of the rifling. Most other rifled guns had peculiarly shaped ammunition which had to be fitted to the grooves, making them relatively slow firers, unless they were breechloaders.

The Ships

C.S.S. Alabama and U.S.S. Kearsarge

The most successful of the Confederate cruisers was C.S.S. *Alabama*, which fought one of the most famous naval duels of the war with U.S.S. *Kearsarge*, off Cherbourg on 19 June 1864.

Alabama was laid down as Hull Number 290 at the Laird shipyard in Liverpool, England. Launched on 15 May 1862 as *Enrica*, it was clear from the start that she was being built as a warship for the Confederacy. Diplomatic representations on the part of the United States resulted in Her Majesty's Government instructing the local authorities at Liverpool to prevent the ship from sailing. Through incompetence—or design—the harbor officials permitted her to go to sea on 29 July with a scratch crew in order to conduct "trials." *Enrica* briefly put in at Port Lynas, on the Anglesea coast, where she took on some stores and a few additional crewmen, and then steamed northwards around Ireland into the open Atlantic, eluding the Union screw sloop *Tuscarora*, which had been lying in wait for her just outside British territorial waters. *Enrica* made for the Azores, putting in at Terceira in early August. There she was met by a vessel carrying guns, ammunition, and the other accoutrements of a warship. As these were transferred aboard, a second ship arrived, carrying Capt. Raphael Semmes, who had skippered the Confederacy's first raider, C.S.S. *Sumter*, along with several of his officers and a sizeable crew of British and American seamen. Semmes supervised the conversion of the ship into a cruiser and on 17 August 1862 took her out into international waters and hoisted the Confederate flag, commissioning her as C.S.S. *Alabama*.

The 1,050 ton *Alabama* had a crew of 25 officers and 120 other ranks. She measured 220 feet in length, had a beam of 31.6 feet, and drew 14 feet. A well designed, well-built vessel with a coppered hull, the barkentine-rigged *Alabama* was steam driven, and fitted with a raisable propeller to reduce drag when operating under sail. Despite this, she was not a fast ship, her best speed under steam being 13-knots and under sail but 10. She had considerable autonomy when using sail, however, and even had a water condenser to permit her to keep to sea for extended periods. *Alabama* was rather poorly armed, having only eight guns, all muzzle loaders—a pivot-mounted 6.4"/100-pounder Blakely rifle on the forecastle, three smooth-bore 32-pounders on each side, and a pivot-mounted 8"/68-pounder smooth-bore aft—but these were sufficient for her primary role, commerce raiding.

Alabama had a active career of 22 months. An accomplished seaman and clever captain, Semmes kept her constantly in motion, rarely lingering in any maritime area for very long. From the North Atlantic he took her into the Caribbean, into the South Atlantic, on into the Indian Ocean, and then back into the Atlantic. With her single stack lowered she could easily be mistaken for a sailing vessel, and she frequently wore the flags of neutrals to further the masquerade. She intercepted 294 ships, of which 69—all save one sailing vessels—were American, which were taken without incident. All but ten of the captured ships were burned. The remaining ships were bonded, released upon promise of payment of an indemnity at the end of the war, and permitted to carry *Alabama's* prisoners to safety. Altogether, *Alabama* destroyed or bonded over $6,500,000 worth of shipping, and was by far the most successful Confederate raider, accounting for 26.2 percent of the 263 Union merchantmen destroyed by the dozen or so Rebel cruisers. During her cruise, *Alabama* fought one engagement, when, on 7 January 1863 she sank the lightly armed blockader U.S.S. *Hatteras* off Galveston, overwhelming the smaller vessel through surprise and superior firepower. During her long cruise, *Alabama* made several landfalls, but was never able to avail herself of the services of a proper shipyard. As a result, by the time she returned to the North Atlantic in the spring of 1864, she was badly in need of a refit. On 11 June 1864 Semmes put in at Cherbourg, hoping to make use of the ship repair facilities there. His arrival was observed by the American consul, who wired the American minister to France, who in turn passed the word to the consul at Flushing, in the Netherlands, where the screw sloop *Kearsarge* lay at anchor.

U.S.S. *Kearsarge*, laid down at the Navy's Portsmouth, New Hampshire shipyard early in 1861, was launched on 11 September of that year, and commissioned for sea on 24 January 1862. Barque-rigged, she displaced about 1,500 tons, was slightly less than 200 feet between perpendiculars, had a beam of a bit more than 33 feet, and drew 15.5 feet. One of a class of four war program vessels based on a successful pre-war design, *Kearsarge* was the sister of *Tuscarora*, which had waited in vain for *Enrica/Alabama* in July of 1862, and of *Wachusett*, which captured the Confederate raider *Florida* as she lay at anchor in the neutral port of Bahia, Brazil, in October of 1864. The single screw *Kearsarge* was a slow ship, being able to do no more than 12 knots under steam, which she could almost equal with sail alone. She had a formidable armament, consisting of two pivot mounted 11"/150-pounder smooth bores, one at each end of the ship, plus a 4.2"/30-pounder Parrot rifle, four 32-pounder smooth bores, and a 12-pounder howitzer for close-in action.

While *Kearsarge's* career was less spectacular than that of *Alabama*, she was a busy ship. Soon after her commissioning *Kearsarge* went on anti-raider patrol in the North Atlantic. She kept at it for nearly three years. It was boring duty, broken only by her participation in the blockade of Semmes' old C.S.S. *Sumter* in Gibraltar in early 1863. In April of 1863 Capt. John A. Winslow assumed command. Winslow (1811-1873) first shipped out as a midshipman in 1827. He rose steadily, if slowly through the ranks thereafter. As a lieutenant in the early 1850s, Winslow became friends with Raphael Semmes while they were both on U.S.S. *Cumberland*. At the outbreak of the war he was serving as lighthouse inspector in the Boston area. He subsequently commanded the river gunboat *Benton* on the Mississippi. Winslow was a man of strong religious convictions and was a confirmed abolitionist. He was also an innovative officer. At the suggestion of some of his officers he arranged to have a six-foot wide network of chains hung over the ship's sides for about 50 feet in the way of her engines, covering these with a light wooden framework to protect them from the weather and detritis. When, on Sunday morning, 12 June word came that *Alabama* was at Cherbourg, Winslow was more than ready.

Kearsarge put to sea as soon as crewmen ashore could be recalled. She steamed southward, clearing for action and putting in at Dover to learn the latest news from the American consulate there. On 14 June she arrived off Cherbourg. Mindful of the 24-hour rule—a neutral power may detain a warship in port if a vessel of a rival power has departed within 24 hours—Winslow stood outside of French territorial waters, from whence he could observe the presence of *Alabama*, within the harbor; tales that the crews of both ships fraternized in waterfront haunts are so much nonsense. Winslow maintained a close watch on his rival, lest Semmes manage to elude him. But his erstwhile friend had no such notions.

Semmes decided to sortie and engage *Kearsarge*. His reasons are unclear, and it was actually a serious error of judgment. *Alabama* was a commerce raider, and even blockaded in Cherbourg she performed a useful service for the Confederacy, for Union vessels would have to be assigned to watch her, and would therefore be unable to perform other duties. By choosing to sortie, Semmes was allowing his instincts to cloud his reason. In any case, he dispatched a message to Winslow requesting that the latter not depart before he was ready to emerge. As Winslow had no such plans, this bit of bravado was perhaps another error, alerting the Yankee skipper to Semmes' intentions.

Escorted by the French ironclad *Couronne*, which intended to ensure that no violation of French territorial waters occur, *Alabama* sortied on Sunday, 19 June 1864, boldly steaming out of the port at about 10:00, as crowds gathered on the breakwater and the English yacht *Deerhound* tagged along to see the sights, and Winslow prepared to conduct divine services as *Kearsarge* lay at anchor about three miles off the harbor mouth.

Superficially the two vessels were well matched. On paper *Alabama* had only about 60 percent of her rival's displacement, but was a trifle faster. Both ships had about the same number of men in their crews, and roughly the same number of guns. But there the resemblance ended. *Kearsarge* was by far the superior vessel. She had a clean bottom, able to make her full speed, whereas *Alabama* was down by a couple of knots due to fouling. *Kearsarge* was using a superior quality gunpowder, and, moreover, had a broadside of 365 pounds, 20 percent heavier than the of *Alabama*, while her gunners had received far more careful training in their art.

The battle between *Alabama* and *Kearsarge* began with the latter steaming up the Channel, putting seven miles between herself and the French coast. To Semmes it appeared that his rival was fleeing, and he gave chase. Then, at 10:50, *Kearsarge* circled about and headed boldly for *Alabama*. At 10:57, with the range at about 2,000 yards, *Alabama* opened fire with her 100-pound pivot gun, and, turning, followed this up with a broadside. Winslow began to turn, to offer his broadside to his rival. Semmes tried to circle, intending to rake *Kearsarge*. As a result, both vessels began to circle, their starboard sides firing on each other. As the range narrowed, they gradually drifted southwestward, sailing on the circumference of a series of circles, right past the harbor entrance, to the delight of the thousands of tourists crowding the sea wall. Altogether the fight lasted nearly two hours, the ships making seven circles, with the range getting down to some 500 yards towards the end. Although *Alabama* delivered some major blows, she was heavily damaged by *Kearsarge's* superior fire, suffering many casualties and being repeatedly holed. Finally Semmes had to admit defeat. With the range down to 400 yards, and with Winslow finally in a position to rake, Semmes struck his flag. What happened next is subject to controversy. As Semmes put a boat over the side to offer his surrender, one or more guns aboard *Alabama* were discharged, possibly accidently or as a result of fires. Suspecting treachery, *Kearsarge* replied with devastating effect. *Alabama* began to settle by her stern. Her crew abandoned ship, most men taking to the water, while one longboat was loaded with wounded. At 12:50 *Alabama* went down, sinking by her stern as her bow rose almost vertically into the air.

During their famous duel neither U.S.S. *Kearsarge* nor C.S.S. *Alabama* demonstrated particularly impressive marksmanship. The former fired 173 rounds, of which about 40 (23.1 percent) found their target, while the latter fired some 370, of which only 42 (11.3 percent) hit something: one unexploded shell lodged in *Kearsarge*'s sternpost, which was later sawn off and is presently on display at the Washington Navy Yard. *Alabama* lost nine killed and 21 wounded, plus a further ten men drowned, while *Kearsarge* lost but one killed and two wounded.

The sinking of *Alabama* did not end the depredations of the Confederate cruisers, but did restore a measure of confidence in the United States Navy's ability to protect American shipping. Moreover, the loss of its most successful raider was a major blow to Confederate morale.

The *Alabama* Claims

After the war the United States dunned Great Britain for the damage caused by the eleven Confederate cruisers which had been built or fitted out in British ports. Although some Jingoists wished to ignore the claims, most Britons believed there was merit in the American position, naval officers in particular observing that the United States was defending Britain's traditional view of the matter. As a result, there was relatively little acrimony as to the validity of the American claims. However, there was a great deal of dispute over the amounts in question. As a result, in 1871 the Treaty of Washington was concluded which provided for a board of five arbiters to be appointed one each by the United States, Britain, Italy, Brazil, and Switzerland, which would meet in Geneva. The board held its first meeting on 15 December 1871. On 14 September 1872 the United States was awarded $15,500,000 in gold in compensation for the depredations of the raiders *Alabama*, *Florida*, and *Shenandoah*, the damage inflicted by the other vessels being considered of negligible importance. Great Britain paid the monies in question promptly, and the last international problem created by the Civil War was concluded.

Afterwards

Upon the loss of his ship Raphael Semmes was rescued by *Deerhound* and eventually made his was back to the Confederacy, where he continued on active duty to the end of the war. John Winslow remained in the Navy until he retired as a rear admiral in 1872, dying shortly afterwards. *Kear-*

sarge had a long career in the Navy which came to an end on 2 February 1894, when she was wrecked in Central American waters. In 1901 the names *Kearsarge* and *Alabama* were given to two new pre-dreadnought battleships, the former being the only American battleship not named after a state. Both names were revived for the Second World War, during which both the battleship *Alabama* and the carrier *Kearsarge* had distinguished careers. At present, however, neither name is represented on the Navy List.

Army Life

Chow

The ration allowances in both armies were quite good given the standards of the times. Officially the daily ration of a Union soldier and, since the Confederacy substantially adopted the U.S. regulations, for his foeman as well, was:

16 ounces of biscuit (hard tack, pilot bread, crackers) or 22 ounces of fresh bread or flour.

20 ounces of fresh or salt meat or 12 ounces of bacon

10 ounces dry measure of dried beans or peas

2.6 ounces dry measure of rice or hominy

5.2 ounces dry measure of potatoes "when practical"

1.3 gills of vinegar

1.6 ounces of green or 1.3 ounces of roasted coffee or .25 ounces of tea

2.4 ounces of sugar

1.3 gills molasses

0.3 ounces of salt

0.04 ounces of pepper

0.2 ounces of candles

0.6 ounces of soap

occasional anti-scorbics (pickles, onions, dried fruits, etc)

On paper this was a fairly good ration, indeed it was superior to that prescribed by any other major power. The only problem was that it often existed largely on paper. Rations were often late, or incomplete, and frequently of poor quality even in the Union Army. For the Confederate troops the situation was usually worse. Moreover, this was the camp ration; there was a separate marching ration—16 ounces of biscuit, 12 ounces of salt or 20 ounces of fresh meat, plus sugar, coffee, and salt—so that when the troops were in the field they ate even less well than when in camp, though they needed it more. Even in the best of times it was unusual for the troops to get more than the biscuit and coffee, without which the war would probably have been impossible. Biscuits or hardtack—occasionally called "flour-tiles," which gives some notion of their nature—were thick, double baked crackers of about 3" square, which had to be soaked to be eaten without danger to the teeth. Since contractors often cheated on the special baking which was required, and since they were often stored improperly, biscuits were almost always inhabited. Green troops usually tried to pick the grubs out, but veterans just ate the whole thing, though finicky ones usually preferred them cooked. Jokes about hard tack were common, as, "The only meat we had for weeks was in the biscuits," and:

"I was eating a piece of hard tack this morning, and I bit into something soft," said a sergeant.

"A worm?" asked a private.

"No, by God, it was a ten-penny nail!"

Confederate troops often got corn bread, but appear to have preferred biscuit, which was more easily carried. The real fuel of the Union armies was coffee, coarsely ground with a rifle butt and made very strong and very black. The Confederate troops liked coffee too, but, since they usually could get it only when they swapped tobacco with their Union counterparts while on picket duty, improvised by using well-roasted peanuts, acorns, rye, chicory, and various other things, and brewed a variety of teas, such as sassafras, ginger, and the like.

Occasionally special rations were authorized in both armies, such as for holidays. In one unusual case, the division of Union Maj. Gen. Louis Blenker, which was composed mostly of men from Central Europe, was issued rye and black bread rather than white, and permitted a beer ration to boot.

During the war the Confederacy had to reduce the prescribed ration level, not that this mattered much, since it was usually incapable of providing even the reduced amounts; by mid-1863 the men of the Army of Northern Virginia were subsisting on 18 ounces of meal or flour and four ounces of bacon a day, well-below the prescribed allowances. The Union was more fortunate, and in June of 1864 increased the individual ration by four ounces of biscuit or six ounces of flour plus three pounds of potatoes each day, along with a twice weekly issue of desiccated vegetables and various canned goods as well. As with the original ration, these were issued as available.

Salted meat was supposed to last for two years and so was rather heavily pickled. Before it could be eaten it had to be soaked to get rid of most of the brine, a process which also removed most of the food value as well. In general the troops much preferred salt pork to salt beef, as the latter salted less well and was often spoiled. Meat was in very short supply in the

Confederacy, which before the war had gotten much of its beef and pork from the mid-West. While domestic production provided some relief, and a little meat came through the blockade—of such poor quality as to prompt Brig. Gen. G. Moxley Sorrel to remark that the Yankees let it through the blockade "in the hope of poisoning us"—the supply never came close to equaling the need. The desiccated vegetables were a good idea, but were usually of poor quality and the troops often lacked time to properly reconstitute them. As a result, the troops resorted to other means to supplement their rations. They could purchase comestibles from a sutler, but the cost was always high, especially in the Confederacy, and the sutlers were often swindlers. Foraging was common in both armies, regardless of locale or official sanction. In addition, packages from home were an occasional help and in friendly territory the troops were often invited to dine with local folks, at least early in the war.

Cooking facilities were poor in both armies. Early in the war the Confederacy had attempted to introduce brigade cooking staffs, but this had not worked out. In 1863 the Union attempted to provide company cooks, but these had little or no training; although the War Department issued an official army cookbook, it suffered from poor distribution and was wholly unsuited to the resources, conditions, and needs of the troops in the field. Fortunately, in both armies there were usually enough bakers around to permit regiments to make their own bread when flour was available. In general the troops, whether Yankees or Rebels, much preferred eating in messes of three to ten men, pooling whatever they had and rotating the cooking chores, or taking on a black servant to handle the business, with the result that some troops fared well and others fared badly on the same rations.

Frying in grease was the preferred method of cooking, which was often the cause of stomach problems and diarrhea among the troops, especially in the early part of the war, before those with weak constitutions died-off.

Some recipes when rations were short included:

Ash Cakes: mix cornmeal with salt and water, wrap in cabbage leaves and cook in ashes until firm.

"Coffee": take one-third measure of green coffee and begin roasting it in the normal fashion. When lightly browned add two-thirds measure of wheat or rye, stirring and roasting it all together until dark. Grind or pound well. Use one measure of this to eight measures of boiling water, stirring well. When done, add a few drops of cold water to lay the sediment. In a pinch, omit the coffee.

Coosh: mix flour or corn meal with water until it "flows like milk" and then fry in a half-pan of boiling grease, adding bits of meat if available, until it looks like dirty brown hash. Also known as "cush" and "slosh," crumbled biscuit or corn bread could be substituted for the flour or meal to produce this delicacy.

Hardtack Pudding: pound biscuits into a powder, add flour if available, mix with water, and knead into a dough. Roll this out until it resembles a pie crust and fill with apples or whatever else is available. Then wrap it in a piece of cloth and boil for an hour.

Hell-Fire Stew: boil hardtack in water and bacon grease.

Lobscouse: stew—or bake—salt meat with hardtack and vegetables. This appetizer was an Old Navy standby.

Skillygalee: soften hardtack in cold water and then fry it in pork fat until brown, salting to taste.

Slapjack: make a thick mixture of corn meal or flour and fry it in half a pan of boiling grease, until the underside is brown, then flip it over to finish the top, forming a sort of cake. A thicker version of coosh.

Slosh: another name for Coosh.

War and the Muses

Hit Tunes of the Civil War

Although neither as large nor as lucrative as the electronicized megabusiness which it has become, the music business was nevertheless well established in nineteenth century America. There were famous song writers and popular singers and hit songs and even groupies. There was also a great deal more participation in music then than now, for with the introduction of the phonograph and still later the radio, music has become a spectator sport for most. And, of course, during the Civil War the armies marched as they went about their business, a practice made easier by song.

While there was no system of record keeping such as that which sustains the "Top Forty" and "Golden Record" nonsense of the contemporary musical scene, a perusal of letters, diaries, and memoirs permits some conclusions to be drawn as to the popularity of various songs during the war. It should be noted, however, that in those simpler times a tune would retain its hold on the public far longer than in the present. As a result, songs which were popular early in the war were still to be heard later. And hoary old tunes, such as "Home, Sweet Home" were perennial favorites, as were hymns.

1861: "Dixie," "Maryland! My Maryland!," and "The Bonnie Blue Flag" in the South; "John Brown's Body" in the North.

1862: "The Battle Hymn of the Republic," "Marching Along," "The Battle Cry of Freedom," "Tramp, Tramp, Tramp," and "We Are Coming, Father Abraham" in the North; "Lorena" and "All Quiet Along the Potomac" on both sides.

1863: "When this Cruel War Is Over" on both sides.

1864: "Tenting Tonight" and "Just before the Battle, Mother" on both sides.

1865: "When Johnny Comes Marching Home" and "Marching Through Georgia" in the North; the South had very little to sing about by this time.

After 1861 the martial airs were less often heard in the ranks of either

army, the men much preferring sad and sentimental, even defeatist tunes
like "Lorena," possibly the most popular song of the war, to the more
stirring songs. Nor were the troops loathe to borrow from the enemy, and
there were often "Rebel" versions of "Yankee" songs and *vice versa*.

Lorena

Possibly the most popular of Civil War songs, the melodious, sentimental *Lorena* was known among the troops on both sides. The origins of the
song are something of a mystery, being attributed to one H.D.L. Webster
and to an anonymous tunesmith who later retired to a monastery. The
authorship cannot be resolved. In any case, it matters little, for the song
itself is very much the eternal soldier's song.

Lorena

The years creep slowly by, Lorena,
The snow is on the grass again;
The sun's low down the sky, Lorena,
The frost gleams where the flowers have been,
But the heart throbs on as warmly now,
As when the summer days were nigh;
Oh, the sun can never dip so low,
Adown affection's cloudless sky.
Oh, the sun can never dip so low,
Adown affection's cloudless sky.
A hundred months have passed, Lorena,
Since I last held that hand in mine;
And felt the pulse beat fast, Lorena,
Tho' mine beat faster for than thine.
A hundred months, 'twas flow'ry May,
When up the hilly slope we climbed,
To watch the dying of the day
And hear the distant church bells chime.
To watch the dying of the day
And hear the distant churchbells chime.
We loved each other then, Lorena,
More than we ever dared to tell;
And what we might have been, Lorena,
Had but our lovings prospered well—
But then, 'tis past, the years are gone,
I'll not call up their shadowy forms;
I'll say to them, "lost years, sleep on!
Sleep on! nor heed life's pelting storms."

I'll say to them, "lost years, sleep on!
Sleep on! nor heed life's pelting storms."
The story of that past, Lorena,
Alas! I care not to repeat
The hopes that could not last, Lorena,
They lived, but only to cheat.
I would not cause e'en one regret
To rankle in your bosom now;
For "if we *try*, we may forget,"
Were words of thine long years ago.
For "if we *try*, we may forget,"
Were words of thine long years ago.
Yes, these were the words of thine, Lorena,
They burn within my memory yet;
They touched some tender chords, Lorena,
Which thrill and tremble with regret.
'Twas not thy woman's heart that spoke;
Thy heart was always true to me;
A duty, stern and pressing, broke
The tie which linked my soul to thee.
A duty, stern and pressing, broke
The tie which linked my soul to thee.
It matters little now, Lorena,
The past is in the eternal Past,
Our heads will soon lie low, Lorena,
Life's tide is ebbing out so fast.
There is a Future! O thank God!
Of life, this is so small a part!
'Tis dust to dust beneath the sod;
But there, *up there*, 'tis heart to heart.
'Tis dust to dust beneath the sod;
But there, *up there*, 'tis heart to heart.

Only One Killed

One day Julia L. Keyes, a minor poet of considerable ability and a resident of Montgomery, Alabama, read a newspaper account of an incident in the war which the phrase "Only one killed" was used to suggest that all was well. Moved, she took the line and used it as the title for a poem which seeks the tragedy which lay hidden by that innocuous line.

Only One Killed
Only one killed—in company B

'Twas a trifling loss—one man!
A charge of the bold and dashing Lee—
While merry enough it was, to see
 The enemy, as he ran.
Only one killed upon our side—
 Once more to the field they turn.
Quietly now the horsemen ride—
And pause by the form of the one who died,
 So bravely, as now we learn.
Their grief for the comrade loved and true
 For a time was unconcealed;
They saw the bullet pierced him through;
That his pain was brief—ah! very few
 Die thus, on the battle-field.
The news has gone to his home, afar—
 Of the short and gallant fight,
Of the noble deeds of the young La Var
Whose life went out as a falling star
 In the skirmish of that night.
"Only one killed! It was my son,"
 The widowed mother cried.
She turned but to clasp the sinking one,
Who heard not the words of the victory won,
 But of him who bravely died.
Ah! death to her were a sweet relief,
 The bride of a single year.
Oh! would she might, with her weight of grief,
Lie down in the dust, with the autumn leaf
 Now trodden and brown and sere!
But no, she must bear through coming life
 Her burden of silent woe
The aged mother and youthful wife
Must live through a nation's bloody strife,
 Sighing, and waiting to go.
Where the loved are meeting beyond the stars,
 Are meeting no more to part,
They can smile once more through the crystal bars—
Where never more will the woe of wars
 O'ershadow the loving heart.

Marching Through Georgia

William T. Sherman's "March to the Sea" in late 1864 inspired Henry Clay

Work, an abolitionist and former Underground Railroad worker, to write "Marching Through Georgia," which rapidly became a popular song in the North. Unlike most war songs, "Marching Through Georgia" gained something of a worldwide popularity; British troops in India sang it while on the march, the Japanese played it when the Russians surrendered Port Arthur in 1905, and it was heard in both World Wars wherever English-speaking troops were to be found.

Marching Through Georgia

Bring the good old bugle, boys, we'll sing another song—
Sing it with a spirit that will start the world along—
Sing it as we used to sing it, fifty thousand strong,
While we were marching through Georgia.
Chorus: "Hurrah! Hurrah! we bring the jubilee
           Hurrah! Hurrah! the flag that makes you free!"
           So we sang this chorus from Atlanta to the sea,
           While we were marching through Georgia.
How the darkeys shouted when they heard the joyful sound!
How the turkeys gobbled which are commissary found!
How the sweet potatoes even started from the ground,
While we were marching through Georgia.—Chorus
Yes, and there were Union men who wept with joyful tears,
When they saw the honored flag they had not seen for years;
Hardly could they be restrained from breaking forth in cheers.
While we were marching through Georgia?—Chorus
So we made a thoroughfare for Freedom and her train,
Sixty miles in latitude—three hundred in the main;
Treason fled before us, for resistance was in vain,
While we were marching through Georgia.—Chorus

Somebody's Darling

One of the most popular poems in the South in the latter days of the war was Marie Ravenel de la Coste's "Somebody's Darling." Probably the best woman poet of the Confederacy, de la Coste effectively conveys some of the tragedy and pathos of the war. Eventually set to music, "Somebody's Darling" became the most popular Southern song by a woman.

Somebody's Darling

Into a ward of the whitewashed halls,
   Where the dead and the dying lay—
Wounded by bayonets, shells, and balls,
   Somebody's darling was borne one day—

Somebody's darling, so young and so brave!
   Wearing yet on his sweet, pale face—
Soon to be hid in the dust of the grave—
   The lingering light of his boyhood's grace!
Matted and damp are the curls of gold
   Kissing the snow of that fair young brow,
Pale are the lips of delicate mould—
   Somebody's darling is dying now.
Back from his beautiful blue-veined brow
   Brush his wandering waves of gold;
Cross his hands on his bosom now—
   Somebody's darling is still and cold.
Kiss him once for somebody's sake,
   Murmur a prayer soft and low—
One bright curl from its fair mates take—
   They were somebody's pride you know.
Somebody's hand hath rested there;
   Was it a mother's, soft and white?
God knows best! He has somebody's love;
   Somebody's heart enshrined him there—
Somebody wafted his name above,
   Night and morn, on the wings of prayer.
Somebody wept when he marched away,
   Looking so handsome, brave, and grand!
Somebody's kiss on his forehead lay—
   Somebody clung to his parting hand.
Somebody's watching and waiting for him,
   Yearning to hold him again to her heart;
And there he lies with his blue eyes dim,
   And the smiling child-like lips apart.
Tenderly bury the fair young dead—
   Pausing to drop on his grave a tear;
Carve on the wooden slab o'er his head—
   "Somebody's darling slumbers here."

VI
1865

If the thing is pressed I think Lee will surrender.
—Philip H. Sheridan

...there is nothing left for me to do but go and see General Grant, and I would rather die a thousand deaths.
—Robert E. Lee

...the nightmare is gone.
—Abraham Lincoln

Now he belongs to the ages.
—Edwin M. Stanton

With the reelection of Lincoln in 1864 the Confederacy was doomed. But too much had been invested in the war for the South to seek, or the Union to accept, a negotiated settlement. And so the armies spent yet another winter in the field. Throughout the South there was terrible hardship, even in areas which had not been marched through and fought over. Nor did the winter of 1864-1865 give the Confederacy a reprieve from its death sentence. Military operations continued, little diminished by the elements.

As the Union naval blockade grew ever tighter, Sherman's armies began marching northwards from Savannah. Charleston fell and Wilmington was sealed so that by the end of February the South no longer possessed a single port. Union troops under Maj. Gen. Philip Sheridan swept through the Shenandoah Valley, while Yankee cavalry raided virtually unhindered through Alabama, and the Mississippi Valley was held in a ever stronger Union grip. And before Richmond and Petersburg the raids and affrays and sniping never ceased, as the Army of Northern Virginia held to its trenches before the increasingly stronger *Army of the Potomac*. As Maj. Gen. William Tecumseh Sherman ground his way through South Carolina and into North Carolina, Lt. Gen. Ulysses S. Grant prepared to deliver the final blows.

The end came quickly. Late in March Grant began to extend his left flank southward, seeking to get around Gen. Robert E. Lee's right and sever his connections with what was left of the interior of the Confederacy. Lee fought back, but to no avail. Seeing his line of retreat threatened, he had no choice but to evacuate Richmond, pulling out on 3 April. A deadly foot race ensued, as Lee sought to escape southward, perhaps hoping to link-up with Gen. Joseph E. Johnston's army confronting Sherman in North Carolina, there to make a final stand. But Grant maintained a close pursuit which Lee was unable to shake. And on 9 April after a brief fight, Lee asked for terms. Within days Johnston did the same. Though some small forces were still in the field in isolated areas, these too would shortly surrender. The war was over. And then on 14 April yet another calamity befell the nation, when John Wilkes Booth murdered Abraham Lincoln in the misguided belief that he was striking a blow for the South. So peace came, but without Lincoln's strong hand to guide the nation.

Incidents of War

"The Reason is . . . ."

The day after Appomattox, Gen. Robert E. Lee was out riding on Traveler, his famous gray, when a Union major general approached him.

"Don't you recognize me, General Lee?" said the man, "I'm George Meade."

Lee smiled, for the two had known each other in the Old Army, and said, "Oh, is that you, Meade? How did you happen to get all that gray in your beard?"

Meade smiled back, "I'm afraid you are the cause of most of it, sir."

The Strange Fate of Wilmer McLean

When I first joined the Army of Northern Virginia in 1861, I found a connection of my family, Wilmer McLean, living on a fine farm through which ran Bull Run, with a nice farm-house about opposite the center of our line of battle along that stream. General Beauregard made his headquarters at this house during the first affair between the armies—the so-called battle of Blackburn's Ford, on July 18. The first hostile shot which I ever saw fired was aimed at this house and about the third or fourth went through its kitchen, where servants were cooking dinner for the headquarters staff.

I had not seen or heard of McLean for years, when the day after the surrender [10 April 1865], I met him at Appomattox Court-house, and asked with some surprise what he was doing there. He replied, with much indignation: "What are you doing here? These armies tore my place on Bull Run all to pieces, and kept running over it backward and forward till no one could live there, so I could live there, so I just sold out and came here, two hundred miles away, hoping I should never see a soldier again. And now, just look around you! Not a fence-rail is left on the place, the last guns trampled down all my crops, and Lee surrenders to Grant in my house." McLean was so indignant that I felt bound to apologize for our coming back, and to throw all the blame for it upon the gentlemen on the other side.

—Edward P. Alexander, "Lee at Appomattox,"
The Century, April 1902

Lee's Farewell to His Troops

General Order, NO. 9
Headquarters, Army of Northern Virginia

April 10, 1865

After four years of arduous service, marked by unsurpassed courage and fortitude, the Army of Northern Virginia has been compelled to yield to overwhelming numbers and resources.

I need not tell the brave survivors of so many hard fought battles, who have remained steadfast to the last, that I have consented to the result from no distrust of them.

But feeling that valor and devotion could accomplish nothing that would compensate for the loss that must have attended the continuance of the contest, I determined to avoid the useless sacrifice of those whose past services have endeared them to their countrymen.

By the terms of the agreement officers and men can return to their homes and remain until exchanged. You will take with you the satisfaction that proceeds from the consciousness of duty faithfully performed, and I earnestly pray that a Merciful God will extend to you His blessing and protection.

With an increasing admiration of your constancy and devotion to your country, and a grateful remembrance of your kind and generous consideration for myself, I bid you an affectionate farewell.

—R.E. Lee

"If We'd Had Your Songs . . . . "

A day or two after Lee's surrender in April, 1865, I left our ship at "Dutch Gap," in the James River, for a run up to Richmond, where I was joined by the ship's surgeon, the paymaster, and one of the junior officers. After "doing" Richmond pretty thoroughly we went in the evening to my rooms for dinner. Dinner being over and the events of the day recounted, the doctor, who was a fine player, opened the piano, saying: "Boys, we've got our old quarter here; let's have a sing." As the house opposite was occupied by paroled Confederate officers, no patriotic songs were sung. Soon the lady of the house handed me this note: "Compliments of General —— and Staff. Will the gentlemen kindly allow us to come over and hear them sing?" Of course we consented and they came.

As the General entered the room, I recognized instantly the face and figure of one who stood second only to Lee or Jackson, in the whole Confederacy. After introductions and the usual interchange of civilities, we sang for them glees and college songs, until at last the General said: "Excuse me, gentlemen, you sing delightfully, but what *we* want to hear is your army songs." Then we gave them the army songs with unction, the "Battle Hymn of the Republic," "John Brown's Body," "We're Coming, Father Abraham," "Tramp, Tramp, Tramp, the Boys Are Marching," through the whole catalogue, to the "Star Spangled Banner"—to which many a foot beat time as if it had never stepped to any but the "music of the Union,"—and closed our concert with "Rally Round the Flag, Boys."

When the applause had subsided, a tall, fine-looking fellow in a major's uniform exclaimed, "Gentlemen, if we'd had your songs we'd have licked you out of your boots! Who couldn't have marched or fought with such songs? While we had nothing, absolutely nothing, except a bastard 'Marseillaise,' the 'Bonnie Blue Flag,' and 'Dixie,'" which were nothing but jigs. 'Maryland, My Maryland' was a splendid song, but the true, old 'Lauriger Horatius' was about as inspiring as the 'Dead March in Saul,' while every one of these Yankee songs is full of marching and fighting spirit." Then turning to the General, he said: "I shall never forget the first time I heard 'Rally Round the Flag.' 'Twas a nasty night during the 'Seven Days' Fight,' and if I remember rightly it was raining. I was on picket, when, just before taps, some fellow on the other side struck up that song and others joined in the chorus until it seemed to me that the whole Yankee army was singing. Tom B——, who was with me, sung out, 'Good heavens, Cap, what are those fellows made of, anyway? Here we've licked 'em six days running and now, on the eve of the seventh, they're singing 'Rally Round the Flag.'" I am not naturally superstitious, but I tell you that song sounded to me like the 'knell of doom,' and my heart went down into my boots; and though I've tried to do my duty, it has been an up-hill fight with me ever since that night."

The little company of Union singers and Confederate auditors, after a pleasant and interesting interchange of stories of army experiences, then separated, and as the General shook hands at parting, he said to me: "Well, the time may come when we can *all* sing the 'Star Spangled Banner' again." I have not seen him since.

-Richard W. Brown, "Memoranda on the Civil War,"
The Century, January 1888

The Men

Jubal A. Early

Born in Virginia, Jubal A. Early (1816-1894) graduated 18th in the West Point class of 1837, entering the artillery. After a tour of duty in Florida against the Seminoles, he resigned from the army to practice law and engage in politics in his native state with considerable success, becoming a member of the House of Delegates and commonwealth's attorney. He served as a major of Virginia volunteers in the Mexican War. In 1861, Early was a delegate to the Virginia secession convention, at which he voted against secession. Nevertheless, he became an ardent Confederate, entering the army as colonel of the 24th Virginia.

Early commanded a brigade under Beauregard during the Bull Run Campaign and was promoted brigadier general shortly thereafter. He led his brigade during the opening phases of the Peninsular Campaign in 1862, until wounded. He returned to duty in time to command a brigade in the Second Bull Run Campaign. Early received a division during the Antietam Campaign, which he led at Fredericksburg. Promoted major general in January of 1863, he led his division during the Gettysburg Campaign, where he was among the officers who convinced Ewell not to attack Culp's Hill simultaneously with Longstreet's attack in the south on 2 July, a matter which seriously affected the outcome of the day's fighting. At Spotsylvania in May of '64 he assumed command of Richard Ewell's II Corps and was soon after promoted to lieutenant general.

Early led the corps at Cold Harbor and then, in July, took it on his famous "raid" down the Shenandoah Valley and into Maryland with the intention of putting pressure on Washington, in the hope of causing troops to be pulled away from Richmond. He was partially successful and repeated the feat a second time in August. This proved less of a success as a strategic diversion, but he did manage to plunder and burn along a broad front, spreading devastation as far as Chambersburg in Pennsylvania. Maj. Gen. Philip Sheridan trounced him later at Cedar Creek and his command was dispersed by Brig. Gen. G.A. Custer early in 1865. Early's performance was so poor that he was relieved by Lee and spent the remaining weeks of the war inactively.

After the war Early fled to Mexico, thinking to take service with the forces of the Emperor Maximilian, but then went to Canada. He eventually returned to Virginia, where he resumed his law practice and became involved in the corrupt Louisiana Lottery. Early became the first president of the Southern History Society, wrote a number of books on the war, and engaged in a rather successful campaign to place all blame for the Confederate reverse at Gettysburg on Longstreet. He remained an ardent Rebel until his death. Nicknamed "Old Jube" and "Jubilee," Early was a fairly good division commander, but lacked the ability to be a really successful corps commander, being stubborn and disloyal. A confirmed bachelor, Early was a notorious misogynist.

Richard H. Anderson

Born into a planter family in South Carolina, "Dick" Anderson (1821-1879) graduated from West Point 40th in the class of 1842 and entered the dragoons. He served in Mexico (one brevet), on the frontier, and in Kansas before resigning as a captain in March of 1861. Anderson entered his state's service as colonel of the 1st South Carolina and served at Fort Sumter. He shortly transferred to Confederate service and was appointed brigadier general in June of 1861, serving briefly at Pensacola before being sent to Northern Virginia.

Anderson commanded a brigade with some skill under Longstreet in early 1862, serving in the Peninsular Campaign. Promoted major general in July, he commanded a division at Second Bull Run, during the Antietam Campaign, in which he was wounded, and at Fredericksburg and Chancellorsville, where he greatly distinguished himself. At Gettysburg, however, his performance was pedestrian. In May of 1864 he assumed command of I Corps when Longstreet was wounded. As an acting lieutenant general he led the corps with some ability, notably at Spotsylvania, until Longstreet returned to duty in October, whereupon he resumed command of his division until virtually the end of the war, when a reorganization left him without a command a few days before Appomattox.

After the war Anderson had difficulties making ends meet, and worked for a time as a day laborer, before being named state phosphate agent by South Carolina, which post rescued him from abject poverty. Anderson was a good division commander, and, although he did well with Longstreet's corps, he was perhaps too cautious to be truly effective as a corps commander. Nevertheless, he suffered only one tactical defeat in his career, at Sayler's Creek (6 April 1865), and even then he managed to extricate most of his troops from a potential disaster.

Nathan Bedford Forrest

One of the more gifted amateur soldiers of the war, Nathan Bedford Forrest (1821-1877) was born in Tennessee. With little formal education, he was early engaged as a small farmer and trader in horses and slaves, by some accounts a dealer in stolen merchandise, later becoming a realtor. He gradually built a considerable fortune, becoming a prosperous planter. At the start of the war he briefly served as a private in the 7th Tennessee Cavalry. In October of 1861 he raised a battalion of mounted infantry at his own expense and was not surprisingly elected lieutenant colonel. Present at Fort Donelson when U.S. Grant's army invested the place in February of 1862, Forrest requested and received permission to attempt to escape and managed to lead some 1,500 mounted troops to safety. Shortly thereafter elected colonel of the 3rd Tennessee Cavalry, he led the regiment during the Shiloh Campaign. In June he was given a cavalry brigade in the Army of Tennessee. The next month he made the first of what would become a series of successful cavalry raids, capturing the Union supply depot at Murfreesboro, Tennessee, for which he was promoted brigadier general.

Forrest's raids proved a major obstacle to the establishment of Union control over western Tennessee and greatly impeded U.S. Grant's efforts to take Vicksburg. Forrest took part in Braxton Bragg's operations in Tennessee from Tullahoma to Chattanooga, his raids complementing those of Joe Wheeler in bringing Union Maj. Gen. William S. Rosecran's army to the edge of dissolution. Shortly after the Confederate defeat at Chattanooga, Forrest had a falling out with Bragg—a not unusual occurrence in the Army of Tennessee—and requested a transfer from Jefferson Davis. Davis gave Forrest a promotion to major general and an independent command in northern Mississippi and western Tennessee.

Forrest's operations over the next 15 months kept alive Confederate resistance in Union occupied areas of Tennessee and Mississippi, as he undertook a series of raids against Union outposts and garrisons, the most notable of which was his capture of Fort Pillow (12 April 1864), during which there occurred a massacre of the largely black garrison after their surrender; although Forrest's admirers deny the charge, it is substantiated by the diaries and letters of a number of the Confederate participants.

Perhaps his most spectacular victories were Brice's Cross Roads (10 June 1864) and Tupelo (13-15 July 1864), at both of which he defeated greatly superior forces through a mixture of guile, aggressiveness, and hard fighting. Numerous tales are told of his adventures including many hand-to-hand combats. On one occasion he even captured a ship on the Tennessee River. Although his irregular operations were of immense value to the Confederacy, in late 1864 Forrest was placed under the command of Gen. John B. Hood, during the latter's disastrous attempt to capture Nashville. With his command almost shattered, Forrest became relatively inactive while he attempted to rebuild his forces. In February of 1865 he was promoted to lieutenant general. Although he shortly afterwards resumed operations, he had little success. In April he was overwhelmed at Selma, Alabama.

After the war Forrest returned to planting and served for a while as president of the Selma, Marion, and Memphis railroad, meanwhile finding the time to become one of the founders of the original Ku Klux Klan, and its first Grand Wizard. Forrest a large, husky man some 6' 2" tall, who rarely drank and never used tobacco, had eight brothers and half-brothers in gray, one of whom died as a brigadier general. A naturally talented commander, he proved a superb partisan, though hardly the best amateur soldier of the war, for he was never tested at the head of larger forces engaged in sustained combat. Perhaps the most perceptive explanation for his success was that of Alan Nevins, who observed that Forrest was "The one Confederate cavalryman who would be absolutely certain to concentrate on hurting the Yankees without having distracting thoughts about his own fame or the glamour of a dashing cavalry raid."

David Dixon Porter

The son of David Porter, naval hero of the War of 1812, David Dixon Porter (1813-1891) was born in Pennsylvania. He had little formal education, went to sea at the age of ten under his father's aegis, and remained active in naval affairs until his death. He had a distinguished and varied career, including a tour in the Mexican Navy which his father commanded for a time, during which he was briefly a prisoner-of-war when his ship was taken by the Spanish fleet. Young Porter formally entered the United States Navy in 1829 and thereafter rose steadily, though slowly up the promotion ladder, serving afloat in the Mediterranean, the Atlantic, and the Gulf of Mexico, becoming a lieutenant by 1861. During the period before the firing on Fort Sumter, Lincoln and Porter contrived to steal the steamer

Powhatan for an expedition to relieve Fort Pickens, off Pensacola, without the knowledge of the Navy Department, which was thought to have been heavily infiltrated by secessionists. Porter commanded *Powhatan* in the Gulf for the balance of the year. Early in 1862 Porter became involved in planning the capture of New Orleans, and commanded a mortar flotilla in the expedition of David G. Farragut, who was, not incidentally, his adoptive brother. The operation was an enormous success.

In October of 1862 Porter was given command of the Mississippi River flotilla and Porter's service for the next 18 months was entirely on the western rivers. He supported the operations of the army against Vicksburg, taking an active part in all of U.S. Grant's efforts to seize the town, for which he received the thanks of Congress and a promotion to rear admiral. He also took part in the capture of Arkansas Post, maintained the interdiction of Confederate communications across the Mississippi, and commanded in the unfortunate Red River Campaign of 1864, an operation which he opposed. In October of 1864 Porter was given command of the North Atlantic Squadron, which maintained the blockade of the Carolina coast and supported army operations against the Confederacy. In this capacity Porter took part in operations against Wilmington and was present at the fall of Richmond.

After the war Porter served four years as superintendent of Annapolis, introducing many innovations and reforms, meanwhile being promoted to vice-admiral. In 1870 he was promoted to admiral upon the death of Farragut, and served thereafter until his death as the senior officer of the navy, though in later years much frustrated by limitations on his ability to influence policy. A big man, with a wonderful sense of humor, Porter was a fine naval officer, with a good imagination and a devotion to hard work.

The Porter Clan

David Porter (1780-1843) had a distinguished career as a naval officer and diplomat, including three years as head of the Mexican Navy (1826-1829). His younger son, David Dixon, of course became the nation's second admiral, while his elder son, William Dixon (1809-1864), rose to commodore after an impressive career in which he established the Lighthouse Service, now part of the Coast Guard, fought in the Mexican War, and commanded the gunboat *Essex*, named for his father's ship, on the Western rivers, until his health put him on the beach, shortly after which he died of a heart attack; surprisingly, his two sons served the Confederacy. The adoptive brother of the Porters, David Glasgow Farragut (1801-1870), of course, had an extraordinary career in the war, becoming the nation's first admiral. In addition, their cousin, Fitz John Porter (1822-1901) led a division and then a corps with considerable distinction during the Peninsular Campaign, but in 1863 was cashiered by court martial on charges of disloyalty, misconduct, and disobedience and spent the rest of his life gradually establishing his innocence.

Oliver Otis Howard

A native of Maine, O.O. Howard (1830-1909) attended various schools before graduating from Bowdoin in 1850, whereupon he entered West Point, graduating 4th in the class of 1854, which also included G.W.C. Lee, J.E.B. Stuart, and William D. Pender, among others who would become prominent in the war. Howard's pre-war career was spent mostly as an assistant professor of mathematics at West Point. In May of 1861 he was elected colonel of the *3rd Maine* and later commanded a brigade during the Bull Run Campaign.

Though Howard was no more successful than any other officer, he was commissioned a brigadier general of volunteers shortly afterwards. During the Peninsular Campaign he lost his right arm at Seven Pines, in an action for which he eventually received the Medal of Honor. He returned to duty in less than three months, serving in the closing part of the Second Bull Run Campaign. At Antietam he took over a division of *II Corps* upon the wounding of its commander, Brig. Gen. John Sedgwick. Promoted major general that November, he led his division at Fredericksburg, and at the end of March of 1863 was given *XI Corps*, the perennial "hard luck" outfit of the *Army of the Potomac*.

At Chancellorsville Confederate Lt. Gen. Thomas "Stonewall" Jackson's flank attack hit *XI Corps*, which constituted the Union right. Due to poor dispositions on Howard's part, the corps broke and was driven from the field in considerable disorder, despite Howard's personal heroism in attempting to rally it. At Gettysburg Howard's corps arrived on the field on the first day. He assumed direction of the battle when Maj. Gen. John Reynolds was wounded and is largely responsible for the attempt to defend north and west of the town, though he did have the foresight to select Cemetery Hill as a fall-back position, rallying *I* and *XI Corps* there after their retreat. When Maj. Gen. Winfield Scott Hancock arrived with orders from Meade to assume direction of the battle, Howard got into an argument about relative rank—both officers were commissioned major generals on the same day but Howard was two or three names ahead of Hancock. His activities for the rest of the battle were satisfactory. The following autumn he took his corps West, fighting under Hooker at Chattanooga.

During the Atlanta Campaign he commanded *IV Corps* and eventually the *Army of the Tennessee* in the closing months of the war. After the war he remained in the army as a regular brigadier general and brevet major general.

Very religious and a dedicated abolitionist, he became head of the "Freedman's Bureau," organizing various services for newly liberated slaves, and was also active in promoting civil rights for blacks. Although there was considerable corruption in the "Freedman's Bureau," Howard was personally honest and defended its numerous critics, many of whom were motivated less by a concern for honest administration and more by a desire to block civil liberties for blacks. He helped found Howard University, established a bank for blacks which failed, served as superintendent of West Point, and in various other military posts until he retired in 1894. Thereafter he wrote and lectured on a wide variety of issues until his death. Howard was neither a great general nor a satisfactory administrator, but his personal courage and devotion to the cause were never questioned.

Henry W. Slocum

Born in a small town in upstate New York, Henry Warner Slocum (1827-1894) graduated from West Point 7th in the class of 1852. After serving against the Seminoles and in garrison, he resigned from the army in 1856 to practice law. He settled in Syracuse, New York, where he held a variety of state and local elective posts, and served as a colonel of artillery in the militia. In May of 1861 he became colonel of the *27th New York*, which he led at Bull Run, where he was wounded.

Promoted brigadier general of volunteers, Slocum was given a brigade in *VI Corps*, which he led with great distinction in the Peninsula, was given a division and promoted major general, serving ably in the Second Bull Run and Antietam Campaigns. He was then given *XII Corps*. At Chancellorsville his corps performed well in heavy fighting. Among the officers who expressed to Lincoln their opposition to the retention of Hooker as commander of the *Army of the Potomac* after Chancellorsville, Slocum graciously consented to serve under Meade, to whom he was senior. At Gettysburg Slocum briefly commanded on the evening of 1 July, but his most distinguished services were as commander of the right wing on the following two days. That autumn, his corps went westward with *XI Corps* to assist in the relief of Chattanooga. As Hooker as given overall command, Slocum promptly offered Lincoln his resignation, but was refused, and a tactful, if clumsy arrangement was arrived at whereby Slocum did not serve directly under Hooker. Early in 1864 he briefly commanded Union forces around Vicksburg, but in August he was given Hooker's *XX Corps* (formed by consolidation of the old *XI* and *XII*) in the *Army of the Tennessee*. Slocum led his corps in the Atlanta Campaign and was afterwards given the *Army of Georgia* during the "March to the Sea" and in the Carolinas.

At the end of the war Slocum resigned his commission and returned to his native New York, eventually settling in Brooklyn, where he practiced law and entered politics, losing the post of secretary of state of New York to former Maj. Gen. Francis C. Barlow. Slocum served several terms in the House of Representatives, was a principal in the corporation which built the Brooklyn Bridge. and served as a member of the board of the Gettysburg Monument Commission. Although an able military administrator and field commander, Slocum never received much public notice nor credit for his considerable achievements.

Edmund Kirby Smith

Born in Florida, Edmund Kirby Smith (1824-1893) graduated from West Point in 1845. He was in the infantry during the Mexican War, serving from the first battle, at Palo Alto, to the fall of Mexico City, and winning brevets for gallantry at Cerro Cordo and Contreras. After the war he taught mathematics at West Point until 1852, when he went west to fight Indians and serve on the Mexican Boundary Commission. He transferred to the cavalry upon the expansion of that arm in 1855 and was a major in the *2nd Cavalry* (now the *5th*), Col. Albert Sidney Johnston's regiment, stationed at Fort Colorado in Texas at the outbreak of the war. Smith chanced to be the senior officer present upon the secession of Texas and, when summoned to surrender the post to a contingent of Texas militia under Col. Ben McCulloch, he refused and expressed his willingness to fight. As a result the garrison was allowed to leave unmolested. Despite this expression of loyalty to the Union, Smith resigned his commission on the secession of Florida on 6 April, entering Confederate service soon after as a lieutenant colonel, and serving under Joseph E. Johnston in the Shenandoah. He was appointed a brigadier general in the provisional army on 17 June 1861 and commanded one of Johnston's brigades at First Bull Run, where he was severely wounded. That October he was made a major general and given a division in the West.

Early in 1862 Smith assumed command of Unionist eastern Tennessee. He took part in Braxton Bragg's invasion of Tennessee later that year, being responsible for the Confederate victory at Richmond (30 August), and even managed to create a threat to Cincinnati through a series of small victories in eastern Kentucky. He fought at Perryville, and was shortly made a lieutenant general. After Murfreesboro he was sent west to command the Trans-Mississippi Department. Smith—who is generally known as "Kirby Smith"—proved highly successful in this theater, keeping alive the Confederate cause, conducting forays into Unionist territory, maintaining a line of supply into Mexico and thence to Europe, and, in the spring of 1864 beating off the Red River Expedition, for which he was promoted to a full generalship. Smith was the last important Confederate commander to surrender, on 26 May 1865.

After the war Smith briefly resided abroad, returning to the United States to serve as president of the Pacific and Atlantic Telegraph Company in 1866-1868, and then took up an academic career, being successively president of the Western Military Academy in Nashville (1868-1870), chancellor of the University of Nashville (1870-1875), and thereafter a professor of mathematics at the University of the South until his death. He was the last Confederate full general to cross the river.

A profoundly religious man, Smith twice considered entering the ministry, once in 1863 and again in 1875. With his wife, whom he married in 1861 after she made him a shirt while he was recovering from his Bull Run wound, he raised eleven children. Although a man of considerable administrative and organizational ability, Smith's rise in the Confederate Army is somewhat inexplicable, since he did not really demonstrate his talents until after attaining high rank and virtually autonomous command.

Ambrose P. Hill

A native of Culpeper Country, Virginia, Ambrose Powell Hill (1825-1865) graduated from West Point in 1847, 15th in the class, and entered the artillery. He served in Mexico, against the Seminoles, on the frontier, and in garrison before resigning as a first lieutenant on 1 March 1861. He entered Confederate service and was immediately commissioned colonel of the 13th Virginia, which he led in West Virginia and during the Bull Run Campaign, though seeing little action.

Appointed a brigadier general in early 1862, Hill led a brigade in the opening phases of the Peninsular Campaign with such ability that he was promoted major general in May and given a division, which he led with great skill, earning for it the nickname "The Light Division" for the speed with which it executed all movements and maneuvers. Due to a personality clash between Hill and Longstreet, the division was transferred from the latter's command to "Stonewall" Jackson's II Corps, with which it fought with considerable distinction during the Second Bull Run, Antietam, and Fredericksburg Campaigns. At Chancellorsville the division formed the bulk of Jackson's striking force during his flank attack. When Jackson was mortally wounded, Hill assumed command of the corps until himself hit. In late May of 1863 he was appointed lieutenant general and given the newly created III Corps, which he led into the Gettysburg Campaign, where he demonstrated little brilliance. His subsequent performance as corps commander was little better, and he was often on sick call at critical times. On 2 April 1865, during the final Union drive at Petersburg, Hill rose from his sickbed to return to the front and was killed trying to rally his men after their lines had broken.

An excellent division commander, Hill suffered from a variety of illnesses, most apparently psychosomatic, and was notoriously touchy, having at various times engaged in open quarrels with both James Longstreet and Stonewall Jackson, who actually had him placed under arrest on one occasion. He certainly did not merit promotion to corps command, for which his principal qualification appears to have been that he was a Virginian. Once he demonstrated his lack of ability at that level of command he ought to have been sacked, a practice common in the Union Army, but rare in the Confederacy.

Joseph Wheeler

"Fighting Joe" Wheeler (1836-1906) was born at Augusta, Georgia, and graduated from West Point in 1859. Commissioned a second lieutenant in the *Regiment of Mounted Rifles* (now the *3rd Cavalry*), Wheeler served on the frontier for a time before resigning in that rank on 22 April 1861 to accept a first lieutenantcy in the Confederate artillery. That September he became colonel of the 19th Alabama.

Wheeler led his regiment at Shiloh in April of 1862, and distinguished himself while covering the Confederate retreat on the 7th. He shortly thereafter transferred to the cavalry and in July was made chief of cavalry in the Army of Mississippi. He served in this capacity during Braxton Bragg's invasion of Kentucky, fighting at Perryville, where he covered Bragg's retreat, for which he was promoted to brigadier general. He again did well at Murfreesboro, which earned him a major generalcy in January of 1863. Wheeler led his cavalry with considerable skill during the Tullahoma and Chickamauga Campaigns, and conducted a spectacular cavalry raid after Union forces under Maj. Gen. William S. Rosecrans were bottled up in Chattanooga, virtually destroying Rosecrans' lines of supply in a nine day sweep (1-9 October 1863), though himself incurring heavy losses. Wheeler was again active during the Atlanta Campaign in 1864, conducting several important raids with the object of disrupting William Tecumseh Sherman's operations and during the "March to the Sea" in late 1864, Wheeler's cavalry continually harassed Sherman's columns.

In February of 1865 the 28-year-old Wheeler was made a lieutenant general, and served under Gen. Joseph E. Johnston in the Carolina Campaign, during which the lack of discipline in his command caused him to be superseded by Lt. Gen. Wade Hampton. Wheeler tried to make his way west after Johnston's surrender, but was captured near Atlanta in May. After the war he settled in New Orleans for a while, and then in Wheeler, Alabama, where he practiced law and raised cotton. He was several times elected to Congress, rising to chair the Ways and Means Committee. On the outbreak of the War with Spain in 1898 Wheeler was made a major general of volunteers by McKinley, who saw the war as a way to heal the "final" wounds of the Civil War, and the old Rebel was given a dismounted cavalry division in *V Corps*, with which he did poorly at Las Guasimas (24 June 1898). Wheeler continued in the service, retiring in 1900 as a brigadier general in the regular army. A dashing cavalryman, one of the best of the war, Wheeler was by no means a great commander.

John C. Breckinridge

A native of Kentucky, John Cabell Breckinridge (1821-1875) was educated for the law and began practicing at Lexington in 1841. After a stint as a major in the *3rd Kentucky Volunteers* during the Mexican War, he jumped into politics and had a remarkable career: Kentucky state legislature, 1849-1851, House of Representatives, 1851-1855, and in 1856—allegedly with some reluctance on his part—became the youngest man ever elected vice president, at 35 years of age, the constitutional limit. In 1859, with 18 months of his term left to run Breckinridge was elected to the United States Senate for a term beginning in 1861! In 1860 Breckinridge was nominated for president by the Southern rump of the Democratic Party, gaining some 845,000 popular votes and 72 electoral votes, not one north of the Mason-Dixon line. During the "Secession Winter" he was involved in a number of compromise proposals in his capacity as vice-president, and then as senator from Kentucky. He remained in the Senate when the shooting war began, and worked to maintain the neutrality of Kentucky, while trying to hamper Lincoln's efforts to conduct the war. Although

Kentucky declared for the Union in September of 1861, Breckinridge's activities caused a warrant to be issued for his arrest. Breckinridge fled in October, accepted a commission as a brigadier general in the Confederate Army, and in December was stripped of his Senate seat. He briefly commanded the "Orphan Brigade," and was then given the Reserve Corps of Gen. Albert Sidney Johnston's army.

Breckinridge led his "corps"—actually a strong division—under Johnston at Shiloh with courage, if not notable skill, and was shortly thereafter promoted to major general. He thereafter led various divisions in Mississippi in mid-1862, in operations against Baton Rouge later that year, at Murfreesboro at the end of the year, during Gen. Joseph E. Johnston's efforts to relieve Vicksburg in the spring of 1863, and at Chickamauga and Chattanooga later that year. In all of these actions Breckinridge did rather well, occasionally very well. He was given a territorial command in western Virginia in 1864, winning the Battle of New Market (15 May), fought at Cold Harbor, took part in Jubal Early's raid on Washington that summer, at Nashville in December, and in early 1865 became Secretary of War.

After the war, Breckinridge lived in England and Canada for a time, before returning to the United States in 1869. He settled in Kentucky and, although quite popular, disclaimed political ambitions and practiced law until his death, which resulted from complications after surgery. Although a "political" general, awarded his commission mostly in an effort to stimulate recruiting among Kentuckians, Breckinridge proved a fairly able soldier, and ought perhaps have been tested in higher commands.

The Battling Breckinridges

The Breckinridges of Kentucky were among the many families split by the Civil War. John C. Breckinridge, the most distinguished member, of course, fought for the South, as did his three sons. Two of his male cousins fought for the Union and a female cousin, Margaret E. Breckinridge, served as a nurse and Sanitary Commission agent with U.S. Grant's army in the West from 1862 to 1864. Another cousin, Robert J. Breckinridge, had two sons on each side, and one of his Yankee sons captured one of his Rebel sons at Atlanta on 22 July 1864.

Philip H. Sheridan

Rather casual about the facts of his life, Philip Henry Sheridan (1831-1888), claimed several different birth dates at various times, and listed his birthplace variously as Boston, Massachusetts and Somerset, Ohio and Albany, New York, which latter place is generally accepted as correct, the family removing to Somerset while "Little Phil" was still an infant. As a youth Sheridan worked for a time as a clerk in a country store, before securing an appointment to West Point, from which he graduated in 1853, after having been suspended for a year when he threatened a fellow cadet with a bayonet. He served eight years on the frontier as a second lieutenant in the *4th Infantry*, not receiving his first promotion until several vacancies occurred on the regimental rolls when a number of officers resigned to join the Confederacy. Thereafter his rise was rather more rapid. He held several staff positions under Maj. Gen. Henry Halleck in late 1861 and early 1862, until appointed colonel of the *2d Michigan Cavalry* on 25 May of that year.

Sheridan served ably at the head of his regiment until September, when he was made a brigadier general of volunteers. He fought with distinction at Perryville and Murfreesboro, and in March of 1863 was promoted to major general, predated to New Year's. He was given a division, which he led in *XX Corps* at Chickamauga, where it incurred 37 percent casualties, at Chattanooga, and at Missionary Ridge, where it swept up the seemingly unassailable heights. All of this activity brought him to the notice of U.S. Grant, who put Sheridan in command of the cavalry of the *Army of the Potomac* early in 1864.

Sheridan launched a series of cavalry blows in conjunction with Grant's Overland Campaign, during one of which famed Rebel cavalryman J.E.B. Stuart was killed. Although not always successful, Sheridan managed to make the best of every action and, unlike several other commanders, welcomed the attentions of the press, which greatly enhanced his reputation. After several Union reversals in the Shenandoah Valley and Jubal Early's raid on Washington in July, Sheridan was given *VI* and *XIX Corps*, three divisions of cavalry, and a considerable reserve of artillery and ordered to clean out the Valley. He accomplished this with ruthless efficiency, delivering a series of deadly blows and adopting a scorched earth policy, at one point riding "twenty miles" to turn a potentially disastrous reverse into a smashing victory. Having devastated the Valley, thus simultaneously closing the "back door to Washington" and denying Robert E. Lee's army its agricultural foundations as well, Sheridan brought the bulk of his command to U.S. Grant's assistance in the final days of the war, winning the Battle of Five Forks, capturing a substantial portion of the Army of Northern Virginia at Sayler's Creek, and closing off Lee's line of retreat at Appomattox.

After the war Sheridan was put in command of 50,000 veterans and sent to the Rio Grande in a successful effort to suggest to the French that they cease interfering in Mexican affairs. He was thereafter involved in a controversy over Reconstruction policies in Louisiana and Texas. In 1869 Sheridan assumed the lieutenant generalcy vacated when Sherman became a full general upon Grant's assumption of the presidency. Over the next few years he served in various administrative posts, was the American military observer with the Prussian Army during the Franco-Prussian War, and fought Indians. In 1884 he became commanding general of the army, and was promoted to full general shortly before his death.

Sheridan, a stocky, 5'5" black Irishman, was one of the most successful commanders of the war, with virtually no failures to mar his record. As a general he knew how to inspire men, was a careful planner, made good use of intelligence, and was aggressive. As a man, he was rather vindictive, and not apparently very personable.

John Wilkes Booth

The most notorious actor in American history, John Wilkes Booth (1838-1865) was born in Maryland, the son of the distinguished actor Junius B. Booth. John followed several of his ten siblings on to the boards, making his debut in Baltimore at the age of 17. Although he never attained the skill of his elder brother Edwin, a noted tragedian and perhaps the best American actor of the nineteenth century, young John was rather successful, particularly in the role of Romeo, which he performed superbly both on and off the stage. At an early age John became a fanatical secessionist, in contrast to the views of the rest of his family, which were decidedly Unionist. His dedication to the notion was considered extreme even by some of the most ardent secessionists, and it is difficult to escape the conclusion that Booth was mentally unstable. A Virginia militiaman, in 1859 he was present at the execution of John Brown. On the outbreak of the war young Booth remained in the North, performing regularly—before Lincoln on a couple of occasions—with excellent reviews, while not giving up his devotion to the South.

The increasingly disastrous situation of the Confederacy as the war dragged on seems to have further unhinged Booth. He began to develop a series of plots designed to save the day for the South. Initially the idea was to arrange for the kidnapping of Lincoln so that the South could use him to ransom the tens of thousands of troops languishing in Union prisoner of war camps. With a few fellow-fanatics, several of whom seem to have been of limited intelligence, Booth actually attempted to carry out this idea in 1864, only to be frustrated by poor planning and bad luck. Frustrated, he revised his goals, settling for nothing less than the assassination of the president, the vice-president, and selected members of the cabinet with the object of "decapitating" the Union. The surrender of Robert E. Lee's Army of Northern Virginia had no effect on Booth's conspiracy.

Booth carried out his plot on the evening of 14 April 1865, as the president and Mrs. Lincoln sat with two guests in their box at Ford's Theater, watching Laura Keene, a noted Anglo-American actress, in the hit comedy *Our American Cousin.* The deed done, he leaped to the stage, breaking his leg in the process, waved a dagger in the air, and cried out " *Sic semper tyrannis!*—Thus ever to tyrants!*", the motto of Virginia. As the theater erupted in chaos, he managed to escape, aided by an accomplice, David E. Herold.

With Herold, Booth stopped briefly at the home of Dr. Samuel Mudd, who set the broken leg. Then the two were off again. For several days they hid out in some woodlands, and then made their way to the farm of Richard Garret, near Bowling Green, Virginia. By this time an enormous manhunt was under way, with military patrols, police agents, and secret service men sweeping the countryside. On 26 April Booth was cornered in Garrett's tobacco barn. Although young Herold surrendered, Booth refused. There was an exchange of gunfire and Booth died, probably shot by Sgt. Boston Corbett. Despite rumors that Booth escaped, there is no reason to doubt that the man whom Corbett shot was indeed John Wilkes Booth, who was, after all, rather well known.

The Aftermath

None of Booth's co-conspirators successfully carried out his mission. Secretary of State Seward's life was saved by a heavy metal brace which he was wearing as a result of an injury incurred when he was thrown from his carriage earlier that year.

Over the next few days Booth's co-conspirators were apprehended. The trial and execution of several people, including Mrs. Mary E. Surratt, who was not a party to the plot, though her son was, and the imprisonment of a number of others, including Dr. Mudd, is now regarded as a gross miscarriage of justice. Similarly, the widespread rumors that high officials of the Confederacy—or indeed of the Union—were involved in Lincoln's death are totally without foundation. Unfortunately, as these are regularly dusted off for the purpose of making a profit, they will be with us for a long time to come.

The Women

"Mother Bickerdyke"

Mary Ann Ball Bickerdyke (1817-1901) was a self-trained nurse and herbalist living in Galesburg, Illinois, at the time the Civil War broke out. When, in June of 1861 word reached Galesburg of the terrible conditions in the military hospitals at Cairo, Illinois, local citizens collected some $500.00 in supplies and selected the widowed Bickerdyke to deliver them; except for an occasional visit to see her children, she did not return until the end of the war. The 44-year-old woman took one look at the filthy, ill-managed hospitals and decided something had to be done. And she proceeded to do it, despite all odds, bringing order out of the chaos in Cairo during the first winter of the war. In doing so she soon became one of the most famous and influential women in the country.

Mrs. Bickerdyke was a dynamic woman who brooked no nonsense and was intolerant of incompetence. She cared nothing for red tape or rank or procedures. A wizard at gathering supplies where none could be had, she also found time to organize proper kitchens and establish army laundries, all the while continuously battling for the welfare of the troops. She went wherever she felt she was needed, working in the Western Theater for the entire war, sometimes with the army and sometimes with the navy. Her acid tongue and tough disposition—she was, wrote one co-worker, "not afraid of anybody"—earned her the hatred of numerous bureaucrats, but the love and devotion of the troops. Once, to resolve a shortage of fresh milk and eggs in army hospitals in Tennessee, she personally led a foraging expedition into the mid-West, where she "recruited" over 100 cows and 1000 chickens, and then commandeered trains to carry the booty back, over the objections of a number of transportation officers. A word from "Mother Bickerdyke" was sufficient to have an errant officer discharged from the army with no possibility of appeal. There is a story, which may be apocryphal, that during the Vicksburg Campaign an outraged surgeon went to U.S. Grant to complain that he had been unjustly dismissed from the service for incompetence. When Grant inquired of the details, Bickerdyke's name came up. At that, the general said, "My God, man, Mother Bickerdyke outranks everyone, even Lincoln. If you have run amuck of her I advise you to get out quickly before she has you under arrest."

In 1864 Sherman requested she accompany his army and she served with him as Sanitary Commission field agent throughout the Atlanta Campaign and the March to the Sea. So popular was "Mother Bikerdyke" with the troops that men of the *VX Corps* placed her at their head in the Grand Review. After the war she became a champion of veterans rights, worked to eradicate prostitution, and was ever welcome in the encampments of the Grand Army of the Republic.

Women in Arms

There were few roles for women in the military life of the Civil War. It was, of course, possible to become a *vivandiere*, a combination den-mother, gofer, and regimental mascot, many of whom served under fire and some of whom seem occasionally to have fired back. And women were also permitted to serve as nurses, who also sometimes came under fire. But such duties were too tame for some women. A few hankered for the real thing. At the start of the war many young women attempted to enlist as combatants. Though earning high praise from some for their zeal, they were turned away by the recruiting officers and frequently ridiculed. However, since the physical examinations given recruits were by no means rigorous, it was not impossible for a woman to join the army if she donned the appropriate garments, adopted male mannerisms, and had a little luck. As a result an unknown number of women—probably several hundred—served in the ranks during the war, many with the connivance of lovers, brothers, or husbands, and sometimes comrades. There unfortunately exists no systematic study of these "soldier girls," nor did any of them leave reliable memoirs. As a result it is rather difficult to develop an accurate notion of the number of women in the ranks and their performance under fire.

Given contemporary standards of dress and modesty, a woman in male clothing could easily pass as a man for extended periods. In most cases the true sex of a female soldier was only discovered when, after as much as two years in the ranks, wounds forced a hospital stay. The identity of most women soldiers was probably never revealed; Albert Cashier *nee* Jennie Hodges was only found out as a result of an auto accident in 1911! Nor is it possible to determine the number of women killed in action. There was no such thing as graves registration during the Civil War and troops were often buried in mass graves on the field, often several days after they had fallen, circumstances unlikely to favor the discovery that a particular "boy" was actually a "girl."

Some Union Women in Arms

Mary Burns: detected and arrested in uniform in Detroit, before her company departed for the front.

Frances Clalin: served in a Missouri militia cavalry regiment.

Sara Collins: of Wisconsin, enlisted, but was discovered before her regiment left for the front.

Lizzie Compton: enlisted at 14 and served in seven different regiments until seriously wounded.

Catherine E. Davidson: of Sheffield, Ohio, enlisted to be with her fiance in the *28th Ohio*. He was killed and she wounded at Antietam, where she was aided by Gov. Andrew Curtin of Pennsylvania, one of many who came to the field to help the wounded. Curtin did not learn her true sex until much later, when Davidson paid him a visit, during which she told her story.

Sarah Emma Edmonds: most famous Federal "soldier girl." Canadian by birth, she enlisted on 14 May 1861 as "Franklin Thompson," a male nurse in *Company F, 2nd Michigan*, serving nearly two years before deserting to avoid hospitalization for malaria. She served in the Bull Run, Peninsular, Fredericksburg, Antietam, and Chattanooga Campaigns as a nurse, soldier, courier, and spy, if her memoirs, *Unsexed, or the Female Soldier* and *Nurse and Spy*—which she partially repudiated—are to be relied upon. With the aid of the regimental veterans association she eventually received a monthly pension of $12.00 from the Federal government.

"Emily": a Brooklynite, her obsession with enlisting prompted her parents to send her to live with relatives in Michigan, but after a few weeks she slipped away and enlisted as a drummer boy in the *Army of the Cumberland*, serving until mortally wounded at Lookout Mountain.

Ellen Goodridge: a Wisconsinite, she accompanied her fiance into the army, fought by his side for three years, and nursed him through a mortal illness, for which she was disowned by her family.

Nelly Graves: enlisted in the *24th New Jersey* with Fanny Wilson (*q. v.*).

Jennie Hodges: in August of 1862 she enlisted at the age of 18 in *Company G, 95th Illinois*, serving for three years as "Albert Cashier," during which she fought at Vicksburg, during the Red River Expedition, and at Nashville. Mustered out undetected in August of 1865, she continued to pass for a man—even getting through an apparently thorough pension physical in 1899—until 1911, when an auto accident led to a hospital stay which revealed her sex. "Albert Cashier" and Catherine E. Davidson are the only known instances of a woman completing a full term of enlistment.

Nellie A. K.: enlisted with her brother and served with *The Army of the Cumberland* until, her sex being revealed, she was discharged.

"The Canadian Low": arrested for drunkness in Memphis in 20 Dec 1862, having served for some time in a Missouri regiment.

"A New Jersey Girl": enlisted with her lover, was later discovered and sent home, where she attempted suicide.

Mary Owens: enlisted with her fiance and served 18 months, until he was killed and she was seriously wounded.

Fanny Wilson: from Williamsburg, New York, Fanny was about 17 and was temporarily resident in Indiana at the outbreak of the war. Learning that her fiance, a New Jerseyite, had enlisted in the *24th New Jersey*, she traveled east with a friend—Nelly Graves—and enlisted in the same regiment, Nelly apparently finding a lover of her own in the ranks, though he was later killed. They served for about 18 months, until Vicksburg, where Fanny's fiance was mortally wounded. By this time both women were suffering from exhaustion, partially due to hard campaigning and to their efforts to nurse the young man back to health. They were sent to a rest hospital in Cairo, where their true sex was discovered. Nelly, her health continuing poorly, went home, but Fanny recovered nicely. For a time she danced in a "ballet company" in Cairo, before enlisting in the *3rd Illinois Cavalry* at Memphis. This time her service was short, only two weeks passing before she was discovered, being drunk while in uniform.

Ida Remington: served as an officer's orderly at South Mountain and Antietam, and later with the *11th New York Militia* in the Gettysburg Campaign, during which her identity was revealed when she was arrested for drunkenness in Harrisburg.

Mary Wise: served at least two years in an Indiana regiment, for which service she received mustering out pay upon being discovered.

Unidentified: served at least two years in a Minnesota regiment, until wounded.

Unidentified: described as a "girl," she served at least 21 months in an Iowa regiment, having in that time been twice wounded, her true sex only being discovered when, in February of 1863 she fainted and was given a warm bath.

Unidentified: had enlisted with her brother; revealed herself to Sara Edmonds (*q.v.*) when dying of wounds at Antietam.

Unidentified Sergeant: "delivered of a baby" whilst serving in the *Army of the Cumberland*.

Unidentified Sergeant: falling ill while on picket duty with the *10th New York Heavy Artillery,* she was "taken to Point of Rocks hospital early in the morning of March 6th [1865], where she delivered a 'bouncing boy'."

Unidentified "Stout and Muscular Woman": captured wounded by Confederate troops and returned to Union lines, where she was interviewed at length by Sanitary Commission volunteer Annie Wittenmeyer.

Unidentified Pair: one serving as a teamster and one as a cavalry trooper in Philip H. Sheridan's division of the *Army of the Cumberland,* exposed in January of 1863 as a result of having gotten drunk together. The teamster was "very large, and so coarse and masculine was her general appearance that she would readily have passed for a man," but the "she dragoon" was a "rather prepossessing young woman." The two had become acquainted in the army.

Some Confederate Women in Arms

Mary and Molly Bell: discovered in October of 1864 in Jubal Early's command, having by then served for two years as "Tom Parker" and "Bob Martin." Although accused of being "common camp followers" who adopted male clothing the better to ply their trade, the fact that they went two years without detection suggests otherwise. Nevertheless, they were tried, convicted, and imprisoned by Early, who was a notorious misogynist.

Malinda Blalock: a North Carolinian, through the collusion of a recruiting officer, she enlisted with her husband in Company A, 26th North Carolina, under the name "Sam Blalock" and served for two months, until her husband was discharged for disability, when she identified herself to the colonel.

Amy Clarke: enlisted with her husband, and continued in the ranks after he fell at Shiloh, her sex only being revealed when, on the occasion of a serious wound, she was captured by Union troops, who gave her a dress and sent her South.

Margaret Henry: captured in uniform by Union troops in Tennessee in March of 1865 while in the company of Mary Wright.

Loreta Janeta Velasquez: the most famous Rebel "soldier girl," her record is rather cloudy, due largely to the extravagant claims which she advanced in her memoirs, *The Woman in Battle:* Jubal Early conceded she may well have served but noted ". . . the book that is given to the public in her name cannot be the truthful narration of the adventures of any person." Velasquez claimed to have raised a battalion in Arkansas, to have served at First Bull Run, Ball's Bluff, Shiloh, and other battles, to have been a spy in Washington, during which she was actually in contact with Lincoln, and even to have masqueraded as a "Lt. Henry T. Buford," in which role she broke a number of hearts throughout the Confederacy. A few of her claims may be accurate, but Early's judgment in this case—though not in others with regard to women—is probably sound. Most of her adventures seem to have been based on those of other women in the service, such as Laura J. Williams.

Laura J. Williams: an Arkansan, she reputedly raised a company of Texans early in the war in the guise of "Lt. Henry Benford," leading it at Shiloh and in several other actions.

Mary Wright: captured in uniform by Union troops in Tennessee in march of 1865 while in the company of Margaret Henry.

Unidentified "Nice Looking Woman": reported to have fought at Perry-ville and Murfreesboro, and was known and accepted in her regiment until she fell into "immoral conduct."

Unidentified Officer: delivered of a "bouncing baby boy" in December of 1864, while held as a prisoner-of-war at Johnson Island.

Women in Command

There were two occasions during the war when women were apparently openly in command of a military operation.

When Col. John Basil Turchin, an expatriate Russian—possibly the only Russian in the war—was wounded while leading his *19th Illinois* in Tennessee one day in 1862, his wife, who, with all the formality of Imperial Russia was always "Madame Turchin," assumed command. One hopes her English was better than her husband's, who was wont to cry "Sharge!" but in any case, she brought the skirmish to a successful conclusion, thus becoming the first woman to lead an American military unit in combat.

Harriet Tubman, the famed fugitive slave and "conductor" on the Underground Railroad, was directly involved in planning a raid along the Combahee River in South Carolina in early June of 1863. Moreover, once the raid got underway, Ms. Tubman accompanied the expedition as a guide and was regularly consulted by its commander as to the measures which she thought appropriate for the conduct of the operation.

Lincoln

The President at Richmond

In late March of 1865, Lt. Gen. Ulysses S. Grant invited the president to spend some time with the troops. Lincoln accepted, and left Washington aboard the steamer *River Queen*, which had been outfitted as the presidential yacht. He was to spend nearly two weeks with the men of the army and navy, his final visit to the front.

The president's stay was a pleasant one. There were visits with the troops in camp and in hospital, during one of which the president gave an encore demonstration of his woodcutting technique. Several reviews were held. As Grant's main base, at City Point, was by this time rather permanent, many officers had brought their wives down, and so several balls and receptions were held in honor of the president and Mrs. Lincoln.

On 25 March the president was able to witness his troops in action, when Lee undertook an attack against Fort Stedman, one of the Union siege works. Although the Rebels assaulted the post with great courage and elan, their efforts proved fruitless, and Lee's last offensive act of the war ended in a disaster, with over 4,000 men killed, wounded, or captured, as against some 1,500 Federal casualties. By then, of course, Grant was preparing for his decisive blow against Lee's army and Lincoln had already arranged for a high level conference to make the final arrangements for winning the war, summoning William Tecumseh Sherman up from Savannah by fast steamer in great secrecy. While waiting for Sherman the president's time was taken up with military reviews, balls, and inspections.

On 28 March the president held a strategy conference with Grant, Sherman, and Rear Adm. David Dixon Porter aboard *River Queen*. He proposed that the most generous possible terms be offered the Confederate armies. "Let them surrender and go home," he said. "They will not take up arms again. Let them all go, officers and all, let them have their horses to plow with, and, if you like, their guns to shoot crows with." His commanders were essentially in agreement, and these became the terms on which the war was ended. When the meeting broke up, Porter asked if the president would like to spend a few days with the fleet. Lincoln accepted. Porter had been one of his favorite naval officers since the start of the war, when they had conspired together to steal a ship from the Brooklyn Navy Yard for a secret mission. In addition, the invitation gave Lincoln a chance to get away from Mrs. Lincoln, who was pestering him because he had been overly attentive to a rather attractive woman at one of the recent receptions. Packing the first lady off to Washington on *River Queen*, the president moved aboard Porter's flagship, U.S.S. *Malvern*.

Refusing the offer of Porter's spacious cabin, Lincoln squeezed his angular form into a spare officers stateroom and spent what he claimed was a comfortable night. The next day, while Lincoln was touring the fleet, Porter had the cabin enlarged, but, having a wit to match the president's, said nothing about the matter when Lincoln returned. The following morning the president emerged and remarked, "A greater miracle than ever happened last night; I shrank six inches in length and about a foot sideways." Noting how care-worn the president looked, Porter screened him from unnecessary intrusions, so that his stay with the fleet would be something of a vacation. Learning that Secretary of State William Seward was looking for the chief executive, Porter asked the president if he wished to receive him. When Lincoln replied that all Seward wanted to do was "talk about Pufendorf," an obscure German philosopher, Porter misdirected the secretary.

On the evening of 1 April, the president was sitting with Porter on *Malvern's* upper deck as she lay at anchor off City Point. After some small talk, Lincoln asked, "Can't the Navy do something at this particular moment to make history?" When Porter observed that by its very presence the fleet was keeping the Confederate James River flotilla bottled up, the president responded, "But can't we make a noise?" Seeing what the president had in mind, Porter summoned an aide.

Instructing the man to proceed to the monitors which were lying upriver, Porter told him to order them to open fire on the Confederate river defense batteries as soon as the moon went down. They were to fire rockets and shells with ten second fuzes, so that the Rebels would think a full scale attack was imminent, concluding by saying, "It is not necessary for any one of the monitors to make any changes in their positions. The only object is to make a noise." The resulting demonstration began at 12:30 a.m. on 2 April and lasted for an hour, much to the president's delight.

Lincoln spent the next night aboard *River Queen*, which had returned from Washington. Early on the morning of 3 April word came that Lee had evacuated Richmond, followed, at about 9:30 a.m., by several loud explosions as the Confederates blew up the ironclads and gunboats of the James River flotilla. Lincoln expressed an interest in visiting Petersburg and Porter accompanied him. They ran into Grant, and spent a pleasant 90 minutes with him, before returning to the fleet to prepare for a visit to Richmond. Secretary of War Edwin M. Stanton soon got wind of the president's intentions, and wired, "Commanding generals are in the line of their duty in running such risks; but is the head of a nation in the same condition?" Lincoln responded with thanks for his concern, recounted his adventures in Petersburg, reiterated his intention to visit Richmond, and added "I will take care of myself."

On the morning of Tuesday, 4 April teams of seamen carefully swept up the "torpedoes" which the Confederates had moored in the James. Shortly before 11:00 Porter received word that the river was clear and the presidential party began to steam upstream, with *Malvern* in the lead, lest an undetected "torpedo" damage *River Queen*, following behind. Not far below Richmond *Malvern* ran aground. As the channel was likely to be too shallow for *River Queen* as well, Lincoln transferred to Porter's barge, accompanied by Porter and three or four military and naval aides. A dozen sturdy bluejackets rowed them on towards the city. A tug carrying a platoon of Marines followed behind, but by the time the admiral's barge landed at The Rockets on the Richmond riverfront it had gone astray.

An enormous mob of newly freed blacks and a few stalwart Unionist whites welcomed Lincoln with great enthusiasm as he came ashore. People crowded around him, attempting to touch his garments, shake his hand, or just say a few words. As Lincoln began to walk towards the center of town, Porter, fearing for his safety, ordered ten carbine-toting tars to surround him and keep the crowd off. It was a mile-and-a-half to army headquarters, aptly enough in the former "White House" of the Confederacy. The streets were heavy with smoke, for the retreating Confederates had fired various installations, including the arsenal, and the flames had spread, abetted by exploding shells and deserters seeking loot, hungry citizens seeking to salvage what they could. The crowd was in a cheerful mood. As Porter put it, "It was a gala day, and no man was ever accorded a warmer welcome. The heat of the weather was suffocating; the president towered a head and shoulders above the crowd, fanning himself with his hat, and looking as if he would give the presidency for a glass of water." Despite Stanton's misgivings, nothing untoward occurred. In about an hour the president reached the headquarters of Maj. Gen. Godfrey Weitzel, commanding the occupation forces.

The president was welcomed at the erstwhile home of Jefferson Davis by Capt. Thomas T. Graves, of Weitzel's staff. Shown Jefferson Davis' office, Lincoln seated himself, remarking "This must have been President Davis' chair." Crossing his legs, he fell silent for a few moments, staring off into space. Then, rather suddenly, he inquired as to whether the housekeeper was about. When told she was out, he jumped up, saying, with a boyish expression, "Come, let's look at the house!" As they were touring the place, Weitzel arrived, a bit out of breath, the presidential visit having caught him by surprise. With Weitzel's arrival, the president had to return to business. Over the next hour or so he held conversations with Weitzel, former Confederate Assistant Secretary of War John A. Campbell and several other dignitaries. Later that day, escorted by Weitzel and Graves, Lincoln visited several notable sites in the city, including the notorious Libby Prison and Castle Thunder, and then returned to Porter's barge. He spent the night aboard *Malvern*. The next day Lincoln paid a second visit to Richmond, dropping in on Confederate Maj. Gen. George E. Pickett's young wife. Later that day he boarded *River Queen* and set out for Washington. A little more than a week later he was shot by John Wilkes Booth.

The Units

The 23rd Ohio

Many regiments had a more impressive combat record than the *23rd Ohio*, but none had a more distinguished alumni. Organized at Columbus, the regiment was mustered into Federal service at Camp Chase on 11 June 1861, 950 strong, under West Pointer Col. William S. Rosecrans, with Eliakim P. Scammon as lieutenant colonel and one Rutherford B. Hayes as major; serving in *Company E* was a young private named William McKinley. Rosecrans was shortly promoted brigadier general. Scammon, a West Pointer and veteran of the Mexican War, was promoted colonel, and Hayes moved up to lieutenant colonel. Scammon, who had served in the Old Army's elite Corps of Topographical Engineers, had been cashiered from the army in 1856 and worked as a teacher for some years before the war. Under Scammon, the regiment took part in the West Virginia Campaign that summer, fighting its first battle at Carnifax Ferry on 10 September, when Rosecrans, commanding a division of some 5,000 men, pinned 2,600 Confederate troops under Brig. Gen. John B. Floyd against the Gauley River after a forced march. Although Floyd took advantage of the fortified landing to get most of his command away, Rosecrans was able to capture his supply train. Scammon was soon assigned to command a brigade, and was replaced by Hayes.

Though Hayes would command the regiment from late 1861, he was not promoted to colonel for nearly a year. By the time he took command the West Virginia Campaign was over. The regiment went into winter quarters and underwent a long period of training and drill, not seeing action again until the spring, when it participated in several small engagements on the fringes of Jackson's Shenandoah Valley Campaign, most notably the series of skirmishes around Princeton, West Virginia, on 15-18 May 1862, as part of Burnside's *IX Corps*, though it was spared participation in the latter's disasters. Much of the regiment's wartime service was in such small affairs, being essentially engaged in security operations in West Virginia, protecting Unionist sympathizers and lines of communication from Confederate raiders and irregulars. Nevertheless, Hayes led the regiment at South Mountain and Antietam in September of '62, for which he was finally promoted colonel on 24 October. Thereafter the regiment went back to its security duties in West Virginia, seeing lots of action but little battle until the spring of 1864, when the Shenandoah again became the scene of major operations.

The *23rd Ohio* took part in the abortive operations of Maj. Gen. David Hunter and the more successful ones of Maj. Gen. Philip H. Sheridan, fighting in a number of skirmishes, and also in the major actions at Winchester (19 September 1864), Fisher's Hill (22 September), and in the brilliantly recovered near-disaster at Cedar Creek (19 October), by which time Hayes was commanding a brigade and the regiment was under Lt. Col. James M. Comley. Thereafter, with the Confederate threat to the Valley decisively crushed, the *23rd Ohio* reverted to its old role as a security force, being mustered out in the summer of 1865. Although the regiment's combat record included few great battles, 290 of the 2,230 men who passed through its ranks died as a result of combat or disease, a death rate of 13 percent, making it one of the 300 hardest hit regiments in Federal service. But the regiment had an even greater distinction: no regiment in either army produced so many high ranking military or political leaders from its ranks. The first colonel, William S. Rosecrans rose to a major generalcy and commanded the *Army of the Cumberland* with some distinction in 1862 and 1863; the second, Eliakim P. Scammon, became a brigadier general; the third, Rutherford B. Hayes, a brigadier general with brevet of major general and president of the United States, and the fourth colonel, James M. Comly, had a distinguished political career crowned by service as minister to Hawaii. And, of course, Pvt. William McKinley, who rose steadily through the ranks to end the war as a captain and brevet major, also became president.

The 9th Louisiana

The Confederate regiment which comes closest to matching the record of the *23rd Ohio* in producing distinguished veterans was probably the 9th Louisiana, which was organized early in the war, and went East to fight in virtually every campaign of the Army of Northern Virginia. Its first commander was Richard Taylor, son of former President Zachary Taylor, who became a lieutenant general. The second commander was Leroy A. Stafford, who became a brigadier general and was mortally wounded at the Wilderness in 1864. The third commander, William R. Peck, who enlisted as a private and rose to colonel, was himself subsequently made a brigade commander and eventually a brigadier general. When surrendered at Appomattox the regiment numbered only four officers and 64 men.

The 2nd Cavalry

The Old Army regiment with the most distinguished alumni was undoubtedly the *2nd Cavalry*, now the *5th Cavalry*. Formed in 1855, shortly before the war the regiment was commanded by Col. Albert Sidney Johnston, who became a full general in the Confederate Army and died at Shiloh in 1862. His second-in-command was Lt. Col. Robert E. Lee, who also became a full general in the Confederacy. The other field officers were Maj. George H. Thomas, who rose to major general in the Union Army and Maj. Earl Van Dorn, who became a Confederate major general. William Hardee, who later became a Confederate lieutenant general had been a major in the regiment before Van Dorn. Among the captains were Edmund Kirby Smith, who became a full general in the Confederate Army; George Stoneman and Richard W. Johnson, who became Union major generals, and Innis W. Palmer, who became a Union brigadier general. Among the lieutenants were four who attained high rank in the Confederacy, John B. Hood, who became a full general; Fitzhugh Lee, later a lieutenant general; and James P. Majors and Frank G. Armstrong, who became brigadier generals.

War and Society

Southern Efforts to Recruit a Black Army

At the outbreak of the Civil War there were over 3,900,000 black slaves in the South, of whom approximately 550,000 were males of military age. In addition, there were some 250,000 free blacks in the Confederacy, of whom perhaps 35,000 were men of military age. While most of the free blacks were poor, some had attained a measure of success in society, and a handful even owned slaves. The South was home to all of these people, and though most disliked slavery, many were almost as ardent secessionists as their white neighbors. As a result, at the start of the Civil War numbers of blacks, both slave and free, volunteered for service in the Confederate armies. Thus, in April of 1861 companies of free blacks volunteered for Confederate service at Nashville and Memphis. In Louisiana the turn-out was impressively large, for the state had a numerous, relatively prosperous, and active free black population with a tradition of having served in the War of 1812. At the onset of the war the free black citizens of New Orleans raised, organized, and equipped the Louisiana Native Guards, a regiment which was accepted as part of the state militia. On 23 November 1861, the 1,400 strong regiment took part in a militia parade and was warmly received by the populace. But neither the Louisiana Native Guards nor any other black volunteer organization was ever accepted for Confederate service.

The Louisiana Native Guards remained active, however, with state approval. When David G. Farragut and the U.S. Navy took New Orleans in early 1862, the Confederate authorities failed to call the regiment out and, indeed, did not even order it withdrawn from the city. As a result, it was soon reorganized under Federal auspices, and eventually became the first black regiment accepted into the United States Army. But the story of black troops in the Confederate Army does not end there.

There were, of course, many individual black men who fought for the South. The body servants of officers were so frequently in the thick of things that they were ever afterwards welcome at reunions of the United

Confederate Veterans, and even drew pensions in Mississippi. But more formal service by black men could also be found. Several states, including Alabama and Tennessee, permitted blacks to serve in the militia and home guard units through to the end of the war. Alabama recruited blacks to help man coast defenses in Mobile Bay, and they were still there when David G. Farragut steamed up in 1864. Blacks even wore Confederate gray; an act of Congress in 1862 permitted the enlistment of black musicians on essentially the same terms as whites.

The idea of large scale enlistment of blacks appears to have first been aired in Alabama, where free blacks had an unusually good existence due to an old treaty with France. A few newspapers were the first to raise the question publicly, amid considerable furor. By mid-1863, with the war growing longer and casualties mounting, the notion grew more popular. Several people began to openly ask that proper use be made of the pool of military aged male slaves, possibly as labor troops, to relieve white manpower for combat. The idea was taken up in a couple of state legislatures, and in January of 1864 Maj. Gen. Patrick R. Cleburne considered that the idea had merit. Indeed, so enthusiastic was he about it that he expressed a willingness to raise, train, and command a division of blacks himself, a sentiment which appears to have been shared by many of the officers in his divison. But the implications of using slaves for military duties were too complex; after all, the principal Southern war aim was the protection of property in slaves, and the conscription of slaves would clearly run counter to that objective. Nevertheless, the idea did not lay dormant long.

Early in 1864 the Confederate Congress enacted a law which authorized the compensated conscription of free blacks and of slaves as labor troops. Later that year, a conference of governors studied the question and made a number of recommendations, including the use of black troops in combat units. Several military leaders, Robert E. Lee among them, expressed support for their proposals. Meanwhile the Confederate government was moving cautiously in the same direction. That November, even as the Confederate Congress strengthened the black labor conscription bill, Jefferson Davis proposed that the Confederacy purchase 40,000 slaves for service as laborers, with the promise of freedom at the end of the war. By then, many other Confederate political leaders had begun to come around to the idea of arming blacks for combat, despite the implications such a move would have on Southern society even if the Confederacy achieved its independence.

Early in 1865 the manpower situation of the Confederacy had become desperate. That February a bill to enlist blacks as soldiers was defeated in the Confederate Congress, despite strong sentiment from the ranks; Maj. Gen. John B. Gordon, of the II Corps of the Army of Northern Virginia, observed that his men were "decidedly in favor of the voluntary enlistment of negroes." The proponents of enlisting black troops tried again the following month with the backing of Robert E. Lee, who, however, observed that the men so recruited ought to be given their freedom. And on 13 March 1865 the Confederate Congress authorized President Davis to enlist as many as 300,000 slaves, some 60 percent of the pre-war military aged black male slave population, with the permission of their owners if possible, but by conscription if necessary.

Recruiting of black troops began almost immediately. Two battalions of four companies each were authorized to be raised in Virginia, another in South Carolina, and separate companies in Florida and Alabama. The first two companies of black troops were mustered into the Confederate Army on 23 March 1865, within ten days of the act. But numbers were small: the two companies numbered less than 100 altogether. And time was running out. The principal service the new black units rendered to the "Cause" was a public display of their drilling prowess in Capitol Square. Many of the onlookers cheered and the Richmond *Dispatch* wrote that the black men had drilled with "aptness and proficiency." But there were those who still opposed the idea, and black soldiers in Confederate gray were splattered with mud by some citizens, as well as by Unionist sympathizing fellow-blacks. A little more than a week later the Army of Northern Virginia evacuated the city. Although in the end the Confederacy had come around to recruiting black men, the measure was far too late to be of help in averting defeat, and was, indeed, an admission of defeat.

The Average Soldier of the Civil War

Not long after the war the bureaucrats began plowing through the records, as a result of which there are mountains of statistical studies about various aspects of the war. Among these is an analysis of the physical characteristics of the typical soldier in the Union armies. As a result, we know that the average recruit accepted for service by the Republic was 5'8.25" tall and weighed 143.5 pounds. Enlisted men averaged 25.8 years old upon mustering in, while officers averaged 30.4. Fully 45 percent of the recruits had blue eyes, 24 percent gray, 13 percent hazel. 10 percent dark, and 8 percent black. Brown hair was most common, 30 percent, followed by 25 percent dark, 24 percent light, 23 percent black, 4 percent sandy, 3 percent red, and 1 percent gray. Fully 60 percent of the men had light complexions, 7 percent medium, and 33 percent dark. Nearly half were farmers, 48 percent, with the next most common occupation being mechanics and craftsmen, 24 percent, followed by 16 percent laborers, 5 percent businessmen and merchants, and 3 percent professionals; no other occupation having as much as 1 percent.

Similar data is not available for Confederate troops. The physical characteristics of Confederate recruits were probably not dissimilar to those of Union troops, though the average age at enlistment may have been lower. Occupational data is known for a sample of some 9,000 Confederate troops from seven states, of whom 62.2 percent were farmers, including members of the planter class, 7.3 percent mechanics and craftsmen, 5.3 percent were students, 5.2 percent laborers, 3.5 percent merchants, and 2.5 percent clerks, with no other occupation accounting for as much as 1 percent.

Note that the average height of the men is virtually the same as that in World War II, when it was 5'8.4", though we are supposed to have grown taller in the interval. It is also interesting to find that no men are recorded as having been bald upon enlistment.

Foreigners in the Armies

There were lots of immigrants in the America of 1860, mostly in the North. Few people fleeing political oppression and slavery in the Old World were inclined to settle in the South, and in 1860 the foreign-born constituted only about 1 percent of its population. When the Civil War broke out, the loyalties of the foreign-born were, with some important exceptions, largely in the Confederacy, pretty much the same as that of their native-born neighbors. Foreigners in both parts of the country flocked to the colors in commendable numbers, as did those immigrants arriving during the war.

In the early part of the war the foreign-born were important in the formation of the armies, particularly in the Union. Many of the recent immigrants possessed considerable military experience from their native lands. More importantly, there were among them veterans of the "Red 1848" revolutions, the Crimea, and the Italian Wars of Independence. They brought their skills and experience to the new war, serving as an example to the green men around them, for bad as well as good, since they conveyed some of the less desirable aspects of Old World military service, such as the severe social class distinction between officers and men.

Many of the foreign-born rose to high rank in the North. Among foreign-born volunteers for the Union Army at the start of the war—thereby excluding men like Irish-born Robert Patterson, who were pre-war veterans—twenty became generals, including Carl Schurz, Julius Stahel, Basil Turchin, and Albin Schoepf, from Germany, Hungary, Russia, and Poland respectively. In the Confederacy far fewer foreign-born men became generals, of whom Irish-born Patrick R. Cleburne and the French adventurer Camille Armand Jules Marie de Polignac were the most distinguished; the latter was the last Confederate major general, dying in 1913.

It is relatively easy to estimate the number of foreign-born Americans who enlisted in the Union armies, but much more difficult for the Confederacy. The foreign-born tended to form their own regiments in the Union Army, while they were generally dispersed in the Confederacy, where, in addition, record keeping was not a strong point. Nevertheless, there existed in the Confederate Army at least 250 companies which were composed largely of foreign-born personnel when first mustered into service, so there is some basis for calculation. As a result, the figures which follow may be considered highly reliable for the Union, and considerably less so for the Confederacy.

Foreign Born Troops

Nationality	Union	Confederate	Notes
	(Figures in 1000s)		
British	60.0	10.0	A
Canadian	53.5	10.0	B
French	1.0	1.0	
German	200.0	10.0	C
Hungarian		0.8	
Irish	144.2	20.0	
Italian	2.0	0.5	
Mexican	4.5	7.5	D
Netherlands	0.1		
Nowegian	6.5		
Polish	4.0	1.0	
Spanish		0.3	
Swedish	3.0		
Swiss	0.5		
Total	478.7	92.8	

Since the figures for both sides are incomplete, it is probably correct to say that perhaps 500,000 foreign-born were enlisted in the Union ranks, about 25 percent of the total individuals serving, while no more than 100,000 probably served the Confederacy, perhaps 10 percent of those enlisted.

Notes to the Table:

A. "British" includes Welsh and Scottish, as well as English.

B. Estimates of Canadians in Confederate service range up to a rather improbable 40,000. Curiously, official Canadian figures put the number who served the Union at only about 40,000. Some 10,000 of the Canadians in Union service were from the Maritimes.

C. Figures for Germans include Austrians, and many Hungarians, Poles, and others living under German-speaking rulers.

D. The term "Mexican" is unfortunate, since Hispanic residents of Texas, New Mexico, and California were technically not foreign-born, though generally treated as such.

Casualties

The number of people who died or were injured in the Civil War is unknown. Published statistics are generally unreliable, even those found in government documents, encyclopedias, and similar works. All figures are fragmentary, even those for the armies and navies, which together enrolled well over 3,000,000 men, and Confederate figures are particularly incomplete. Thus, figures given for Union battle deaths vary from about 95,000 to 140,000, while those for the Confederacy range from about 75,000 to about 92,000. Deaths from disease and other causes are usually given as about 250,000 for the Union and a little over 59,000 for the Confederacy, a figure which is absurdly small, given the slender medical resources of the South. Despite this confusion, it is possible to arrive at a logical approximation of the actual figures. The figures which follow are modified from those generated by Thomas L. Livermore, in his classic *Numbers and Losses in the Civil War in America: 1861-1865.*

Military Casualties of the Civil War

	Union (%)	Confederate (%)
Killed in Action	67,058 (3.4)	52,934 (5.3)
Mortally Wounded	43,012 (2.2)	34,000 (3.4)
Battle Deaths	110,070 (5.5)	86,934 (8.7)
Other Deaths	249,458 (12.4)	124,000 (12.4)
Total Deaths	359,528 (17.9)	200,934 (20.9)
Wounds not Mortal	275,175 (13.7)	137,000 (13.7)
Total Casualties	634,703 (31.7)	337,934 (33.8)

Figures for Union casualties are those reported by the Medical Department, modified through addition of Navy and Marine Corps casualties, which include 1,804 dead or mortally wounded. The only firm figure for the Confederacy is the 52,934 killed-in-action reported by Gen. Samuel Cooper, the Adjutant General of the Confederate Army. The figure for mortally wounded is derived from this, using the same percentage of mortal wounds to deaths as prevailed in the Union ranks. The Confederate figures for other deaths, which are primarily from disease, but also including accidents, murders, suicides, and executions, are based on the assumption that such could not have been lower than those suffered by the Union. Indeed, it is reasonable to assume that the figures for "Other Deaths" should be higher, perhaps 200,000, given the poverty of Confederate medical resources and the increasingly poor diet of the troops as the war dragged on.

Percentage figures are based on the total manpower enrolled, which in the Union forces was somewhat above 2,000,000 and in the Confederate about half that. The higher battle death rate for the Confederate forces reflects the greater strain which the war placed on the South's slender manpower resources. It is probable that more than 86 percent of the Confederacy's military-aged white manpower served.

Civilian Casualties

The number of civilian casualties in the Civil War, including deaths from combat, atrocities, starvation, or exposure, and injuries of all sorts, has never been satisfactorily calculated.

The Ships

C.S.S. Shenandoah

The South sent many raiders to sea during the war in an effort to disrupt Union commerce. A number of them were outfitted in Britain through various ruses and subterfuges, including three of the most famous, *Florida*, *Alabama*, and *Shenandoah*. Of this distinguished trio, none had a stranger career, and only a handful a more successful one, than did C.S.S. *Shenandoah*.

If was James D. Bulloch, the most successful Confederate procurement agent in Europe, who set *Shenandoah* on her destructive course. In 1863 he was looking about for another vessel to fit out as a raider. *Sea King*, a newly completed auxiliary steamer, seemed to fill that need quite well. Her 222 foot hull had an iron frame, with a teak hull and a coppered bottom. The ship could make nine knots with her 850 horsepower engine, and nearly 14 under sail alone, with as much as 16 possible under both steam and sail. Given an "A-1" by the ship raters, *Sea King* was designed for the Indian Ocean trade, characterized by long voyages with few landfalls. When *Sea King* shoved off on her maiden voyage in late 1863 Bulloch began to lay plans for her acquisition and conversion into a raider. By the following autumn all was in readiness. On 8 October 1864 *Sea King* sailed from Liverpool, eluded some Union naval vessels posted to stop her, for rumors of what was afoot had begun to circulate, and made for the Desertas, a group of small uninhabited islands off Madeira.

On 18 October *Sea King* rendezvoused in the Desertas with *Laurel*, an iron-hulled steamer which was carrying guns and munitions and the 34 officers and men who would constitute the nucleus of a crew. Within three days the work of transferring the guns and stores was completed and *Sea King* was commissioned as *C.S.S. Shenandoah*, Lt. James I. Waddell, C.S.N., in command, with a crew of 43, several British citizens of the *Laurel* and *Sea King* crews having volunteered to serve. After a few days spent fitting out the ships armament, *Shenandoah* sailed for its assigned operating area, the North Pacific.

Shenandoah began to make captures almost as soon as she put to sea. By the time she reached Melbourne, Australia, in late January of 1865, she had already taken five ships. Given a tumultuous welcome by the largely pro-Confederate populace of Australia, *Shenandoah* remained in Melbourne for nearly a month, effecting repairs to a cracked propeller shaft and secretly recruiting about 40 additional crewmen. When he sailed, in mid-February, Waddell took his ship out of the normal shipping lanes and essentially "lost" her for a month, to lay a cold trail for expected Union pursuers. He need not have bothered, as there was not a single Federal warship in the Pacific capable of taking on *Shenandoah's* impressive armament: two 32-pounder Whitworth rifles, among the finest in the world, six 8-inch 68-pounder smoothbores, and two 12-pounders. *Shenandoah* began making captures in late March. Pickings were slim, however. Over the next three months no more than nine vessels were taken. But aboard one of those ships Waddell discovered notes and charts describing the principal whaling areas of the North Pacific. And aboard another vessel he came away with a prize indeed, in the person of one Thomas Manning, a Marylander who agreed to join the ship and serve as a guide to the whaling grounds. With that, Waddell shaped course for Arctic waters. There his luck improved.

Shenandoah arrived in the Bering Sea on 22 June 1865—by which time Appomattox was over two months in the past. Over the next six days 24 vessels were taken, 21 of which were burned and three released under bond to carry prisoners, save for eight men who enlisted, the last men to take up arms for the Confederacy. The best day was 28 June 1865, when eight whalers were burned and two bonded. It was on this day that *Shenandoah* fired the last round of the war, a blank warning shot. But there was a cloud over the ship's success. Newspapers aboard the captured vessels revealed that Lee had surrendered.

News of Appomattox was a shock, but Waddell considered that the war was not yet over, for those very same newspapers revealed that Confederate armies were still in the field in the Carolinas, the Trans-Mississippi, and the Deep South. Having cleaned out all the Yankee whalers he could find, Waddell took his ship south, looking for prey in warmer waters. And on 2 August he raised a British bark which confirmed that the war was indeed over.

Waddel stripped the ship, stowing the guns, raising the propeller, and set sail for England. After a remarkable voyage of 17,000 miles in 122 days—during which she incidently became the only Confederate warship to circumnavigate the globe—without once raising a ship, *Shenandoah* reached Liverpool on 4 November and there surrendered to British authorities.

Altogether, in a career of little more than nine months, *Shenandoah* had taken 38 vessels worth well over a million dollars, fully two-thirds of them after the war was over. In a surprising development, the insurers paid up. But the fate of *Shenandoah* and her crew was less easily settled, for technically their actions qualified them for charges of piracy. Such charges were never brought, however, and the crew soon dispersed. James I. Waddell spent some years as skipper of a merchant ship on the Pacific coast and later working in fisheries protection for Maryland.

Shenandoah was turned over to the United States. She remained at dockside in Liverpool for some time, but was eventually sold to the Sultan of Zanzibar, who put her into the tea trade until she was wrecked in the Arabian Sea in 1879.

C.S.S. Stonewall

The desperate shortage of shipbuilding facilities in the South early forced the Confederate authorities to contemplate securing warships abroad, and particularly ironclads which would be capable of breaking the Federal blockade. Altogether contracts were let for some two dozen vessels, most notably by Cdr. James D. Bulloch, C.S.N., who proved an extraordinarily capable agent for the Confederacy. But of this armada, sixteen cruisers, three gunboats, and five ironclads, only a handful ever took to sea wearing Confederate colors. And of these, the only ironclad was C.S.S. *Stonewall.*

Stonewall, originally named *Sphinx*, was one of two ironclad rams laid down at Arman's of Bordeaux, in France. Contracts were concluded in July of 1863 and the ship was launched the following June. She had a composite hull of iron and wood, displaced 1,400 tons, was 171.8 feet long, 32.7 feet in the beam, and drew 14.3 feet. The ship used a sandwich armor of 3.5" of iron, one inch of teak, and another inch of iron at its thickest on her sides; her forward "turret" had 4.5" face plates on this method and the after one, which was octagonal in plan, but 4". Her armament consisted of one 10"/300-pounder Armstrong muzzle loading rifle forward and two 6.4"/70 pounder Armstrongs aft. The gun positions did not rotate, each having several gun ports, to permit fire on various bearings. Like most early ironclads, Stonewall was under-powered, her two boilers generating only 1,200 horsepower, which could drive her at about 10 knots. Although rigged as a two-masted ship, she was an indifferent and slow sailer.

While the ship was being built, Napoleon III, noting the declining fortunes of the Confederacy, decided to avoid further difficulties with the United States—relations were already bad because of his Mexican adventures—and prohibited her sale to the Confederacy. The builders promptly "sold" the ship to a Swede who was allegedly purchasing her as an agent of the Danish government. She sailed for Denmark, which was just then imminently about to become involved in a war with Prussia, Austria, and the rest of Germany. The outbreak of the Schleswig-Holstein War prevented her delivery, which would have been a violation of international law, and so she lay at anchor in Copenhagen for a time. The war being over, the Danes canceled their order—if it had ever existed—and the builders transferred the ship to the Confederacy in December of 1864. This entire episode is rather cloudy; at various times the ship was known as *Staerkodder* and *Olinde*, but precise explanation of these events is lacking. Whatever the case, in January of 1865 she was commissioned into the Confederate Navy as C.S.S. *Stonewall*, under the command of Capt. Thomas J. Page, who soon took her to sea.

Stonewall was a lemon. The Bay of Biscay being its normally unpleasant self, the ship proved a poor sea boat, handling badly in virtually any weather, and she suffered a good deal of damage. As a result, Page brought her into El Ferrol, in northwestern Spain to effect repairs, a matter which required some time. While *Stonewall* was lying in El Ferrol, a small Union squadron showed up under Com. Thomas T. Craven, U.S.N, a veteran of over 40 years in the Navy. Craven set up a blockade, which effectively bottled Page up. This went on for some time, until, in March, news from the Confederacy being bad, Page determined to take his ship to sea. Emulating Semmes at Cherbourg, on 24 March Page issued a formal challenge.

At this point in the blockade, Craven had two ships, U.S.S. *Sacramento*, a two-year old screw sloop mounting 10 guns, including six 100-pounders, and the ten year old U.S.S. *Niagara*, a screw frigate mounting a dozen guns. Both vessels were wooden-hulled. After careful consideration, Craven decided that his ships were no match for the impressive ironclad and declined, for which he was severely criticized afterwards. As a result, *Stonewall* slipped away to sea and soon eluded the shadowing Union warships. Page set course for Havana. The Atlantic crossing proved difficult, and the ship did not make port until May of 1865. In Havana, Page discovered that the war was over. He turned the ship over to the Spanish government, who shortly afterwards gave it to the United States. The Navy, not just then in the market for additional warships, even ironclads, of which it had several dozen, laid her up. In 1867 the ship was sold to the

Japanese *Shogun*. The ship reached Japan after the Meiji Emperor had staged his *coup d'etat* to overthrow the shogunate, and as a result, the former Confederate warship became the first ironclad in the Imperial Japanese Navy. Commissioned as *Kotetsu* ("Iron Ship") she saw some action in the wars against the feudal faction. In 1871 the ship was renamed *Adzuma*, but, her hull being found rotten, she was placed in reserve. Stricken in 1888, the ship was scrapped about 20 years later.

Although great hopes had been placed in C.S.S. *Stonewall*, they were false hopes. The ship was impressive on paper, but she would not have proven particularly effective as an instrument with which to break the blockade. Of course, her mere existence might have greatly improved Confederate morale. But that alone would not have been sufficient to carry the South for very long.

The European Ironclads

Aside from *Stonewall*, five other ironclads were built in Europe under contract to the Confederacy or with the Confederacy in mind. All of these ships saw service in various navies. Peculiarly, several vessels being built for the Confederate Navy to use against the United States Navy became the first ironclads in two fleets which would later prove impressive opponents of the U.S.N., those of Japan and Germany.

The Arman Rams. *Stonewall* and a sister to have been named *Cheops* were both laid down in 1863 and launched in mid-1864. When, in May of 1864 Napoleon III prohibited the transfer of the two ships to the Confederacy, the builders sold the second vessel to Prussia. Since the Schleswig-Holstein War broke out shortly afterwards, she was not delivered until the following year. Commissioned as S.M.S. *Prinz Adalbert*, the ship had the same design and construction flaws as her sister. In 1871 her hull was found to be rotted and she was taken out of service, to be broken up in 1878.

The Glasgow Frigate. A broadside ironclad pierced for 20 guns, she displaced 4,670 tons, measured 270 feet between perpendiculars, had a beam of 50 feet, and drew 19.5 feet. Severely underpowered, she could make no more than eight knots. The ship's hull was entirely of iron and she was fully armored above the waterline, with plates as thick as 4.5". The builders, Thompson's of Glasgow, terminated the contract in late 1863 while she was still on the ways and sold her to Denmark in 1864. Named *Danmark* she served until 1893, after which she was in reserve until broken up in 1907.

The Laird Rams. Two double turreted ships, C.S.S. *North Carolina* and C.S.S. *Mississippi*, were laid down at Laird's of Birkenhead ostensibly for Egypt. Extremely well built, they displaced 2,750 tons, measured 224.5

feet between perpendiculars, had a beam of 42.3 feet, and drew 16.25 feet. Although capable of only 10.5 knots, they were excellent seaboats. They had an armor belt of 4.5 inches at its maximum, tapering to 2 inches at the ends, backed by as much as 10 inches of wood, and the turret faces had 10 inches of iron. Mounting four 9" rifled muzzle loaders, the two ships would have proven a problem for the Union Navy. Although technically building such vessels was not a violation of the British neutrality laws—which took no account of armored ships—since their guns were not to be mounted in Britain, under pressure from the United States, the British government ordered them detained in September of 1863, and they were seized by the Crown the following month. As H.M.S. *Scorpion* and H.M.S. *Wivern* they served in the Royal Navy for many years, but were for some reason never considered quite satisfactory, and both were relegated to harbor defense duties for many years. *Scorpion* was expended as a target in 1901; later raised, she sank whilst en route to the United States. *Wivern* became an auxiliary in 1898 and was sold for scrap in 1922.

The Samauda Turret Ship. Built by Samauda's of London, this 1,800 ton vessel, was laid down as a speculative venture, apparently in the hope that the Confederacy would buy her. Confederate interest never materialized, and in April of 1865 she was sold to Prussia. The ship, which measured 207.3 feet over all, with a beam of 35.8 feet and a draught of 14.9 feet, could make about 11 knots. Armed with four 72-pounders in two double turrets, she would have proven an impressive opponent. Commissioned as S.M.S. *Arminius*, she served for many years as a harbor defense ship, training vessel, and auxiliary, until scrapped in 1902.

Army Life

Pay

No matter how patriotic they are, soldiers do like to get paid occasionally, and in this regard the boys in blue and the boys in gray were no different. At the outbreak of the war the Union already possessed, and the Confederacy rapidly established, regulations for the payment of their troops.

| | **Monthly Pay** | |
	Confederate	Union
Pvt.	$ 11.00	$ 13.00
Corp.	13.00	13.00
Sgt.	17.00	17.00
1st Sgt.	20.00	20.00
QM Sgt.	21.00	21.00
Sgt. Maj.	21.00	21.00
2nd Lt.	80.00	105.50
1st Lt.	90.00	105.50
Capt.	130.00	115.50
Maj.	150.00	169.00
Lt. Col.	170.00	181.00
Col.	195.00	212.00
Brig. Gen.	301.00	315.00
Maj. Gen.	301.00	457.00
Lt. Gen.	301.00	758.00
Gen.	301.00	

For both armies, officer figures include some, but not all benefits, such as additional ration, forage, and fuel allowances, usually commutated in cash: a Union infantry colonel, for example, received the cash value of six human and three horse rations each day, which amounted to $78.00 a month.

The figures for Confederate generals require some explanation. Under Confederate army regulations there was only one grade of officer in the

Regular Army above colonel, general. The other grades—brigadier general, major general, and lieutenant general—existed in the Provisional Army only: this was the reason there was only one collar badge for all generals, regardless of rank. As a result, all generals received the same base pay. However, additional compensation was provided to generals holding certain commands. Thus, regardless of rank, a general received an extra $100.00 a month while commanding an army in the field, plus other cash payments in lieu of additional rations, fodder, and fuel, a quarters allowance, and seniority pay. As a result, in mid-1864 Robert E. Lee was drawing at least $604.00 a month: $301.00 base pay, $108.00 ration allowance (twelve per day), $32.00 fodder allowance (four horse rations per day), $63.00 seniority pay ($9.00 a month for each five years in the service, including that of the United States), plus $100.00 as an army commander, nor does this include his fuel and quarters allowance. Confederate figures for lower ranks are for the infantry, artillery, and Marine Corps; enlisted men in other branches received a few dollars more and officers an additional $10.00 to $15.00 a month.

Union officer figures are for the infantry and artillery only, other branches receiving about $15.00 a month more. In addition, black enlisted men, regardless of rank, were paid only $10.00 a month for most of the war, of which $3.00 was deducted for clothing allowance, an inequity which was not abolished until September of 1864, by which time the *54th Massachusetts*, which had refused to accept pay until granted equality, was owed $170,000.

In May of 1861 the Confederacy set the pay for chaplains at $85.00 a month, but reduced it to $50.00 two weeks later. That fall chaplains were permitted to draw rations. The following April their pay was raised to $80.00, at which it remained. Union chaplains got a much better deal, being treated as officers and getting $100.00 a month, plus rations for themselves and a horse, unless they were black, in which case they treated as enlisted men and subject to the same fiscal inequities as other black troops. In both armies medical officers were paid according to their respective ranks. Union Army hospital stewards received $30.00 a month and women nurses about $12.00.

Both sides eventually gave the troops a raise. In October of 1862 Confederate Marines were given an additional $4.00 a month, while army enlisted men had to wait until June of '64, when their pay was raised by $7.00 a month, at which time they moved ahead of the Marines, though by then the Confederate dollar had declined to the point that $18.00 was worth only about a dollar in gold. That same June the Union gave its enlisted men $3.00 a month more, a sum that, if paid in greenbacks, was worth only about $5.00 or $6.00 in gold, which substance was, of course much preferred by the troops.

In both armies pay was supposed to be every two months, but was often in arrears, particularly in the Confederate Army, where instances are known of regiments which had not been paid in over a year.

The Navy

Pay for seamen in both navies was roughly comparable with that for soldiers. Union recruit seamen—called "Landsmen"—received $12.00 a month, ordinary seamen got $14.00, able seamen $18.00, and third class petty officers $20.00. A senior petty officer, however, could make considerably more than his army equivalent, as much as $45.00 a month. And on top of their pay all sea going enlisted men over 21 received a half-pint of wine or quarter-pint of grog each day, until September of 1862, when some blue noses managed to get the ration replaced by a cash payment of $1.50 a month.

What Was It Worth?

A direct conversion of 1861 dollar values into money of 1992 is impossible, as increased industrialization has greatly reduced prices relative to earnings, with a contingent considerable increase in the quality of the goods and services received: in 1861 a newspaper cost one cent and a horse car ride two or three, while a good overcoat could run $7.50 and a pair of shoes $2.00. Nevertheless, some notion of the relative value of the sums involved can be obtained. Consider that on the eve of the war a common laborer received about a dollar for a ten-to-twelve hour day, and usually worked a 55 to 65 hour week, for a monthly income of about $30.00, roughly twice what a private made in the Union Army. An income of $300.00 a year was considered pretty good, but few laborers actually earned this much since employment was seasonal and job security non-existent. On this basis, a Union private's $156.00 a year was competitive with civilian wages, given that his rations, clothing, and quarters were at least partially provided for. Nevertheless, this was insufficient to support a family, and there was considerable suffering among soldier's dependents as a result. In contrast, the pay of an officer was extraordinary. A Union lieutenant pulled in over eight times what a private did, and a major general over 35 times; the comparable figures today are about 2:1 and 6.5:1.

A very rough idea of comparable dollar value in money of 1992 can be obtained by multiplying Civil War figures by 35. This yields some interesting results. On this basis a private's monthly pay amounts to $455.00, lower than what the Armed Forces are currently paying, but pretty close after taxes. In contrast, on this basis Lee would be pulling down over $21,000 a month and Grant $26,530, also after taxes.

War and the Muses

When Johnny Comes Marching Home

The only upbeat song to become popular in the latter part of the Civil War was "When Johnny Comes Marching Home." A mindless paean to military glory which began making the rounds as the struggle neared its end, "When Johnny Comes Marching Home" appears to be a genuine folk song, which had several forms, the most common being now the standard. The tune has endured, having a notable popularity during the Spanish American War and, though surpassed by others, during World War I as well.

When Johnny Comes Marching Home

When Johnny comes marching home again,
    Hurrah! hurrah!
We'll give him a hearty welcome then,
    Hurrah! hurrah!
The men will cheer, the boys will shout,
The ladies, they will all turn out,
    And we'll all feel gay,
When Johnny comes marching home.
Chorus: The men will cheer, the boys will shout,
The ladies, they will all turn out,
    And we'll all feel gay,
When Johnny comes marching home.
The old church-bell will peal with joy,
    Hurrah! hurrah!
To welcome home our darling boy,
    Hurrah! hurrah!
The village lads and lasses say,
With roses they will strew the way;
    And we'll all feel gay,
When Johnny comes marching home.
Get ready for the jubilee,
    Hurrah! hurrah!
We'll give the hero three times three,

Hurrah! hurrah!
The laurel-wreath is ready now
To place upon his loyal brow;
    And we'll all feel gay,
When Johnny comes marching home.
Let love and friendship on that day,
    Hurrah! hurrah!
Their choicest treasures then display,
    Hurrah! hurrah!
And let each one perform some part,
To fill with joy the warrior's heart;
    And we'll all feel gay,
When Johnny comes marching home.
Chorus: The men will cheer, the boys will shout,
The ladies they will all turn out,
    And we'll all feel gay,
When Johnny comes marching home.

O Captain! My Captain!

The death of Lincoln was a national tragedy of enormous proportions, and his passing was deeply mourned, both North and South, and in Europe as well as America. The enormous shock of his loss was perhaps best expressed by Walt Whitman.

O Captain! My Captain!

O Captain! my Captain! our fearful trip is done,
The ship has weathered every rack, the prize we sought is
    won,
The port is near, the bells I hear, the people all exulting,
While follow eyes the steady keel, the vessel grim and daring;
But O heart! heart! heart!
    Where on the deck my Captain lies,
    Fallen cold and dead.
O Captain! my Captain! rise up and hear the bells;
Rise up—for you the flag is flung—for you the bugle trills,
For you bouquets and ribboned wreaths—for you the shores
    acrowding,
For you they call, the swaying mass, their eager faces turning;
Here Captain! dear father!
    This arm beneath your head!

It is some dream that on the deck
    You've fallen cold and dead.
My Captain does not answer, his lips are pale and still,
My father does not feel my arm, he has no pulse nor will,
The ship is anchored safe and sound, its voyage closed and done,
From fearful trip the victor ship comes in with object won;
Exult O shores, and ring O bells!
   But I, with mournful tread,
  Walk the deck my Captain lies,
    Fallen cold and dead.

VII

Aftermath

Furl the Banner!
—Abram Joseph Ryan

I mourn, and yet shall mourn, with ever returning spring.
—Walt Whitman

Every time I read a book about that war, I have the far-off hope that maybe this time, just this one time, we will win it.
—Mac Hyman

The sacrifice was not in vain.
—Booker T. Washington

What happens to a dream deferred...?
—Langston Hughes

I say segregation now, segregation tomorrow, segregation forever!
—George Wallace

I have a dream.
—Martin Luther King, Jr.

Afterwards

*T*he war was over, but what was to become of the South? Lincoln had believed leniency was the best course. But Lincoln was dead and his successor, Andrew Johnson, lacked the political and moral strength to carry on Lincoln's plan for Reconstruction. As a result, the balance of political power in the nation fell into the hands of the so-called "Radical Republicans." A more rigorous plan of Reconstruction was adopted. Military rule was instituted, blacks enfranchised. The famed "Carpetbaggers and Scalawags" rose to prominence. Abuses abounded. Reconstruction is depicted as a disastrously oppressive, corruption-ridden conspiracy to inflict vengeance upon the South. It was hardly that. Though rigorous, it was at best a half-hearted effort, perhaps the least vigorous vengeance for rebellion in history. Despite the desires of the most radical anti-Southern fanatics, there were no treason trials and mass executions. Only one person was executed, Henry Wirz, commandant of the notorious Andersonville prison, and only one person, Jefferson Davis, was jailed for more than a few months. True, former Confederate political and military officials were stripped of their civil rights, but in every case these were restored immediately upon individual petition. Myth to the contrary, the Carpetbaggers— Northerners who settled in the South after the war—and the Scalawags—Southerners who collaborated with Reconstruction—often worked for the benefit of the region, but the extreme secessionist fanatics were incapable of seeing that.

To be sure, there were abuses. Efforts to relieve the great suffering caused by the war were disorganized and poorly implemented and some Union commanders on occupation duty acted mean spiritedly. And there was corruption in Reconstruction governments, but it was the age of the Tweed Ring and the Louisiana Lottery and the *Credit Mobilier*, an era of corruption unparalleled save for the Harding and Reagan years. Reconstruction was at most a feeble, ineffective effort, which caused some discomfort, but hardly affected most people, save in one area, race relations, for the Radicals did make serious efforts to assist the newly liberated blacks in adjusting to freedom. And there were blacks in the state houses, often ignorant men, very much in the spirit of their white predecessors, who had not been shy about shooting at each other in moments of heated debate. Nor were blacks in control politically: black delegates were in the minority in virtually every one of the state constitutional conventions held under Reconstruction. But it was the enhanced status of blacks which rankled most throughout the South, calling forth radical resistance, such as the Ku Klux Klan, and the flourishing myth of "The Lost Cause."

The Civil War secured for black Americans their personal freedom, but nothing more. No effort was made to ensure the former slaves their civil rights nor compensate them for the enormous wealth which they had generated through their centuries in bondage, wealth which had not benefitted them. As a result, the freedmen were left politically impotent and economically dependent, so that freedom was as dysfunctional an experience as slavery had been. The end of Reconstruction—which had at least initially attempted to provide social, educational, and economic assistance to the freedmen—saw the start of a protracted decline in the fortunes of black Americans. It was slow because for many years after Reconstruction the leadership of the South was provided by the old aristocratic class, the former slaveholders themselves, who curiously found political support among their former bondsmen as well as among the "poor white trash" whom they had led into the war. But this was an unstable situation. As the rest of the nation—which itself had never been devoted to racial equality— gradually lost interest in the war and the freedmen, the leadership of the South passed into new hands and the political situation of black citizens deteriorated. It was a long process, and as late as the mid-1890s there were still some elected black officials in some Southern states. The nadir was reached in the administration of Woodrow Wilson when Federal offices were segregated, when the Ku Klux Klan enjoyed an enormous popularity, and when black men in the uniform of their country could be lynched with impunity.

By the 1930s the romantic myth of the "Lost Cause" had come to dominate American thought on the Civil War, with a steady stream of books and films which glorified the Confederacy, denigrated the Union, and depicted blacks in blatantly racist terms. The road back has been long and difficult. Beginning almost contemporaneously with the centennial of the Civil War, there was a reevaluation of the struggle and a prodigious cooperative effort by all types of Americans from which blacks have regained a measure of political influence. But the nation still has a long road to travel before the Civil War can truly be said to be over.

Incidents of War

War Debts

On 9 July 1864 Lt. Gen. Jubal A. Early led 14,000 of the Confederacy's doughtiest into Frederick, Maryland, en route to Washington in an effort to draw Yankee manpower away from the Army of Northern Virginia and, just possibly, to liberate 18,000 Confederate prisoners-of-war held at Point Lookout, Maryland. Early made the city fathers an offer: come up with $200,000 in hard money and he would forego the pleasures of putting the place to the torch. The good burgers of Frederick perceived the elegant good sense of Early's offer and immediately began raising the money. Several local banks patriotically lent a hand, though capitalistically asking for interest bearing notes in return. Thus, when Early marched off towards Washington and greater things, the city was saddled with a considerable debt, perhaps $7,200,000 in money of 1988. Taking the reasonable view that this burden had been incurred in the national interest, the city fathers quite logically petitioned Washington for some relief.

What with one thing and another, no one in Washington seemed very interested in the problem. For some time after the war the citizens of Frederick persisted in their efforts to secure recompense, but after a while even the slow learners could see that they were getting nowhere. And so, the city accepted its fate and gradually retired the notes, paying off the last of them in 1951, some 87 years after Early paid his call. And there the matter rested. At least for a while.

In the early 1960s the district which included Frederick elected a new representative to Congress, Charles Mathias, Jr. Representative Mathias happened to know something about the "Early Loan" which had cost Frederick so much. And, like the city fathers of so-long ago, he too believed the debt had been incurred in the national interest. So he began to pester the Congress to do something about the matter. It took a while, for, like the rest of the nation, Congress was not interested in anything serious about the Civil War. But Mathias doggedly kept at it. Indeed, he kept at it for thirteen Congresses. Finally, in October of 1986 Congress approved repayment of the original debt, though, alas, without interest and carrying charges. Thus, after 122 years the books were finally closed on this fiscal footnote to the Civil War. Unless, of course, the tenacious Mathias is inclined to go after all that accumulated interest.

The Oregon Claims

When the Civil War broke out, Federal troops were summoned from a number of outlying posts in order to help in the struggle for the Union. This left some areas without military protection. One such was the state of Oregon, which had what was quaintly termed an "Indian problem." In order to secure protection from the Indians, the state legislature coughed up enough money to maintain some of the militia on active duty as state troops. When the war was over, the state petitioned Washington for redress. The matter dragged for generations, eventually reaching the Supreme Court. And in 1980 the Court ruled that the Federal government not only owed Oregon for the monies expended in the "common defense" but also additional funds by way of interest, for a total amount in the several millions. Truly do the wheels of justice grind slowly. But at least Oregon got a better deal than Frederick.

The Penultimate Engagement of the Battle of Gettysburg

Over 25 years after the great battle, the Gettysburg Battlefield Memorial Association, a private organization which had begun to acquire land on the field to preserve it for posterity, got into a legal dispute with the veterans of the *72nd Pennsylvania*. The Pennsylvanians argued that their regimental monument deserved to be on the front line on Cemetery Ridge. Since the regiment had shown itself rather reluctant to advance at the moment the spearhead of Pickett's Charge breached the Union line at The Angle, the directors of the association were in turn rather reluctant to grant the request, offering instead a site on the reserve line, from which the regiment certainly had not budged, either to retreat or to advance. The regimental veterans association sued. The case dragged through the courts for a number of years. Scores of witnesses were called, including Brig. Gen. Alexander Webb, who had commanded in The Angle. Webb's testimony was devastating to the regiment's pride; only the color sergeant had done his duty, advancing immediately, without regard for what his comrades were doing, for which he paid the ultimate price. Indeed, over all there was significant evidence that the *72nd Pennsylvania* had been lacking in intestinal fortitude at that fateful moment in '63. However the regiment won its case on a technicality. As a result, the Gettysburg Battlefield Memorial Association was forced to permit a monument to be erected on the front line. And so, to this day it stands, an heroic figure with a clubbed rifle, perhaps the most combative monument on the field, on the front line, where no man of the regiment stood until the enemy had been driven off.

The Ultimate Engagement of the Battle of Gettysburg

Some years after the Civil War, Union and Confederate veterans began holding joint reunions, often on the very fields where they had in former times striven mightily to kill each other. Among the most celebrated of these reunions were those of the Gettysburg veterans. The survivor's of Pickett's Charge met regularly with those of Alexander Webb's *Philadelphia Brigade*, which had received and repulsed their attack, at various places for some years in good comradeship and with much rhetoric. On the occasion of their 50th anniversary reunion, held on the "hallowed ground" itself, their good fellowship is reported to have broken down. As one version of the story goes, on 3 July 1913 some of Pickett's elderly veterans started walking up the ridge once more, giving forth emphesymic versions of the famed "Rebel Yell." This annoyed some of the aged Philadelphians atop the Ridge, who are reported to have cried out, "We didn't let you up here in '63 and we ain't gonna let you up now!" After much pushing and shouting and shaking of walking sticks the geriatric warriors from the Union once more held the line. Fortunately, no one was hurt.

The Civil War and the War with Spain

In 1898, 33 years after Appomattox, the nation found itself once more at war. The Spanish-American War, which lasted but four months, was something of a Civil War veterans' reunion. Virtually the entire higher level leadership of the American forces were Civil War retreads. And, while it has generally been fashionable to consider the war as something of a joke, it was actually one of the most well-managed wars in the nation's history, due largely to the enormous experience which the veterans of 1861-1865 brought with them.

Consider the war policies of President William McKinley, who had risen from private to captain and brevet major during the Civil War. At the outbreak of the Spanish War, McKinley issued calls for an enormous number of troops, over 300,000 being enrolled in less than four months. When the war ended, in mid-August, no more than 15% of these men had managed to go overseas. McKinley has been widely criticized for calling up so many men, not least because of the resultant pension costs. But his Civil War experience was at work. There were well over 100,000 Spanish troops in Cuba, some 15,000 in Puerto Rico, and another 45,000 in the Philippines, not to mention the men in Spain itself. Spanish armies have historically often proven tenacious in the defense, and no one could predict how long the war would last. Recalling the nearly disastrous recruiting problems which began to plague the Union as the Civil War dragged on, McKinley wanted enough troops on hand before the shooting started; once the casualty lists began to grow the supply of enthusiastic volunteers might well dry up. McKinley also viewed the new war as a final step in the process of healing the wounds of the Civil War. As a result, he was extremely generous in handing out Volunteer Army commissions to former Confederates, and even readmitted a number of them to the Regular Army.

Virtually all of the general officers involved in the war were Civil War veterans. The most distinguished of these was Maj. Gen. Nelson A. Miles, the commanding general of the Army. One of the most successful volunteer soldiers of the Civil War, Miles had risen from second lieutenant to major general of volunteers by 1865. Miles supervised mobilization in 1898 and himself commanded the expedition which seized Puerto Rico. Other Civil War veterans serving in Puerto Rico—which was the theater in which American troops displayed the greatest degree of tactical finesse— were Maj. Gen. John R. Brooke, a brigadier in '65, Maj. Gen. Guy V. Henry, who came out of the Civil War as a colonel and went on to win a Medal of Honor fighting Indians, and Maj. Gen. John H. Wilson, "boy wonder" cavalryman who was a major general five years after graduating from West Point in 1860. Only one of the four brigadier generals who served in Puerto Rico—one of the most "over-generalled" campaigns in American history—was not a Civil War veteran, and he had joined the Regular Army in 1866. Maj. Gen. William R. Shafter, who commanded *V Corps* in Cuba, had emerged from the Civil War as a brevet brigadier general. One of his division commanders, Maj. Gen. Joseph Wheeler, was the most notable former Confederate to get into action during the war: he held only two ranks in Regular Army, second lieutenant and brigadier general. All of the eleven other generals in Cuba were Civil War retreads as well, of whom the most notable were Brig. Gen. Samuel B. Young, and Brig. Gen. Edwin Vose Sumner, Jr., whose father had been one of the best corps commanders in the *Army of the Potomac*, and was himself a Civil War brevet brigadier.

Maj. Gen. Wesley Merritt, who commanded *VIII Corps* in the Philippines, had led a cavalry brigade at Gettysburg and emerged from the Civil War with brevets as a major general in both the volunteer and regular service. Two of his subordinates where Civil War veterans of some note, Brig. Gen. Francis V. Greene and Brig. Gen. Arthur MacArthur. Of the many generals who saw no action, the most distinguished was undoubtedly Maj. Gen. Fitzhugh Lee, commander of *VII Corps*, which was earmarked for a expedition against Havana, who had been a Confederate lieutenant general and went on to retire as a brigadier general in the Regular Army in 1901. Other notable Civil War veterans who saw no action were Maj. Gen. Alexander McD. McCook of the "Fighting McCooks of Ohio," Maj. Gen. Grenvill Dodge, who had not only been a fine combat officer during the war, but had supervised the construction of the Union Pacific Railroad, and former Confederate Maj. Gen. Matthew C. Butler, who held that rank as one of the American commissioners overseeing the Spanish evacuation of Cuba after the war.

The presence of these seasoned veterans seems to have been of some importance in the conduct of the campaigns. Of a half-dozen or so open field engagements which involved a thousand men or more on at least one side, all but one—the nearly disastrous frontal attack at Las Guasimas, Cuba (24 June 1898)—were characterized by American movements to flank or envelop the Spanish forces. In addition, men like Lee were important in sorting out the muddle which resulted when the too-hasty mobilization dumped enormous numbers of green men at ill-prepared encampments such as the Chickamauga Battlefield Park, which threatened for a time to become a pesthole. On the whole, the management of the Spanish American War was far superior than that of the Civil War over a comparable period. Had the war lasted longer, the experience of the Civil War would have been even more evident.

The *6th Massachusetts*

Generals were not the only veterans of the Civil War to serve in the Spanish War, a number of the old regiments also turned up. The Regular Army, of course, was well represented, the first ten infantry regiments, the first six cavalry regiments, and the first five artillery regiments all having served in the Civil War. But so were the old militia outfits. Although New York's famed "Silk Stocking" *7th Regiment*, which had been among the first volunteer outfits to reach Washington during the Civil War, decided not to bother taking part in the new war, many of the volunteer units which were mustered into service were descendants of Civil War outfits. One of these was the *6th Massachusetts*, which had an unusual career during the war with Spain. Almost as soon as it was mustered into service, the *6th Massachusetts* was sent South. En route, someone had the bright idea that, in the interests of national unity, it might be nice for the regiment to parade through the streets of Baltimore, where its Civil War predecessor had been given a less than hearty welcome on 19 April 1861. Remarkably, the heavily segregated city gave the regiment a warm reception, despite the fact that it had two companies of black troops, officers and all, making it the first "integrated" outfit in the United States Army since the Revolutionary War. Although the regiment went on to have a number of interesting adventures during the Puerto Rican Campaign, its march through the streets of Baltimore was undoubtedly the high point of its war service.

The Navy

As with the Army, so too many of the senior officers of the Navy were Civil War veterans. George Dewey, hero of Manila Bay and the only Admiral of the Navy in American history, served as a junior officer on the Mississippi and the East Coast during the Civil War, and fought in a naval brigade of Fort Fisher. Rear Adm. William T. Sampson and Commodore Winfield Scott Schley, who commanded at Santiago, and who afterwards quarreled mightily about who was responsible for the American victory, were both veterans of blockade duty during the Civil War, Sampson having the distinction of having been aboard the monitor *Patapsco* when she was mined in Charleston harbor in early 1865. As promotion in the Navy was slower than that in the Army, there were a number of Civil War veterans who commanded ships during the Spanish-American War. Three of the most prominent had all fought at Mobile Bay under Farragut, Capt. Charles V. Gridley of Dewey's flagship *Olympia*, who was the only American casualty at Manila, dying of a heart attack, Capt. Charles D. Sigsbee of the ill-fated *Maine*, and Capt. Charles C. Clark, who skippered the battleship *Oregon* on her famed voyage from the West Coast around South America to join the fleet off Cuba.

The Men

George Armstrong Custer

Though born in Ohio, George Armstrong Custer (1839-1876) was raised in Michigan, where he briefly taught in a local school before going to West Point. He was close to expulsion for excessive demerits all four years he was in the Academy, and was actually under detention when he graduated at the bottom of his class in June of 1861.

Commissioned a second lieutenant of cavalry, Custer's first assignment was as a courier between Lt. Gen. Winfield Scott, the general-in-chief, and Brig. Gen. Irvin McDowell during the Bull Run Campaign. He later served on the staffs of Maj. Gen. George B. McClellan and Maj. Gen. Pleasanton, rising to first lieutenant, acting captain. Custer distinguished himself in a number of engagements and on 29 June 1863 was jumped to brigadier general of volunteers and given a cavalry brigade in the *Army of the Potomac.* He led his brigade, comprising the *1st, 5th, 6th,* and *7th Michigan Cavalry Regiments,* with great dash during the Gettysburg Campaign and then fought with considerable courage and aggressiveness through to October of 1864; the command suffered the highest losses of any Union cavalry brigade in the war, 525 killed or mortally wounded. In late 1864 he commanded the *3rd Cavalry Division* under Maj. Gen. Philip Sheridan in the Shenandoah Valley. In the final days of the war it was his division which completed the encirclement of the Army of Northern Virginia at Appomattox, though it is reported that an effort on his part to "accept" the surrender of a portion of the Army of Northern Virginia was rebuffed by a clever ruse on the part of one Confederate general. During the war, from which he emerged as a major general of volunteers, Custer had eleven horses shot out from under him, but was himself wounded only once.

Custer remained in the Regular Army after the war and was named lieutenant colonel of the newly authorized *7th Cavalry.* As the colonel of the regiment was almost never present, Custer was the effective commanding officer. He led the regiment for many years, usually with considerable friction between himself and his superiors and his subordinates. Responsible for the brutal attack on a Cheyenne village at the Washita in late 1868, he was also directly responsible for the loss of himself and a third of his regiment at the Little Big Horn on 26 June 1876. The tall, spare Custer, who wore his curly blond hair in long flowing locks, was nicknamed "Curly" or "Fanny" in the army. Not a cerebral soldier, his basic battle plan was to charge into action and then figure out what to do afterwards. It is only his spectacular death which preserves his memory, when many far more capable cavalrymen have been long forgotten.

War and Society

Demobilization

The demobilization of the Confederate Army began even before the war ended. Literally tens of thousands of men abandoned the cause in its dying weeks. On paper, Confederate strength was still well over 300,000 men at the beginning of April of 1865, yet only 174,223 men were formally paroled in the last few weeks of the war. The Army of Northern Virginia, which numbered about 55,000 in March, surrendered barely 28,000 on 14 April. Most of the men just walked away from the colors. One officer, who witnessed the dissolution of a Texas outfit, said there was "a widespread and immediate decamping of soldiers with whatever army property they could lay their hands on." A small number of Confederate soldiers, mostly senior officers, were briefly held as prisoners of war, but even they were paroled by the end of summer.

Union demobilization was rather more difficult, as there were areas which had to be patrolled—even before the war ended some Confederate guerrillas had found banditry more to their taste than war—and the occupation of the South had to be taken in hand. Despite this, the Federal armies dissolved with remarkable speed.

Strength of the Army	
1 May 1865	1,000,516
7 Aug	359,710
22 Aug	281,178
14 Sep	259,409
15 Oct	215,311
15 Nov	199,613
1 May 1866	80,000

After May of 1865 the strength of the army declined at a slower pace. Nevertheless, by the end of 1866 the army was down to an authorized strength of less than 55,000 men. It was not much considering that it had to patrol the frontier and maintain the occupation of the South, but it was all that a war weary nation was willing to support and in the end proved sufficient. In the space of 18 months, the United States Army went from being the largest—and finest—in the world in the spring of 1865 to one smaller than that of Egypt.

The Veterans' Organizations

Soon after the war a number of veterans organizations were established, most notably the Grand Army of the Republic, founded in 1866, which was open to all Union veterans, and the Military Order of the Loyal Legion of the United States, an association of former officers established in 1865. In addition, there were a number of associations for veterans of particular organizations, such as the *Army of the Potomac* and the *Army of the Tennessee*. However, these rather quickly became dormant, as the immediate enthusiasm of the newly discharged veterans waned. In a pattern characteristic of other wars, not for nearly a decade was there very much success in getting a serious veterans movement going, by which time the worst memories of the war were fading, and the veterans were being resocialized into remembering how glorious it had all been. Thereafter growth was explosive, as figures for the Grand Army of the Republic demonstrate.

The Grand Army of the Republic
1878-1890

Year	Members
1878	c. 30,000
1883	c. 146,000
1884	c. 233,000
1887	c. 320,000
1890	427,981

At its peak in 1890 the G.A.R. probably included nearly a quarter of the total number of men ever enrolled in the Union forces, and, considering wartime losses and actuarial probabilities, perhaps as many as half of the Union veterans then living. The G.A.R. was by far the largest and most influential of Union veteran's organizations, invariably backing Republican candidates and proving an effective lobby for veteran's causes until well into the twentieth century. The last G.A.R. national encampment was held in 1949, 84 years after the war, with six of the 16 surviving members in attendance. The last member, and the last Union veteran, was Albert Woolson, a former drummer boy from Minnesota, who died in 1956.

Confederate veterans were understandably rather slow in getting organized. Although a number of local, regimental and even army veterans associations were formed in the years following the war, no nation-wide organization was established until the United Confederate Veterans was formed in 1889, with former Maj. Gen. John B. Gordon as its first president. The U.C.V. never equalled the G.A.R. in numbers, but did eventually include a respectable proportion of surviving Confederate veterans: it peaked at about 160,000 in 1904, perhaps half of those still living at the time. While the U.C.V. had little political influence on the national level, it was of considerable importance in the South. Like the G.A.R., the U.C.V. lobbied for veterans' benefits, securing pensions from states of the *soi disant* Confederacy, promoted the erection of monuments, published memoirs, and held annual reunions, the last of which, in 1951, was attended by three of the approximately two-dozen surviving members.

While Union and Confederate veterans organizations were in a sense rivals, a degree of cooperation and ultimately comradeship eventually developed between them. Union and Confederate veterans first met informally in Boston in 1875 at the Bunker Hill centennial celebration. More formal contacts soon followed. By the early twentieth century joint G.A.R./U.C.V. reunions were regular occurrences, the last being held at Gettysburg in the mid-1930s.

The G.A.R. and the U.C.V. were the first mass-based veterans organizations in American history, and the most successful.

The Auxiliaries

Both the G.A.R. and the U.C.V. had satellite organizations for the wives and children of their members. Several of these survive. The Sons of Union Veterans of the Civil War, the Sons of Confederate Veterans, and the United Daughters of the Confederacy continue to thrive. Open to the descendants of veterans, these organizations help to keep alive the memory of the war and aid in the struggle to preserve Civil War historic sites.

The War and the White House

Having one's "ticket punched" by serving a tour in the armed forces has always been a help when running for political office, and it was no different in the aftermath of the Civil War. Indeed, in the generation following the war it was difficult to find anyone occupying political office in the North who had not served in the war, and virtually impossible in the South, where service to "The Cause" was an absolute prerequisite for political office. The big prize, then as now, was, of course, the presidency. The Civil War yielded more presidents than any other, seven, 43.7% of the presidents with wartime military service, though only three of the ten generals to become chief executive. For only eight of the 36 years following the war was the White House not occupied by a veteran.

Andrew Johnson (National Union Party [a Republican-War Democrat "popular front" fusion ticket], 1865-1869): a Tennessee senator before the war, Johnson stuck by the Union, and was appointed brigadier general of volunteers on 4 March 1862 in consequence, serving as military governor of his home state. He resigned on 3 March 1865 to become vice-president, succeeding Lincoln when the latter was assassinated.

Ulysses S. Grant (Republican, 1869-1877): West Point, 1839-1843; Regular Army, from 1843, with a distinguished record in Mexico (two brevets and a citation for merit), rising to captain before resigning on 31 July 1854 to become an inept civilian. Appointed lieutenant colonel of volunteers on 17 June 1861, Grant rose thereafter to lieutenant general and commanding general on 12 March 1864, and then to full general on 25 July 1866, before resigning on 3 March 1869 to become president.

Rutherford B. Hayes (Republican, 1877-1881): a lawyer and early Republican activist, Hayes was commissioned a major in the *23rd Ohio* on 27 June 1861, rising thereafter to brigadier general on 19 October 1864, serving creditably as a brigade and division commander, most notably in Sheridan's Valley Campaign. Elected to Congress in 1864, he did not take his seat. Breveted major general on 13 March 1865, he resigned on 8 June to take his seat in the House. Hayes was wounded four times during the war.

James A. Garfield (Republican, 1881): an Ohio politician before the war, Garfield was commissioned lieutenant colonel of the *42nd Ohio* on 21 August 1861, and rose steadily through the ranks by distinguished service at Shiloh, and Corinth, and as chief-of-staff of the *Army of the Cumberland,* until he was made a major general of volunteers on 19 September 1863. He resigned shortly thereafter upon being elected to Congress.

Chester A. Arthur (Republican, 1881-1885): became attached to the infant Republican party as a young lawyer in New York City. On the outbreak of the war he was appointed assistant quartermaster general of the state militia, responsible for procuring supplies for regiments being raised for both state and federal service, rising by the war's end to quartermaster general and inspector general, ranking as a major general.

Grover Cleveland (Democrat, 1885-1889 and 1893-1897): a lawyer and Democratic politician in his Buffalo, Cleveland did not serve, providing a substitute when drafted in 1864.

Benjamin Harrison (Republican, 1889-1893): great-grandson and namesake of Benjamin Harrison, a signer of the Declaration of Independence, and grandson of Indian fighter and ninth president William Henry Harrison, Benjamin Harrison was a lawyer in Indianapolis when the war came. He enlisted as a second lieutenant in the *70th Indiana*, mustering in on 14 July 1862, and became colonel 24 days later, on 7 August. Harrison was a firm taskmaster and his regiment quickly became proficient, though he never became popular as a result. Leading the regiment in the *Army of the Cumberland* at Resaca, Golgotha, New Hope Church, and Peach Tree Creek, he was made a brigade commander. Thereafter, he commanded various brigades, at Nashville and—after being made a brevet brigadier general on 23 January 1865— during the Carolina Campaign. Harrison mustered out on 8 June 1865, to resume his law practice.

William McKinley (Republican, 1897-1901): a teacher in Ohio at the start of the war, on 23 June 1861, 19 year-old McKinley enlisted as a private in *Company E, 23rd Ohio* (See Rutherford B. Hayes, above). He served in West Virginia, at Antietam, and in the Shenandoah, rising to captain on 25 July 1864, and brevet major on 13 March 1865.

War Babies

Theodore Roosevelt, Jr. (Republican, 1901-1909): Little Teddy was only three when the war began, but rapidly became an enthusiastic war hawk, with his own uniform. Much to Teddy's annoyance, his father, Theodore Roosevelt, Sr., a wealthy New Yorker, did not serve, choosing instead to provide a substitute. This may explain Theodore's thirst for military glory.

William Howard Taft (Republican, 1909-1913): Billy Taft was four when the war began. His father, Alfonso Taft, a prominent lawyer and Republican politician in Cincinnati, did not serve, supplying a substitute in his stead.

Woodrow Wilson (Democrat, 1913-1921): Little Thomas Woodrow was almost five when the war began. He spent some time in Richmond, where he witnessed some of the horrors of war, and, at the age of nine, watched as Jefferson Davis was being taken under arrest to Washington after his capture. His father, The Rev. John R. Wilson, a Virginian, was an ardent secessionist and racist—opinions reflected in his son's later writings and actions—who served as a chaplain in the Confederate Army.

Some Also Rans

1864: George B. McClellan, the erstwhile General-in-Chief and commander of the *Army of the Potomac*, carried the Democratic banner to crushing defeat at the hands of Lincoln.

1880: This was the big year for Civil War aspirants to the White House, with a field of four. Winfield Scott Hancock, a highly successful major general and corps commander in the *Army of the Potomac*, ran as a Democrat and was narrowly defeated by James A. Garfield in a race which also saw former Union Brig. Gen. John W. Phelps on the Anti-Masonic line and former Union Brig. Gen. Neal Dow on the Prohibition ticket, who garnered all of 10,000 votes.

1884: This was the year in which Gen. William Tecumseh Sherman, annoyed at incessant pressure to run, declared "If nominated, I will not run, if elected, I will not serve." Maj. Gen. Benjamin Butler, one of the most prominent "political generals" in the war, however, ran on the Greenback ticket and was never heard from again.

1888: Union Brig. Gen. Clinton B. Fiske tried his luck on the Prohibition line.

1896: John McC. Palmer, a former Union major general, ran on the so-called "Gold Democrat" ticket, with former Confederate Lt. Gen. Simon Bolivar Buckner as his running mate, thereby helping to defeat Democrat William Jennings Bryan's "Free Silver" campaign and elect brevet Maj. William McKinley.

The Brooklyn Bridge

The Brooklyn Bridge, built between 1870 and 1883, is inseparably linked to the Battle of Gettysburg, fought on 1-3 July 1863. The bridge was designed by John A. Roebling in 1867 under the sponsorship of the East River Bridge Corporation. In 1869 Roebling died as a result of an accident while surveying the site and his son, Washington A. Roebling, assumed supervision of the project. During construction the younger Roebling's health was seriously impaired as a result of the bends and his wife, Emily Warren Roebling, acted as his factotum thereafter, personally supervising the work as Roebling watched through a telescope from a distant window.

At Gettysburg, Washington Roebling had been a lieutenant of engineers on the staff of Brig. Gen. Gouverneur K. Warren, Chief Engineer of the Army of the Potomac and one of the heroes of the campaign. In the two or three days immediately before the battle Roebling had traveled from Baltimore to Washington and thence to the *Army of the Potomac* in the field, collecting the maps which Warren believed necessary for the battle. He arrived on the field on 2 July and accompanied Warren on all his adventures during the fighting that day, when the latter hastily collected troops to defend Little Round Top during the most critical hours of the battle.

Emily Warren Roebling was Gouverneur K. Warren's sister. The Gettysburg connection does not end with the Roeblings.

Union Maj. Gen. Henry Slocum, who commanded the *XII Corps* and the right wing during the Gettysburg Campaign, was a director of the Great East River Bridge Corporation and one of its principal stockholders. In addition, Brig. Gen. Horatio Gouverneur Wright, who commanded a division in *VI Corps* during the Campaign, served as a engineering consultant on the bridge, as did Maj. Gen. John Newton, who commanded a corps during part of the battle. And then, of course, many of the thousands of workers who helped build the bridge were themselves veterans of the battle.

"Pave Paradise and Put Up a Parking Lot"

The nation is in danger of losing a significant part of its heritage, the physical relics of the Civil War. More Civil War sites of historical importance have been lost to "development" in last dozen or so years than in all the previous years since 1865. And there seems no end in sight.

The greatest danger is to the battlefields in Northern Virginia and Maryland, as a result of increasing suburbanization contingent upon the growth of Washington, but the problem is one which affects virtually every Civil War site. Indeed, only Pea Ridge of all the hundreds of Civil War battlefields remains largely unchanged. A few examples may serve to illustrate the extent of the impending disaster to the nation's heritage.

At Antietam, scene of the bloodiest single day's fighting in the nation's history, a cable television company wishes to erect a relay tower on a hill which will be visible from much of the battlefield, while a local builder is planning some condos for a nearby ridge which also overlooks the field. Meanwhile, significant portions of the Chantilly battlefield have been cut up into housing tracts, though monuments to commemorating the gallant Phil Kearny and Isaac Ingalls Stevens—who fell that day in '62— will be "allowed" to remain in small park of about 2.3 acres to be established by the developers. Virtually all of the Fair Oaks/Seven Pines battlefield now lies under a shopping mall with its attendant service roads and parking lots. Meanwhile, recently important sites within, but not part of the Manassas Battlefield Park—including Lee's headquarters during Second Bull Run— were threatened by another proposed shopping mall, and local authorities wished to widen two historic roads through the heart of the park itself, forever changing the appearance of the field; one official saying that preservationists are "being really silly about the whole thing." At Gettys-

burg, the city fathers—grown prosperous off the events of 1-3 July 1863—
are resisting the transfer of the Taney farm, a tract of 31 acres owned by the
private Gettysburg Battlefield Preservation Association to the Gettysburg
Battlefield Park because the town stands to lose about $250.00 a year in
taxes! A similar dispute is hampering efforts to preserve certain portions of
the South Mountain battlefield. Nor is the problem confined to sites and
relics which are in private hands. Even things which have been preserved,
are threatened.

The State of Louisiana recently closed some Civil War historic sites as
an economy measure, thereby realizing a savings on the state's utility bills
of the enormous sum of $6,000 a year. Similarly, the Confederate Naval
Museum, at Columbus, Georgia, which preserves two of the three surviving Confederate warships, has lost public funding in an economy move,
while the Museum of the Confederacy in Richmond is down to one full
time employee. Perhaps most disgraceful of all, the Federal government—
which spent over $100,000,000 on military bands last year and recently
designated the home of Whitaker Chambers as a National Historic Site—
refused to provide funds to restore and preserve several flags which flew
over Fort Sumter in April of 1861.

Meanwhile, in a misguided and largely mercenary effort, the wholly
undistinguished building in which Margaret Mitchell had a small apart-
ment while writing *Gone With the Wind* is being preserved, as is a plantation which she herself observed has no relationship to her fictional "Tara."

The situation is grave, but not hopeless. Civil War interest groups such
as the Round Tables and the reenactors, local historical societies, the Sons
of Confederate Veterans, the Sons of Union Veterans, the United Daughters of the Confederacy, and some public officials have begun to take
action. The problem has received increasing journalistic attention, not
only in Civil War-related publications, but also in such important newspapers as *The New York Times* and *The Washington Post*. As a result, some
victories have been won. The shopping mall on the Bull Run/Manassas
battlefield was blocked by government action, while a proposal to widen a
highway through the Chattanooga-Chickamauga Military Park was defeated and certain additional lands preserved from "development" by a
coalition of concerned citizens. Public opinion in New Mexico successfully
pressured the state into assisting in the preservation of privately owned
portions of the Glorieta Pass battlefield. Several states, notably Pennsylvania, New York, and North Carolina, have begun to take measures to
preserve their memorials at various battlefields, such as Gettysburg. The
Fort Sumter flags have been preserved through public donations raised in

a campaign coordinated by various Civil War journals, while efforts of the Civil War Round Tables have financed the restoration of Union Maj. Gen. George Thomas' gravesite.

Several organizations have been established to help in the task of preserving the physical remains of the war. The Civil War Sites Fund (c/o National Park Foundation, Washington, DC., 20240) was created in 1973 so that the public can contribute to the purchase of lands to be added to various Civil War parks. The Association for the Preservation of Civil War Sites (POB 23, Arlington, Virginia, 22210) has been formed with the object of coordinating the activities of the many Civil War interest groups, such as the Round Tables, with those of local historical associations, the Civil War descendants organizations, and the like in order to strengthen their efforts to preserve the nation's past. It remains to be seen as to how successful such efforts will be in the face of greed, indifference, and ignorance. If they fail, far more Civil War sites will be lost. And truly will we have fulfilled the prediction of the old '60s song, "Pave paradise and put up a parking lot," with our national heritage buried under concrete and asphalt, and the memory of the Civil War will linger only in the Battlefield Business Park, the Stonewall Acres Estates, and the Lee-Grant Burger Bar.

War and the Muses

"The Conquered Banner"

Abram Joseph Ryan (c. 1839-1886) was born in Limerick, Ireland, and came to the United States at the age of seven or eight, during the "Potato Famine." Educated to the priesthood, he was assigned to various parishes in the South, beginning in Nashville. Serving in Georgia at the outbreak of the Civil War, Fr. Ryan became an ardent supporter of the Confederacy, lecturing and writing poetry. After the war, Fr. Ryan continued in the priesthood, lectured, wrote, and edited his works. A poet of some ability, his style marks him as very much a man of his times. "The Conquered Banner," a lament for the defeated Confederacy, is his most notable effort, and among the best Southern poems on the war. The piece was quite popular in the South well into the twentieth century. Running through several editions, it was regularly recited in schools throughout the South and even performed on the stage as a pantomime.

The Conquered Banner

Furl the Banner, for 'tis weary;
Round its staff 'tis drooping dreary.
Furl it, fold it, it is best;
For there's not a man to wave it,
And there's not a sword to save it,
And there's no one left to love it
In the blood which heroes gave it;
And its foes now scorn and brave it.
Furl it, hide it—let it rest!
Take the Banner down! 'tis tattered;
Broken is the staff and shattered.
And the valiant hearts are scattered
Over home it floated high.
Oh! 'tis hard for us to fold it;
Hard to think there's none to hold it;
Hard that those who once unrolled it
Now must furl it with a sigh.

Furl the Banner! furl it sadly!
Once ten thousands hailed it gladly,
And ten thousands wildly, madly
Swore it should forever wave;
Swore that foeman's sword should never
Hearts like theirs entwined dissever
Till that flag should float forever
O'er their freedom or their grave!
Furl it! for the hands that grasped it
And the hearts that fondly clasped it,
Cold and dead are lying low.
And that Banner—it is trailing!
While around it sounds the wailing
Of its people in their woe.
For, though conquered, they adore it!
Weep for those who trailed and tore it!
But, oh!, wildly they deplore it.
Now who furl and fold it so.
Furl the Banner! True, 'tis gory.
Yet, 'tis wreathed around with glory
And 'twill live in song and story
Though its folds are in the dust;
For its fame and brightest pages,
Penned by poets and by sages,
Shall go sounding down the ages—
Furl its folds though now we must.
Furl that Banner! softly, slowly!
Treat it gently—it is holy—
For it droops above the dead.
Touch it not—unfold it ever,
Let it droop there, furled forever,
For its people's hopes are dead.

Cycloramas and Panoramas

An unusual genre of painting became immensely popular in both the
United States and Europe in the period around the Civil War, panoramas
and cycloramas. Panoramas were flat or somewhat curved works, while
cycloramas were designed to entirely encircle the viewer. These works were
enormous, most being 50 or so feet high and 400 feet long. Many such
were executed on a variety of themes, such as "The Mississippi"—which at
1000 feet probably holds the record as the largest painting ever executed—

and a "Paradise Lost" which was making the rounds shortly after the war. By far the most popular themes were battle scenes.

A number of panoramas and cycloramas were completed on Civil War themes in the two decades after the struggle by teams of about a dozen artists working under the direction of a master. Many were highly accurate portrayals of the most spectacular moments in the battle being depicted. A number of artists took considerable pains to include as many portraits as possible, often working from wartime photographs of officers and men who had played significant roles in the action. In 1881 French artist Paul Philippoteaux—a veteran of seven European battle cycloramas executed in ten years—and five assistants invested months touring and photographing the battlefield and interviewing participants before executing his Gettysburg cyclorama—in Paris, incidently—, which depicts the climactic moment of Pickett's Charge on the afternoon of the third day. Similarly, Frenchman Theophile Poilot, who did eight panoramas on war themes in Europe and America, incorporated over 2,000 individual portraits in his depiction of the "Hornet's Nest at Shiloh," one of three Civil War works which he executed, the others being a Manassas and a *Monitor-Merrimac.*

An admiring public paid $0.50 a head—a considerable sum in those days—to view these works and hear lectures by learned authorities on the subject; Maj. Gen. Benjamin Prentiss, who had defended "The Hornet's Nest" once did a stint as a lecturer for Poilot's Shiloh cyclorama, during which he ran into his former Confederate opponent, Maj. Gen. John S. Marmaduke, with whom he had a pleasant chat going over old times. Whole families would visit, much as people now go to the movies. War panoramas and cycloramas were considered educational and uplifting for young people, though veterans, in between looking for familiar faces, would often carp about inaccuracies, of which there were always a few. Most errors were inadvertent, such as the haystacks in Philippoteaux's Gettysburg cyclorama, which are more appropriate to his native Normandy than Pennsylvania, but there were occasional deliberate ones: Philippoteaux painted himself into Gettysburg in the guise of a Federal officer.

Despite the popularity of these enormous works time has taken a heavy toll. Several were burned, a number simply lost. Only two now survive intact, Philippoteaux's Gettysburg and one of the Battle of Atlanta, each on permanent exhibit in the appropriate battlefield parks, though a copy of the Gettysburg—three were later executed—is rumored to be in storage somewhere. Poilot's Shiloh is preserved in a remarkable set of photographs taken before it disappeared, but most of the others have vanished, save for portions preserved in photographs, engravings, sketches, and small scale copies.

"The Unsung Heroes"

Although there had been considerable resistance to the employment of black troops during the Civil War, they had quickly made themselves a reputation once in action. The war was no sooner ended, however, when—despite the continued excellent service rendered by black regiments in the Regular Army—the fighting qualities of black troops began to be denigrated. By the beginning of the twentieth century is was unusual to find mention of the military service by blacks in the war. In his "The Unsung Heroes," from which the piece below has been taken, Paul Lawrence Dunbar (1872-1906), a black poet and novelist from Ohio, attempted to recall the services of black troops. Dunbar first gained public attention with his dialect verses and stories about black life, beginning with *Oak and Ivy* in 1893. Later proving as capable a hand with standard English verse and novels which focussed on white characters, Dunbar produced fourteen volumes of verse and fiction in his brief life. Though now little read, his works were quite popular in his day, earning him the sobriquet "The Poet of his People."

The Unsung Heroes

A song for the unsung heroes who rose in their country's need,
When the life of the land was threatened by the slaver's cruel greed,
For the men who came from the cornfield, who came from the plough and the flail,
Who rallied round when they heard the sound of the mighty man of the rail.
They went to the blue lines gladly, and the blue lines took them in,
And the men who saw their muskets' fire thought not of their dusky skin.
The gray lines rose and melted beneath their scathing showers,
And they said, " 'Tis true, they have forced to do, these old slave boys of ours."
Ah, Wagner saw their glory, and Pillow knew their blood,
That poured on a nation's altar, a sacrificial flood.
Port Hudson heard their war-cry that smote its smoke-filled air,
And the old free fires of their savage sires again were kindled there.

Afterwards

They laid them down where the rivers the greening valleys
gem.
And the song of the thund'rous cannon was their sole
requiem,
And the great smoke wreath that mingled its hue with the
dusky cloud,
Was the flag that furled o'er a saddened world, and the
sheet that was their shroud.
Oh, Mighty God of Battles Who held them in Thy hand,
Who gave them strength through the whole day's length,
to fight for their native land,
They are lying dead on the hillsides, they are lying dead on the
plain,
And we have not the fire to smite the lyre and sing them one brief
strain.
Give, Thou, some seer the power to sing them in their
might,
The men who feared the master's whip, but did not fear the
fight;
That he may tell of their virtues as minstrels did of old,
Till the pride of face and hate of race grew obsolete and
cold.
A song for the unsung heroes who stood the awful test,
When the humblest host that the land could boast went forth to
meet the best;
A song for the unsung heroes who fell on the bloody sod,
Who fought their way from night to day and struggled up to God.

The Civil War Today

The Reenactors

One of the most unusual phenomena of history as a hobby in the contemporary world is the reenactor. Beginning several years before the Civil War centennial, groups of black powder enthusiasts began holding informal skirmishes on Civil War themes. Out of this has emerged an enormous network of "recreated" regiments, both Union and Confederate, which can be found all over the United States, in Canada, and even in England. While at first reenactors made do with vague approximations of Civil War uniforms and equipment, such are now considered "farby"—derived from observations about such beginning, "Far be it for me to say, but...." Most veteran reenactors are virtually indistinguishable in appearance from the original boys in blue and gray, so much so that they are regularly called upon to do their stuff in motion picture and television epics, and can readily be distinguished from the Hollywood variety of Civil War soldier by their realistic slovenliness; some extremists have even taken to wearing Civil War style underclothing in the interests of verisimilitude. It should be noted that this is essentially a male hobby, wives and daughters preferring to dress in what would have been rather elegant fashions for the Civil War; sooner or later, of course, some woman will make an issue of exclusionary policies, rightfully observing that there were women in the ranks during the Civil War.

Reenactments of battles are now regularly scheduled. Several, such as the annual Champion's Hill reenactment in Mississippi, have become regular affairs. A number of reenactments have involved truly enormous numbers of men, some thousands being by no means unusual. Some extremely devoted reenactors have actually cobbled together a *Monitor* and a *Merrimac* to have a little naval action. Whenever possible reenactments are staged on the very ground over which the original battle was fought, but as blind development engulfs an increasing proportion of important Civil War sites, many restagings have to be held on "similar" ground, a practice which English reenactors find relatively easy, given the resemblance of much of the English countryside to the Shenandoah Valley. Notices of reenactments regularly appear in such publications as *Blue and Gray* and *Civil War Times Illustrated*, as well as in newspapers, frequently coordinated by the North-South Skirmish Association (P.O. Box 12122, Richmond, Virginia, 23241).

In general, reenactors rarely attempt to recreate actions from the period after 1863, by which time the romance had largely gone out of the war. It is not unusual for men to show up at a reenactment with several uniforms, so that they can fight for the Union or the Confederacy as the situation, and manpower shortage, dictates. There are, however a number of devotees—mostly in gray—who so strongly identify with the times that they refuse to engage in such "treasonous" activities. Indeed, a few neo-Confederates have been known to load their muskets with something other than blanks, though there have been no fatalities so far.

In addition to recreating battles, reenactors regularly camp out in proper Civil War fashion, cooking up period breakfasts, sleeping in tents, and so forth, though even the most devoted prefer the port-o-san to the Civil War alternative. While most reenactors are infantry, there are a few cavalry and artillery groups, and one engineer regiment, the *15th New York*, which builds pontoon bridges and engages in other engineering works. The reenactors perform a useful service, not only helping to strengthen the public's interest in history, but also increasing awareness of the need for historic preservation. In addition, they maintain skills which would otherwise be lost.

Civil War Round Tables and Other Interest Groups

In a nation not noted for its concern with the past, the Civil War stands out as the historical event which has attracted the greatest amount of popular interest. While the many battlefield parks and the increasingly popular reenactment groups receive by far the greatest amount of attention, the most active and most important Civil War interest groups are undoubtedly the numerous Round Tables. The first Civil War Round Tables began forming shortly before World War II and they have thrived ever since. Today there are well over 100 Civil War Round Tables scattered all across the United States, and one or two in Canada, plus more than a dozen Lincoln groups and a number of other related organizations; in contrast, there is but one American Revolution Round Table.

The members of the Civil War Round Tables are mostly interested laymen, with a liberal seasoning of people with a professional interest in the subject, such as social studies teachers, college professors, historians, and even a few soldiers. Many of the lay people are themselves creditable amateur historians, antiquarians, biographers, or collectors, and not a few have conducted serious, useful research. Most groups meet monthly, often at a local site with some Civil War connection—the New York group meets in the trophy-bedecked armory of the erstwhile *7th New York*—for dinner and a presentation. The more active groups have extremely varied programs, including lectures, slide shows, and even sing-alongs. Most groups sponsor battlefield tours, help in the increasingly important task of protecting and preserving historic sites, and work to promote better education in history in the schools. Several groups have annual awards which they present to authors or other people working in the field.

The Civil War Round Tables are loosely affiliated through the Civil War Round Table Associates (P.O. Box 7388, Little Rock, Arkansas, 72207), which serves as coordinating body, information service, and umbrella organization for the sponsorship of regional activities, such as conferences.

The Best Civil War Simulation Games

Out of the many hundreds of Civil War simulation games which have seen print, there are a few which are generally considered to be outstanding. What follows is a list of the ten most popular Civil War simulation games based on a survey conducted by *Volunteers*, the largest journal of Civil War gaming.

Game	Publisher	Complexity(0-5)
1. *Terrible Swift Sword*	TSR/SPI	4.2
2. *The Civil War*	Victory Games	4.6
3. *A House Divided*	GDW	3.5
4-5. *Ironclads*	Yaquinto	4.1
A Gleam of Bayonets	TSR Hobbies/SPI	4.4
6. *Chickamauga*	West End Games	4.2
7. *Blue & Gray*	TSR Hobbies/SPI	3.5
8. *Devil's Den*	Avalon Hill	4.0
9-10. *Pea Ridge*	SPI	4.3
Gettysburg '77	Avalon Hill	2.6

The Civil War Scholar

Some Extraordinary Civil War Source Collections

These journals and collections were devoted primarily to the publication of reminiscences, reports, and documents about the Civil War, in most cases by the actual participants. A perusal of any of them can be a rewarding experience, not the least for the often heated quarrels which were sometimes fought out in their pages. As a result, they provide a rich source of historical, personal, and anecdotal materials. Several of these have been reprinted from time to time and are available in several editions.

The Bivouac. Boston, 1883-1885.
Battles and Leaders of the Civil War edited by Robert V. Johnson and Clarence C. Buell. Four volumes. New York, 1887.
The Century Magazine. New York, 1870-1930.
The Confederate Veteran. Nashville, 1893-1932.
The Rebellion Record edited by Frank Moore. Eleven volumes. New York, 1861-1864.
Southern Bivouac. Louisville, 1882-1887.
Southern Historical Society Papers. Richmond, 1876-1952.

Some Indispensible Old Reference Works on the Civil War

The originals of any of these are horrendously expensive. Fortunately, many exist in reprint, although the quality of these is often poor and the price often equally prohibitive.

Commanders of Army Corps, Divisions, and Brigades, United States Army, During the War of 1861 to 1865. Philadelphia, 1887.

Confederate Military History, edited by Clement Anselm Evans. Thirteen volumes. Atlanta, 1899.

Dyer, Frederick H., *A Compendium of the War of the Rebellion.* Three volumes. Des Moines, 1908.

Fox, William Freeman, *Regimental Losses in the American Civil War, 1861-1865.* Albany, 1889.

Heitman, Francis Bernard, *Historical Register of the United States Army from Its Organization, September 29, 1789 to September 29 1889.* Washington, 1890. [Second edition *to March 2, 1903.* Two volumes. Washington, 1903.]

Livermore, Thomas L., *Numbers and Losses in the Civil War in America, 1861-1865.* Boston, 1900.

Official Army Register of the Volunteer Force of the United States Army, 1861, 1862, 1863, 1864, 1865. Eight volumes. Washington, 1865.

Official Records of the Union and Confederate Navies in the War of the Rebellion. Thirty volumes. Washington, 1894-1927.

Personnel of the Civil War edited by William Freyne Ammen. Two volumes. New York, 1961. Despite its relatively recent date, this consists of reprints of several uncirculated War Department documents dating from the turn of the century.

The Surgeon General of the United States Army, *Medical and Surgical History of the War of the Rebellion.* Six volumes. Washington, 1870-1888.

The Union Army: A History of Military Affairs in the Loyal States, 1861-1865. Eight volumes. Madison, Wisconsin, 1908.

War of the Rebellion...Official Records of the Union and Confederate Armies edited by the War Department. Seventy volumes in 128 parts. Generally known as the *Official Records.*

Wright, Marcus J., *List of Field Officers, Regiments and Battalions in the Confederate States Army, 1861-1865.* Washington, 1891. As this is almost completely unavailable, only 25 copies having been issued, try Claude Estes' *List of Field Officers, Regiments and Battalions in the Confederate States Army, 1861-1865* (Macon, Georgia, 1912), which was a rip-off reprint.

Atlases to the Civil War

Atlas to Accompany the Official Records of the Union and Confederate Armies. Three volumes. Washington, 1880-1901. This has been reissued several times, most often in one volume.

Atlas for the American Civil War edited by Thomas E. Greiss. Wayne, New Jersey, 1987.

Steele, Matthew Forney, *American Campaigns, Vol. II: Atlas.* Washington, 1909.

Symonds, Craig, and William L. Clipson, *A Battlefield Atlas of the Civil War.* Annapolis, 1983.

The West Point Atlas of American Wars edited by Vincent J. Esposito. Two volumes. New York, 1959.

Important Civil War Photographic and Pictorial Works

While several of the older items listed have been reissued in recent years, the quality of such reprints has frequently been poor and the price ridiculous.

The American Heritage Century Collection of Civil War Art, edited by Stephen W. Sears. New York, 1974.

Blay, John S., *The Civil War: A Pictorial Profile.* New York, 1958.

Catton, Bruce, *The American Heritage Picture History of the Civil War.* New York, 1960.

The Confederate Image, edited by Mark E. Neely, Jr., Harold Holzer, and Gabor S. Boritt. Chapel Hill, North Carolina, 1987.

Davis, William C. and William A. Fassantino, *Touched by Fire.* Two volumes. Boston, 1986.

Gardner, Alexander, *Photographic Sketch Book of the Civil War.* New York, 1866.

Harper's Pictorial History of the Civil War, edited by Alfred H. Guernsey and Henry M. Alden. Two volumes. New York, 1866-1868.

Humble, Richard, *The Illustrated History of the Civil War.* New York, 1986.

Images of War, edited by William C. Davis. Six volumes. New York, 1981-1984.

Lossing, Benson J., *A History of the Civil War.* New York, 1912.

Meredith, Roy, *The Face of Robert E. Lee.* New York, 1981.

Francis T. Miller, *The Photographic History of the Civil War.* Ten volumes. New York, 1911.

The Soldier in Our Civil War: A Pictorial History of the Conflict, 1861-1865 edited by Paul F. Mottelay and T. Campbell-Copeland. Three volumes. New York, 1884-1885.

Wertstein, Irving, *1861-1865.* New York, 1962.

Five Invaluable Civil War Journals

Blue & Gray: a profusely illustrated, serious bimonthly journal devoted to Civil War history and memorabilia, published by Blue & Gray Enterprises, Box 28625, Columbus, Ohio, 43228

Civil War History: a scholarly quarterly devoted to the "middle period" of American History, published by The Kent State University Press, Kent, Ohio, 44242.

Civil War Times Illustrated: an extensively illustrated, well written, serious magazine of the Civil War, appearing ten times a year from Historical Times, Inc., 2245 Kohn Rd, Harrisburg, Pa., 17105-8200.

Military Images: a bimonthly journal devoted particularly to Civil War era military photographs, frequently with excellent articles on a variety of subjects, published by Military Images, 205 West Miner St., West Chester, Pa, 19380.

Volunteers: a quarterly newsletter of Civil War simulation gaming, with game and book reviews, news, surveys, and short historical pieces, published by *Volunteers*, 146 Chimney Lane, Wilmington, N.C., 28403.

Some Useful Modern Civil War Reference Works

Bartleson, John D., Jr., *A Field Guide for Civil War Explosive Ordnance*. Indian Head, Maryland, 1972.

Boatner, Mark M., *The Civil War Dictionary*. Second edition. New York, 1979.

Brown, John C., *The Civil War Almanac*. New York, 1983.

Coggins, Jack., *Arms and Equipment of the Civil War*. New York, 1962.

Crute, Joseph H., Jr., *Units of the Confederate Army*. Gaithersburg, Md., 1988.

Edwards, William B., *Civil War Guns*. Harrisburg, Pennsylvania, 1962.

Haythornthwaite, Philip, *Uniforms of the American Civil War*. New York, 1975.

Hazlett, James C., *et al.*, *Field Artillery Weapons of the Civil War*. Newark, Delaware, 1983.

The Historical Times Illustrated Encyclopedia of the Civil War, edited by Patricia Paust. New York, 1986.

Hogg, Ian V., *Weapons of the Civil War*. New York, 1986.

Krick, Robert K., *Lee's Colonels*. Dayton, Ohio, 1979.

Long, Everette Beach, with Barbara Long, *The Civil War Day by Day: An Almanac, 1861-1865.* Garden City, New York, 1971.

Neely, Mark E., Jr., *The Abraham Lincoln Encyclopedia.* New York, 1982.

Ripley, Warren, *Artillery and Ammunition of the Civil War.* New York, 1970.

Rogers, H.C.B., *Confederates and Federals at War.* New York, 1983.

Wakelyn, Jon L., *Biographical Dictionary of the Confederacy.* Westport, Connecticut, 1977.

Warner, Ezra J., *Generals in Blue.* Second edition. Baton Rouge, 1984. *Generals in Gray.* Second edition. Baton Rouge, 1983.

Who Was Who in the Civil War edited by Stewart Sifakis. New York, 1987.

Zimmermann, Richard J., *Unit Organizations of the American Civil War.* Paris, Ontario, 1982.

The Most Important Recent Works on the Civil War

These books have been included here for a variety of reasons. Several of them represent critical break-throughs in Civil War scholarship. A couple develop unusual and insightful ideas, while some demonstrate innovative approaches to the study of the Civil War and its various aspects. And a few present controversial perspectives which have resulted in stimulating scholarly exchange.

Adams, Michael C.C., *Our Masters the Rebels: A Speculation on Union Military Failure in the East, 1861-1865.* Cambridge, Massachusetts, 1978.

Beringer, Richard E., Herman Hattaway, Archer Jones, and William N. Still, Jr., *Why the South Lost the Civil War.* Athens, Georgia, 1986.

Blight, David W., *Frederick Douglass' Civil War: Keeping Faith in Jubilee.* LSU, 1989.

Bussy, John W., and David G. Martin, *Regimental Strengths and Losses at Gettysburg.* Highstown, New Jersey, 1986.

Connelly, Thomas L., *The Marble Man: Robert E. Lee and His Image in American Society.* New York, 1977.

Current, Richard Nelson, *Those Terrible Carpetbaggers: A Reinterpretation.* New York, 1988.

Fishel, Edwin C., "Myths That Never Die," *International Journal of Intelligence and Counterintelligence,* Vol. II, No. 1 (Spring, 1988), pp. 27-58.

Frassanito, William A., *Gettysburg: A Journey in Time.* New York, 1975.

Hattaway, Herman, and Archer Jones, *How the North Won: A Military History of the Civil War.* Urbana, 1982

Linderman, Gerald F., *Embattled Courage: The Experience of Combat in the American Civil War.* New York and London, 1987.

McPherson, James C., *Battle Cry of Freedom.* New York, 1988.

McWhiney, Grady, and Perry D. Jamieson, *Attack and Die: Civil War Military Tactics and the Southern Heritage.* University, Alabama, 1982.

Sutherland, Daniel E., *The Confederate Carpetbaggers.* LSU, 1988.

Index

Army Life:

Civil War Scholar:

Civil War Today:

Incidents of War:

Lincoln:

The Men:

The Ships:

The Units:

War and the Muses:

War and Society:

Ways of War:

The Women: